Changing Societies, Changing Party Systems

How do changes in society that increase the heterogeneity of the citizenry shape democratic party systems? This book seeks to answer this question. To do so, it focuses on the key mechanism by which social heterogeneity shapes the number of political parties: new social groups successfully forming new sectarian parties. Why are some groups successful at this while others fail? Drawing on cross-national statistical analyses and case studies of Sephardi and Russian immigration to Israel and African American enfranchisement in the United States, this book demonstrates that social heterogeneity does matter. However, it makes the case that in order to understand when and how social heterogeneity matters, factors besides the electoral system – most importantly, the regime type, the strategies played by existing parties, and the size and politicization of new social groups – must be taken into account. It also demonstrates that sectarian parties play an important role in securing descriptive representation for new groups.

Heather Stoll is associate professor of political science at the University of California, Santa Barbara. She holds a M.Phil. in politics from the University of Oxford and both a M.S. in statistics and a Ph.D. in political science from Stanford University. She is a 1996 Harry S. Truman Scholar and a 1997 British Marshall Scholar. Her Stanford dissertation, on which this book is loosely based, was the co-recipient of the Seymour Martin Lipset Award for the best comparative politics dissertation in 2005. She has published a number of articles in a variety of journals, including the *Journal of Politics*, *Comparative Political Studies*, *Party Politics*, and *West European Politics*.

Changing Societies, Changing Party Systems

HEATHER STOLL
University of California, Santa Barbara

Shaftesbury Road, Cambridge CB2 8EA, United Kingdom

One Liberty Plaza, 20th Floor, New York, NY 10006, USA

477 Williamstown Road, Port Melbourne, VIC 3207, Australia

314–321, 3rd Floor, Plot 3, Splendor Forum, Jasola District Centre, New Delhi – 110025, India

103 Penang Road, #05-06/07, Visioncrest Commercial, Singapore 238467

Cambridge University Press is part of Cambridge University Press & Assessment, a department of the University of Cambridge.

We share the University's mission to contribute to society through the pursuit of education, learning and research at the highest international levels of excellence.

www.cambridge.org
Information on this title: www.cambridge.org/9781107030497

© Heather Stoll 2013

This publication is in copyright. Subject to statutory exception and to the provisions of relevant collective licensing agreements, no reproduction of any part may take place without the written permission of Cambridge University Press & Assessment.

First published 2013

A catalogue record for this publication is available from the British Library

Library of Congress Cataloging-in-Publication data
Stoll, Heather, 1976–
Changing societies, changing party systems / Heather Stoll.
Includes bibliographical references and index.
ISBN 978-1-107-03049-7 – ISBN 978-1-107-67574-2 (pbk.)   1. Political parties.   2. Political participation.   3. Democracy.   I. Title.
JF2051.S765   2013
324.2 – dc23   2012029516

ISBN   978-1-107-03049-7   Hardback
ISBN   978-1-107-67574-2   Paperback

Cambridge University Press & Assessment has no responsibility for the persistence or accuracy of URLs for external or third-party internet websites referred to in this publication and does not guarantee that any content on such websites is, or will remain, accurate or appropriate.

To my family,
both two- and four-legged,
and especially Wim

Contents

List of Tables	ix
List of Figures	xi
Acknowledgments	xiii

1 Introduction — 1
  1.1 The New Institutionalism — 2
  1.2 A New Societalism? — 6
  1.3 What This Book Does — 13

2 Social Heterogeneity and the Number of Parties: A Theory — 22
  2.1 Setting the Stage: The Franchise in the West — 23
  2.2 Getting Started: Literature and Theory — 26
  2.3 Defining Social Heterogeneity — 28
  2.4 Relating Social Heterogeneity to Party System Fragmentation — 32
  2.5 Conclusion — 56

3 Describing Social Heterogeneity: Measures and Testable Hypotheses — 59
  3.1 Historical Dimensions of Social Heterogeneity in the Advanced Industrial Democracies — 61
  3.2 A Cross-Sectional Index of Social Heterogeneity — 77
  3.3 Conclusion — 87

4 Social Heterogeneity and Party System Fragmentation: Empirical Evidence across Space and Time — 90
  4.1 Changing Societies, Changing Party System Fragmentation in Legislative Elections? — 92
  4.2 Social Heterogeneity and Presidential Party System Fragmentation — 101
  4.3 Conclusion — 120

5 Israel: New Parties for New Groups? — 124
  5.1 Social Heterogeneity in Israel — 127

Contents

    5.2 Party System Fragmentation in Israel 138
    5.3 Conclusion 159

6 *Israel: Testing Hypotheses about Sectarian Party Success* 161
    6.1 Nonexplanatory Factors 162
    6.2 Explanatory Factors 165
    6.3 Conclusion 194

7 *The United States: New Parties for New Groups? Testing Hypotheses* 198
    7.1 Social Heterogeneity in the United States 200
    7.2 Party System Fragmentation in the United States 209
    7.3 Explaining Sectarian Party (Un)Success 216
    7.4 Conclusion 232

8 *Conclusion: Party System Fragmentation and Beyond* 235
    8.1 Social Heterogeneity and Party System Fragmentation . . . 236
    8.2 Social Heterogeneity and Other Dimensions of the Party System 239
    8.3 Descriptive Representation: Changing the Sociodemographic Face of Politics? 241
    8.4 The Role of Sectarian Parties 252
    8.5 Quo Vadis? 257

A *Additional Material for the Quantitative Analyses in Chapter 4* 263

B *Demography in Israel* 273
    B.1 Sephardim 273
    B.2 Russians 278

C *Sephardi and Russian Sectarian Parties and Their Success in Israel* 280
    C.1 Sephardi Parties 280
    C.2 Russian Parties 280
    C.3 Measuring Party Success I: Assumptions for Comparing Electorate Shares to Vote Shares 280
    C.4 Measuring Party Success II: Survey Data 286

D *Demography and the Franchise in the United States* 292
    D.1 National-Level Estimates 292
    D.2 State-Level Estimates 293
    D.3 House District Estimates 299

E *African American Descriptive Representation in the United States* 300

Bibliography 307

Index 335

List of Tables

2.1	Hypotheses about the eight factors that condition the effect of social heterogeneity on party system fragmentation	57
3.1	Periods of universal suffrage for the advanced industrial democracies	69
3.2	Social heterogeneity index values for presidential democracies	85
3.3	Descriptive statistics for the social heterogeneity index	86
4.1	Legislative elections analysis results, Models 1 and 2	97
4.2	Descriptive statistics for the index of presidential powers	106
4.3	Presidential elections analysis results, Models 3 and 4	112
5.1	Immigration to Israel by period	129
5.2	Estimates of the Sephardi share of Israel's population, the Sephardi share of Israel's electorate, and the effective number of ethnic groups in Israel	135
5.3	Estimates of the Russian share of Israel's population, the Russian share of Israel's electorate, and the effective number of ethnic groups in Israel	138
5.4	The entry and electoral performance of Sephardi sectarian parties	146
5.5	The success of Sephardi parties in Israel evaluated using two approaches	148
5.6	The entry and electoral performance of Russian sectarian parties	154
5.7	The success of Russian parties in Israel evaluated using two approaches.	157
6.1	Results of the 1996 and 1999 direct prime ministerial elections in Israel	173
7.1	Estimates of the African American share of the population, the African American share of the electorate, and the effective number of ethnic groups for selected election years	203
7.2	Estimates of the African American share of the population and electorate of each state for selected election years	206
7.3	The vote and seat shares of African American political parties at the federal level	212

List of Tables

7.4 Logistic regression analysis of African American party entry and success in federal elections, Models 1–3, and entry in state elections, Model 4 226
8.1 The representation of women in democratic legislatures for selected advanced industrial democracies 244

List of Figures

2.1	The theory: the factors conditioning the effect of social heterogeneity on party system fragmentation	36
2.2	Stylized examples of the hypothesized relationship between social heterogeneity and party system fragmentation	55
3.1	The electorate as a percentage of the adult population in the advanced industrial democracies	66
3.2	Net cumulative territorial gains for the twelve advanced industrial democracies experiencing territorial change	72
3.3	The foreign-born as a percentage of the population in the advanced industrial democracies	75
4.1	The estimated marginal effect of social heterogeneity on the effective number of presidential candidates for regimes with varying degrees of horizontal centralization (index of presidential powers operationalization)	114
4.2	The estimated marginal effect of social heterogeneity on the effective number of presidential candidates for regimes with varying degrees of horizontal centralization (ordinal regime typology operationalization).	115
4.3	The estimated conditional effect of social heterogeneity on the effective number of presidential candidates for regimes with varying degrees of horizontal centralization (index of presidential powers operationalization)	118
4.4	The estimated conditional effect of social heterogeneity on the effective number of presidential candidates for regimes with varying degrees of horizontal centralization (ordinal regime typology operationalization).	119
5.1	The raw and effective number of electoral political parties in Israel	140
6.1	The number and collective success of Sephardi and Russian sectarian parties in Israeli elections	170
6.2	Percentage of Sephardi and Russian MKs by Knesset and political party	179
6.3	Percentage of Sephardi and Russian cabinet ministers by government and political party	181

List of Figures

7.1 The African American proportion of the population, theoretical electorate, and actual electorate of the United States 204
7.2 The African American proportion of the population and of the theoretical electorate for selected states 208
7.3 The effective number of electoral political parties in the United States 210
7.4 The African American share of major party state and federal representatives for selected states 223
8.1 The percentage of Sephardi and Russian MKs, in total and from sectarian parties 246
8.2 The percentage of Sephardi and Russian cabinet ministers, in total and from sectarian parties 247
8.3 The percentage of African American members of the federal House and Senate, in total and for sectarian parties 250
8.4 The percentage of African American state representatives for Mississippi and Alabama, in total and for sectarian parties . . 251

Acknowledgments

This book has been a very long time coming. Its genesis lies in my Stanford University dissertation. While a comparison of the two reveals that only some of the introductory material was directly carried over from the dissertation to the book, a few of the book's core insights, although certainly not all of them, and a part of its quantitative empirical analysis build upon the dissertation.

As a result, the first debts of gratitude I owe are to the Stanford Department of Political Science and to my Stanford dissertation committee: David Laitin, Mo Fiorina, Beatriz Magaloni-Kerpel, and Jonathan Wand. The department provided a stimulating and pleasant (yes, really!) graduate experience. Besides being grateful to my committee members for their suggestions and support, which contributed greatly to the dissertation, I am grateful to them for (somewhat unusually) telling me at my defense to shelve the book project for a few years. I followed this advice, and although the reader is the ultimate judge, I think that the book is infinitely better for it. If I had written the book right away, it would not have been the book that I wanted to write—which is this book. Particular thanks is owed to David Laitin, who has always pushed me to think about the big picture "why we should care" questions. I hope I have at least somewhat answered those questions here.

With the book project on the back burner for a few years, I worked on various other projects, some related to the dissertation and some not. This work ultimately enriched the book, sometimes in surprising ways. I owe much to the many scholars (too many to name them all here) with whom I have collaborated or otherwise engaged regarding this work over the years. Chief among these colleagues are Jim Adams, who is surely one of the nicest people I have had the pleasure to know, and Allen Hicken. My long-running collaboration with Hicken deserves special note: the many theoretical and empirical issues we have grappled with in the course of our joint work have certainly made their way into this book. I thank him for these intellectual exchanges as well as for the use of some of the data, most notably on presidential powers, that we developed.

Needless to say, many colleagues have directly contributed to the book itself. Amit Ahuja, Kate Bruhn, Matthew Shugart, and two anonymous Cambridge University Press reviewers read the entire draft manuscript and pro-

Acknowledgments

vided very useful feedback that I didn't always want to hear, but which strengthened the book. Thank you. At the risk of committing a sin of omission, in addition to the individuals already mentioned, Sarah Anderson; the late Asher Arian, who is sorely missed; Lee Ann Banaszak; Walter Dean Burnham; Michael Coppedge; Kevin Deegan-Krause; Garrett Glasgow; Reuven Hazan; Kent Jennings; Mark Jones; Cynthia Kaplan; Ken Kollman; Scott Mainwaring; Lorelei Moosbrugger; Robert Rauchhaus; Ethan Scheiner; Rein Taagepera; and Stephen Weatherford either read and commented on portions of the draft manuscript or otherwise provided advice about various aspects of the project. I thank them for this. I also thank participants in the forums where I have presented drafts of chapters, ranging from conferences such as the Annual Meeting of the American Political Science Association to works-in-progress seminars at the University of California, Santa Barbara, for the helpful feedback. Of course, I apologize to all of these colleagues who have so generously given of their time for any remaining flaws in the book, for which I bear sole responsibility.

I am also grateful to those who shared or otherwise assisted me with data. Again at the risk of committing a sin of omission, I thank Matt Golder for his replication data; Orit Kedar, Michal Shamir, and Rafi Ventura for assistance with the Israeli National Election Studies; Nir Atmor for assistance with compiling and translating complete Israeli election returns; Ofer Kenig and Shlomit Barnea for their data on the ethnicity of Israeli cabinet ministers; staff of the Israeli Central Bureau of Statistics's Tel Aviv and Jerusalem offices for assistance obtaining Israeli electoral and demographic data; and staff of the United States Census Bureau for assistance with United States census and other demographic data. I also thank the many Israelis, from the politicians and their staff to ordinary people on the street, who spoke with me about ethnic politics in Israel, and Asher Arian (yet again!) for facilitating aspects of my field research in Israel. Michael Citron, Molly Cohn, and Katie Swann provided excellent research assistance at different stages of the project.

The project would not have been possible without funding from the Academic Senate of the University of California, Santa Barbara, and the Hellman Foundation's Hellman Family Faculty Fellowship, for which I am grateful. At the University of California, two Regent's Junior Faculty Fellowships; a Faculty Career Development Award; and a sabbatical provided leave time initially for the field research and later for writing. I thank both Dean Melvin Oliver and Political Science Department Chair John Woolley for helping to make these things possible. Colleagues at the University of California provided an unusually collegial and intellectually stimulating environment, as previous paragraphs suggest. Also at the University of California, Susan d'Arbanville, Sharon Terry, and Helen Deshler assisted admirably with various administrative aspects of the project, while Florence Sanchez provided excellent editorial assistance. Last, but certainly not least, I thank Lewis Bateman and everyone else at Cambridge University Press for their support

Acknowledgments

throughout the publication process. In particular, the production team, led by Russell Hahn, graciously accommodated delays due to the birth of my daughter, Branwen. It has been both a privilege and a pleasure to work with them.

Finally, of course, there is my family. They have put up with my preoccupation with first the dissertation and then the book for close to a decade now. Yet they have always understood. I thank my parents, Mark and Grace; sister Lona and family; and brother Nathan and family for all of their love and support over the years. But most of all, I thank my husband, Wim, who has contributed to this project in innumerable ways, from discussions about third-order polynomials to the LaTeX layout to extra dog walks and cooking. I could not have done it without him, and now that it's done, he has earned the right to say "I told you so" on many fronts.

1 *Introduction*

Voice is "a basic portion and function of any political system"(Hirschman 1970, 30). But it is particularly important in political systems that aim for some sort of responsiveness of the government to its citizens—the type of political system that Dahl (1971) has called polyarchy, and that others have more commonly called democracy.

In his classic work, Dahl (1971) conceptualized voice as developing along two dimensions in democratic systems. The first dimension, contestation, concerns the extent to which opposition to the government is allowed. For example, are there free and fair elections for both the chief executive and the legislature? The second dimension, inclusion, concerns the proportion of the population that is allowed to participate in the contestation. For example, are women allowed to vote in elections? Another way of looking at this is that we should distinguish between *how* voice may be exercised (contestation) and *who* exercises it (inclusion). Voice *in toto* is ultimately shaped by both this "how" and this "who."

Many scholars of democratization such as Alvarez and colleagues (1996) have focused heavily on the first of these dimensions of voice, which is institutional in nature.[1] Yet even they have acknowledged the importance of the second of these dimensions, which is societal in nature. This societal dimension of voice may alternatively be conceptualized in terms of preferences. Just as the institutional framework for exercising voice varies, so too do the preferences that are its content. For example, the working class was denied the franchise for many years in most countries. When the franchise was extended to these lower-class individuals, new demands, such as demands for safer working conditions, were voiced, holding constant the institutional setting. Accordingly, the kind of issues that a polity's citizens have cared about and the positions that they have taken on these issues, which may be said to characterize their preferences, have varied over time. In this example, as the electorate has changed, so too have preferences.

Turning from the process of democratization to the working of democracy itself, few political scientists would disagree with the claim that pref-

---

[1]Studies accordingly have embraced topics ranging from the existence of contested elections to the rules governing the translation of votes into legislative seats. See, for example, Doorenspleet (2000).

erences (the "who" or societal dimension of voice) interact with institutions (the "how" or institutional dimension of voice) to produce the outcomes of the democratic political process. Originally put on the map by Plott (1991), others have called this claim the fundamental equation of politics (Hinich and Munger 1997). In other words, if politics is about who actually gets what, when and how (Lasswell 1936), or in Lenin's maxim, about who can do what to whom, then *both* preferences and institutions are essential to understanding politics.

1.1 THE NEW INSTITUTIONALISM

Since the late 1980s, the new institutionalism has focused scholarly attention on one half of the fundamental equation of politics: political institutions.[2] Political institutions, either as enforcers of agreements that give rise to collective benefits or as "weapons of coercion and redistribution" (Moe 1990, 213), are the "constraint[s] that human beings devise to shape human interaction" (North 1990, 4). As such, they structure the incentives that guide individual actions, which in turn underlie the aggregate outcomes—such as election results and legislation—that political scientists observe.

In comparative politics, the new institutionalism has spurred the growth of a vast literature studying the variance in institutional arrangements across both space and time. Particular attention has been paid to eliciting institutional differences from country to country. To illustrate briefly, scholars have studied the system of government (democracy versus dictatorship); the type of democratic regime (presidential versus parliamentary, as well as federal versus unitary); the cameral structure of the legislature (unicameralism versus bicameralism); the electoral system (proportional representation versus majoritarian); and central banks (independent versus constrained), to name just a few.[3] An overview, at an undergraduate level but nevertheless reflecting the breadth of the literature, is found in Lijphart (1999). It is true that most of the attention has been paid to democratic institutions, as Laitin

---

[2]The "new institutionalism" is understood here to mean the methodologically individualist meta-research program that explains macro-level phenomena using the strategic behavior of individuals. This encompasses two substantive research programs in the social sciences: that of rational choice (e.g., Shepsle and Weingast 1987; Moe 1990; Knight 1992) and that of bounded rationality (e.g., Bendor 2001). This book places itself within this methodologically individualist tradition. What is not meant is work from a different meta-research program, the institutional school of organizational sociology (e.g., Cohen, March, and Olsen 1972; March and Olsen 1984). Studies in this tradition explicitly reject methodological individualism but are still labeled as belonging to the "new institutionalism" (Moe, Bendor, and Shotts 2001).

[3]To identify just a few examples of scholarly studies exploring each of these institutions, Alvarez et al. (1996) and Przeworski et al. (2000) discuss the broadest possible classification of regimes: democracy and dictatorship. Shugart and Carey (1992) provide a classic treatment of presidentialism, while Chhibber and Kollman (2004) have more recently addressed the centralization of policy-making authority in the national level of government. Tsebelis and Money (1997) deal with the structure of legislatures, while Tsebelis (1995) offers a more general argument about both partisan and institutional veto players. On electoral systems, Cox (1997) is the modern classic. Central banks are tackled by Hall and Franzese (1998) and Iversen (1998), among many others.

(2001) notes.[4] Nevertheless, the ultimate goal is to link the differences in a polity's political institutions, whether the polity is democratic or not, to differences in the outcomes of the political process.

A prominent example is the comparative politics literature seeking to relate differences in a democracy's political institutions to different characteristics of its party system, the dependent variable with which I am concerned in this book. The party system is the way in which political competition is organized by political parties in modern representative democracies. In Sartori's (1976, 44) famous phrase, it is the "system of interactions resulting from inter-party competition." For example, are there few parties or many parties, and are the positions parties take as they compete for votes generally extremist or centrist? Political scientists have sought to gain explanatory leverage over the determinants of the party system because "democracy is unthinkable save in terms of parties" (Schattschneider 1942, 1). Political parties give voice to a democracy's citizens via the functions they perform in the electorate, as organizations, and in government (Key 1964). As such, they are important from the normative perspective of democratic theory. Moreover, the party system, in turn, has been shown to relate to many other consequential outcomes of the political process, from government stability to macroeconomic policy outcomes to the type of democracy, over which political scientists would like to gain leverage.[5]

The dimension of the party system that has received the most attention to date is the number of political parties, which has also been referred to as the fragmentation of the party system.[6] An observer of contemporary world politics might naturally ask why some countries tend to have few parties while other countries tend to have many. For example, since World War II, two political parties, the Democrats and the Republicans, have dominated elections in the United States. No more than a handful of seats in the lower house of the legislature, the House of Representatives, have been won by other parties.[7] By way of contrast, elections in Israel have been fought by an average of approximately six parties, with the two largest parties averaging only about 60 percent of the seats in the legislature. Similarly, an observer of a particular country's politics might ask why that country has had more

---

[4]In a sense, the field of comparative politics that is described here is a compilation of Laitin's (2001) "Political Institutions" and "Comparative Politics" subfields. Like his "Political Institutions" subfield, it is concerned with how institutions work; like his "Comparative Politics" subfield, it is concerned with outcomes that vary across countries and the exogenous factors that account for such variance.

[5]For some of these consequences and others, see King et al. (1990); Wolendorp, Keman, and Budge (1993); Alt and Lowry (1994); Tsebelis (1995); Alesina, Roubini, and Cohen (1997); Lijphart (1999); Thomson (1999); and Powell (2000).

[6]See, for example, the prominence of this dimension in the classic typologies of party systems developed by scholars such as Dahl (1966), Sartori (1976), and Ware (1996).

[7]For example, one seat out of 435 went to other parties from 1940 to 1952; no seats from 1954 through 1988; and nine seats from 1990 through 2006 (all but one of which were won by Bernie Sanders, an Independent from Vermont, during his eight terms of service in the House). See Chapter 7 for more information.

parties at some times than at others. Israel is again a good example: only approximately five parties contested its 1992 election, but a record high of approximately ten parties contested its 1999 election.[8] Why did the number of parties *double* over the course of two elections and seven years?

The electoral system is the political institution that political scientists have primarily turned to as the explanatory factor.[9] All else being equal, countries with majoritarian electoral systems are expected to have fewer political parties in equilibrium than countries with proportional representation systems. For example, building upon Duverger's (1963) well-known arguments, Cox's (1997) influential book argues that restrictive or "majoritarian" electoral systems place a constraining upper bound on the equilibrium number of parties competing in an election. The most prominent example of this type of electoral system combines a first-past-the-post (or plurality) electoral formula with single-member districts. Under these electoral rules, both political elites and ordinary voters have an incentive to strategically engage in electoral coordination, supporting less preferred but stronger contenders in order to make their votes and resources count. Specifically, the incentive is to support one of the two front-runners. At the other end of the spectrum are permissive or "proportional representation" electoral systems. These electoral systems combine multimember electoral districts with an electoral formula that awards seats in each district in proportion to the votes received by the parties. Under these electoral rules, there are no incentives for conventional seat-maximizing strategic behavior. Political elites and ordinary voters instead support the contender they sincerely prefer.

Returning to the stylized examples just discussed, the electoral system seems capable of accounting for the difference in the number of political parties between the United States and Israel. The United States employs a restrictive electoral system—specifically, single-member plurality. Conversely, Israel employs a nonrestrictive electoral system—specifically, a proportional formula (today, the d'Hondt) and one nationwide district of 120 legislators. And as already discussed, the United States on average has far fewer parties than Israel does, in accordance with the theoretical predictions.

But the electoral system does not seem capable of accounting for variation over time within each country. Israel has always employed a proportional representation electoral system, yet its number of parties increased sharply in the mid- to late 1990s.[10] Similarly, earlier in the United States'

---

[8]See Chapters 5 and 6 for more information.

[9]In comparative politics, prominent cross-national and quantitative studies exploring the relationship between the electoral system and the number of political parties include Duverger (1963), Rae (1967), Sartori (1976), Grofman and Lijphart (1986), Taagepera and Shugart (1989), Lijphart (1990), Lijphart (1994), Ordeshook and Shvetsova (1994), Cox (1997), Sartori (1997), Mozaffar, Scarritt, and Galaich (2003), Clark and Golder (2006), Singer and Stephenson (2009), and Moser and Scheiner (2012), among many, many others. There are also numerous case studies of single countries, such as Reed (1990).

[10]Other if less stark changes in the fragmentation of the Israeli party system can also be identified. Note that the minor changes that Israel has made to its electoral system over time have all moved it in a more restrictive direction, such as switching to the d'Hondt from the

history, more than two parties commonly contested elections (think, for example, of the American Party and the Progressives), yet the United States, too, has effectively always employed the same electoral system at the national (federal) level. Obviously, a constant cannot explain variation. Are there other political institutions that might provide an explanation?

The answer is "yes": the type of democratic regime. More recently, scholars have begun linking this political institutional variable to the number of political parties. For many years, as part of the literature debating the merits of presidential versus parliamentary systems of government, scholars simply compared the number of political parties under the two types of regimes, finding that "presidential systems, all other factors being equal, will have smaller effective numbers of parties than non-presidential systems of government" (Lijphart 1994, 131). Subsequent studies have refined this presidential–parliamentary dichotomy. The effect of presidentialism, also referred to as the presidential coattails, is now known to be mediated by the fragmentation of the presidential party system itself and by the electoral cycle (e.g., Shugart and Carey 1992; Amorim Neto and Cox 1997; Cox 1997; Golder 2006; Hicken and Stoll 2011).[11] Specifically, when a presidential election is held in temporal proximity to a legislative election and there are few presidential candidates, the presidential election casts a deflationary shadow over the legislative election, which consolidates the legislative party system. By way of contrast, when a presidential election is held in temporal proximity to a legislative election and there are many presidential candidates, the presidential election casts an inflationary shadow over the legislative election, which fragments it.[12]

However, the existence of a separately elected president is not the only feature of the regime type that shapes the number of political parties. Very recently, political scientists have taken a fresh look at other potentially consequential ways in which democratic regimes vary across space and time. For example, in their pioneering work, Chhibber and Kollman (1998, 2004) argue that the more centralized policy-making authority is at the national level of government vis-à-vis subnational levels of government, the greater the incentive political elites and ordinary voters have to coordinate across electoral districts to form political parties capable of winning many legislative seats. This process of party system aggregation leads to fewer, more nationalized political parties.[13]

LR-Hare formula. Accordingly, these changes cannot account for the *increase* in the number of political parties in Israel in the 1990s.

[11] More recently still, the size of the presidential prize, that is, the centralization of policy-making authority in the presidency vis-à-vis the legislature, has been identified as an additional conditioning variable (Hicken and Stoll 2013). These other features of the regime type will be discussed in more detail later.

[12] Note, though, that the empirical evidence for the deflationary effect is stronger than that for the inflationary effect (Hicken and Stoll 2011).

[13] Another important recent study that takes a novel look at the democratic regime is Samuels and Shugart (2010). However, this work explores how the regime type shapes a different dependent variable: the internal organization of political parties.

More generally, Hicken and Stoll (2008, 2009) and Hicken (2009) argue that it is the type of regime, not the electoral system, that provides the incentives for combining the many party systems existing in the electoral districts together into one national party system. While the electoral system primarily provides incentives to coordinate within electoral districts, shaping the district-level party system (e.g., Singer and Stephenson 2009), the type of regime provides incentives to coordinate across electoral districts in order to become the largest party in the national legislature, shaping the national-level party system. The more the democratic regime centralizes policy-making authority in the hands of the largest party in the national legislature, the more valuable it is to be this largest party, and hence the greater these incentives. Better cross-district coordination or aggregation, in turn, usually results in fewer political parties nationally (Hicken and Stoll 2011). Specifically, these scholars have proposed studying how the regime type distributes policy-making authority along two dimensions: vertically among the different levels of government, à la Chhibber and Kollman (1998, 2004), as well as horizontally among different institutional actors within the national level of government. These lines of inquiry have been facilitated by the increased availability of data at the level of the electoral district over the past decade.[14]

Again returning to the stylized examples introduced earlier, in the United States, the increase in the vertical centralization of policy-making authority in the national level of government in the mid- to late 1800s helps to explain the decrease in the number of political parties over this same period (Chhibber and Kollman 1998, 2004). And as a later chapter will argue, Israel's 1996 switch from a parliamentary regime to a unique hybrid regime, classified by some as a president–parliamentary regime (Hazan 1996) and by others as an elected prime ministerial regime (Samuels and Shugart 2010), helps to explain the spectacular fragmentation of the Israeli party system in the late 1990s. Moreover, like the electoral system, the United States' presidential regime seems capable of contributing to the explanation of why this country on average has fewer political parties than nonpresidential Israel does.

Hence, the new institutionalism has identified variation in two political institutions, the electoral system and the democratic regime type, and linked this variation to variation in the number of political parties competing in democratic elections.

1.2 A NEW SOCIETALISM?

However, institutions do not—and cannot—tell the whole story: as I initially argued, preferences have work to do as well. Conventional understandings of the world go hand in glove with very old and fundamental philosophical

---

[14]In addition to the previously referenced studies, such as Chhibber and Kollman (2004) and Moser and Scheiner (2012), see also Caramani (2004), Brancati (2008), and Jones (2009). Of particular note, the Constituency Level Electoral Archive (CLEA) at the University of Michigan now serves as a valuable repository for district-level electoral returns.

1. Introduction

debates to tell us this.

To illustrate, one need only compare the writings of the ancient Greek philosophers to those of the early scholars of the Christian tradition to understand how different ideas about political life can be. For Aristotle, politics existed to facilitate human flourishing: it was the crucible where man, a political animal, realized his particular excellence on earth (*areté*).[15] For Paul, on the other hand, politics existed as a terror to evil works, to control the wicked and minister to the good until the imminent day of salvation finally dawned.[16] A thought experiment can easily conjure up two imaginary states, Aristotelia and Paulia, each dominated by the respective perspective on politics. While one might argue that each state would naturally be inclined towards a certain set of political institutions, accepting for the sake of the thought experiment that the same set of democratic institutions exists in each, the mind boggles at the many ways in which political life would differ in the two states. Dissimilarities would likely range from the issues framing political campaigns to the activities ultimately undertaken by the governments. For example, education would likely be a major focus of the Aristotelian state whereas the Paulian state would likely put its energies into law enforcement, particularly of the "Thou Shalt Not Kill" type of commandments. Further, if Aristotelians woke up one morning to find themselves coexisting in a single state with many Paulians, the political sparks would surely fly.

The number of political parties, the dependent variable with which I am primarily concerned in this book, is a good example. It is hard to imagine the Aristotelians and Paulians being able to work together within a single political party: the radically different worldviews of the two groups would almost certainly give rise to radically different interests. If a number of Paulians, for whatever reason, did suddenly find themselves citizens of the Aristotelian state, or vice versa, it is accordingly likely that these new citizens would strike out on their own, forming a new political party to give voice to their own unique interests. The result would be the fragmentation of the original party system.

While the prior paragraphs have deliberately drawn an exaggerated contrast between two sets of beliefs and the likely consequences each would have for political life, the lesson has hardly been lost upon modern political scientists. Some new institutionalists controversially claim that "generally speaking, the institutions of politics provide a larger part of the explanation than do preferences" (Dowding and King 1995, 7),[17] but most of the

---

[15] For an elaboration of these ideas, consult Aristotle's *Nicomachean Ethics* and *Politics*. Plato, of course, also viewed the ultimate goal of politics as the development of human excellence; however, he viewed politics itself as a necessary evil, not constitutive of human nature. In fact, he consigned it to the realm of experts: his philosopher-kings.

[16] These ideas are developed most forcefully in Romans 13; similar themes pervade the writings of other early Christian philosophers such as St. Augustine.

[17] Dowding and King (1995) offer in support of their contention work by scholars such as Hall (1986), who, they argue, explains different policy outcomes in France and Britain not

new institutionalism still leaves a role for preferences to play. In fact, the political situations of the greatest interest to contemporary political scientists are those that are characterized by disagreement.[18] Social choice theory provides a vivid illustration: the rationality or irrationality of group preferences (e.g., the presence or absence of voting cycles) is jointly determined by the structure of and the method of aggregating individual preferences. Similarly, game theory formalizes institutions and their effects on interdependent individual decisions, where one critical structure of a game is individual preferences over outcomes. Hence, comparative politics must not only concern itself with variance in institutions when explaining variance in outcomes. It must also concern itself with variance in preferences.

Consider again the topic that I am concerned with in this book: party systems. A number of scholars have recognized the need to go beyond political institutions when explaining why some countries and elections have more political parties than others. This countervailing perspective has long-standing scholarly antecedents: for example, a close reading of Duverger (1963), typically portrayed as an institutionalist, reveals a view of political parties as reflections of social forces (Clark and Golder 2006). For another example, one need look no further than Lipset and Rokkan's (1967) famous treatise. For Lipset and Rokkan, the party systems of the 1960s were products of countries' salient social cleavages, which in turn were largely products of how the national and industrial revolutions had earlier played out in each country.[19] More recently, in his modern classic work, Cox (1997) argues that the number of political parties in a country is the product of *both* the restrictiveness of its electoral system and its social cleavage structure. Specifically, he argues that many political parties will be the result of a heterogeneous society combined with a permissive electoral system; by way of contrast, few political parties will be the result of either a homogeneous society or a heterogeneous society combined with a restrictive electoral system.[20] In the latter case, downward pressure is applied on the country's

---

by differences in interests, but by differences in institutions. This may be somewhat of an overstatement of Hall's position regarding the role played by interests, ideas, and ideology in economic policy making, but there is some merit to Dowding and King's characterization.

[18] For example, Hinich and Munger (1997, 6-7) playfully describe the collective choice that the hypothetical Hun-Gat tribe must make about where to find food: to stay put; to go north; or to go south. The inherent boredom political scientists feel when confronted with unanimity emerges clearly from their writing: "If everyone wants to go north or south, they all go. If all want to stay, they stay." Conversely, their excitement is barely disguised when different Hun-Gats want different things: "Disagreement tests collective choice mechanisms; conflict strains the ties that gather a group of individuals into a society." In fact, the rest of their introductory text—like the spatial theory it is designed to explicate—is devoted to analyzing what the Hun-Gats should do in this situation.

[19] The "largely" is critical here in that Lipset and Rokkan (1967) also allow political institutions to play a role, even if this component of their argument is not as well developed or as prominent as the societal component. In their account, the primarily institutional thresholds faced by the social groups that sought representation determined which social cleavages were politicized and hence which party families were present in a country.

[20] How this social heterogeneity should be defined and operationalized is obviously a critical

1. Introduction

"natural" (given its cleavage structure) number of parties by the strategic responses of voters and elites to the restrictive electoral system. Following Cox, most scholars have both argued for and found empirical support for an interaction between the electoral system and the social heterogeneity of the country.[21]

Applying these arguments to the stylized example of the previous section, Israel is viewed by most commentators as a plural, deeply divided society (e.g., Kop and Litan 2002). Individuals are divided by sociodemographic criteria ranging from ethnicity to religion, as well as by the non-sociodemographic criterion of their stance towards Israel's foreign policy. This social diversity gives rise to a large "natural" number of political parties. Given Israel's permissive electoral system, there are few incentives for either political elites or ordinary voters to engage in electoral coordination, which means that its natural number of political parties becomes its actual number of political parties. In other words, it is the combination of its social heterogeneity and its permissive electoral system that explains Israel's fragmented party system; taking both of these variables into account provides more explanatory leverage than does the electoral system alone. There is less consensus about the social heterogeneity of the United States.[22] Regardless of whether the United States should be viewed as socially heterogeneous or homogeneous, however, its restrictive electoral system ensures that only a few political parties will contest American elections.

Accordingly, it would be setting up a straw man to make the case that students of party systems have exclusively sought political institutional explanations. Yet both theorizing about and empirical measurement of preferences have lagged behind that of political institutions. Take again the stylized examples and the party systems literature just described. As I will argue in a later chapter, Israel is a country of immigration. Many different groups of immigrants have made their way to its shores over the past sixty years. For example, in the 1950s and 1960s, large numbers of non-European Jews from the Middle East and North Africa, known as Sephardim, immigrated to Israel, and in the 1990s, close to a million Russian Jews did. These two groups of immigrants differed from Israel's existing citizens in a variety of ways, from their native tongues to their religiosity. Given Israel's permissive electoral system, the state-of-the-art literature just described would predict that these increases in Israel's social heterogeneity would lead to an increase in its number of political parties: it is natural to think that these

---

question, one to which I will turn later.

[21] Examples include Ordeshook and Shvetsova (1994), Amorim Neto and Cox (1997), Jones (1999), Mozaffar, Scarritt, and Galaich (2003), Chhibber and Kollman (2004), Jones (2004), Clark and Golder (2006), Golder (2006), and Singer and Stephenson (2009). There are some prominent exceptions, however. For example, Powell (1982) tested only for an additive relationship; Jones (1997) held the electoral system constant by design; and both Stoll (2008) and Moser and Scheiner (2012) have found limited empirical support for the posited interaction.

[22] Contrast, for example, the portrait of heterogeneity in Stoll (2004, 2011) with the portrait of homogeneity in Lijphart (1999).

9

new groups of immigrants would demand and be supplied with new political parties designed to give voice to their unique interests. Yet while Russian Jews have successfully formed their own parties, the Sephardim for the most part have not. Hence, the number of political parties has only sometimes increased as a result of changes in Israeli society that have increased its social, and specifically its ethnic, heterogeneity. But what can explain the different political trajectories of these two immigrant group? Why, in other words, have these different waves of immigration had different impacts upon the Israeli party system? The existing literature gives no leverage over these questions.

Similarly, African Americans were emancipated from slavery and enfranchised after the American Civil War of the 1860s. The inclusion of this new ethnic group in the citizenry, an event so revolutionary that it took military force to see it through, is also an example of an increase in social heterogeneity. Because of the United States' restrictive electoral system, however, one conventional reading of the literature predicts that this increase in social heterogeneity should not lead to an increase in the number of political parties. Specifically, the implication of existing theories is that political parties aiming to uniquely represent African Americans should not have emerged. And indeed, as a later chapter will argue, effectively no African American political parties were successful in the 1870s, a period known as Reconstruction. But following African Americans' subsequent disenfranchisement around the turn of the last century and later re-enfranchisement as part of the Civil Rights movement, African American political parties did successfully appear in some states and elections in the twentieth century. What can explain the appearance of these parties, despite the United States' use of a restrictive electoral system throughout this period, and why did they emerge in some states and elections but not in others? Again, the existing literature does not provide sufficient empirical leverage over these questions.

More generally, there have been many changes in both Israeli and American society, some of which have shaped the number of political parties and some of which have not—yet in each country, the electoral system has not changed in any meaningful way over time. Given the two countries' electoral systems, the state-of-the-art literature predicts only that changes in American society should have little impact on the number of American political parties, and that changes in Israeli society should have a substantial impact on the number of Israeli parties. It does not explain the variation over time within each country: why only *some* increases in social heterogeneity have increased the number of parties in these countries. Put differently, the literature does not shed any light on *which* of the many social changes that democracies might experience should be expected to impact the number of parties. Hence, to increase our empirical leverage over how changes in societies (preferences) shape the party system, we need better conceptualizations and measures of this variable, as well as theories that go beyond the conditioning effect of the electoral system. The following paragraphs elaborate upon each of these points.

To begin, take the closely entwined issues of conceptualization and measurement. The societal counterpart of political institutions, preferences, has largely been conceptualized as the heterogeneity or diversity of a democracy's society. But beyond this very abstract level, there has been surprisingly little discussion of how to conceptualize and measure this variable.[23] What exactly does it mean for one society to be more or less heterogeneous than another? Or, phrased longitudinally, what are the ways by which an individual society may become more or less heterogeneous as the years pass? For example, at times some scholars have taken heterogeneity to mean the number of social cleavages, with more cleavages equaling greater heterogeneity, while other scholars at other times have taken it to mean the number of social groups, with more groups equaling greater heterogeneity. Moreover, all existing measures of social heterogeneity are cross-sectional rather than longitudinal, despite a longitudinal perspective being better suited to testing causal hypotheses; almost all measure only a society's ethnic heterogeneity, despite the obvious existence of other types of heterogeneity, from the socioeconomic to the religious; and almost all operate at the national level, despite the modifying effect of electoral systems actually operating at the level of the electoral district. This begs the question: do the conceptualization and measurement matter? Evidence presented by scholars such as Stoll (2008) and Moser and Scheiner (2012) suggests that they do: that the conclusions we draw are sensitive to the way in which social heterogeneity is conceptualized and measured.[24]

Contrast this thin conceptualization with the much thicker conceptual schema that have been developed for political institutions such as the electoral system. For example, Cox (1997, 37) devotes an entire chapter (Chapter 2) to developing a "consistent set of abstract, non-country-specific terms that can be used to describe and classify electoral systems." There is no such comparable chapter for social heterogeneity. Also contrast the impoverishment of the measures of social heterogeneity with the many detailed, longitudinal, and multilevel measures of political institutions that have become available to researchers in recent years. Examples include the CLEA at the University of Michigan (discussed earlier) and the data set on political institutions and party systems recently compiled by Golder (2005). While there is certainly still room for improvement,[25] several decades of scholarly

---

[23]See Stoll (2004, 2008) for elaborations of this point and for reviews of the major conceptual and measurement issues raised by the literature. For many years, the most prominent exception was Jones (1997, 1999, 2004), who drew initial attention to these issues and developed some solutions. More recently, Moser and Scheiner (2012) have made important strides in the areas of both measurement and theory (see the following discussion for more about the latter). It should also be noted that Powell's (1982) important early work devoted significantly more space to measurement issues than is the norm.

[24]Stoll (2008) employs different measures of ethnic, religious, and linguistic heterogeneity. Moser and Scheiner's (2012) study is the first cross-national study of legislative electoral coordination to employ district-level measures of ethnic heterogeneity.

[25]See, for example, recent work by Kedar (2011) on measures of electoral system restrictive-

debate have resulted in relatively tighter connections between theories, concepts, and measures for political institutions.

Now take the issue of theory. How does an increase in the independent variable of social heterogeneity produce an increase in the dependent variable of the number of political parties? Thinking this through begs several questions. First, there are a variety of possible mechanisms and microfoundations for linking social heterogeneity to the number of parties. Recent work by Moser and Scheiner (2012), the most extensive study of social heterogeneity to date next to Stoll (2004), highlights this point. Which of these mechanisms is studied may in turn have implications for the precise nature of the relationship—for example, whether it is linear or not.[26] Second, are all increases in social heterogeneity alike in their capacity to contribute to the fragmentation of the party system? To provide just one example, almost all scholars have studied ethnic heterogeneity, Moser and Scheiner (2012) among them, as noted earlier. But it may be fruitful to hypothesize about how different types of heterogeneity shape the number of parties. Work by Stoll (2008) suggests that they do, in fact, have different effects. Third, are there other systemic factors besides the electoral system that might determine how social heterogeneity affects the number of political parties? For example, does the strategy adopted by existing parties towards a new social group shape its chances of successfully forming its own political party? Work by scholars such as Chandra (2004) and Meguid (2005, 2008) suggests that it might.[27] And is the electoral system the only political institution that conditions the effect of social heterogeneity, as the literature has held to date? Given the interest the type of regime has attracted from comparativists in recent years, it seems a logical candidate for consideration—yet thus far, no work systematically addresses this issue.

The contrast with the political institutional literature, with its deep and systematic body of theory, is again stark. As before, a good illustration is provided by Cox (1997). His book devotes several chapters to explicating the microfoundations or mechanism by which the electoral system shapes the number of parties—for example, through the strategic entry of candidates at the elite level and strategic voting at the mass level. By way of contrast, there are at most a few pages (certainly fewer than twenty) devoted to the variable of social heterogeneity.

Accordingly, we currently lack a conceptual scheme for describing and classifying the heterogeneity of democratic societies. We also lack a compre-

---

ness.

[26]For example, Moser and Scheiner (2012) suggest that both the size of a new ethnic group and the extent to which the group disperses its votes over the competing parties condition its effect on the number of political parties. This leads them, like Stoll (2004), to argue for a nonlinear relationship between social heterogeneity and the fragmentation of the party system.

[27]Meguid (2005, 2008) has explored the effect of mainstream party strategy on the success of single-issue "niche" (green, radical right, and ethnoterritorial) parties in Western Europe, while Chandra (2004) has explored the effect of the internal structures of political parties on the success of ethnic parties in India.

hensive theory, grounded in the actions of both political elites and ordinary voters, of how social heterogeneity shapes the number of political parties. Last but not least, we are missing the measures of social heterogeneity that we would need to test any such theory. Again, this is not to say that there is no scholarly work tackling the relationship between social heterogeneity and the number of political parties, or that there is no scholarly work taking steps towards addressing the issues raised in the prior paragraphs. There is. However, many studies have addressed only one piece of the often narrowly defined puzzle—for example, theorizing about a single potential conditioning variable or drawing evidence from a single country. The theoretical and empirical contributions of these different scholars, often working in different literatures, need to be both synthesized and built upon. In other words, comparativists now need to do for preferences what the new institutionalism has done for political institutions.

1.3 WHAT THIS BOOK DOES

In this book, I turn my lens on the other, relatively neglected half of the fundamental equation of politics: preferences. I first identify variation in the heterogeneity of democratic societies across both space and time. I then link this variation to variation in the party system, with my primary focus being the number of political parties competing in democratic elections. Accordingly, I study how democratic voice is shaped by *both* preferences and political institutions.

An extreme, although certainly not rare, example of how a democratic society can change is through the redrawing of the state's borders. Most significantly, countries may disintegrate, like the former Union of Soviet Socialist Republics (USSR), or unite, like the former East and West Germanies. Almost inevitably, change in the territory of a democratic state brings with it change in the state's citizenry. These are the individuals who by the modern understanding of democratic citizenship may exercise voice: full and equal members of the political community as adults, they have the right to participate in the democratic process, which at a minimum includes the right to vote. By changing the composition of this set of individuals, territorial changes are likely to change the state's party system. Extensions of the legal franchise, the tearing down of barriers to participation such as poll taxes, and immigration also alter the composition of a democracy's citizenry and hence who exercises voice, but they do so without altering borders. Of course, these are not the only ways in which societies can change, shaping who is exercising voice to what end. Over time, individual citizens' identities, beliefs, and values can shift; generations with new sociological characteristics and perspectives can replace their predecessors; and the balance among groups of citizens with divergent views can be upset by the groups' differing rates of natural increase, among others.

All of these societal changes have implications for the party system in democracies. However, here I focus upon the former type of changes, which are more likely to be exogenous to the party system: the addition of sets of individuals to and the subtraction of individuals from the citizenry through processes other than natural increase and generational replacement. This will usually change the heterogeneity of the citizenry. Specifically, the addition of a new group to the citizenry through historical processes such as territorial expansion, the extension of the franchise, and immigration will usually, but not always, increase societal heterogeneity. By extension, the subtraction of a group from the citizenry through these same processes will usually, but not always, decrease it. Because societal changes like these may be large in scale and tend to be sudden in nature, they should make an obvious mark on the party system.

Identifying and measuring these societal changes across space and time, isolating their impact upon the party system, and then exploring their implications more broadly for democracy itself are this book's goals. Many scholars have studied individual pieces of the general puzzle, as already noted. For example, scholars from Lipset and Rokkan (1967) to Bartolini (2000) have studied the extension of the franchise to the working class in Western Europe; scholars such as Lovenduski (1986) have examined women's suffrage; and scholars such as Van Cott (2005) have studied the entry of Latin America's indigenous peoples into the political arena. Other scholars have worked from the other end of the research question. For example, Hug (2001) has traced the formation of new political parties in advanced industrial democracies back to changes in society. Yet in order to develop a general theory about the likely effects of adding new groups of individuals to a democracy's citizenry, the insights of these numerous studies of particular places, times, and processes need to be pulled together. This is what I attempt to do here.

Accordingly, my research question in this book is how social heterogeneity shapes the party system, and primarily the number of political parties, in democracies. Throughout, however, I direct my attention to the classic mechanism by which an increase in social heterogeneity shapes the number of political parties. This mechanism is a new social group both demanding and being supplied with a political party that seeks to represent it to the exclusion of existing social groups—in other words, successfully forming what I will henceforth call a sectarian party. The alternative is that this new social group receives representation from existing catch-all parties. This leads to the secondary, yet perhaps ultimately more fundamental, research question that I ask in this book: why some new social groups successfully form sectarian political parties in some places and times (e.g., Russian Jewish immigrants to Israel in the late 1990s), while others in other places and times do not (e.g., African Americans in the United States during Reconstruction). By taking this approach, I follow Geddes's (2003, 40) advice about how to construct and test theories addressing "big" questions: by breaking the big question up into the smaller processes that contribute to it.

1. Introduction

To answer my research questions, I theorize about the conditioning effects of two types of factors. First are factors specific to the polity. These factors are both political institutional in nature—specifically, the electoral system and the regime type—and noninstitutional in nature, with the key factor here being the strategies existing parties play towards a new social group. Second are factors specific to the new social group itself, most importantly its size and politicization. My central argument is that the electoral system alone cannot explain whether sectarian parties successfully emerge to represent a new social group, and hence how social heterogeneity shapes the number of political parties. This is not to say that the electoral system is unimportant: I agree with the existing literature that it *is* an important conditioning factor. However, taking into account other factors greatly increases our explanatory leverage.

After developing my theory, I subject it to empirical scrutiny. To do so, I provide the first multi-method, cross-national, and longitudinal book-length analysis to date of the relationship between social heterogeneity and the party system.[28] In brief, as I will discuss in greater detail later, case studies of Israel and the United States are combined with time series cross-national analyses of both legislative and presidential elections. A critical step is to develop new measures of social heterogeneity, such as measures with a longitudinal dimension, which are used in the empirical analyses.

I find that, as hypothesized, social heterogeneity sometimes shapes the number of political parties. But with respect to the all-important "sometimes," several factors matter as much if not more than the electoral system, the conditioning variable upon which the existing literature has focused. An increase in social heterogeneity is most likely to lead to an increase in the fragmentation of the party system when the polity is not too socially diverse to begin with; when the new social groups are larger, politicized, ethnically defined, and originating internally; when existing mainstream political parties fail to accommodate the group; and when policy-making authority is not too centralized by the type of regime. By way of contrast, I find mixed empirical support for the conditioning effect of another systemic factor: party system openness.

To elaborate regarding the conditioning effect of political institutions, restrictive electoral systems do not preclude the equilibrium success of a sectarian party when the group is large in at least some electoral districts. The regime type is often the more important constraint.[29] The incentive to link across electoral districts in order to become the largest party in the national legislature, a function of the way in which the regime type distributes policy-making authority among different levels of government and within the national level of government, determines the extent to which the group's size in the national electorate will act as a constraint upon its successful par-

---

[28] For example, even the focus of Moser and Scheiner's (2012) recent manuscript is primarily upon the electoral system: only one chapter in their book is devoted to social heterogeneity.

[29] African Americans are a case in point here, as I will argue in a later chapter.

ticization. In other words, the less centralized policy-making authority is, the more likely it is that a new social group will successfully form its own sectarian political party. My exploration of how the regime type constrains the effect of social heterogeneity complements the recent surge of interest in this less studied political institutional variable. Further, by bringing the regime type into the story, I for the first time differentiate between the effects of social heterogeneity at two levels: the electoral district and the aggregate (national) level. This complements the recent surge of interest in analyzing subnational political outcomes.

Finally, I close by briefly investigating dimensions of the party system other than the number of political parties. While the number of political parties has received the lion's share of the scholarly attention to date, as noted earlier, scholars have identified other dimensions of the party system that are both practically and normatively important. To name just a few, there is the set of ideological or issue dimensions that are salient to the competing political parties, which some have called the political agenda (e.g., Stoll 2004, 2011); the positions that the parties take on these dimensions, as well as characteristics of these positions such as their polarization (e.g., Sartori 1976; Powell 2004); and, last but not least, the descriptive characteristics of political parties' personnel (e.g,. Rule and Zimmerman 1994; Jones 2009; Moser and Scheiner 2012).

Just as social heterogeneity may shape the number of political parties, I argue that it may also shape these other dimensions of the party system. Here, I focus upon arguably the most normatively important of them: the descriptive representation offered to different social groups by the competing political parties. For example, I explore how well women and the lower socioeconomic classes are represented across space and time. In general, changes in the social heterogeneity of the citizenry do eventually change political parties' personnel and hence the sociodemographic face of politics. However, the extent of this change varies with the type of the new social group, from country to country and with the passing of time. As part of this inquiry, I also explore the role new sectarian political parties play in shaping descriptive representation. Ultimately, I argue and present evidence that while sectarian political parties are not *necessary* in order for new social groups to secure descriptive representation, these parties have often played an important role. Because the success or failure of new social groups in forming sectarian parties has implications for democratic representation, I also argue that political institutions should not be engineered to preclude the success of sectarian parties seeking to represent at least reasonably large new social groups.[30] Yet when engaging in this kind of constitutional engineering, the devil is in the details of the electoral system. Moreover, the way

---

[30]The caveat "at least reasonably large" is important because constitutional engineers must take into account the oft-noted trade-off between representation and efficiency (e.g., Lijphart 1999). A polity's citizens must debate at which size of group the line should be drawn, and hence which balance between representation and efficiency they would like to strike.

1. Introduction

in which the regime type distributes authority is just as critical, even though it is often overlooked.

1.3.1 RESEARCH DESIGN

As mentioned earlier, the research design of the book is multi-method: observational, cross-national, and longitudinal quantitative analyses are combined with two within-case studies. I will now briefly elaborate upon each component of the design.

The cross-national quantitative analysis has two parts. The first is a study of all minimally democratic and partisan legislative elections in the advanced industrial democracies since the early 1800s. The second is a study of all minimally democratic presidential elections in the post–World War II era. For these analyses, new measures of social heterogeneity are developed. These measures range from longitudinal measures of the extensiveness of the franchise in a country to a cross-sectional index of heterogeneity encompassing six historically important divisions. This is the most extensive cross-national compilation, and the only longitudinal compilation, of data on social heterogeneity to date; as such, one of the book's major contributions is this original data.

Most studies—particularly the more recent ones—tackling this research question employ a purely quantitative research design.[31] Yet there are several reasons for mixing methods. The first is that adding a qualitative component increases a study's internal validity by compensating for certain inherent weaknesses of an observational and quantitative design (Kinder and Palfrey 1993, 3; see also King, Keohane, and Verba 1994, 479–480). A second reason for adding a qualitative component is that it provides additional tests of the hypotheses. That is, case studies may collectively provide great variance on the independent and dependent variables, with pairs of them capable of being matched and contrasted for empirical leverage (Munck 2004). The more the conclusions drawn from the case studies match those drawn from the quantitative analysis, the stronger the empirical support for the hypotheses and the more "dependable" our knowledge (Kinder and Palfrey 1993, 3). This process is also known as triangulation. Third and finally, while the necessary data was not available for testing a few of my hypotheses in the cross-national and quantitative analyses, it could be gathered for the two case studies. The case studies accordingly allow me to test hypotheses that I otherwise could not have tested.

The first case study is immigration to Israel. The second is African American enfranchisement in the United States. Both are examples of democratic citizenries undergoing rapid, fairly large-scale ethnic change—change that is relatively exogenous to the number of political parties.[32] Specifically, in

---

[31] A small minority employ instead a purely qualitative research design. The classic example of this is Lipset and Rokkan (1967); a more recent example is Van Cott (2005).

[32] Ethnicity is used here to refer to hard-to-alter, descent-based attributes. It accordingly subsumes race. These matters are dealt with at grater length in the following chapter.

each country, at least one new set of ethnically distinct individuals has been added to or subtracted from the citizenry. In Israel, two ethnic groups are studied. One of these groups consists of the Sephardim, Middle Eastern and North African Jewish immigrants who arrived in several large waves during Israel's first two decades; the other consists of Russian Jewish immigrants, who arrived in one small wave in the 1970s and one large wave in the 1990s. Given both the group- and polity-specific factors that I hypothesize condition the effects of increasing social heterogeneity, the Israeli case study explores the variation over both groups and time in these groups' success at forming their own sectarian parties. In the United States, by way of contrast, only one ethnic group is studied. African Americans were emancipated from slavery and enfranchised in the 1870s, disenfranchised in the South by 1910, and re-enfranchised in the 1960s. The case study is nevertheless able to test my hypotheses about both group- and polity-specific factors by leveraging the country's federal structure: the variation in African American sectarian party success is explored from state to state as well as over time.

Both are quasi-experimental, within-case studies that trace changes in the independent and dependent variables over time. Relative to the cross-national quantitative analyses, these analyses allow me to process-trace the hypothesized causal mechanism. In each country, social heterogeneity has varied over time, but several other important factors are effectively held constant. These include the electoral system, the conditioning factor upon which the existing literature has focused. The observed variations in social heterogeneity accordingly approximate experimental treatments, with the number of political parties being measured both before and after each change (Campbell and Ross 1968). To the extent that there is variation in how social heterogeneity has shaped the number of political parties, this means that factors other than the electoral system, such as the other conditioning factors about which I have hypothesized, must have a role to play. Moreover, measures that more validly isolate the causal process of interest are developed for each case. For example, in contrast to the cross-national quantitative analyses, it is possible to identify the sectarian political parties that emerged to represent the new social groups in each country, as well as to measure the extent to which existing parties accommodated these new social groups. As a result, as argued earlier, the case studies both triangulate the quantitative analyses and enable the testing of hypotheses that could not otherwise be tested.

There are several reasons for the choice of these cases. First, both countries are advanced industrial democracies, which holds constant many potentially confounding factors such as the degree of democratic consolidation.[33] Second, these are arguably the only two advanced industrial democracies to have experienced rapid, large-scale and exogenous change in the

---

[33]While Israel is a newer democracy than the United States, it had almost thirty years of limited self-government under its belt prior to its independence in 1948.

1. Introduction

ethnic composition of their citizenries.[34] Third, the two countries vary in the restrictiveness of their electoral systems, the key political institutional independent variable that is hypothesized by the existing literature to constrain the effect of social heterogeneity. Fourth, the two cases also vary on the dependent variable: new sectarian parties have emerged to represent the new social groups more successfully in Israel than in the United States, but there is also great variation within each case, as alluded to earlier. Fifth, quite unusually for an advanced industrial democracy, Israel has changed its regime type. It accordingly serves as a natural experiment for testing my hypothesis about how this political institution conditions the effect of social heterogeneity. Finally, by focusing upon ethnic heterogeneity in the qualitative analysis, that is, by holding this factor constant at the value most likely to favor sectarian party success, the cases serve as most likely cases for testing the hypotheses regarding the remaining factors. A similar rationale lies behind the focus upon African Americans instead of immigrant groups in the United States. In later chapters, I elaborate upon all of these issues.

The case studies draw upon the secondary literature, survey data, newspaper articles, and, in the Israeli case, several months in the field, which encompassed activities ranging from archival research at the Central Bureau of Statistics to interviews with politicians from a variety of political parties. I undertook significant original data collection for each. For example, surprisingly, longitudinal data did not exist on the descriptive representation of either African Americans in American state legislatures or the Sephardim and Russians in the Israeli parliament. This original data, like the original time series cross-national data described earlier, is another major contribution of the book.

1.3.2 ORGANIZATION OF THE BOOK

Naturally, the book begins with theory. In the second chapter, I develop a theory about how social heterogeneity shapes the number of political parties in a democracy. I first define the concept of social heterogeneity. I then turn to the relationship between social heterogeneity and the fragmentation of the party system. My focus is upon the most prominent mechanism by which social heterogeneity shapes party system fragmentation: a new social group successfully forming its own sectarian party. Moving beyond the electoral system, the explanatory factor that has drawn the bulk of the political science literature's attention to date, I both synthesize and build upon a variety of scholarly works to identify seven additional factors that condition the effect of social heterogeneity on party system fragmentation. These factors are the politicization of a new social group; the type of attribute defining the group; the group's size; the strategies played by existing

---

[34]This will become apparent in a later chapter, where I present data regarding the nature and magnitude of the major processes that have historically altered the social heterogeneity of democracies.

parties; the openness of the party system; the type of regime; and the prior social heterogeneity.

The third chapter turns from the theoretical to the empirical: measuring social heterogeneity. The two measurement strategies I develop in this chapter provide greater empirical leverage than existing approaches in that both move beyond a focus upon ethnic heterogeneity, and one is longitudinal. The first measurement strategy identifies and develops measures of three historical processes that have shaped the heterogeneity of the citizenry of the advanced industrial democracies from the early 1800s through the present day: changes in the franchise, changes in territory, and immigration. The second measurement strategy assesses a polity's heterogeneity on six key dimensions, ranging from ethnicity to foreign affairs. It then additively combines these individual dimensions into an overall index of social heterogeneity. This cross-sectional measure is constructed for all presidential democracies in the post–World War II era.

In the fourth chapter, I employ these new measures in two quantitative, cross-sectional time series analyses that test several of my hypotheses. The first analysis consists of modern, minimally democratic, and partisan legislative elections in the advanced industrial democracies, where social heterogeneity is measured longitudinally at the aggregate level. The second analysis consists of minimally democratic presidential elections in the post–World War II era, where social heterogeneity is measured cross-sectionally at the district level. I find that social heterogeneity is sometimes, but not always, related to party system fragmentation. Specifically, I find that the relationship is nonlinear, which means that the prior heterogeneity of the polity conditions the effect of an increase in social heterogeneity, as hypothesized. Moreover, I find that different historical processes and hence characteristics of the new social groups have also had a conditioning effect, again as hypothesized, as have the type of regime (that is, the centralization of policy-making authority) and, in some circumstances, the electoral system.

The fifth chapter is the first of two chapters that together constitute the within-case study of Israel. I begin by describing the changes in Israel's social heterogeneity from Sephardi and Russian Jewish immigration. I then explore the consequences of these increases in social heterogeneity for the fragmentation of the party system in Israel. To do so, I identify the Russian and Sephardi sectarian political parties that have contested legislative elections from 1949 through 2009. While political entrepreneurs have consistently attempted to supply these new ethnic groups with their own sectarian parties in Israel, I draw upon official election returns, demographic data, and the Israeli National Election Survey to demonstrate that the ability of these parties to attract the votes of a majority of their target audience has varied both over time and across groups. Because Israel has always employed one of the world's most permissive electoral systems, the Israeli case accordingly provides support for my argument that factors other than the electoral system also shape the likelihood of new social groups successfully forming

1. Introduction

their own sectarian parties.

In the sixth chapter, the second of the two Israeli case study chapters, I seek explanations for this variation in sectarian party success in Israel across both groups and time. The electoral system cannot be an explanatory factor because it is effectively held constant. Drawing upon both original and secondary data, I argue that the primary factors that contribute to an explanation of why the Russians have been more successful than the Sephardim at forming their own sectarian parties, as well as to an explanation for the specific timing of both groups' successes, are the type of regime, existing parties' responsiveness to the groups, and the politicization of the new immigrant groups. Notably, I am able to leverage a quasi-experimental design against my hypothesis about the regime type.

The seventh chapter continues the qualitative analysis with a within-case study of the United States. Initially, I describe the changes in the social heterogeneity of the United States resulting from African American enfranchisement. I then identify and estimate the success of the African American sectarian parties that have contested national political office (either the presidency or the legislature) from 1860 through 2006. Leveraging the federal structure of the United States, and drawing upon both original and secondary data, I finally conduct a quantitative analysis at the level of the states in order to test my hypotheses. I find that three factors explain the observed variation in African American party entry and success: the size of the group, the group's politicization, and the responsiveness of existing political parties. All other factors, such as the electoral system, are effectively held constant. I also argue that the equilibrium failure of African American parties is best explained by the small African American share of the national electorate, and hence by the regime type, instead of by the restrictive electoral system.

In the eighth and final chapter, I summarize the findings of the quantitative and qualitative analyses regarding the relationship between social heterogeneity and party system fragmentation. I then identify other dimensions of the party system to which social heterogeneity can be linked, with a focus upon descriptive representation. Using evidence from the Israeli and United States case studies, as well as cross-national evidence regarding the representation of women and the lower socioeconomic classes, I both argue for and present evidence for a relationship between social heterogeneity and descriptive representation. Moreover, again drawing upon evidence from the two case studies, I argue that sectarian parties have played an important role in securing this representation: either they have spurred existing catch-all parties to accommodate the new groups, or they have themselves supplied representation in the absence of this accommodation. I close by sketching some directions for future research and discussing the implications of my findings for constitutional engineers.

2 Social Heterogeneity and the Number of Parties: A Theory

In this chapter, I develop a theory about how changes in the heterogeneity of society affect one important facet of democratic party systems: the number of political parties. For both normative and practical reasons, this relationship has been the primary focus of the literature seeking to link society to the party system.[1] Yet more specifically, my goal in this chapter is to grapple with the question of whether new groups of citizens added to democratic societies by processes such as extensions of the franchise successfully form their own sectarian political parties, and why. These are newly formed political parties that seek to represent new social groups to the exclusion of other groups.

Drawing from the existing literature, I argue that the electoral system has an important role to play in this process. But I also argue that our explanatory leverage is greatly increased if we take into account several additional variables. Focusing on the electoral system alone leaves us unable to explain whether sectarian parties will successfully emerge to represent new social groups in most real-world situations. As I will argue in a later chapter, an example is Israel, where some groups of Jewish immigrants have successfully obtained sectarian representation but others have not. Moreover, both the existence and the electoral success of sectarian parties seeking to represent these new social groups in Israel have varied over time. Yet Israel has had an extremely proportional electoral system throughout its history, which means that the electoral system cannot help us to explain the outcomes of the Israeli case.

Accordingly, in this chapter, I undertake the first systematic identification of the factors other than the electoral system that condition the relationship between social heterogeneity and the number of political parties. I identify seven additional factors in total. Six of these factors exert their effect upon

---

[1] As noted in the previous chapter, this is not the only dimension of the party system to consider. A later chapter will accordingly tackle the issue of how changes in social heterogeneity shape facets of the party system other than the number of parties, from the types of issues on the political agenda to the sociodemographic face of politics.

2. Social Heterogeneity and the Number of Parties: A Theory

this relationship by shaping the specific mechanism that is my focus: the successful emergence of sectarian parties to represent new social groups. These factors include three characteristics of a new social group itself: a group's size; the type of attribute defining it; and its politicization. The remaining three factors are features of the democratic political system: the extent to which existing parties accommodate a new group; the openness of the party system; and the type of regime. While the latter is introduced here for the first time, the other factors have received some attention in the literature, upon whose insights I build. A final, seventh factor that is also introduced here for the first time conditions the relationship between social heterogeneity and the number of political parties, but not by shaping the mechanism of interest. This factor is the prior or initial social heterogeneity of the polity.

2.1 SETTING THE STAGE: THE FRANCHISE IN THE WEST

To begin, consider an example of a historical process that added large numbers of individuals to the citizenries of many countries: the extension of the franchise in the West in the nineteenth and early twentieth centuries.[2] States that have democratized in the post–World War II era, often hand in hand with achieving independence, have usually accepted that the franchise should be granted to all adult citizens.[3] However, the same cannot be said for earlier democratizers such as the United Kingdom. For most of these countries, contestation preceded inclusion (Dahl 1971), which meant that "the struggle for democracy...concerned suffrage primarily: the right to participate" (Alvarez et al. 1996, 5). Studying this historical process is one way to glean some theory-building insights.

In the West, barriers to participation have been built around a variety of sociological characteristics. The extension of the franchise to individuals outside of a small aristocratic and male elite—that is, the shift from a limited franchise to today's universal adult franchise—took place in two broadly defined stages.[4] The first stage enfranchised working-class and poor adult men by eliminating property and income qualifications for male voters. The second stage enfranchised adult women, which mostly occurred in the aftermath of World War I. Bartolini (2000) suggests comparing coun-

---

[2] The discussion that follows refers to national elections; the franchise was often different for sub-national (state and local) elections. Overviews of franchise reforms in this period are provided by Carstairs (1980), Flora (1983), Bartolini (2000, 206–221) and Aidt, Dutta, and Loukoianova (2006) for Western European countries, as well as by Mackie and Rose (1991) and Acemoglu and Robinson (2000) for the West in general.

[3] For example, India's constitution, which governed its first independent general election in 1952, instituted universal adult suffrage.

[4] Despite the use of the term "universal," most democracies today (Western and otherwise) still deny the franchise to some individuals, such as felons. Also, the definition of adulthood has shifted over time. While by the mid-1900s, the usual voting age had fallen to twenty-one from somewhere in the thirties, in the 1970s, many countries lowered it further still to eighteen. Some (such as Austria in 2007) have recently gone further by lowering it to sixteen.

tries on two characteristics of this historical process: how early or late they came to a relatively large male suffrage (timing) and how gradually or suddenly enfranchisement proceeded (tempo). For example, in some countries, economic enfranchisement took place gradually, with an extensive male suffrage appearing only in the late 1800s or early 1900s; conversely, in other countries, a large proportion of adult men were abruptly enfranchised in the mid-1800s. This same period also saw the franchise extended to many previously excluded religious, ethnic and racial groups. Examples include African Americans in the United States and the Maori in New Zealand.[5] However, this has generally received less attention in cross-national studies because few countries have employed such restrictions on the franchise on a large scale.

Take as an example the case of the United Kingdom, a process of enfranchisement that was both gradual and on the late side.[6] The First or Great Reform Act of 1832 both reduced and standardized the income and property qualifications for the franchise in England and Wales.[7] Upper-middle-class suffrage was provided by giving the vote to all men in more urban districts (boroughs) who occupied property with an annual value of at least ten pounds, while also extending the franchise to well-to-do tenant farmers in the more rural districts (counties). The effect of these reforms was to increase the electorate from approximately four hundred thousand to more than six hundred fifty thousand (Phillips and Wetherell 1995, 413–414). The Second Reform Act of 1867 further reduced the income and property qualifications and enfranchised part of the urban working class for the first time, increasing the electorate from one million to two million (Rallings and Thrasher 2007, 85–89). The Representation of the People Act of 1884, also known as the Third Reform Act, extended the borough franchise to the counties and hence introduced a largely uniform male franchise, although a stringent residency requirement was maintained. This reform expanded the electorate from two and a half million to almost four and a half million (ibid.). Universal suffrage for men of at least age twenty-one, subject to a reduced residency requirement, arrived only with the 1918 Representation of the People Act (or the Fourth Reform Act), when suffrage was also granted

---

[5]The case of African Americans in the United States reminds us that enfranchisement does not always proceed linearly: this group's enfranchisement was effectively reversed around the turn of the twentieth century with the end of Reconstruction. It was not until the ratification of the Twenty-fourth Amendment to the U.S. Constitution in 1964 and the passing of the Voting Rights Act in 1965 that African Americans were effectively re-enfranchised. I return to this case in later chapters. Significant reversals of this sort have been rare, however (e.g., Bartolini 2000, 220–221).

[6]Enfranchisement was also accompanied by reforms to the electoral system itself, such as standardization of the constituencies (e.g., eliminating "rotten boroughs") and the introduction of the secret ballot. However, my focus here is upon the franchise.

[7]Although today's Ireland was a part of what is now called the United Kingdom from 1801 to 1922, and Scotland is still a part of it, neither the Scottish nor the Irish franchise evolved in quite the same manner as the British franchise, not the least because each passed its own reform acts. For example, see Hoppen (1985) for a discussion of Ireland.

2. Social Heterogeneity and the Number of Parties: A Theory

to women aged thirty and older who were either householders or wives of householders. This expanded the electorate to approximately seventeen million from six million (ibid.). Finally, in 1928, universal female suffrage was granted to women of at least age twenty-one, increasing the electorate from almost nineteen million to twenty-five million (ibid.). Accordingly, the Fourth Reform Act was the most consequential of these reforms in that it almost tripled the size of the British electorate.

Elites of the day expected the extension of the franchise to affect the party system. They certainly believed it would work against their interests, which is why it took the threat of revolution to convince them to extend the franchise (Acemoglu and Robinson 2000). For example, in the British case, Lord Elcho (a leading Liberal Adullamite) argued that democracy meant "handing the country over to the Trade Unions and the rule of numbers, enabling the poor to tax the rich" (ibid., 1190).[8] More specifically, Saunders (2007, 574) argues that elites in mid-1800s Britain[9] viewed further extensions of the franchise and other electoral reforms as inevitable, but they disagreed over exactly which kind of reforms should be passed when because of the anticipated implications for partisan politics: "Depending on *who* was enfranchised and *where*, reform could...alter the balance between town and country or church and chapel, and swing a constituency from one party to another."[10]

The reformers who fought to see suffrage extended to the excluded groups also expected it to alter the political landscape. For example, pamphlets produced by the British reform movement in the 1840s and 1850s spoke of reform dealing "an irrevocable blow to the inordinate power... [of] the aristocracy" (ibid., 574–575). Similarly, early socialist movements in many countries fought to achieve universal suffrage out of the belief that it would lead socialist parties to victory at the polls, which in turn would enable them to replace capitalism with socialism (Przeworski and Sprague 1986). However, it is not clear that either side foresaw the appearance of new parties to represent the newly enfranchised masses, as opposed to existing parties simply accommodating the newcomers (e.g., Walton 1993).

So did new parties successfully emerge to represent the groups newly enfranchised during this period? A brief survey of the literature reveals that the evidence seems mixed. On the one hand, a large number of scholars have found the enfranchisement of both the rural and urban working class "intimately tied" to the emergence and the electoral success of social demo-

---

[8] A more humorous example is the famous March 1776 correspondence between Abagail Adams and her husband, John Adams, the future president of the United States. To her plea that the male delegates to the Continental Congress in Philadelphia (including her husband) should "remember the ladies" in the new laws that they were drafting, he responded, "Depend upon it, we know better than to repeal our Masculine systems" (Paxton and Hughes 2007, 32).

[9] See Acemoglu and Robinson (2000) for similar arguments about the West as a whole.

[10] For example, a reform bill that failed to pass the Commons in 1866 (the predecessor to the 1867 Second Reform Act) was described by the Conservative leader, Lord Derby, as a bill that would "extinguish the Conservative party for the next 20 years" (Saunders 2007, 574).

25

cratic parties and other parties of the left (e.g., Dahl 1971, 23)—at least, that is, the enfranchisement of the *male* rural and urban working class (Bartolini 2000). Hence, we have Lipset and Rokkan's (1967, 35) famous observation that all Western European countries developed lower-class parties at some point before World War I: the "uniform divisiveness" of the class cleavage. Similarly, some scholars have argued that successful confessional parties in Western Europe countries with large Catholic populations were a response, if an unplanned one, to the rise of mass democratic politics following the extension of the franchise (e.g., Kalyvas 1996). On the other hand, while the enfranchisement of women bolstered the fortunes of conservative parties, at least until late in the last century (e.g., Lipset 1960; Bartolini and Mair 1990; Paxton and Hughes 2007), the emergence—let alone the successful emergence—of women's parties was the exception rather than the rule (Paxton and Hughes 2007, 145–147).[11]

Hence, new political parties sometimes, but not always, emerged to represent the newly enfranchised groups of individuals during this period. What can explain why some of these new social groups achieved representation through their own sectarian political parties but others did not?

2.2 GETTING STARTED: LITERATURE AND THEORY

It is important to emphasize initially that the dependent variable that is the subject of this and subsequent chapters is the number of *electoral* as opposed to the number of *legislative* or *parliamentary* political parties. The number of legislative parties is produced by the electoral system's translation of votes into seats, the mechanical effect of Duverger (1963). But my primary interest lies not in this purely mechanical effect. Rather, I am interested in explaining how society and institutions jointly produce what is called the number of electoral parties, a concept that combines how voters distribute their votes over the competing parties with elites' decisions about whether to put a party on the ballot.[12] This is the psychological effect of Duverger.

The literature in comparative politics most relevant to my research question is that which studies both the institutional and societal determinants of the number of political parties in democracies.[13] The foundation of most

---

[11] Further, even the former, seemingly supportive evidence is complicated by a closer examination. For example, the role played by the "franchise factor" in the rise of the Labour Party and the decline of the Liberal Party in Britain is contested by historians (e.g., Matthew et al. 1976; Tanner 1983; Laybourn 1999). Similarly, Kalyvas (1996) points to the failure of a confessional party to emerge in France despite the fact that all of the right structural conditions obtained.

[12] Benoit (2002) in fact argues that using the number of legislative parties as the dependent variable when social heterogeneity is one of the independent variables is likely to yield a biased estimate of the relationship.

[13] Key works in this literature include Duverger (1963), Lipset and Rokkan (1967), Powell (1982), Ordeshook and Shvetsova (1994), Amorim Neto and Cox (1997), Cox (1997), Jones (1997), Filippov, Ordeshook, and Shvetsova (1999), Jones (2004), Clark and Golder (2006), and Golder

2. Social Heterogeneity and the Number of Parties: A Theory

recent scholarly work was laid by Cox (1997). He hypothesized that the heterogeneity of society interacts with the restrictiveness of the electoral system to produce the equilibrium number of electoral parties in a country. Specifically, there will be few parties either if society is homogeneous or if the electoral system is restrictive, where the microfoundation of the latter is strategic behavior by both voters and elites. Conversely, there will be many parties only if *both* the electoral system is permissive *and* society is heterogeneous.

But this account can be recast in a way that is more in keeping with my research question, which has the added benefit of illuminating the causal relationship between the variables. For example, Clark and Golder (2006) argue in their "rehabilitation" of Duverger's (and Cox's) theory that Duverger viewed political parties as a reflection of social forces or "spiritual families," which consist of individuals with a set of socially determined interests. As social developments such as industrialization and the expansion of the franchise increase the number of spiritual families that are politically mobilized, so too will the number of political parties increase—if and only if the electoral system is sufficiently permissive. In other words, Clark and Golder argue that when the electoral system is permissive, political entrepreneurs are more likely to form new, sectarian parties to represent new social groups demanding representation, just as new social groups are more likely to support these new parties. By way of contrast, when the electoral system is restrictive, neither elites nor voters are likely to back the formation of such new sectarian parties. Hence, there should be a positive relationship between social heterogeneity and the number of electoral parties in the former case, but no relationship in the latter case.

In what follows, I build upon this theory positing a conditional relationship between the number of electoral parties, social heterogeneity, and the electoral system. To do so, I first explore the conceptualization of the independent variable of social heterogeneity. I then identify the independent variables that condition the effect of social heterogeneity, which are expressly not limited to the electoral system. Throughout, two levels of analysis are considered: the elite level, that is, the strategic entry and exit of political parties, and the mass level, that is, voter support for political parties at the polls.[14] However, the focus is on political elites for two reasons: first, elites make the first move in the coordination game (Cox 1997, 26–27, 29–30, 151–172); second, elite behavior is more amenable to rational choice analysis than is mass behavior (Fiorina 1995).

(2006). An even larger literature has solely studied the influence of institutions, and most importantly the electoral system, on the number of political parties. A prominent example of this literature is Lijphart (1994).

[14] In Hug's (2001) terms, these are two separate research questions: explaining the formation of new parties versus explaining their success.

2.3 DEFINING SOCIAL HETEROGENEITY

A well-known Shakespearian adage holds that "a rose by any other name would smell as sweet." However, the variety of labels that the variable of social heterogeneity has acquired—for example, ethnic heterogeneity in Ordeshook and Shvetsova (1994), social cleavages in Jones (2004), and latent diversity in Stoll (2004)—suggests that greater conceptual clarity is needed. A theory about the effect of social heterogeneity upon the party system will be meaningful only to the extent that it is clear what social heterogeneity means, as well as what it does *not* mean.[15] My initial task is therefore to specify how I conceptualize this variable, drawing upon the work of Stoll (2004, 2008).

First, social heterogeneity is conceptualized as the diversity or heterogeneity of a polity's social groups—*not* the heterogeneity of its cleavages or divisions, which are the large-scale ways in which members of a society divide from and associate with one another (Zuckerman 1975, 232).[16] For example, what is of interest is how many ethno–religious groups there are in Israel (such as Jews of European ancestry, Jews of non-European ancestry, Christian Arabs, and Muslim Arabs) instead of the more basic fact that Israel is both ethnically and religiously heterogeneous. While the literature has vacillated between conceptualizing heterogeneity in terms of divisions and groups, it has always operationalized heterogeneity in terms of groups. My preference is for the group-based conceptualization because it provides the more theoretically compelling story linking social heterogeneity to the number of electoral parties, as Clark and Golder's (2006) "rehabilitation" of Duverger's theory makes clear.[17] Simply put, it is new groups, not new

---

[15] In the words of G. K. Chesterton in *As I Was Saying* (1936), "A man does not know what he is saying until he knows what he is not saying." An essential part of a social science that seeks to "make descriptive and causal inferences about the world" (King, Keohane, and Verba 1994, 7) is the testing of hypotheses that posit relationships between abstract concepts. This requires scholars to define concepts in a way that allows them (or their implications) to be observed and measured, what some have described as "maximizing concreteness" (ibid., 109). Such an approach to social science views concepts as neither right nor wrong but as more or less useful, where utility is determined by balancing theoretical importance and empirical precision (Zuckerman 1975).

[16] Zuckerman (1975) points out that the more standard term "cleavage" has semantic baggage: it usually denotes a specific kind of large-scale division within society, one along natural lines. This is why I employ the term "division" instead of "cleavage" in what follows. See Deegan-Krause (2007) for a recent review of the concept of political cleavages. Another term that I will sometimes employ is "category set," which is from Sacks (1992). Attributes are mapped onto "groups" or "categories," which can then be sorted into divisions or category sets. See Chandra and Boulet (2003), Stoll (2004), and Posner (2005) for useful discussions of these concepts. Other terms still are "dimension" and "conflict."

[17] One might retort that this is much ado about nothing because there is a relationship between the number of divisions and the number of groups. Each division must be anchored by at least two distinct social groups, so more divisions will equal more groups as long as the divisions do not perfectly overlap. However, because divisions may at least partially overlap, and because more than two groups may form around a division, the relationship between the number of groups and the number of divisions is likely to be weak. The former is the bigger empirical problem. For example, Rae and Taylor (1970, 14) argue that "virtually all extant

2. Social Heterogeneity and the Number of Parties: A Theory

divisions, who are the actors giving rise to new sectarian political parties. More specifically, I define social heterogeneity as the *number* of social groups: more groups equals more heterogeneity.[18]

Second, I define social heterogeneity inclusively. Social groups can be defined in terms of a myriad of types of attributes,[19] from language spoken to opinions about the European Union. Of course, these types of attributes differ in their "stickiness" (e.g., van der Veen and Laitin 2004) or "ethnicness" (e.g., Chandra and Boulet 2003), which is the amount of difficulty an individual has in changing them.[20] Types of attributes that are sticky, such as race, will be referred to as "sociological" here. This variation suggests that an attribute's stickiness may influence which groups are likely to succeed at forming their own sectarian political parties, an issue that is revisited in the next section. Accordingly, my analysis is confined neither to groups defined solely by sociological types of attributes, à la Lipset and Rokkan (1967), nor to groups defined even more specifically by ethnicity, a single sociological type of attribute, à la Ordeshook and Shvetsova (1994)—the groups that have been the primary focus of the literature to date.[21] To paraphrase Zuckerman (1975, 236), this less restrictive definition leaves the tie between the sociological nature of a group and its successful formation of a sectarian party to hypothesis.

Third, these social groups are *latent* or potential groups. A latent group defined by a sociological type of attribute consists of "the nominal members of an ascriptive [inherited] category such as race, language, caste, tribe or religion" (Chandra 2004, 2–3). For example, Jews who immigrated to Israel from a European country such as Poland are European Jews, regardless of whether they think of themselves that way, just as women with blonde hair are blondes, regardless of whether this ascriptive trait is constitutive of their identities. Conversely, a latent group defined by a nonsociological type of attribute arises from individuals' reactions to objective features of

---

cleavage systems result in some cross-cutting and...none result in complete cross-cutting; the pertinent question is not whether cleavages cross-cut each other, but rather how much they cross-cut each other." In general, for j divisions with n_j groups generated by the jth division, the number of joint groups (accounting for the relationships between the divisions) ranges from a minimum of $\max(n_1, \ldots, n_j)$ to a maximum of $n_1 \times \ldots n_j$, depending on the precisely how the divisions relate (Stoll 2008).

[18]While I agree that ideally we should also take into account how different the groups are, as originally suggested by Fearon (2003), the empirical difficulties in doing so lead me to focus primarily on the more straightforward number of groups.

[19]A type of attribute is a class of attributes with mutually exclusive values (Chandra and Boulet 2003). For example, "religion" is a type of attribute; in Israel, one possible set of mutually exclusive values or attributes belonging to this class is "Jewish," "Muslim," and "Other."

[20]For example, Chandra and Boulet (2003) place types of attributes on a scale according to the difficulty of changing them. Physical features such as skin color are placed at the high end of the scale, and occupation and place of residence are placed at the low end. The types of attributes that range from the high to the middle portion of the scale are called "ethnic" and the remaining types falling on the low end of the scale are called "nonethnic."

[21]Some scholars such as Rae and Taylor (1970) and Stoll (2004), however, have broken with the dominant approach in the literature, laying the groundwork for what I do here.

the world. An example is a country's decision to engage its troops in a foreign conflict. A hawk agrees with this decision, while a dove does not, but their opinions do not necessarily lead them either to identify with others with similar opinions or to act upon their opinions. Hence, membership in a latent group "does not imply active participation in a common group identity" (ibid.). Some scholars such as Chandra have used the word "category" to refer to this type of group precisely in order to signal its lack of groupness. Whether or not a group identity emerges, and how this relates to the formation of sectarian political parties, are other matters entirely—ones that are also revisited in the next section.

A complicating factor is that individuals are members of many latent groups, some of which are nested within one another. This is because there are infinitely many types of attributes that may be used to define groups, and accordingly infinitely many latent divisions or category sets into which groups may be sorted. On the sociological front, for example, possible types of attributes include hair color, body type, and shoe size. Moreover, there are infinitely many ways of constructing each division's set of groups, which is equivalent to saying that a particular type of attribute can take infinitely many values. For example, with respect to the religious division, Muslims, Protestants, and Catholics may be arrayed against one another, or Muslims may face off against a more encompassing group: Christians. From this constructivist perspective, *anything* can define a latent group; there is theoretically no end to how finely societies can be sliced and diced when assessing their latent heterogeneity. Consequently, which of these types of attributes and sets of groups become salient, that is, with which groups individuals ultimately choose to identify, is an issue that is also central to my research question.[22] At the same time, this theoretically appealing constructivist perspective poses great empirical challenges, as I will discuss in the next chapter.

Latent social groups can be contrasted with three additional types of groups that represent higher stages in a group's political evolution or salience (Stoll 2004).[23] The first is a politicized group, a latent group where members do participate in a common identity that encompasses shared beliefs and interests, as well as where an organization facilitating collective action by the group exists.[24] The second is a particized group, a latent

---

[22]This constructivist approach can be contrasted with the "election as census" approach of Horowitz (1985), who views ethnic demography as fixed and hence views elections in ethnically divided societies as akin to conducting an ethnic census.

[23]It is important to differentiate this schema from the dominant schema in the literature, which conflates what I have called politicized and particized groups by requiring that the organizational life of a politicized group take the form of a political party (e.g., Bartolini and Mair 1990). Note that normative value does not intrinsically attach to higher stages on this evolutionary scale. In a later chapter, I will weigh in on the issue of how empirically beneficial particization has been for a variety of real-world new latent groups.

[24]The distinction between latent and politicized groups is an old one. Consider, for example, the distinction Marx drew between "a class in itself" (*Klasse en sich*) and a "class for itself" (*Klasse fuer sich*). While Marx viewed it as axiomatic that the potential for class conflict inheres

group that has given rise at least one sectarian political party. The third is a successfully particized group, a particized group where the sectarian party not only contests elections but also receives substantial support from the group on election day. Some but not all latent groups will be politicized; some but not all politicized groups will be particized; and some but not all particized groups will be successfully particized.[25] Examples of latent groups that have been neither politicized nor particized are legion—for example, groupings of individuals around the trait of shoe size. There are also many politicized groups that have not been particized, such as Cuban Americans in the United States. Likewise, there are many examples of unsuccessfully particized groups, such as Jews of Middle Eastern ancestry in Israel—at least until recently, as I will argue in a later chapter. Hence, out of the "billions of potential conflicts in modern society...only a few become significant" (Schattschneider 1960, 64). In my terms, out of the infinitely many latent groups, only a few are successfully particized. Why this is so is the million-dollar question, the topic of the following sections.

But why focus on latent groups here? That is, why should I ask whether new latent groups are successfully particized instead of asking whether newly politicized groups are successfully particized? The reason is simple: doing so is the only way to make the claim that the arrow of causality runs from society to political competition, as I would like to do.[26] By definition, latent groups are *exogenous* to political competition. Politicized groups, by way of contrast, may be *endogenous* to both political competition and factors such as political institutions (e.g., Posner 2005). A long and distinguished line of scholars have convincingly argued that even seemingly natural and exogenous political divisions such as class do not "happen spontaneously as reflections of objective conditions in the psyches of individuals" (Przeworski and Sprague 1986, 7). Rather, someone—political entrepreneurs, for example, or even political parties themselves—must "politically forge" them (Laitin 1986, 159–160). Newly politicized groups may accordingly be

---

in all differentiated societies, that is, those where individuals' relationships to the means of production grant unequal access to scarce resources and power, he was careful to argue that differentiation need not always lead to conflict. Common interests must first develop among similarly situated individuals, which occurs when such individuals repeatedly interact in particular social circumstances. In the constructivist literature, the development of these common interests and hence of a shared identity, one important component of the process of politicization, is often described as a category becoming either salient (e.g., van der Veen and Laitin 2004) or activated (e.g., Chandra and Boulet 2003). Note that the organizational life of a politicized group may take many forms, such as schools, unions, interest groups, clubs, and newspapers.

[25] Hence, I reject what Zuckerman (1975, 237) describes as the deterministic approach of viewing social divisions as a "necessary and a sufficient condition" for the emergence of political divisions: that is, that latent divisions are objectively and automatically translated one-on-one into political divisions. Astute observers of late 1980s film might term this the Ray Kinsella approach: build it (a baseball diamond in an Iowa cornfield or a latent group) and they (the Chicago White Sox or a political party) will come. I instead side with the nondeterministic camp that views the former as a "necessary but not a sufficient condition" for the latter.

[26] Przeworski and Sprague (1986) famously pointed out the untenability of assuming that the arrow cannot run in the other direction.

Changing Societies, Changing Party Systems

the product of new parties instead of the cause of new parties, an issue to which I will return. Moreover, a newly politicized group may be rooted in an existing latent group instead of in a newly introduced one, divorcing its appearance from the sort of fundamental changes in a state's citizenry that are of interest. The most straightforward way to proceed is therefore to study the exogenous sources of social heterogeneity, which means to study changes in the diversity of a polity's latent groups. This is probably the reason why the literature has largely chosen exactly this research strategy.[27]

Fourth, I study increases in social heterogeneity that result from the emergence of entirely new latent groups: latent groups that are created by either new groups or new divisions cross-cutting (as opposed to the overlapping) existing ones. An example may help to illustrate. Let the citizens of a hypothetical country be partitioned into three ethno-class-religious groups. More specifically, let individuals be members of a single religious group, two ethnic groups and three class groups such that individuals in the first ethnic group exclusively belong to the first class group (call this Group 1), and individuals in the second ethnic group are divided between the second and third class groups (call these Groups 2 and 3, respectively). Now let a new religious group appear, but let every one of its members be a member exclusively of Group 1. Has a new latent group appeared or not? From one perspective, it has not: citizens are still partitioned into the same set of latent groups; it is simply that the set of attributes defining Group 1 has changed. However, from another perspective, it has: the country has moved from religious homogeneity to heterogeneity. Now let a new religious group appear that partitions Group 1 into two groups, giving rise to an entirely new fourth group. My interest lies in the likelihood that the genuinely new Group 4 from the second scenario will be successfully particized, not the redefined Group 1 from the first scenario.

2.4 RELATING SOCIAL HETEROGENEITY TO PARTY SYSTEM FRAGMENTATION

Having defined social heterogeneity, it is time to turn to its relationship to the number of electoral parties, my primary research question in this book. To begin, assume that the electoral system, the political institution upon which the literature has focused as a conditioning factor, does not provide incentives for seat-maximizing strategic behavior.[28] Under these institutional conditions, the simple hypothesis borrowed from the literature that

---

[27]However, see Mozaffar, Scarritt, and Galaich (2003), Jones (2004), and Posner (2004a) for some (arguable) exceptions by design, as well as Stoll (2008) for some examples of exceptions in execution.

[28]This is the most studied type of strategic behavior, which is aimed at affecting the allocation of legislative seats. A good example of a country where this assumption might hold is the Netherlands, which elects all 150 seats in the lower chamber of its legislature in a single, nationwide electoral district; has no formal threshold for attaining representation; and employs a list proportional representation formula for translating seats into votes.

2. Social Heterogeneity and the Number of Parties: A Theory

serves as my starting point is that the more socially heterogeneous a country is, the more electoral political parties that country will have.[29] Adopting a more dynamic perspective, an increase (decrease) in social heterogeneity should increase (decrease) the number of electoral parties.

The mechanism of this relationship upon which I focus is the one that underpins the conventional account in the literature: latent groups newly added to the citizenry being supplied with and electorally supporting their own sectarian political parties. An example discussed in a later chapter is Russian Jewish immigrants to Israel, who launched several Russian political parties that have done well at the ballot box. By extension, latent groups removed from the citizenry can no longer electorally support sectarian parties that have been representing them; unless these sectarian parties find a new modus vivendi, they will accordingly disappear.[30] An example is how Irish sectarian parties advocating for home rule, such as the Irish Parliamentary Party (Nationalists), vanished from the United Kingdom's electoral scene after Ireland (save Northern Ireland) obtained its independence in 1922.

How, though, does social heterogeneity relate to *party system fragmentation?* Party system fragmentation is a concept that encompasses both the raw number of competing political parties and the distribution of votes over those parties: that is, how dispersed or concentrated votes are, given the parties that entered the race. This is what most comparativists, myself included, have in mind when they speak of the number of electoral parties. What is meant is *not* simply how many parties there are, but how many parties there are *after taking their size (in terms of votes) into account*. The effective number of electoral parties, a statistic that weighs each party by its vote share when counting it, is the standard operationalization of party system fragmentation.[31] This concept is obviously closely related to, yet distinct from, a simple count of the number of electoral parties. My primary research question, accordingly, should be rephrased as follows: how does social heterogeneity shape party system fragmentation?

Despite this rephrasing, the basic hypothesis remains the same: that under the institutional conditions described above, an increase in social heterogeneity should increase party system fragmentation. Moreover, the mechanism described earlier linking social heterogeneity to the number of electoral parties is also a mechanism linking social heterogeneity to party system

---

[29] Here I paraphrase Cox (1997, 141–142), who argues that "the more cleavages there are in a society, the more parties it will have."

[30] The former is the well-known phenomenon of "goal displacement" (Selznick 1949). Alternatively, it may be viewed through the lens of the "iron law of oligarchy," which predicts that parties will be led away from their founding ideology by the desire of leaders and bureaucrats to preserve their power (Michels 1911). Hence, just as all new latent groups will not go on to successfully found a sectarian party, as I will argue, so too will all sectarian political parties not disappear following the disappearance of the group that they initially represented. This process should generally be shaped by the same systemic factors that I argue shape the likelihood of a new latent group successfully obtaining sectarian representation, my focus in what follows; however, organizational characteristics of the party itself are likely to play a larger role.

[31] I will say more about this statistic in subsequent chapters.

fragmentation: a new sectarian party both entering an electoral contest and gaining a reasonable share of a new latent group's vote, that is, the new latent group being successfully particized, will increase the effective number of electoral parties and hence the fragmentation of the party system. For example, if two parties had previously split the vote evenly between them, the effective number of electoral parties was equal to two. If a new sectarian party appears and splits the vote evenly with the original two parties, the effective number of electoral parties is now equal to three—a more fragmented party system.

But this is not the *only* mechanism linking social heterogeneity to party system fragmentation; there are others. For example, Madrid (2005) argues that a new group may fragment the party system even if there is no sectarian party to represent it. By dispersing its votes over previously existing smaller parties, it increases the effective number of electoral parties, and hence party system fragmentation, even though a simple count of the number of electoral parties remains the same.[32] More generally, Moser and Scheiner (2012) argue that once we stop assuming that each group will be represented by its own distinct party, an assumption that underlies the conventional hypothesis of a positive linear relationship between social heterogeneity and party system fragmentation, different relationships are possible. Specifically, these scholars make a compelling case that how increases in social heterogeneity affect party system fragmentation depends upon several factors, such as the number of social groups and their relative sizes, and how these groups either disperse their votes over several parties or concentrate them upon a single party.[33]

In this and subsequent chapters, I primarily focus upon the first of these mechanisms by which social heterogeneity shapes party system fragmentation, as discussed earlier. Hence, my secondary, if ultimately more fundamental, research question in this book is whether new sectarian political parties successfully emerge to represent new latent social groups. Under the institutional conditions also discussed earlier, the basic hypothesis drawn from the literature is that they will.[34] This makes my conceptualization of party system fragmentation narrower than most of the literature's, something that distinguishes this study from that of Moser and Scheiner (2012).

This brings me back to the million-dollar questions. Will *all* new latent groups be able to obtain political representation via their own sectarian parties when the electoral system is favorable, as described earlier? That is,

---

[32] Madrid (2005) provides evidence for this mechanism by studying the indigenous population in Latin America: effectively only recently enfranchised, this group has voted for smaller populist and leftist parties in countries where a sectarian indigenous party did not emerge, the result of which has been a more fragmented party system.

[33] Moser and Scheiner's (2012) argument is actually about *ethnic* heterogeneity, but the argument generalizes to social heterogeneity writ large.

[34] As will become clear later, this does simplify the existing literature's position. Nevertheless, it is the logical consequence of the state-of-the-art hypothesis relating social heterogeneity to the number of electoral parties already described.

will increases in social heterogeneity always fragment the party system under these institutional conditions? Contrary to the existing literature, the answer is, surely not. Of course, even if some new latent groups fail to turn themselves into particized groups, at least some will succeed. This will result in a positive relationship between the number of latent groups, my operationalization of social heterogeneity, and the fragmentation of the party system. Yet this still begs the question of *which* new latent groups are likely to succeed, and hence *when* an increase in social heterogeneity will lead to party system fragmentation.

In the following sections, I provide an answer to these questions by identifying the factors that condition the effect of social heterogeneity on party system fragmentation. In addition to the electoral system, seven factors are identified. Some of these factors are characteristics of the new latent group itself, while others are systemic characteristics of the polity in which the group is located. Specifically, six of the additional factors shape the likelihood of a new latent group's successful particization. These factors are a new latent group's politicization; the type of attribute defining a new latent group; a new latent group's size; the strategies played by existing political parties; the openness of the party system; and the type of regime. By shaping sectarian party success, which increases the fragmentation of the party system, these variables *indirectly* condition the relationship between social heterogeneity and party system fragmentation. However, the seventh additional factor *directly* conditions the relationship between social heterogeneity and party system fragmentation. That is, it does not affect the likelihood of sectarian party success. This factor is the prior or initial social heterogeneity of the polity. Figure 2.1 summarizes the theory that I develop.

2.4.1 Group Characteristics

I begin with the characteristics of the new latent group itself. By synthesizing arguments from the existing literature and then building upon them, I explore three such characteristics that shape the likelihood of a new latent group's successful particization: the politicization of the group; the type of attribute defining the group; and the group's size.

Group Politicization

Cox (1997, 16) suggests one answer to the question of "which latent groups" by arguing that "a belief that socially defined groups will always be able to organize in the political arena seems to ignore the problem of collective action." He then hypothesizes that the groups that will succeed are those that are "organized, that have leaders who can speak for their interests in an authoritative and public fashion, and that are perceived as usually voting as a bloc" (ibid., 142). Building upon this argument, my first hypothesis is that a group's politicization will facilitate its successful particization. A politicized group will be better able to overcome the collective action problem inherent

Changing Societies, Changing Party Systems

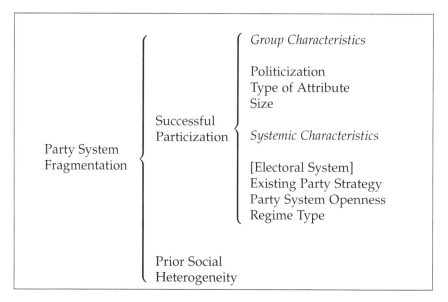

Figure 2.1: Summarizing the theory: the factors conditioning the effect of social heterogeneity on party system fragmentation.

in creating the collective good that is a political party.

Olson (1965) famously argued that the existence of a large collection of individuals with a common interest is not a sufficient condition for collective action. Contrary to the arguments of early group theorists such as Truman (1958), groups do not spontaneously emerge to provide their members with public goods. Rather, entrepreneurs must develop either the rewards or the coercive elements that motivate individual participation and administer these selective incentives.[35] Additionally, although Olson's analysis presumes a common interest, this, too, must initially be cultivated—again, usually by entrepreneurs.

Accordingly, elites, and specifically political entrepreneurs, have an important role to play in both the politicization and particization of a latent group.[36] Entrepreneurs help to politicize groups by encouraging the growth of a common group interest,[37] as well as by developing the organizational

---

[35] Wagner (1966), Salisbury (1969), Frohlich and Oppenheimer (1970), Frohlich, Oppenheimer, and Young (1971), and Walker (1994) developed the concept of the entrepreneur. See Olson (1971, 174–178) for a discussion of some of this work and how it complements his own.

[36] This emphasis upon the supply side stands in contrast to the emphasis on the demand side that pervades much of the literature, including other parts of Cox's (1997) own work. See, for example, the discussion in Stoll (2004).

[37] Many examples abound. One is how early socialist activists fostered the growth of a working-class consciousness (Przeworski and Sprague 1986). Another is the creation of the idea of "Tumbukaness" in the Tumbuka people of Malawi during the colonial period by missionaries and a small group of missionary-educated intellectuals (Posner 2004b).

2. Social Heterogeneity and the Number of Parties: A Theory

structures that allow the group's interest to be expressed.[38] Similarly, entrepreneurs play an important role in particizing groups. They must initially create a new sectarian political party and then rally the group around that party on election day. Perhaps not surprisingly, this entrepreneurial role has often been played by politicians,[39] who particize the divisions within society that will bring them power and suppress those that will not (Schattschneider 1960).[40]

There are two specific levels at which politicization, that is, a preexisting capacity for collective action, will aid political entrepreneurs in successfully particizing a new latent group.[41] First is the level of new party formation. Consider, for example, how much easier it is to gather the number of signatures required to register a party if there are existing group organizations upon which the entrepreneur can draw. Second is the level of new party success. Here, take as an example how pre-existing group organizations can aid in "get out the vote" drives. More generally, a sectarian party is more likely to attract the votes of group members if they are active participants in a common group identity. Politicization will also encourage entrepreneurs and other political elites such as media figures to coordinate on a single sectarian political vehicle, thereby avoiding the group's votes being split across several competing parties on election day.

Yet it is important to recognize that despite the advantages to particizing an already politicized group, particization may either precede or occur simultaneously with a group's politicization. In fact, it may be precisely the existence of a political party seeking to represent the group that both encourages the growth of the group's consciousness and develops its organizational backbone, as in Przeworski and Sprague's (1986) account of the rise of electoral socialism.[42] For example, a sectarian party may initially fail to attract a significant number of votes because of a group's lack of politicization. But by putting issues relevant to the group on the political agenda,

---

[38] Many examples again abound; see, for example, Kalyvas (1996) on the role played by Catholic activists in the development of Catholic lay organizations.

[39] Usually, entrepreneurs have a personal incentive to help organize efforts to provide a collective good. For example, Wagner (1966) argued that politicians may provide an otherwise unorganized group with political representation in exchange for votes. More generally, politicians may be motivated by the perks of office, policy, or both (Strom 1990a).

[40] Riker (1986) used the term "heresthetics" to refer to this form of strategic behavior.

[41] The literature on this general point is voluminous. One recent example is Van Cott's (2005) work on indigenous peoples' parties in Latin America: she finds that viable (successful) indigenous parties emerged only in countries where well-institutionalized, mature, and unified (that is, politicized) indigenous social movements existed. Another example is the relationship between Green parties and environmental movements (e.g., Hug 2001). Lessons can also be drawn from the literature on social movements themselves. For example, the availability of resources and elite cohesion are identified as factors that account for social movement mobilization (e.g., Foweraker 1995; Kitschelt 1986).

[42] Sartori (1969, 84) offers an eloquent, if extreme, argument along these lines: "It is not the 'objective' class (class conditions) that creates the party, but the party that creates the 'subjective' class (class consciousness).... The party is not a 'consequence' of the class. Rather, and before, it is the class that receives its identity from the party."

and thereby underscoring the failure of existing parties to meet the groups' representational needs, it may gradually manage to instill a shared identity in group members. This type of party is what scholars of new parties such as Harmel and Robertson (1985) call a "protest" or "promoter" party. Such parties do not anticipate voter support and electoral success as do "contender" parties; rather, their goal is to bring attention to particular issues and hence to influence other actors, from parties to voters.[43] Future sectarian parties will then reap the benefits in the form of greater group support at the ballot box. Hence, while politicization is necessary for successful particization in equilibrium, in the short term it is not.

Type of Attribute Defining the Group

Given my conceptualization of social heterogeneity, groups may be defined by many different types of attributes, from religiosity to opinions about foreign conflicts. That does not mean, however, that all of these groups are equally likely to be successfully particized, controlling for their politicization. Some scholars have argued that divisions where groups are marked by great cultural differences are good candidates for particization, while others have argued for certain types of divisions such as race (e.g., Posner 2004b). Evidence that the groups defined by different types of attributes do in fact vary in the extent to which they are successfully particized is provided by Stoll (2008), who found that ethnic, linguistic, religious, and cultural heterogeneity had different relationships with party system fragmentation. Specifically, only various measures of ethnic heterogeneity generally had the hypothesized positive relationship with the effective number of electoral parties. This suggests that new latent ethnic groups are the most likely to successfully form their own sectarian parties.

An explanation for these findings is that ethnic groups are better able to engage in collective action than other types of social groups. This makes them more likely to succeed at providing public goods such as sectarian political parties. Consider, for example, recent work by Habyarimana and colleagues (2007). Using experiments to identify the mechanisms that account for the well-known failure of ethnically diverse communities to provide public goods, this study found evidence for two mechanisms: strategy selection and technology. These mechanisms provide ethnic groups with the norms and networks, respectively, for sanctioning members who fail to contribute to collective endeavors.[44] Latent ethnic groups should accordingly be more easily politicized by entrepreneurs than other types of latent social groups, and already politicized ethnic groups should be primed for successful par-

---

[43] See also the classic treatment in Downs (1957) and a more modern example in Posner (2004b).
[44] The mechanism that they did *not* find evidence for is preferences: that is, group members either having concern for the welfare of fellow group members or sharing tastes (that is, agreeing about which outcomes are preferred to others).

ticization.[45] Groups defined in terms of other relatively "sticky" attributes such as religion should be similarly privileged, but to a lesser degree. Hence, the lower position of religion on the "stickiness" scale may explain the divergent findings regarding religious and ethnic heterogeneity.[46] In general, this argument probably underlies Cox's (1997, 142) hypothesis that ethnic, linguistic and religious minorities should be the leading examples of social groups that are able to overcome the problem of collective action and organize in the political arena. It might also explain the focus of the large social cleavages literature dating back to Lipset and Rokkan (1967) upon the "structural" or sociological divisions within societies.

Hence, I hypothesize that ethnic attributes are such potent observable markers of difference, ones that hold so many implications for the ways in which individuals interact with one another, that ethnically defined new latent groups are more likely to be particized than groups defined by other attributes, ceteris paribus.[47] More generally, the stickier the attribute defining the group, the more likely its particization. However, a cautionary note is warranted: like Posner (2004b), I believe that the trump card is held by other factors such as a group's politicization and its size. This is accordingly an argument only about propensities. Many scholars have demonstrated that a particular type of attribute is neither necessary nor sufficient for successful particization.

Group Size

Most political parties are vehicles for furthering immediate office- and policy-seeking goals. Political entrepreneurs therefore behave strategically in deciding whether or not to supply a new latent group with a sectarian party. The expected benefits of entry will outweigh the costs only if there is a reasonable chance that the new sectarian party will be large enough to exercise political influence. This generally means playing some sort of governing role, which brings both influence over policy and the plummest perks of office. If entry occurs, similar calculations at the mass level lead group mem-

---

[45] In contrast to the preferences mechanism, which should be at work only in an already politicized group (or at least in a partially politicized group that has developed a common identity), the technology and strategy selection mechanisms may function even in latent ethnic groups. The technology mechanism, in particular, merely requires group members to share certain ascriptive characteristics such as language or to interact more frequently; hence, it involves little in the way of "groupness."

[46] For example, Fearon (2003) argues that an ethnic group is a group that is larger than a family and in which membership is reckoned by a descent rule. Accordingly, religious groups may be viewed as ethnic or "sticky" if membership is primarily by descent instead of by public confession of faith. However, he argues that in many countries and time periods, such as the contemporary United States, religion does not have this ethnic character.

[47] In the modern world, prominent ethnic attributes are skin color and language. Interestingly, skin color (and race more generally) was a less salient ethnic attribute in the ancient world than language and cultural markers such as tattooing. Race vaulted into its current preeminent position only somewhere in the seventeenth century as a result of European colonialism and the African slave trade. See, for example, Smith (2008) on ethnicity in ancient Egypt.

bers to strategically decide whether to support the party with their votes, the anticipation of which feeds into elite calculations. The desire to govern accordingly provides an incentive to win a reasonable number of legislative seats, not just a few.[48]

At the same time, the size of latent groups varies greatly. At one extreme, a group may possess only a single member. At the other extreme, it may consist of the entire electorate. One answer to the question of how large a group should be in order to be successfully particized in equilibrium is therefore "large enough to play a governing role," a claim that can be made precise only after considering the political institutional setting—my task in a later section. Nevertheless, my basic hypothesis is that strategically minded entrepreneurs are more likely to particize groups that are large than groups that are small, just as strategically minded group members are more likely support a sectarian party if their group is large instead of small, ceteris paribus.

Moreover, I hypothesize that group size is a *necessary* factor for successful particization in equilibrium. Both Chandra (2004) and Posner (2004b) argue that *only* groups large enough to exercise political influence will be successfully particized. Recently, Posner (2005) has even more specifically argued that successfully particized groups will be minimal winning in size (see also Chandra and Boulet 2003), which means that they will be just large enough to secure political victory and no more.

Of course, even small groups may be successfully particized if their members do not behave strategically. For one, they may cast a sincere ballot for their preferred sectarian party, either because they are expressively motivated or because they overwhelmingly prefer it to others (see, for example, Moser and Scheiner 2012). For another, their strategic behavior may have a long instead of a short time horizon: they may support their sincerely preferred party in the near term with the strategic goal of altering the behavior of other political parties in future elections, turning their sectarian party into what I earlier called a protest or promoter party. I will return to this issue later. However, the latter type of small group will not be successfully particized in equilibrium. And with respect to the former type of small group, while the existence of expressive, nonstrategic behavior cannot be denied, I believe that there is enough evidence that individuals, and particularly elites, do often behave strategically that the successful particization of small groups in equilibrium will be the exception rather than the rule.

---

[48]This might be thought of as a version of what Cox (1997, 181–202) calls linkage in states with more than one electoral district. Linkage results when the pursuit of national policy and executive office provides strategic incentives for elites to come together under a common banner across electoral districts in order to control more legislative seats. Note that a party need not be a part of the formal governing coalition to play a governing role. I will later return to these issues in greater depth.

2.4.2 SYSTEMIC FEATURES

Characteristics of the group are obviously not the only factors that matter. Systemic features of the polity in which a new latent group is located also shape the likelihood of its successful particization; further, some systemic factors determine the ultimate impact of this particization upon the fragmentation of the party system.

I initially develop arguments about the role of two noninstitutional systemic variables: the strategies played by existing political parties and the openness of the party system. I then turn to political institutions: the electoral system and the type of regime. Last but not least, I discuss the prior social heterogeneity of the polity, which conditions the effect of social heterogeneity upon party system fragmentation but does not shape the likelihood of sectarian party success. My arguments about the regime type and the prior social heterogeneity are introduced here for the first time. For the other variables, I again synthesize the insights of the existing literature and then build upon them.

Existing Party Strategy

As Hug (2001) argues, the successful emergence of a new political party is one possible outcome of the interaction between existing parties and a new latent group. An alternative is that existing parties employ strategies to head off the entry of new parties, or if entry is not deterred, to weaken the new entrant at the ballot box.

How can this be done? Two possibilities are suggested by the literature. The first is that existing parties ignore the new group *qua* group, downplaying the salience—even perhaps the legitimacy—of its identity and demands. This corresponds to what Meguid (2005) calls a dismissive strategy. The second possibility is that existing parties reach out to the new group, the catchall (e.g., Kirchheimer 1966) or accommodative (Meguid) strategy. That is, they appeal to it, staking out favorable positions in response to its demands, while simultaneously continuing to appeal to their existing constituencies.[49] By way of contrast, existing parties facilitate the success of a new party when their response takes the form of what Meguid calls an adversarial strategy. Here, they batten down the hatches and defend the interests of their existing constituencies. By acknowledging the new group *qua* group but at the same time opposing its demands, they raise its salience.

First consider the entry of new sectarian parties. This is a topic that has unfortunately received little empirical attention: existing party behavior does not feature in the empirical analyses of either Hug (2001) or Tavits (2006), and both Chandra (2004) and Meguid (2005) black-box new party entry to focus on new party success. Hug (2001, 15–24) does provide an extended example of an accommodative strategy heading off the entry of a

---

[49]Chandra (2004) calls existing parties that employ these strategies nonethnic and multiethnic, respectively, to be contrasted with her sectarian ethnic parties.

Green party in the Netherlands for many years. Drawing upon the work of Inglehart and Andeweg (1993), he argues that the openness of established parties to the new post-materialist demands served as a deterrent: existing parties both acknowledged the importance of post-materialist issues and adopted the desired post-materialist policies precisely because they wanted to "take the wind out of the sails" of nascent Green parties contemplating entry (Inglehart and Andeweg 1993, 358). But why this accommodative strategy? Inglehart and Andeweg postulate that the permissive political institutional structure in the Netherlands, like that assumed here, led existing parties to anticipate new party entry and hence to react preemptively to deter it, although this still leaves the question of why an accommodative instead of a dismissive approach was the strategy of choice. An example of a dismissive strategy heading off the entry of a working-class party for almost two decades is provided by Britain in the aftermath of the Second Reform Act of 1867: the existing Conservative and Liberal parties did not compete for the favor of the newly enfranchised component of the working class by appealing to class issues; rather, with few exceptions, the new voters were incorporated within the two parties' local organizations, and the parties kept dangerous items off of the political agenda by pursuing orthodox policy programs and raising the salience of cross-cutting religious issues (e.g., Walton 1993, 33-50).

Now consider the success of new sectarian parties where entry has occurred. Meguid (2005, 2008) finds empirical support for her arguments that mainstream party strategies matter in determining the electoral success of what she calls "niche" (that is, radical right and Green) parties in post-1970 Western Europe. Specifically, any combination of dismissive and accommodative strategies reduces niche party success. However, if at least one existing party plays either an adversarial strategy with more fervor than another plays an accommodative strategy, or an adversarial strategy against another's dismissive strategy, niche party success increases. Similarly, existing parties' adoption of an accommodative strategy accounts for Ahuja's (2008) seemingly counterintuitive finding that Dalit parties in Indian states with strong Dalit social movements have been less successful than Dalit parties in states that lack strong Dalit social movements. By raising the salience of the issues of concern to the group, the strong social movements have encouraged existing parties to adopt accommodative strategies, reducing the appeal of sectarian parties when they finally appeared on the political scene; however, in these movements' absence, existing parties have felt no pressure to adopt accommodative stances, leaving open the door to future sectarian party success.

An interesting operational approach to accommodative strategies is offered by Chandra (2004, 82–98). She hypothesizes that voters in patronage democracies develop preferences over parties by "counting the heads" of co-ethnics among party personnel. In a limited-information setting, the ethnic identity of party personnel provides a better guarantee of the delivery

2. Social Heterogeneity and the Number of Parties: A Theory

of both psychological and material benefits than either the issue positions of parties or the nonethnic characteristics of party personnel, such as their character, reputation, and influence. Party strategy accordingly takes the form of offering different amounts of descriptive representation to different social groups. However, because information is a scarce resource in all democracies, this argument should also generalize to nonpatronage democracies, even if it will have less force there.[50]

Accordingly, my hypothesis is that the use of accommodative and/or dismissive strategies by existing parties will head off sectarian party entry, as well as dampen the electoral success of any entrants, ceteris paribus. Equivalently, to the extent that existing parties neither dismiss nor accommodate new latent groups, they leave the door open to the successful particization of these groups. This situation is particularly ripe for exploitation by a promoter sectarian party: it can enter and enjoy success in the short run, aiming in the long run to convince the original parties to adopt more accommodative strategies. If at least one original party then accommodates the group, the promoter party will bow out, and the new group will not be successfully particized in equilibrium. If the nonaccommodative behavior persists in equilibrium, however, then the promoter party will turn itself into a contender party, and the group will be successfully particized in equilibrium. This makes the response of existing parties a necessary factor for the successful particization of new latent groups. More specifically, I operationalize accommodation by hypothesizing that a sectarian party will experience electoral success only to the extent that it offers more descriptive representation to the new group's members than existing nonsectarian parties do. Further, the greater this differential, the greater the sectarian party's success.

This begs the question of what can explain how much representation a new group receives in existing parties. Pushing the causal chain back another step, Chandra (2004) argues that if existing parties employ competitive rules for intraparty advancement, which means holding elections for organizational posts and opening membership to all interested individuals, they will be open to elites from a new group. Her hypothesis is accordingly that a sectarian party's likelihood of entry and electoral success will be reduced the more competitive existing parties' internal selection procedures are. Yet uncompetitive internal selection procedures do not necessarily preclude groups from obtaining representation within existing parties. Even dictatorial party leaders may ensure balance in the representation of different groups in the belief that balance will yield electoral dividends, increasing the size of the office and policy pie available for distribution. The game, in other words, is not necessarily zero-sum. And in fact, some scholars have argued that noncompetitive selection procedures yield more equitable results (e.g., Hazan and Rahat 2000; Rahat, Hazan, and Katz 2008).[51] Other

---

[50]See, for example, Birnir (2007, 9) on how ethnicity provides a "stable yet flexible information shortcut for political choices" in all (both new and mature) democracies.

[51]But see Bruhn (2009) for evidence from Mexico suggesting that competitive procedures such

43

scholars have studied other organizational characteristics of parties such as their centralization and institutionalization (that is, clarity of rules). Both the arguments and the empirical results about which characteristics are favorable to the representation of new and underrepresented groups such as women have again been mixed (e.g., Norris 1993; Caul 1999; Matland 2003).

These competing arguments and evidence suggest that there should not be a strong relationship between party organization, candidate selection procedures, and descriptive representation, contrary to Chandra's argument. This in turn supports an operational focus on the actual representation that different groups obtain, which is my approach in the later empirical chapters.

Party System Openness

The existence of entrenched, long-established political parties reduces the likelihood that new sectarian parties will successfully emerge to represent a new latent group. Dealignment and the decline or fragmentation of existing parties are all processes that open up space in a formerly frozen party system for new parties. By detaching some members of the electorate from existing parties, making them available as potential supporters, they provide incentives for political entrepreneurs to form new parties (Van Cott 2005, 33). More generally, moments of change and turbulence are held to provide entrepreneurs with the opportunity to exercise agency: to create new identities, which I have called politicization, and to forge new political coalitions, which I have called particization (Enyedi 2008).

While I am generally sympathetic to this argument, I do not believe that it is always applicable. A closed party system is likely to preclude the successful particization of a new latent group only when the group's members are either already citizens—for example, converts to a new religion—or long-standing residents, such as the previously disenfranchised. Citizens and long-term residents should both have been socialized to identify with existing parties to some extent if the party system is closed. However, existing citizens are likely to be more strongly attached to existing parties than mere residents, who have been barred from the ballot box in the past. Yet even citizens in a closed party system may switch their party allegiance if other factors are favorable enough. By way of contrast, when the members of a new latent group, such as immigrants, are completely new to the polity, it does not seem plausible to hypothesize that party system openness will have an effect. The members of this type of new group are already detached from existing parties, which means that they are available for particization. My hypothesis is accordingly that party system openness is not a necessary factor for the successful particization of a new latent group, but it may

---

as primaries do produce more representative candidates, although her focus is upon ideological rather than descriptive representation. She also provides a good review of the long-running debate over the relative representativeness of candidates chosen by competitive (that is, selection by primary) and noncompetitive (that is, selection by party leadership) procedures.

2. Social Heterogeneity and the Number of Parties: A Theory

facilitate successful particization when the group's members are long-term inhabitants of the polity, ceteris paribus.

Electoral System

Elections can be viewed as coordination games (Cox 1997) with two distinct levels: the first occurring within electoral districts and the second occurring across them (e.g., Hicken and Stoll 2011). The political institution that determines the amount of coordination required to win an electoral district's legislative seats is the electoral system. A commonly encountered definition of the electoral system is that it is the set of rules governing the translation of votes into seats. As such, it determines the threshold of representation, which is the minimum percentage of the vote that a party must win in a district in order to be assured of being awarded at least one of the district's seats (Lijphart 1994, 25–30).[52]

Consider first the situation when the threshold of representation is high, as in a single-member district with a majoritarian electoral formula. Electoral systems with high thresholds are those that I have called restrictive or majoritarian. In this setting, groups have an incentive to engage in pre-election coordination. In other words, to have a reasonable chance of winning in this kind of electoral district, it is necessary to build a large coalition that consists of a reasonable share of the district's electorate. Now consider the situation where the threshold of representation is low, as in a multi-member district with a proportional representation electoral formula. I have called this type of electoral system permissive or proportional. Here, groups have little or no incentive to engage in pre-electoral coordination. Because even very small groups have a reasonable chance of winning, there is no need to make the compromises that must be made to build a large coalition.

The existence of strategic incentives for coordination when the electoral system threshold is high is the foundation of the well-known hypothesis of Reed (1990) and Cox (1997): that in equilibrium, the effective number of electoral parties in a district will be equal to the district magnitude (M), the number of seats that the district elects, plus one (that is, $M + 1$). This is known as the carrying capacity of the electoral system in that district, an upper bound on the number of parties that are viable competitors in equilibrium. For example, in a single-member district, the expectation is that the equilibrium effective number of electoral parties will equal two. Accordingly, the key feature of the electoral system that determines the threshold of representation and hence its position on the restrictiveness-

---

[52] Many different ways of formally calculating this threshold, as well as a broader "effective threshold," have been proposed (e.g., Taagepera and Shugart 1989; Lijphart 1994; Taagepera 2007). However, I use the term loosely here. This is because all actual calculations of the threshold obviously must (and do) take into account the number of parties, which has the downside of turning the threshold from an exogenous into an endogenous variable. I accordingly follow the common practice of focusing upon the key institutional determinant of the threshold instead of upon the threshold itself, as will be discussed.

to-permissiveness continuum is the district magnitude.[53] The microfoundations of the relationship are strategic entry and exit by elites and strategic voting by voters. However, this strategic behavior and hence the $M + 1$ relationship breaks down when the district magnitude is greater than five: the informational assumptions that one must make about voters in order for them to be able to vote strategically, and to a lesser degree about elites in order for them to be able to engage in strategic entry, become unrealistic (Cox 1997, 100). A district magnitude of five therefore demarcates the two types of electoral systems.

What are the implications for increases in social heterogeneity? As I have already discussed at length, it is the conditioning effect of the electoral system that has received the lion's share of the literature's attention to date. The arguments are accordingly well known and need only be briefly reviewed here. The social structure of a country gives rise to a certain "natural" number of parties. As was argued earlier, more socially heterogeneous countries will have a larger natural number of parties. If a country's natural number of parties exceeds the district's carrying capacity of $M + 1$ parties and the district magnitude is less than five, strategic behavior by voters and elites will winnow down the partisan field, reducing the number of parties below the natural number to the carrying capacity (Cox 1997). Hence, an increase in social heterogeneity should increase party system fragmentation if the electoral system is permissive, but not if it is restrictive.[54] By extension, under a restrictive electoral system, unless a large proportion of a district's electorate belongs to a new latent group, it is unlikely that in equilibrium, elites will supply the group with its own sectarian party (strategic entry) or that voters will support such a party (strategic voting) in that district. Conversely, under a permissive electoral system, elites will not be deterred from supplying and voters will not be deterred from supporting a sincerely preferred sectarian party, even if the group consists of a small fraction of the district's electorate.[55]

---

[53] There is substantial empirical evidence for this effect. For example, at the elite level, scholars such as Hug (2001), Rice and Van Cott (2006), and Tavits (2006) have found the typical district magnitude in a country to be positively related to that country's aggregate number of new parties. Combining the elite and mass levels, numerous scholars from Ordeshook and Shvetsova (1994) to Clark and Golder (2006) have also found the typical district magnitude to be positively related to a country's aggregate party system fragmentation. Similarly, other scholars such as Hug (2001) and Rice and Van Cott (2006) have found it to be related to the share of the national vote that new parties obtain.

[54] There is also substantial empirical evidence for this conditioning effect (e.g., Cox 1997; Mozaffar, Scarritt, and Galaich 2003; Clark and Golder 2006). But for evidence against it, see Jones (1997), an analysis of Louisiana state legislative elections at the level of the electoral district; Van Cott (2005), a study of the emergence of successful indigenous parties in Latin America; and Moser and Scheiner (2012), a district-level analysis of five polities employing mixed-member electoral systems. However, with rare exceptions, empirical analyses have been conducted at the national level. As a result, most both gloss over variance from district to district and fail to measure social heterogeneity where it matters for testing the hypothesis: in the electoral district. The next chapter revisits these issues.

[55] For example, Lipset and Rokkan (1967, 29–33) argue that where the early electoral systems set a high threshold for gaining representation, it was difficult for the newly enfranchised

2. Social Heterogeneity and the Number of Parties: A Theory

In sum, then, the hypothesis that I draw from the literature is that a low district magnitude will reduce the likelihood of a new latent group being successfully particized in an electoral district, ceteris paribus. However, this constraint will operate only when the group is small. One way in which group size matters is therefore at the level of the electoral district. To elaborate, consider the maximally restrictive case of a single-member district. Exactly how large a new latent group must be for both elites and voters to view a potential sectarian party as viable will depend upon the sizes of the other, preexisting groups in the district. Yet accepting the arguments advanced earlier that the ideal group is one that is minimal winning in size, I more specifically hypothesize that new latent groups are likely to be successfully particized under restrictive electoral systems if their sizes range from a near-plurality to a bare majority of the district's electorate, and that they will not be successfully particized in equilibrium if they are smaller than this.[56] Conversely, when the district magnitude is large, a sectarian party seeking to represent even a very small group still has a good chance of winning at least one of the district's seats. An example is the Netherlands, where a group with slightly less than one percent of the country's electorate might still reasonably expect its party to win one seat in the single national electoral district. Accordingly, the electoral system is a necessary factor for a new latent group's successful particization, unless the group is large: smaller groups will be successfully particized in equilibrium only under a permissive electoral system.

Of course, the conditions for Duvergerian equilibria must be satisfied if the electoral system is to constrain the effect of social heterogeneity in an electoral district, as just hypothesized.[57] But it may be the case that these conditions are *not* satisfied in a given election. Elites in a single-member

---

working class to attain representation on its own. An example is the series of "Lib-Lab" pacts in Britain around the turn of the last century, such as the secret agreement between Labour Representation Committee Secretary Ramsey MacDonald and Liberal whip Herbert Gladstone that the two parties would not compete in approximately thirty British districts in the 1906 election. The districts where Labor did successfully run candidates were primarily industrial, meaning that the party's targeted constituency, the working class, made up a significant share of the electorate (Pugh 1982; Laybourn 1999; Searle 2004). By way of contrast, where the early electoral systems set a lower threshold for gaining representation, the working class was more inclined to part ways with liberal parties and to strike out on its own. An example is Sweden, where the Social Democratic and Liberal alliance that had formed to advocate for the extension of the franchise collapsed when proportional representation was introduced (Eley 2002, 67). Further, not only did the Swedish Social Democrats largely fight elections alone, they successfully campaigned in most districts, even those where the working class made up a small share of the population (Berman 1998; Svarlik 2002; Caramani 2004).

[56] See, for example, Butler and Stokes (1969, 146–148), who found that working-class support for Labour in the United Kingdom increased curvilinearly with the percentage of workers in a district.

[57] Cox (1997) lays out these conditions in his now-classic work. For example, incentives for strategic voting are undermined by a lack of information about the rankings of parties, particularly the absence of a clear distinction between the second-place (or first loser) and third-place contenders, and an expectation that one party will almost certainly win. If elites anticipate this, the incentives for strategic entry will also be undermined.

district may then behave nonstrategically by supplying a small-ish new latent group with a sectarian party, and voters may behave nonstrategically by backing it. Changes in social heterogeneity are particularly likely to undermine the conditions for Duvergerian equilibria. For example, they will often result in uncertainty about the rankings of parties (e.g., it may not be known how a new latent group will vote or exactly how large the group is), although this should be the case only in the short run. It is also possible that citizens simply behave expressively instead of strategically, as discussed earlier, with the same end result of small-ish new groups being successfully particized under restrictive electoral systems, as argued by Moser and Scheiner (2012). Accordingly, successful particization may sometimes occur when political institutional conditions are not optimal—for example, under a restrictive electoral system—contrary to the equilibrium arguments offered here. But these should be exceptions rather than the rule.

I note in closing that there are other features of the electoral system that determine the threshold of representation. These features have received less empirical attention, however, particularly in the quantitative literature. They include formal legal thresholds, such as the two percent of the vote that a party must currently win in Israel to participate in the allocation of legislative seats; the electoral formula actually translating the votes into seats; and the existence and size of a compensatory upper tier of seats. The most important of these features is the legal threshold. Requiring that a party receive a minimum share of a district's votes in order to be allocated seats obviously precludes the successful particization of new latent groups whose share of the electorate falls below this threshold. A reasonably large and compensatory upper tier of seats is another important feature.[58] An example is the increasingly popular mixed-member electoral system employed by Germany. This type of electoral system combines single-member districts with a large number of compensatory upper-tier seats, which are distributed to parties so that the ultimate distribution of seats is proportional to the national-level distribution of votes (Shugart and Wattenburg 2001). Even if a new latent group is too small in one district to produce a viable party there, a compensatory upper tier like this one means that the votes cast for such a party are not necessarily wasted. Yet the effect of compensatory upper tiers is not limited to electoral coordination within districts: both they and vote thresholds at the national level also encourage coordination across electoral districts (Cox and Knoll 2003; Hicken and Stoll 2009), the second level of the coordination game to which I now turn.

Regime Type

How are individual electoral districts stitched together into a national party system? While the district magnitude determines how much coordination is needed to win a legislative seat in a single district, it contains no informa-

---

[58]However, for evidence against the importance of upper tiers, see Clark and Golder (2006).

tion about the value of that seat. As argued in an earlier section, political entrepreneurs, other elites, and voters all have an incentive to back parties that are large enough to play a governing role at the national level. This means that parties must command a reasonable number of legislative seats, not just a few. Building such aggregated or nationalized parties, particularly when there is a large number of districts that each elect a small number of legislators, involves coordinating across districts, bringing individual candidates or parties from different districts together under one of a few common party banners (Cox 1997; Chhibber and Kollman 1998, 2004; Cox 1999; Cox and Knoll 2003; Hicken 2009; Hicken and Stoll 2009, 2011).

Exactly how large, and hence how aggregated, political parties must be in order to play a governing role depends upon the centralization of policy-making authority in the polity, a concept that I view as including the perks of office. If this authority is centralized in the hands of the largest party in the national legislature, both elite and mass-level actors have an incentive to engage in extensive strategic coordination across districts in a bid to be that largest party, which means being able to win at least a plurality of legislative seats.[59] Conversely, if this authority is widely shared among most if not all of the parties that win seats in the legislature, actors have little incentive to engage in extensive cross-district coordination. Even if there is only a single nationwide district, the greater the centralization of policy-making authority, the greater the incentive to be the largest party, which entails coordinating behind one of a few party labels. And the political institution that determines the centralization of policy-making authority is not the electoral system. Rather, it is the type of democratic regime.

The regime type can be decomposed into two dimensions. The first, which has received the most attention to date, is the vertical distribution of policy-making authority between the national and subnational levels of government (Chhibber and Kollman 1998, 2004; Hicken and Stoll 2008).[60] This encompasses both political and fiscal decentralization, one important

---

[59] This kind of strategic behavior falls into the broader class of policy-related strategic behavior. Examples include the portfolio-maximizing strategic behavior identified by Cox (1997, 194) and the compensational and policy-balancing strategic behavior identified by Kedar (2005, 2006). See Bargsted and Kedar (2009) for a recent review of some of this literature. Note that the party system will also play a role here: depending upon the sizes of existing parties—for example, whether a single party is large enough to govern alone—sometimes even fairly small parties may be able to play a governing role, as in Israel. Vote share and the likelihood of membership in the governing coalition consequently combine to determine a party's influence (Austen-Smith and Banks 1988).

[60] Using case studies of the United States, Canada, and Great Britain, three countries that have all employed a restrictive electoral system (that is, a plurality formula with single-member districts), Chhibber and Kollman (2004) show that in each, the transfer of policy-making authority from the local to the national level of government beginning in the nineteenth century encouraged candidates to come together under common party banners to gain control of the national policy-making apparatus. This coordination across electoral districts gave rise to the modern, nationally competitive political party; to nationalized or aggregated party systems; and hence to fewer electoral parties at the national level.

indicator of which is federalism (Brancati 2008).[61] The second is the horizontal distribution of authority within the national level of government. Here two factors must be considered: (i) the distribution of authority between the legislature and other national-level institutional actors, such as a president, and (ii) the distribution of authority within the legislature between the largest or governing party and other parties (Hicken and Stoll 2008; Hicken 2009; Hicken and Stoll 2009, 2011). For example, the policy-making authority of the largest legislative party is constrained by powerful legislative committees that smaller parties are regularly allowed to chair, as well as by a nonconcurrently elected president who may veto legislation. Combined, the extent to which policy-making authority is vertically centralized in the hands of the national government and horizontally centralized in the hands of the largest party in the national legislature determines the overall payoff to being that largest party, which I call the "size of the legislative prize" (ibid.).

This brings me to my key political institutional hypothesis. The existing literature paints the successful particization of new latent groups as constrained by only one political institution: the electoral system. By way of contrast, I argue that another political institution, the type of regime, also acts as a constraint. The more policy-making authority is horizontally and vertically centralized in the hands of the largest party in the national legislature, the less incentive both elites and voters have to back a new sectarian party that is locally competitive but too small nationally to win a plurality of seats, ceteris paribus. Many voters who sincerely prefer such a party will nevertheless cast their ballots for a more nationally competitive party that they prefer to the front-runner (strategic voting). Anticipating this, political entrepreneurs and other elites will not support such a party, which maximally includes not doing the necessary legwork to initially enter it in the race (strategic entry). In other words, I hypothesize that unless a new latent group is large relative to the national electorate, policy-making authority *not* being concentrated in the hands of the largest party in the national legislature is a necessary factor for the group's successful particization: groups that are small nationally, even if they are large relative to the electorate in a single electoral district, will succeed at obtaining sectarian representation in equilibrium only when policy-making authority is decentralized. A second way in which group size matters is therefore at the national or aggregate level.[62]

---

[61] Another perspective on decentralization is that subnational elections, where the stakes are not as high, provide new sectarian parties with a launching pad: they can demonstrate their viability and raise their visibility at the lower level, leveraging successes there into future successes at higher levels (e.g., Dalton, Flanagan, and Beck 1984; Kitschelt 1989). Yet another perspective is that by providing more access points to the state, decentralized regimes provide groups with a more favorable political opportunity structure (e.g., Kitschelt 1986).

[62] See, for example, Bartolini (2000, 145–151) for arguments for and evidence of a positive relationship between the size of the working class in Western European countries and the electoral success of the left (that is, socialist and communist parties). The classic work of Przeworski and Sprague (1986) makes a similar case. However, neither argue that the effect

2. Social Heterogeneity and the Number of Parties: A Theory

Of course, the successful particization of new latent groups that are large relative to the national electorate, such as groups that command a plurality, will not be constrained by the type of regime. But because few new groups will be this large, increases in social heterogeneity are predicted to generally have less effect on the number of electoral parties when policy-making authority is both vertically and horizontally centralized. It is also the case that both voters and elites may sometimes fail to behave strategically for the reasons discussed earlier. In such situations, the regime type will not act as a constraint on social heterogeneity. Again, however, I expect these situations to be the exception rather than the rule.

To illustrate regarding the horizontal dimension, first take the explanation for the failure of socialism in the United States offered by Lipset and Marks (2000). They argue that the presidential system of government is one factor that impeded the success of sectarian parties formed to represent the new working class that emerged from the Industrial Revolution. Because the working class lacked a national majority, the coordination incentives provided by the restrictive nature of the nationwide American presidential electoral contest shut these parties out of the presidential race. While a straightforward application of the argument just developed suggests that the existence of the presidency should dilute the size of the legislative prize, giving sectarian parties a leg up in the legislative contest, the concurrence of presidential and legislative elections in the United States must also be taken into account. With concurrent elections, the campaign for the plum prize that is the American presidency casts a shadow over the legislative race.[63] The result is that working-class parties were hamstrung in elections for *both* the presidency and the legislature by the horizontal distribution of policy-making authority in the United States. Conversely, consider Lipset and Marks's explanation for the success of socialist parties under the Keiserreich, which—like the United States—also employed a restrictive legislative electoral system. With the electoral system held constant, an explanation for the variation in the success of these sectarian parties must be found elsewhere. And that elsewhere is the type of regime: Lipset and Marks point to the weakness of democracy itself as the explanation for the German Social Democratic party's success. The fact that the legislature had little power to influence policy devalued electoral outcomes. This encouraged recently enfranchised working-class voters to sincerely express their preferences for

---

of group size is conditional upon the size of the legislative prize. While Posner (2004b, 2005) has likewise recently argued that the size of groups in the national political arena shapes their political salience, only his later work links group size to political institutions. Yet the political institution that he focuses upon is the whether the system of government is democratic or authoritarian (technically, whether it is a period of multiparty or one-party rule), whereas this study confines itself to democratic systems of government.

[63] The effect of presidentialism upon the size of the legislative prize is actually contingent upon the number of presidential candidates and the powers of the president, in addition to the temporal proximity of the presidential and legislative elections, also known as the electoral cycle (e.g., Shugart and Carey 1992; Cox 1997; Golder 2006; Hicken and Stoll 2011, 2013). I return to this topic in a later chapter.

working-class parties at the ballot box.

To illustrate regarding the vertical dimension, take Hug's (2001) argument about the formation of new political parties. He argues that as policy-making authority is centralized at the national level of government, new parties are less likely to form; similarly, he argues that federalism—which decreases the centralization of authority at the national level of government—should facilitate the emergence of new parties. Interestingly, his empirical evidence supports only the former proposition. Many other examples of the vertical distribution of policy-making authority conditioning the impact of increases in social heterogeneity can be supplied, however. To name just one, Van Cott (2000) argues that decentralization has facilitated the success of parties representing indigenous peoples in Bolivia and other Latin American countries. To the extent that the conditioning effect of the regime type has received attention from scholars studying social heterogeneity, it has been with respect to this vertical dimension.

Prior Social Heterogeneity

In polities that are initially very heterogeneous, the sectarian parties of new latent groups will often not be large enough to play a governing role, even if they are large enough to win seats in the legislature. This suggests that new latent social groups are less likely to be successfully particized in countries that are already very diverse.

To illustrate, consider the following examples. First take Country A, which has two approximately equally sized latent groups along a single division, say class. Let a new division, say ethnicity, appear, which could result from an extension of the franchise. Also let the members of the new ethnic group be roughly equally divided between the two original class groups. Each of the resulting two new ethno-class groups is large enough for both political entrepreneurs and group members to believe that a sectarian party is viable: a coalition with just one of the other parties, that of either the fellow ethnic or class group, would enable the party to govern. It is therefore plausible that both of the new latent groups will be successfully particized in Country A.

Now consider Country B, which has four approximately equally sized latent groups around two divisions, say class and religion. As before, let a new ethnic division equally partition the original groups. Sectarian parties of the four new groups that result are unlikely to play meaningful governing roles: putting together a coalition with three other parties is a more difficult and less rewarding proposition than putting together a coalition with one other party. Political entrepreneurs accordingly have an interest in engaging in pre-electoral coordination in order to construct more viable new sectarian political parties—for example, forming one party to jointly represent several of the new groups. Hence, because the new groups in Country B are too small for their parties to play a governing role, it is less plausible that all of them will be successfully particized, in contrast to Country A.

2. Social Heterogeneity and the Number of Parties: A Theory

As these two examples make clear, the prior social heterogeneity affects the likelihood of a new latent group's successful particization through its influence on the size of the group. Group size is therefore an intervening variable. However, the relationship between prior social heterogeneity and group size is only a weakly probabilistic one. It is possible for a large new latent group to be added to an already diverse country like Country B. Given my earlier hypotheses, such a group will not be deterred from pursuing sectarian representation by the polity's prior diversity. Because it is possible to study group size directly when seeking to explain sectarian party success, as I do in the later case studies, I accordingly do not view the prior social heterogeneity to be an explanatory factor, let alone a necessary factor, for the successful particization of new latent social groups.

Rather, I hypothesize that the prior social heterogeneity directly conditions the relationship between social heterogeneity and party system fragmentation, my primary dependent variable. There are two reasons for this. First, the prior social heterogeneity can serve as a useful, if imperfect, proxy for the size of the group in the absence of the appropriate cross-national measures, a matter to which I return in a later chapter. In initially heterogeneous polities, the group is likely to be small enough that even if a new sectarian party does successfully emerge, its effect on the fragmentation of the party system will be small. Second and more importantly, we still need to take into account how existing groups and their parties react to the new entrant. These reactions determine the ultimate impact of sectarian party success upon the fragmentation of the party system. Political entrepreneurs often treat moments of substantial change in a society's social heterogeneity as an opportunity to restructure the links between existing groups and parties, developing larger, more viable political vehicles.[64] In an initially heterogeneous polity, existing parties are likely to engage in a reactionary consolidation to counterbalance a new sectarian entrant, particularly if the new group (and hence its party) is a large one. The end result will depend critically upon the exact size of the new group[65] and the extent of the reactionary consolidation, but even some consolidation should lead to the fragmentation of the party system either not changing or decreasing, despite the entry of the new sectarian party.

But what about the other extreme, initially very homogeneous polities? Using a formal model of social group representation, Dickson and Scheve

---

[64]Consider, for example, the alliance between the Liberal Unionists and the Conservatives in the United Kingdom, which was begun in the 1880s in the wake of the broadening of the franchise by the 1867 Second Reform Act. This alliance was eventually formalized in the 1912 merger of the two parties.

[65]For example, say that a large new latent group is added to Country B. Assume that the new group's members support a new sectarian party and that the original four groups continue supporting their own original parties. Then with a new group that is 40 percent of B's population, leaving the original four groups commanding 15 percent of the population each, the effective number of electoral parties will be unchanged at four. However, a new group larger than this will decrease the effective number of parties, while a new group smaller than this will increase it.

(2010) find that in homogeneous polities where one group has a share of the population in excess of two-thirds, the dominant group will be represented by more than one party in equilibrium: political entrepreneurs compete for the benefits of leadership and office without any fear of electoral consequences following from the failure to present a joint group front. However, once the dominant group's population share falls below two thirds, these political entrepreneurs will coordinate on one party.[66] Accordingly, the addition of a reasonably sized latent group to an initially homogeneous polity will reduce the dominant group's population share. This in turn will deter the entry of some of the parties that were originally competing for the dominant group's votes. The overall impact of an increase in social heterogeneity on party system fragmentation will therefore be either negligible or negative, even if a new sectarian party successfully emerges to represent the new group.

Hence, combining these arguments, I more specifically hypothesize that the relationship between social heterogeneity and party system fragmentation takes a particular nonlinear form. Ceteris paribus, an increase in social heterogeneity from an initially low level of heterogeneity is predicted to lead to a decrease in fragmentation, but once the initial level of heterogeneity rises sufficiently, an increase in social heterogeneity is predicted to begin increasing fragmentation. Eventually, once the initial level of heterogeneity becomes high enough, a further increase in social heterogeneity is predicted to either decrease or have a negligible effect upon fragmentation. Graphically, the function capturing this relationship should have a local minimum and a local maximum, which implies that it should be at least a third-degree polynomial.[67] Figure 2.2 shows two such stylized functions.

The contrast with conventional accounts such as Cox's (1997), which argue for a positive linear relationship between social heterogeneity and party system fragmentation, is stark. In fact, the latter lead to a reductio ad absurdum. To see why, consider the extreme case of a country where social heterogeneity increases over time until the country becomes perfectly heterogeneous: that is, until each citizen forms his or her own group. Taking the linear argument literally, each citizen is then predicted to form his or her own political party. Yet no interest aggregation is taking place in this situation. This is not democratic politics as we know it in the modern world, a costly situation for all involved—costly enough, in fact, to have historically spurred the formation of political parties to aggregate previously unaggre-

---

[66]The model technically assumes a relatively restrictive electoral system (plurality and majority run-off). Specifically, these results are obtained under plurality rule. However, the logic seems to generalize to permissive electoral systems. Portfolio-maximizing strategic behavior of the sort described here can still provide incentives for the dominant group to coordinate in order to become the largest party in the legislature. Similarly, the model assumes only two social groups, but this, too, seems to generalize.

[67]This argument builds upon that of Stoll (2004), who argued for a nonlinear, and specifically a concave parabolic, relationship between social heterogeneity and fragmentation of the party system.

2. Social Heterogeneity and the Number of Parties: A Theory

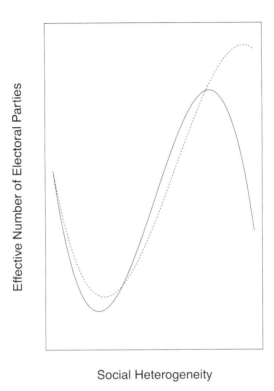

Figure 2.2: Two stylized examples of the hypothesized relationship between social heterogeneity and party system fragmentation (the effective number of electoral parties).

gated interests (e.g., Aldrich 1995). In other words, the continued successful emergence of sectarian parties to represent ever-smaller groups as heterogeneity approaches its maximum is unlikely.[68]

However, it is important to stress again that while the prior social heterogeneity of the polity may condition the relationship between social heterogeneity and the fragmentation of the party system, it does not shape the likelihood that a new latent group will be successfully particized.

---

[68] A real-world example is provided by Papua New Guinea, which has the highest level of ethnic fractionalization in the world and which approximates a perfectly fractionalized state (Fearon 2003, 205). Citizens' primary ethnic attachments are to one of the several thousand separate communities, most with only a few hundred people. But contrary to what a linear relationship would predict, although in accordance with what a nonlinear relationship would predict, the effective number of electoral parties in Papua New Guinea is much smaller than the effective number of ethnic groups, even if the effective number of electoral parties is comparatively quite large.

2.5 CONCLUSION

This chapter has built upon the insights of a diverse set of literatures to offer a theory about how changes in a democracy's social heterogeneity shape the most studied dimension of political competition: the number of electoral political parties, also known as the fragmentation of the party system. Throughout, I focused upon relatively exogenous increases in social heterogeneity resulting from historical processes such as extensions of the franchise. I also focused upon the classic mechanism by which increases in social heterogeneity shape party system fragmentation: when new latent social groups of individuals added to the citizenry are successfully particized, which means having successfully formed their own sectarian political parties.

In contrast to the literature's narrow focus upon the electoral system as the sole factor conditioning the relationship between social heterogeneity and party system fragmentation, I argued for a broader theory. Characteristics of the new groups and other systemic features of the polity should matter as much as if not more than the electoral system. Specifically, I argued that six additional factors shape the likelihood that a new latent social group will be successfully particized in equilibrium. These factors are the politicization of the group; the size of the group; the type of attribute defining the group; the strategy adopted by existing parties towards the group; the openness of the party system, at least when the members of the group are long-term inhabitants of the polity; and the type of democratic regime. Because these factors determine how likely it is that a new latent social group will successfully form its own sectarian political party, they indirectly condition the relationship between social heterogeneity and party system fragmentation. Further, I argued that a seventh additional factor, the prior social heterogeneity of the polity, directly conditions this relationship without shaping the likelihood of sectarian party success.

Table 2.1 summarizes my hypotheses about all of these variables. In this table, I draw attention to the five variables that I argued are the necessary factors, and hence that I view as the most important, by italicizing them. These factors range from the size of a new latent social group to the regime type. Further, it would not do to close this chapter without drawing special attention to the interaction between three of these factors, which the table also notes: I have argued that the effects of the political institutional variables depend upon a new group's size, and vice versa. In light of the complicated interactive relationship between these key factors, I close the discussion by reviewing my arguments about them.

Most importantly, as part of my case for moving beyond the electoral system, I argued that the electoral system is not the only *political institution* that conditions the relationship between social heterogeneity and party system fragmentation: the type of regime, and particularly the horizontal dimension of the regime, was introduced for the first time here as a conditioning variable. To summarize my argument, powerful subnational levels

2. Social Heterogeneity and the Number of Parties: A Theory

Variable	Hypothesis	Effect on Fragmentation
Group Politicization	More politicized new groups are more likely to be successfully particized.	Indirect
Type of Attribute	New groups defined by stickier attributes such as ethnicity are more likely to be successfully particized.	Indirect
Group Size	Larger new groups (specifically, minimally winning groups) are more likely to be successfully particized when the electoral system is more restrictive and the regime type centralizes policy-making authority more.	Indirect
Existing Party Strategy	The more existing parties fail to play either an accommodative or a dismissive strategy, the more likely it is that new groups will be successfully particized.	Indirect
Party System Openness	The more open the party system is, the more likely it is that internally originating new groups will be successfully particized.	Indirect
Electoral System	The more permissive the electoral system is, the more likely it is that new groups will be successfully particized when groups are smaller in the electoral districts.	Indirect
Regime Type	The less centralized policy-making authority is, the more likely it is that new groups will be successfully particized when groups are smaller in the national electorate.	Indirect
Prior Heterogeneity	An increase in heterogeneity is likely to decrease fragmentation if the prior heterogeneity is very low, decrease or have no effect upon fragmentation if the prior heterogeneity is very high, and increase fragmentation otherwise.	Direct

Table 2.1: Hypotheses about the eight factors that condition the effect of social heterogeneity on party system fragmentation, either directly or indirectly via their effect on the likelihood of a new latent social group's successful particization. Necessary factors, which are the most important, are italicized.

of government, whether formally federal or not; presidents who wield at least some meaningful powers and whose elections are not held concurrently with legislative elections; and powerful legislative committees are all features of the regime type that reduce the stakes of a legislative election, which I call the size of the legislative prize. By diluting the policy-making authority of the largest party in the national legislature, these institutional features allow smaller, less aggregated parties to play a governing role. Accordingly, they decrease the incentives for coordination across electoral districts in order to win a large number of legislative seats. This means that elites are likelier to supply and voters are likelier to support sectarian representation for new latent social groups when policy-making authority is more decentralized. However, the constraint imposed by regime types that centralize authority will bite only if the new group is small relative to the national electorate.

Combining the arguments regarding the electoral system and the regime type, when there is not a single nationwide electoral district, the size of a new latent group matters in a more subtle way than the existing literature has recognized: at the level of the electoral district *and* at the aggregate or national level. Predictions based solely on the electoral system are accordingly likely to be in error. To be successfully particized, a new latent group must be large enough relative to other groups in at least one electoral district to win seats there, and it must also be large enough in the polity as a whole to win seats in enough districts to play a governing role. How large is "large enough" at the district level is a function of the restrictiveness of the electoral system. At the national level, it is a function of the size of the legislative prize. For example, if policy-making authority is not too centralized, a group that is a minority in the overall polity but a majority (or at least a plurality) in a particular geographic area will not be constrained by, and may even benefit from, a restrictive electoral system (e.g., Ware 1996, 192). However, if policy-making authority is reasonably centralized, the incentive to form an extensive alliance across districts in order to become the largest party in the national legislature will mitigate against the successful particization of such a group. Of course, when there is a single national electoral district, a real-world example of which is Israel, only the group's size relative to the national electorate matters.

3 Describing Social Heterogeneity: Measures and Testable Hypotheses

In the prior chapter, I developed a theory about how changes in the heterogeneity of democratic societies should shape party system fragmentation. To empirically assess this theory, measures of the independent variable of social heterogeneity—and hence testable hypotheses—are needed. In other words, which democracies are more socially heterogeneous than others? And what are the ways in which a country's citizenry can change with the passing of time, increasing its social heterogeneity? Answering these questions is my goal in the present chapter.

Yet measuring social heterogeneity is a difficult task. As I argued in the last chapter, there are an infinite number of ways in which the citizens of a polity can be divided into latent groups. For example, the types of attributes that may be used to define groups include the quality and pitch of a person's voice; the speed and accuracy with which a person types; and a person's passion for scuba diving. And even given a particular type of attribute such as vocal pitch, there is no end to the ways in which people can be sorted into groups for the purposes of assessing heterogeneity, such as sopranos versus all others, on the one hand, and sopranos, altos, tenors, and basses, on the other.

How can empirical leverage be gained over such a theoretically intractable concept? In the qualitative literature, scholars have used their knowledge of a particular country or region to narrow down this theoretically infinite menu of possibilities. Posner's (2005, 21–22) elegant metaphor for this process is identifying which cards players hold in their hands. For example, he tells a convincing story of how the colonial state and its allies slowly built up two ethnic divisions in Zambia, one around language and the other around tribe. Similarly, in their classic work, Lipset and Rokkan (1967) studied divisions related to the national and industrial revolutions in Western Europe, where the groups worth focusing upon varied from country to country, depending upon how the industrial and national revolutions had played out there. In the quantitative literature, social heterogeneity has been primarily operationalized either as the size-weighted (effective) number of ethnic groups or, equivalently, as ethnic fractionalization at a single point in time.[1] All of these empirical solutions rely on particular analysts' expert judgments (usually historically grounded) as to which of the infinitely many latent divisions and groups are likely enough to become politically relevant to be worthy of study.[2]

But each of these solutions comes at a price. The Achilles' heel of the qualitative literature's solution is its lack of generalizability. Insights about how to assess the heterogeneity of society in specific places and at specific times must somehow be synthesized into a broadly applicable approach. There are two main problems with the quantitative literature's solution. The first is that it is purely cross-sectional: I am not aware of any existing study that includes a time dimension for social heterogeneity. For example, Country A is compared to Country B, but developments over time within these countries are ignored. This makes it difficult to confidently make claims about causality. The second issue is its focus upon ethnic heterogeneity. While increases in the ethnic heterogeneity of the citizenry should be particularly likely to lead to an increase in the fragmentation of the party system, as I argued in the prior chapter, new ethnic groups are not the only type of new social group that may be particized. Tapping a single dimension of the multidimensional concept of social heterogeneity is likely to result in biased estimates of the relationship of interest. Also, it precludes the testing of the hypothesis that some types of heterogeneity have stronger effects on party

---

[1] Examples of studies employing this measurement strategy include Powell (1982); Ordeshook and Shvetsova (1994); Amorim Neto and Cox (1997); Cox (1997); Filippov, Ordeshook, and Shvetsova (1999); Jones (1999); Mozaffar, Scarritt, and Galaich (2003); Chhibber and Kollman (2004); Clark and Golder (2006); Golder (2006); Hicken and Stoll (2008); Singer and Stephenson (2009); and Moser and Scheiner (2012). Reviews of this literature are found in Stoll (2004, 2008), from which this and the following discussions draw. Only Powell (1982), Ordeshook and Shvetsova (1994), Jones (1997, 2004), Stoll (2004, 2008), and Moser and Scheiner (2012) have employed different operationalizations. Two of these are closely related to the dominant approach: the effective number of linguistic groups in both Ordeshook and Shvetsova and Moser and Scheiner and the effective number of racial groups in Jones (1997). The more novel alternatives are the effective number of religious groups in Ordeshook and Shvetsova; ordinal indices based on the Catholic and agricultural proportions of the population in Powell; level of urbanization in Moser and Scheiner; and ideological (left–right) fractionalization in Jones (2004). While Taagepera (1999) alternatively employed the number of issue dimensions as his operationalization, this is not a measure of *latent* heterogeneity—an argument that may also be made, if less forcefully, about Jones's measure of ideological fractionalization. Stoll (2008) employed a variety of measures ranging from ethnic fractionalization to religious polarization in a sensitivity analysis that was discussed in the last chapter. The composite measure developed in the second half of this chapter, which taps latent heterogeneity along several divisions in addition to the ethnic, draws upon the work of Stoll (2004).

[2] The lack of generalizable hypotheses may be attributed to the many idiosyncratic factors that shape the process of politicization, as well as to the role played by random events (Stoll 2004, 193–194). In fact, Fearon (1999, 12) goes so far as to opine that "perhaps little can be said at a general level...the best answers may just be historical accounts of how political identities developed and changed in particular cases." I believe that *some* comparative empirical (if not theoretical) leverage can be gained, however, as I will argue.

3. Describing Social Heterogeneity: Measures and Testable Hypotheses

system fragmentation than others.

Accordingly, in this chapter, I develop two new ways of measuring social heterogeneity. By synthesizing the findings of a variety of studies that range from the qualitative to the quantitative, both of my broadly applicable measurement strategies identify the types of social heterogeneity that have been consequential for political competition in many contemporary democracies. Of particular note, neither of them solely focuses upon ethnicity. However, while the measures developed here are more general than those that have come before, they are still historically contingent, as all measures of social heterogeneity are likely to be given the theoretical intractability of the concept.

To preview the two approaches, I first identify the three major processes that have historically shaped social heterogeneity in the world's longest-standing democracies: changes in the franchise, territory, and volume of immigration. I then construct measures of each of these processes that vary across both space and time. My second approach more closely mirrors that taken by existing quantitative studies. For both new and long-standing democracies, I assess a country's heterogeneity with respect to each of six key latent divisions, such as religion and class. I then combine these individual indicators into an overall index of social heterogeneity. The resulting measure varies across space but not across time.

3.1 HISTORICAL DIMENSIONS OF SOCIAL HETEROGENEITY IN THE ADVANCED INDUSTRIAL DEMOCRACIES

My first task is to assess how the heterogeneity of the citizenry has evolved in the world's longest-standing democracies, the countries that are known today as the advanced industrial democracies. Specifically, I focus upon the twenty-two advanced industrial democracies that have populations of at least one million. These countries are listed in Table 3.1.[3] For each, I identify changes in social heterogeneity over time through the present day,[4] beginning with the country's first (minimally) procedurally democratic and partisan election.[5] These elections, identified by Mackie and Rose (1991), are also listed in Table 3.1. The date of the first election ranges from 1828 for the earliest democratizer, the United States, to 1976 for the latest democratizer, Portugal.

---

[3] Of the countries conventionally viewed as advanced industrial democracies, only Iceland and Luxembourg are excluded by confining the study to countries with populations of at least one million. Practical concerns regarding data availability combined with a concern about comparing apples and oranges led me to this threshold.

[4] Technically, the study ends with the most recent election prior to 2006. More recent data was difficult to obtain for many variables.

[5] These are elections in which the great majority of seats were contested; when reasonably nationalized parties existed; and for which national electoral returns by party exist.

3.1.1 The Approach

Given that the defining feature of democratic citizenship is the right to exercise political voice as an adult, the operational goal is to identify changes in the heterogeneity of countries' electorates, as opposed to their resident populations. Further, the operational goal is also to identify only reasonably exogenous and clearly identifiable (that is, measurable) changes in heterogeneity, *not* changes resulting from more endogenous processes such as natural growth and generational replacement. In the modern era, two dimensions of this kind of change in advanced industrial democracies' electorates can be identified.[6] The first of these dimensions is *internal*: change in which adults resident within the boundaries of a state are granted the franchise in national elections and hence citizenship as I have defined it. Because the franchise controls who can exercise the most important democratic act of voice, it is a central component of democracy (see, for example, Kleppner 1982). The second historical dimension is *external*: change in the set of citizens that occurs in ways other than through changes in the franchise. This means either change in the territory of the state, which adds citizens to or subtracts them from a polity, or immigration and emigration, which does the same without territory changing hands.

Accordingly, in the remainder of this section, I discuss the three historical processes that have played important roles in either increasing or decreasing social heterogeneity in the advanced industrial democracies since the early nineteenth century. These historical processes are changes in a state's franchise (internal); changes in a state's territory (external); and changes in the volume of immigration to a state (external).

---

[6] A third dimension can also be identified: change in the attributes of a given set of citizens, such as their religion or occupation. However, three issues preclude the consideration of this dimension of change here. First, some major historical changes precede the modern era. For example, with the Protestant revolution occurring in the sixteenth century, religious affiliation has been remarkably stable over the last two centuries in most Western European countries. To see this, one needs only to consult the historical data in Flora (1983). Second, historical data on some of these changes does not currently exist. For example, while there has been a decline in religiosity in the post–World War II era in most advanced industrial democracies, longitudinal data on this trend is spotty. Third, some major historical changes that have occurred are coterminous with one of the other dimensions. For example, two major political conflicts emerged out of the Industrial Revolution (Lipset and Rokkan 1967): the socioeconomic or class conflict and the struggle between the urban and rural sectors. Yet the growth of both the industrial working class and the urban population increased the heterogeneity of the electorate (as opposed to the resident population) only when the franchise was extended to the lower socioeconomic classes in the late nineteenth and early twentieth centuries. These changes in the citizenry's attributes are therefore coterminous with changes in the franchise. For these reasons, I solely study the three historical processes identified here (changes in the franchise, territory, and immigration). Future work should nevertheless seek to gather the historical data on changes in attributes that we currently lack with the goal of revisiting this issue. For some of the particularly hard-to-measure attributes, one operational approach might be to instead gather data on proxies, such as the state features that have historically shaped the attributes. Examples include the growth in a state's wealth, which has spread post-materialist values, and events such as wars, which have altered beliefs about foreign policy. The next section provides some guidance for how this might be done.

3. Describing Social Heterogeneity: Measures and Testable Hypotheses

3.1.2 THE FRANCHISE

There are two ways to operationalize what I have called *internal* change in the citizenry. The first and most general is to assess what percentage of a country's adult population is granted the franchise at the time of each election.[7] Increases in this percentage signal either the addition of a previously excluded group, such as women, to the electorate or an increase in the size of a group that was previously receiving token representation—for example, the franchise being extended from wealthy to lower-class women. Either of these changes in the composition of the electorate might spur elites to supply and members of the new groups to support sectarian parties. Similarly, decreases in this percentage signal the exclusion of a previously included group. Accordingly, one testable hypothesis is that higher percentages of the adult population with the franchise will be associated with greater party system fragmentation, ceteris paribus.[8]

A wrinkle is that the definition of adulthood, as reflected in franchise laws, has varied. Take as an example the Netherlands, which lowered the voting age to twenty-three for the 1946 election, to twenty-one for the 1967 election, and to eighteen for the 1972 election. If the electorate as a percentage of the adult population was calculated using a moving benchmark of adulthood (that is, the minimum voting age at the time of a given election),[9] changes in heterogeneity resulting from the inclusion in or exclusion

---

[7] An alternative would be to assess the absolute size of the electorate. Just as countries with large populations tend to be more heterogeneous than countries with small populations, so too countries with large electorates are likely to be more heterogeneous than countries with small ones. For example, both Hug (2001) and Tavits (2006) find a positive relationship between a country's population and the number of new political parties. Yet there are several problems with this approach. To point out just one, consider change within a single country over time. An increase in the size of the electorate may be due to natural growth, or it may be due to a change in the franchise. But my interest is only in the former. The solution is to compare the size of the electorate relative to (that is, as a percentage of) the adult population across both space and time.

[8] One objection to this line of argument is that extensions of the franchise are endogenous to the number of electoral parties: that new sectarian parties emerged to campaign for the inclusion of previously excluded groups, not that new sectarian parties emerged in response to the inclusion of previously excluded groups. The case of socialist parties and the economic extension of the franchise certainly provides some historical fuel for this fire (e.g., Bartolini 2000). However, in the long run, these sectarian parties could not flourish electorally without the excluded groups gaining political voice. Their *successful* emergence accordingly followed the addition of the previously excluded lower classes to the citizenry, regardless of which (franchise extension or sectarian party) technically came first. The operationalization of the dependent variable that is employed in the next chapter's quantitative analyses explicitly captures both the elite-level supply of new parties *and* their mass-level electoral support. Moreover, in most other cases (e.g., African Americans in the United States), sectarian parties did not pave the road to the franchise. And even where socialist parties did play a role in the eventual attainment of universal manhood suffrage, they did not emerge until extensive franchise reforms had already taken place. An example is the United Kingdom, where the first three reform acts preceded the birth of the contemporary Labour party's forerunner.

[9] For examples of this approach to calculating what is called the "voting-age population," see many United States Census Bureau publications and data sets (e.g., the Current Population Reports).

from the electorate of younger persons would be overlooked. Consequently, I adopt one of the approaches taken by Flora (1983), from whom some of the data for this variable is drawn, in that the threshold of adulthood is fixed at twenty. This means that the electorate is calculated as a percentage of a country's twenty-and-over population. The recent (since the 1970s) lowering of the voting age to eighteen in most advanced industrial democracies does not pose any difficulties for this operationalization: when the voting age is under twenty and no other restrictions on the franchise exist, the electorate as a percentage of the twenty-and-over population will simply exceed one hundred.

For all Western European advanced industrial democracies with the exception of Greece, Portugal and Spain, data through 1975 is taken from Flora (1983). For all other countries and for the latter countries post-1975, I calculated this percentage myself. To do so, I compiled data on both the number of persons in the electorate and the twenty-and-over population, linearly interpolating the latter for election years as necessary, from a variety of primary and secondary sources. Secondary sources included the International Institute for Democracy and Electoral Assistance (IDEA 2009); the United Nations Demographic Yearbook (UN SD 1997); the United States Census Bureau's International Database (U.S. Census Bureau 2009b); and Mackie and Rose (1991). Primary government sources were used exclusively for Israel (one of my case studies) and for other countries as needed; these sources included publications of government statistics bureaus and electoral commissions, such as the *Historical Statistics of Canada* (Canada SC 1983). The one country for which such data does *not* exist, however, is the United States.

In contrast to all other advanced industrial democracies, the registration of electors in the United States is not in any way a responsibility of the central government. Rather, the states are sovereign in all matters of registration, with very few exceptions, and registration requirements have varied greatly from state to state as well as over time. As a result, no official, longitudinal compilation of the adults eligible to vote in federal elections exists for most American states, let alone for the country as a whole. The pioneering work of Walter Dean Burnham, who has devoted more time to collecting historical data related to voter turnout in the United States than anyone, illustrates the problem.[10] His estimates of the number of individuals theoretically eligible to vote, which he calls the "potential electorate," are based primarily on federal census data and take into account state legal qualifications regarding sex, age, race, and citizenship. However, they fail to incorporate state property qualifications that existed through the mid-1800s; poll taxes, literacy tests, and other Jim Crow laws enacted by southern states after the end of Reconstruction that were not dismantled until the civil rights movement of the 1960s; personal registration requirements put into

---

[10] An excellent overview of these and other issues that one must confront in compiling historical data about the United States' electorate is found in Burnham (1986, 2007).

3. Describing Social Heterogeneity: Measures and Testable Hypotheses

place around the turn of the last century that are largely still in effect today; and other specialized barriers to participation. While it is well known that these legal barriers thrown up around the ballot box have reduced (often by substantial amounts) the actual electorate as compared to the potential electorate, there is no way of systematically quantifying exactly how much they have reduced it.[11] Accordingly, because Burnham's measure of the potential electorate does not capture many of the important ways in which the United States' electorate has changed over time, such as through the post-Reconstruction disenfranchisement of African Americans, it cannot be used here.

Figure 3.1 displays the data for each advanced industrial democracy, with the exception of the United States. Specifically, it graphs the electorate as a percentage of the adult (twenty-and-over) population at the time of each minimally democratic and partisan election from the early nineteenth century to the present day.[12] The two distinct stages of enfranchisement, which were discussed in the prior chapter, can be seen from these graphs for the early democratizers. The first, the economic enfranchisement of lower-class men, took the electorate to around 50 percent of the adult population by the early 1900s. The second, the enfranchisement of women, then took the electorate to around 100 percent of the adult population in the early to mid-1900s. One can also see the different patterns of economic enfranchisement discussed earlier: the early and sudden extension of the franchise to lower-class men in countries such as France and Germany, in contrast to the late and gradual extension in countries such as the United Kingdom. The minimum observed percentage of the enfranchised adult population is 2.8, obtained by Japan in the early 1900s, while the maximum percentage is 121, obtained by Portugal in the 1990s.

The second approach to operationalizing internal changes in the citizenry distinguishes between changes in the franchise with respect to three key types of attributes: socioeconomics, gender, and ethnicity (race). For each type of attribute, the simplest approach is to compare elections where adults are excluded from the franchise for having particular attributes, such as not being owners of property, to elections where they are not. That is, elections held under a universal socioeconomic franchise are compared to

---

[11] But see Kousser's (1975) classic work for estimates for some southern states. It is these "potential electorate" figures that appear in the *Historical Statistics of the United States* (U.S. Census Bureau 1975) and that are used for the electorate in Mackie and Rose's (1991) well-known historical election almanac. They are closely related to the "voting-age population" figures used by the United States Census Bureau and many scholars in calculating voter turnout in the United States. See McDonald and Popkin (2001) for an overview as well as for some recent improvements.

[12] While 1885 is the date of the first British election that should be included under the case selection rules described here, data for earlier British elections (beginning in 1832) is shown for two reasons: because these earlier elections only barely fall short of satisfying the criteria, and because they illustrate the late and gradual pattern of franchise extension that Britain exemplifies. Similar results are obtained if these early British elections are included in the next chapter's quantitative analyses.

65

Changing Societies, Changing Party Systems

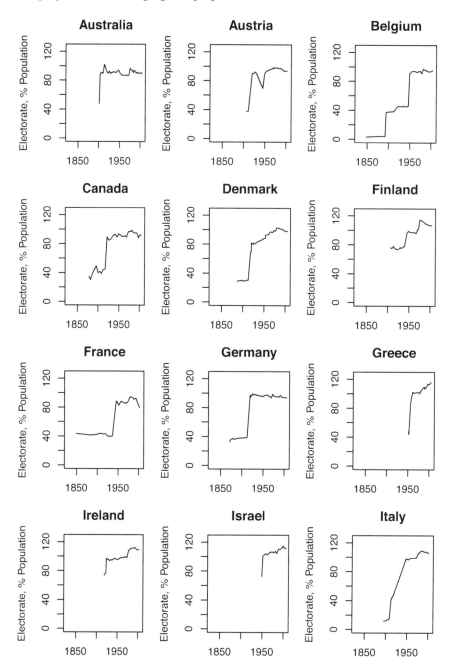

Figure 3.1: The electorate as a percentage of the adult (twenty and over) population in twenty-one advanced industrial democracies throughout the modern era. Continued on next page.

3. Describing Social Heterogeneity: Measures and Testable Hypotheses

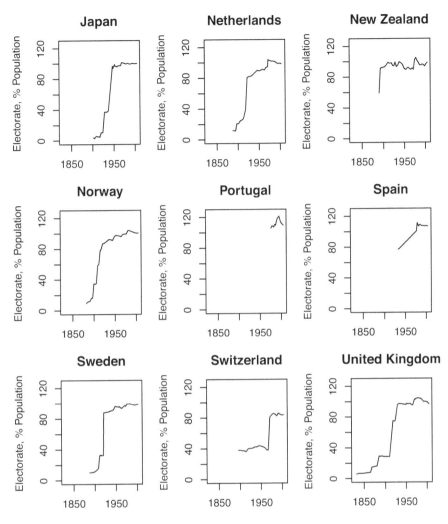

Figure 3.1: Continued from previous page.

elections that are not; elections held under a universal gender franchise are compared to elections that are not; and elections held under a universal ethnic franchise are compared to elections that are not. The electorate under the universal franchise is more heterogeneous than the electorate under the nonuniversal franchise because the former includes a group that is excluded from the latter, at least in part. Another testable hypothesis, accordingly, is that elections with universal socioeconomic (or gender or ethnic) suffrage should experience greater party system fragmentation than elections with nonuniversal suffrage, ceteris paribus.

For each country, I drew upon a variety of primary and secondary sources to identify the periods of universal suffrage for each of the three types of attributes, most prominently Carstairs (1980), Flora (1983), and Mackie and Rose (1991).[13] The first three columns of Table 3.1 display these periods of universal suffrage. An advantage of this operationalization is that data can be obtained for the United States.[14]

One notable observation drawn from this table is that only four countries have employed ethnic restrictions on the franchise, one of which did so extremely briefly: Australia, Canada, Israel (two elections only), and the United States.[15] Because three of these countries have employed majoritarian electoral systems throughout their history, it will consequently be difficult to say much about how the effect of expanding the ethnic franchise has

---

[13]See also Bartolini (2000, 206–221) and Aidt, Dutta, and Loukoianova (2006) for descriptions of franchise laws in Western European countries. My only significant disagreements with the latter, who also identify the election years in which universal economic and gender franchises first applied, concern Sweden and Norway. Aidt, Dutta, and Loukoianova state that Swedish elections were first held under a universal economic franchise in 1919, but all other sources that I have consulted instead identify 1921 as this year (moreover, lower-chamber elections were held only in 1917, 1920 and 1921). The disagreement over Norway is more understandable because there were few economic restrictions on the franchise from the 1900 election onwards; however, bankrupts and those receiving public assistance were excluded prior to the 1921 election, which means that the economic franchise for the 1900–1918 elections falls short of the criterion of "universal." Country-specific sources that I consulted included Australia EC (2006) for Australia; Canada OCEO (2007) for Canada; Bloomfield (1984) for New Zealand; and Kousser (1975), Kleppner (1982), and Keyssar (2001) for the United States. The dates offered for the United States are the most controversial by far. Nevertheless, the scholarly consensus is that effectively all economic restrictions on the franchise had been removed by the 1860s (see, for example, Mackie and Rose 1991, 457), and specifically by 1855 (Keyssar 2001, 29). Similarly, I date the rollback of universal economic as well as ethnic suffrage to 1878, following the Compromise of 1877 that ended Reconstruction, even though the process of disenfranchisement would take approximately thirty years (until 1910) to complete (Kousser 1975, 224). Coding the Reconstruction elections of 1870–1876 as taking place under a universal ethnic franchise ignores the special position of Native Americans, many of whom were denied citizenship until 1924 (Keyssar 2001, 132–134); however, I choose to err on the side of generosity here out of a desire that my measure capture the remarkable experiment in biracial democracy that was Reconstruction, as discussed more fully in a later chapter. The alternative, coding these elections as being held under a nonuniversal ethnic franchise, does not substantively alter the conclusions of the quantitative analyses undertaken in the next chapter. The disproportionate impact that personal registration requirements and felon disenfranchisement have had on the lower class, immigrants, and racial minorities in the United States is also ignored (e.g., Keyssar 2001, 50–53, 122–132).

[14]While it is not possible to pinpoint exactly how many persons were included in the electorate in the United States at any given time, I can pinpoint when explicit socioeconomic, gender, and racial restrictions on the franchise existed and when they did not, as discussed in note 13. Eliminating the United States from this part of the next chapter's quantitative analyses, commensurate with its absence from the prior part, does not substantively affect the conclusions.

[15]Subsequent chapters contain more details about the ethnic restrictions on the franchise in Israel (Arabs) and the United States (African Americans). In Australia, most aborigines were disenfranchised prior to the 1962 Commonwealth Elections Act, although it was only in 1983 that they became subject to compulsory enrollment and voting like other Australians (Australia EC 2006). In Canada, Asians were disenfranchised until 1948, and most Inuits and First Nations were effectively disenfranchised prior to the 1960 Elections Act (Canada OCEO 2007).

3. Describing Social Heterogeneity: Measures and Testable Hypotheses

Country	Universal Socio-economic Franchise	Universal Gender Franchise	Universal Ethnic Franchise	First Democratic and Partisan Election
Australia	1903–	1903–	1963–	1901
Austria	Always	1919–	Always	1907
Belgium	1919–	1949–	Always	1848
Canada	1921–	1921	1962–	1878
Denmark	1918–	1918–	Always	1887
Finland	Always	Always	Always	1907
France	Always	1945–	Always	1849
Germany	Always	1919–	Always	1871
Greece	Always	1956–	Always	1926
Ireland	Always	1923–	Always	1918
Israel	Always	Always	1955–	1949
Italy	1919–	1946–	Always	1895
Japan	1928–	1946–	Always	1902
Netherlands	1918–	1922–	Always	1888
New Zealand	Always	1893–	Always	1890
Norway	1921–	1915–	Always	1882
Portugal	Always	Always	Always	1976
Spain	Always	Always	Always	1933
Sweden	1921–	1921–	Always	1887
Switzerland	Always	1971–	Always	1896
United Kingdom	1918–	1929–	Always	1885
United States	1856–1876, 1966–	1920–	1870–1876, 1966–	1828

Table 3.1: Periods of universal suffrage with respect to socioeconomics, gender, and ethnicity for twenty-two advanced industrial democracies. Years are elections, so "1903–" means that 1903 was the year of the first election held under universal suffrage, not that legislation eliminating restrictions on the franchise was passed in 1903. Note that "Always" means that while democratic, a country has not restricted the franchise since its first minimally democratic and partisan election, the election year of which is presented in the last column.

been conditioned by the restrictiveness of the electoral system.

Second, another notable observation is that during the period analyzed here, only the United States has contracted its franchise. The latter's "antidemocratic reaction" to the profound social changes that it experienced in the mid-nineteenth century is particularly surprising given its broadening of the franchise in the first half of that century (Keyssar 2001, 53). For all other countries during this period, by way of contrast, the expansion of the franchise proceeded linearly, as democratic theorists such as De Tocqueville (1969, 59–60) had long believed that it would. In Figure 3.1, this is illustrated by the effectively monotonic increases in the electorate's share of the adult population.

Third and finally, digressing from the table, of the three types of attributes, the biggest impact has come from women's suffrage. Given the well-known ratio of the genders in most countries, this franchise extension approximately doubled most countries' electorates, which can be seen by locating the years of universal gender suffrage on Figure 3.1. By way of contrast, the smallest impact has come from ethnic extensions of the franchise. For example, the largest ethnic group that has been disenfranchised in the advanced industrial democracies is African Americans in the United States, and they made up only approximately 11 percent of the population in 1960 (U.S. Census Bureau 2002), just prior to their re-enfranchisement.[16]

3.1.3 TERRITORY

But changes in the franchise are not the only ways in which the heterogeneity of the citizenry can change. A prominent alternative source of change is the alteration of a country's borders. Examples of territorial change include Germany's loss of Alsace-Lorraine to France as part of the peace settlement concluding World War I and the reunification of East and West Germany following the end of the Cold War.

Territorial gains and losses matter because they bring with them changes in a country's electorate. This is because the residents of newly acquired territories have usually been extended the franchise on the same basis as existing residents. These new citizens are often distinguished from a country's original citizens by many types of attributes, such as language, religion, and the more basic sense of a shared history. There are accordingly many ways in which they can be viewed as a distinctly new social group. The same may be said of ex-citizens from territories that have been lost. Moreover, many of these distinguishing types of attributes, such as language, have been ethnic. An example is the post–World War I Belgian annexation of the German cantons of Eupen and Malmedy (the East Cantons). Although the territory in question was small, its acquisition introduced a German-speaking minority into Belgium. The testable hypothesis is accordingly that territorial gains will be associated with greater party system fragmentation, ceteris paribus.

Accordingly, I collected data on a country's cumulative net territorial gain (or loss) in square kilometers at the time of each minimally democratic

---

[16]The First Nations and Inuit in Canada constituted 1.2% of the population in 1961 on the heels of their enfranchisement, while Asians constituted 0.52% of the population on the heels of theirs in 1951 (based on Canada SC 1983, Series A125-163). Similarly, aborigines are estimated to have constituted 1.1% of the Australian population in 1961, the year before they were enfranchised (based on Australia Bureau of Statistics 2008, Tables 2.1 and 4.1).

3. Describing Social Heterogeneity: Measures and Testable Hypotheses

and partisan election. Net gains in total area, not just in land area, were used because this was the data that was most consistently available.[17] A variety of primary and secondary sources were used for this task. The most important secondary sources were historical editions of *The Statesman's Yearbook* and *The New International Yearbook*.

Figure 3.2 shows this data for the twelve advanced industrial democracies that experienced territorial change during the period under study.[18] The largest net cumulative territorial loss, approximately three hundred thousand square kilometers, was experienced by Germany between World War II and reunification in 1990. By way of contrast, the largest cumulative net territorial gain, almost eight million square kilometers, was experienced by Canada when the final portion of the Northwest Territory was granted parliamentary representation for the 1962 election. With the United States included in the data set, the average net cumulative territorial gain is just under eight hundred thousand square kilometers; with it excluded, it is about three hundred thousand square kilometers. Yet these averages, skewed upwards by the United States and Canada, do not reflect the typical change experienced by most countries: with both of the latter countries excluded, the maximum gain is only approximately thirty-two thousand square kilometers.[19]

---

[17]The exception is the United States, for which historical data was available only as land area. The *cumulative* net territorial gain is calculated instead of the net gain since the previous election because the impact of a territorial change should be long-lasting. This is comparable to the way in which changes in the franchise are operationalized. One alternative operationalization is a country's total area at the time of an election. This has the drawback of conflating territorial gains with a country's initial size. Moreover, the United States and Canada then become even greater outliers. If these two countries are either excluded from the next chapter's quantitative analysis or coded as having no territorial gains (see note 19) and this alternative measure is employed, similar results are obtained with one exception: majoritarian electoral systems are predicted to increase instead of decrease the effect of a territorial expansion. This finding is consistent with the argument that the successful particization of territorially concentrated new groups, as new citizens from a territorial acquisition by definition are, should not be constrained and may even be facilitated by a majoritarian electoral system. Another alternative operationalization is the net cumulative population gain resulting from territorial changes. While theoretically appealing, this data was much harder to come by and is less reliable. (The difficulty of obtaining even this data is the reason why data was not collected on the net cumulative gain of members of the electorate, the more theoretically compelling operationalization.) Nevertheless, this alternative measure also yields reasonably similar conclusions, with the same exception regarding the conditioning effect of the electoral system.

[18]The ten countries experiencing no territorial change during this period are Australia, Ireland, Israel, the Netherlands, New Zealand, Norway, Portugal, Spain, Sweden, and Switzerland. Given the small number of persons involved, I ignore the minor changes to Israel's territory between the 1949 and 1951 elections that resulted from the signing of the various armistice agreements later in 1949; the lack of political representation (that is, the effective exclusion from Australian territory) of the inhabitants of Australia's Northern Territory and Federal Capital Territory from the 1913–1919 and 1913–1946 elections, respectively; and the Dutch annexation of the German municipality of Selfkant for the 1952–1963 elections. Note that Israel's territory is not considered to have expanded following the 1967 Six Day War: because the residents of the occupied territories have, with rare exceptions, not been given the right to vote in Israeli elections, they have not become part of the Israeli citizenry.

[19]Either dropping these two countries from the next chapter's quantitative analysis or cod-

Changing Societies, Changing Party Systems

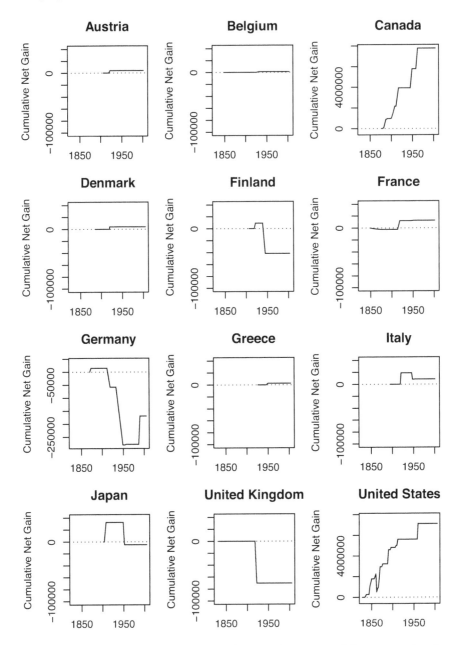

Figure 3.2: Net cumulative territorial gains in square kilometers for the twelve advanced industrial democracies experiencing territorial change throughout the modern era. Note that three scales are used: one for the United States and Canada; one for Germany; and one for the remaining countries.

3. Describing Social Heterogeneity: Measures and Testable Hypotheses

3.1.4 Immigration

The final way in which individuals may be brought into the citizenry from the outside world is through immigration. Existing citizens may likewise exit through emigration. An example is the massive wave of immigration that Israel experienced in the the decade and a half following its statehood, when the population doubled from immigration alone in a mere three years.

As with the inhabitants of newly acquired territories, immigrants who become citizens constitute a new social group simply due to their status as newcomers, reflected in the history that they and the existing citizenry do not share. Nevertheless, differences in other types of attributes such as language and religion have often overlapped with this basic division. An example is contemporary Muslim immigrants to Western European countries such as France. Emigrants are also likely to differ from their former compatriots in key types of attributes. Accordingly, because immigration will usually if not always increase the heterogeneity of the electorate (more on this "usually" later), the final testable hypothesis is that immigration will be associated with greater party system fragmentation, ceteris paribus.

Unfortunately, however, historical data on the net immigration of citizens cannot be compiled for even this relatively small number and data-rich set of countries. The next-best solution is to employ a proxy for net immigration: the percentage of the electorate that is foreign-born. Yet this data also does not exist in comparative perspective. Instead, only the percentage of the *population* that is foreign-born can be identified.[20] Accordingly, due to the practical limitations of data availability, my approach to operationalizing external changes in the citizenry from the processes of immigration and emigration is to collect data on the percentage of a country's population that is foreign-born at the time of each minimally democratic and partisan election.

Data for most Western European countries prior to 1960 is taken from Flora (1983); from 1960 onwards, it is taken from the United Nation's International Migrant Stock database (UN PD 2009). The latter is also the source for data from 1960 onwards for all other countries with the exception of Israel and the United States (my two case studies), for which primary government sources are utilized. For the countries not covered by Flora, I

---

ing them as having experienced no territorial gains yields broadly similar results. The only difference of note concerns the relative impact of territorial gains under nonmajoritarian and majoritarian electoral systems, as discussed in note 17. One might make the case for coding the United States and Canada as not having experienced territorial gains on the theoretical grounds that their newly acquired territories were primarily populated by existing citizens and those citizen–settlers' descendants. That is, because territorial expansion did not lead these two countries to acquire distinctively new citizens, their territorial gains should not lead to the fragmentation of their party systems. This is consistent with the finding that including these two countries, both of which employ majoritarian electoral systems, in the quantitative analysis reduces the effect of territorial gains under majoritarian electoral systems.

[20] The percentage rather than the absolute number of foreign-born is calculated because it is a group's size relative to other groups, not its absolute size, that matters, as discussed in the previous chapter. This is consistent with the approach taken regarding the franchise.

compiled historical data (prior to 1960) from primary government sources.[21] Data for election years was linearly interpolated as necessary using the closest surrounding years for which data was available. In a few cases, data was backwards extrapolated.[22]

Figure 3.3 displays this data for the twenty-two advanced industrial democracies over the elections studied. It shows that the foreign-born as a percentage of the population ranges from a high of 66 percent in Israel's 1951 election to a low of zero percent (an approximation) in early Danish, Finnish, Greek, Italian, Japanese, Spanish, and United Kingdom elections. More generally, three distinct types of countries emerge from this figure with respect to both the average size of the foreign-born population and the trend in immigration over time. The first, countries of immigration such as Australia, Canada, Israel, New Zealand, and the United States, had initially high levels of immigration that gradually decreased over time before picking up again in the last few decades. On average, these countries, not surprisingly, have had large foreign-born populations.[23] The second group, most of the remaining countries in the sample such as Belgium and Norway, had very low levels of immigration in their early years but moderate levels more recently, yielding small foreign-born populations on average.[24] Finally, the third group consists of countries with an effectively nonexistent foreign-born population and little growth in immigration over time: Japan most prominently, but arguably also Finland and Italy.

---

[21] However, data was sometimes available only for foreign nationals rather than for the foreign-born. Moreover, in some cases, there is ambiguity as to which is reported. Unfortunately, the percentage of foreign nationals underestimates the percentage of the foreign-born, the quantity of interest: foreign nationals are the subset of the foreign-born who have not naturalized. Evidence for this is provided by Sweden, which enumerated both the foreign-born and foreign nationals in its 1880 to 1910 censuses (Flora 1983, 54). When compiling my data set, I obviously used data on the foreign-born if it was available and data on foreign nationals only as a last resort. This is the same approach taken by the United Nations (UN PD 2009), the source of my data beginning in 1960.

[22] For example, there is no historical Finnish government data on the foreign-born population because Finland's first population census was for the year 1950. The United Nations data shows only 0.7% of the population being foreign-born in 1960 (UN PD 2009), and the 1950 Finnish census shows this figure to be only 0.3%. Combining this data with the fact that Finland has not historically been a country of immigration (the foreign-born population has slowly grown over time, reaching a maximum of 3.0% in 2005), it seems reasonable to backwards extrapolate a foreign-born population of 0.0% for pre-1950 Finnish elections. Note that eliminating all eighty-nine extrapolated cases from the next chapter's quantitative analysis yields results even more favorable to the hypothesis: when the electoral system is majoritarian, the foreign-born percentage of the population no longer attains conventional levels of significance using a two-sided test.

[23] Of this group of countries, the United States has the smallest foreign-born population on average: approximately 11 percent. Israel has the largest: 44 percent. Despite not being conventionally viewed as a country of immigration, Switzerland arguably belongs in this group as well based on its high average foreign-born population, as well as the trend in its foreign-born population over time.

[24] An example is Norway, where the foreign-born have averaged just under three percent of the population but have increased from under two percent in 1882 to under seven percent in 2005.

3. Describing Social Heterogeneity: Measures and Testable Hypotheses

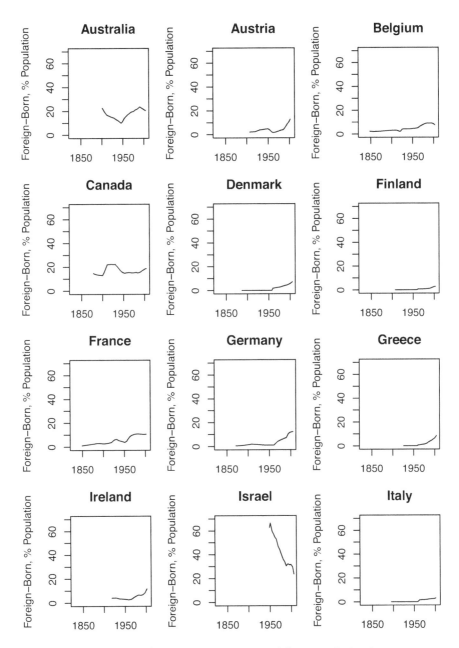

Figure 3.3: The foreign-born as a percentage of the population in twenty-two advanced industrial democracies throughout the modern era. Continued on next page.

Changing Societies, Changing Party Systems

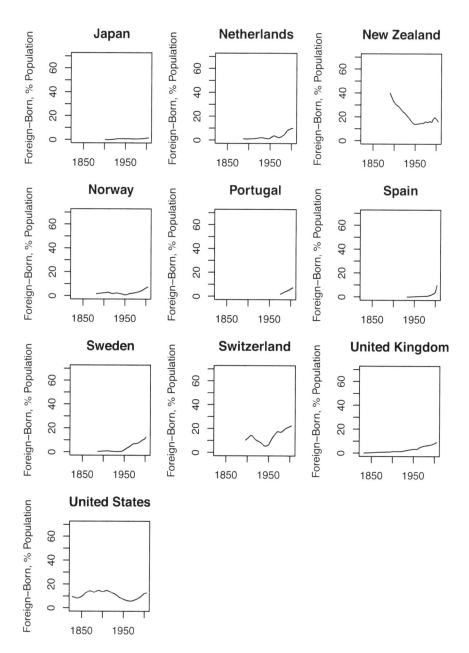

Figure 3.3: Continued from previous page.

3. Describing Social Heterogeneity: Measures and Testable Hypotheses

There is one additional complication that must be kept in mind regarding this data, however. Some countries, particularly those that employ the *jus sanguinis* principle of citizenship, make it difficult for immigrants who are not fellow ethnics to become citizens (Brubaker 1992).[25] Germany is the classic Western European example: until recently, neither the Turks who had immigrated to Germany in the 1960s and 1970s nor their German-born children were allowed to acquire German citizenship. By way of contrast, ethnic Germans who had immigrated from Eastern Europe and the former Soviet Union following the fall of communism were automatically granted citizenship. This introduces a potentially problematic but unavoidable slippage between theory and measure: if immigrants are not allowed to acquire citizenship, they cannot successfully form their own sectarian political parties. Accordingly, measuring immigrants as a percentage of the population rather than as a percentage of the electorate, as I do here, will lead me to overestimate the number of electoral parties in *jus sanguinis* countries like Germany. The exception is if immigration has led existing citizens to form reactionary anti-immigrant political parties that have done well at the polls. Examples of the latter include countries such as Austria and Switzerland.[26]

3.2 A CROSS-SECTIONAL INDEX OF SOCIAL HETEROGENEITY

My second task is to step back from identifying the specific historical processes that have shaped social heterogeneity in the world's long-standing democracies. Instead, I seek to holistically measure the heterogeneity of democratic societies. Like the measure of social heterogeneity commonly employed by existing quantitative studies, and in contrast to the measures developed here earlier, the measure I develop in this section does not identify changes in social heterogeneity over time. Rather, it statically assesses the overall social heterogeneity of the sample of democracies listed in Table 3.2: specifically, the minimally democratic countries with presidents in the post–World War II era.[27]

---

[25] Even in countries traditionally viewed as "countries of immigration" such as the United States, the political incorporation of immigrants is "uneven and halting" for several reasons, prominent among them the simple fact that many immigrants never naturalize. For example, only approximately 60 percent of the legal permanent residents of the United States have acquired citizenship over the past few decades (Hochschild and Mollenkopf 2009, 9).

[26] Indeed, in the next chapter's regression models, countries such as Germany with high recent levels of immigration, low naturalization levels for immigrants but effectively no anti-immigrant parties have reasonably large and negative residuals for recent elections. Conversely, countries such as Austria with high recent levels of immigration, low naturalization levels for immigrants but successful anti-immigrant parties generally have positive residuals for recent elections. This means that, as expected, the models overestimated the effective number of electoral parties for the former but not for the latter countries.

[27] I will explain the reason for focusing upon presidential democracies in the next chapter. In that chapter, I will also discuss the additional case-selection criteria that produced this sample.

3.2.1 THE APPROACH

A seemingly straightforward way of operationalizing social heterogeneity writ large, given how I defined the concept in the previous chapter, is the number of latent groups in a country. The corresponding testable hypothesis is that a greater number of latent groups will be associated with greater party system fragmentation, ceteris paribus. However, for the reasons discussed earlier, identifying these latent groups is no easy task. Most fundamentally, because there are infinitely many latent groups, it is impossible even to conceptually define the population of them.[28]

There are two solutions to this problem. One is proposed by Laitin and Posner (2001, 15): to focus on the groups that are actually "doing the competing" relevant to the outcome of interest at a given time. This might match the measure to the mechanism, to paraphrase Posner (2004a), but the downside when the dependent variable is party system fragmentation (as opposed to, say, economic growth) is the loss of precisely the exogeneity that is needed. Another solution is to focus on historically relevant groups, an approach akin to Fearon's (2003) suggestion to use lagged measures of ethnic heterogeneity. That is, we can identify the divisions or category sets that have been judged to be historically important by the literature because they have been particized in some but not all democracies in the modern era. For each of these divisions, we can then identify the historically important categories or groups associated with it.

It is this second approach that I, like Stoll (2004), take here: measuring heterogeneity with respect to historically important divisions or category sets. There are six such divisions that seem to merit focus: the ethnic (center–periphery); religious (church–state); rurality (urban–rural); socioeconomic (class); post-materialist; and foreign policy. All have been the subject of numerous studies.[29] Most notably, the first four constitute Lipset and Rokkan's (1967) classic set of foundational political conflicts. For each of these divisions, I then develop a measure of a country's latent heterogeneity that theoretically ranges from zero to one, with higher values denoting greater heterogeneity. This identical scale ensures that each component exercises approximately equal influence. The more heterogeneity a country exhibits with respect to a division, the more likely it is that at least one sectarian party will have formed to represent at least one of the division's groups—at least up to a point.

The final step in this approach is to additively combine the individual indicators, which yields an overall index of social heterogeneity. This index theoretically ranges from zero to six, with higher values again denoting greater heterogeneity. For example, a country that is both religiously

---

[28]See Fearon (2003) regarding the difficulty of identifying even the population of latent *ethnic* groups.
[29]Take, for example, Lijphart (1999), who assessed the salience of all six of these conflicts over the post-war period in order to construct his well-known measure of the effective issue dimensionality of party systems.

3. Describing Social Heterogeneity: Measures and Testable Hypotheses

and ethnically homogeneous will be scored by the index as less heterogeneous than a country that is religiously homogeneous but ethnically heterogeneous. In turn, the latter country will be scored as less heterogeneous than a country that is both religiously and ethnically heterogeneous. The testable hypothesis is accordingly that higher scores on this index of social heterogeneity will be associated with a larger number of electoral parties, ceteris paribus.

Before turning to the measures of heterogeneity for each of the index's six component divisions, four general comments regarding this index are in order. First, because longitudinal data is not available for several divisions (e.g., religion), for those divisions for which it is available (e.g., the urban–rural division), either data is averaged over the post–World War II period or the earliest data available is used to maximize exogeneity. As discussed earlier, the result is both individual index components and an overall index that are time invariant (cross-sectional). Second, because the index additively combines the different divisions into one overall measure, hypotheses about how the characteristics of new latent groups shape the likelihood of their particization cannot be tested using this measure. Third and fourth, the potential overlapping of the different lines of division is ignored, and relatedly, the operational focus is shifted from groups to divisions. Unfortunately, I am aware of no way of gathering data on how the six historically important divisions cross-cut (Stoll 2008).[30] In other words, while it is possible to assess how many historically important latent groups there are for each historically important division, it is not possible to assess how many overall groups there are after taking into account the cross-cutting of the divisions. This means that the index essentially counts how many latent divisions are present in a society, instead of how many latent groups there are. As I noted in the prior chapter, a mitigating factor is that perfectly overlapping divisions are rare: generally, if there are more divisions, there will be more groups. This measurement strategy should accordingly not grossly overestimate social heterogeneity.[31] However, it is important to acknowledge even such a practically necessitated and plausible shift away from the theoretically ideal operationalization.

---

[30] The one recent empirical exception is Selway (2009), who has developed measures of the cross-cuttingness of any two of ethnicity, religion, region, and income for a number of countries using survey data. The major drawback to his approach from my perspective is that it does not directly measure the concept of interest: the number of latent cross-cutting groups. Other drawbacks are: (i) that it omits several of the key divisions that have historically been of interest to comparativists studying party politics; and (ii) that it is limited to the cross-cutting of at most two lines of division. Nevertheless, this is a promising approach upon which future work should build.

[31] Famously, Rae and Taylor (1970, 14) argued in their classic work that "virtually all extant cleavage systems result in some cross-cutting and...none result in complete cross-cutting; the pertinent question is not whether cleavages cross-cut each other, but rather how much they cross-cut each other."

3.2.2 INDEX COMPONENTS

The natural place to begin is with the two divisions that have received the most empirical attention: ethnicity and religion. The most intuitive measure of heterogeneity for both of these divisions is the size-weighted or effective number of historically important groups (e.g., Ordeshook and Shvetsova 1994; Amorim Neto and Cox 1997; Clark and Golder 2006). The more ethnic or religious groups there are, the more ethnically or religiously heterogeneous the country is and the larger that country's effective number of groups will be, generally speaking. However, I instead employ the less intuitive index of fractionalization, a simple transformation of the effective number, as the measure. This is because of its less skewed distribution and its natural zero-to-one range.[32]

Various scholars have constructed lists of the important ethnic groups in a number of countries, while also calculating these groups' population shares. The earliest or most historical set of these measurements should be the most exogenous, so it is this set that I use here: the well-known ethnolinguistic fractionalization index (ELF) created by Soviet geographers in 1961, as modified by Roeder (2001) to make use of data on sub-groups. This version of ELF takes into account racial divisions within ethno-linguistic groups. Accordingly, it has the advantage of not defining ethnicity narrowly in linguistic terms. For example, African Americans and Caucasians in the United States are treated as separate ethnic groups by Roeder's variant of ELF, but as a single ethnic group by the original ELF due to their shared language. The former seems desirable for obvious reasons. For countries not in existence in the early 1960s (e.g., Russia), the Roeder variant of ELF, calculated using Soviet measurements from 1985, is used instead.[33]

---

[32] If the index of fractionalization is represented by F and the effective number by N, then $F = 1 - 1/N$. The effective number of ethnic (or religious) groups is calculated as follows: $N = 1 \backslash \sum_{i=1}^{n} p_i^2$, where p_i is the group's population share in the ith country. For the religious division, Powell (1982) alternatively employed the percentage of the population that was Catholic as his operationalization. In contrast to his study, this study includes many non-European countries where Catholics effectively do not appear as a latent category. A more general operationalization is therefore needed. More recently, for both the religious and ethnic divisions, Stoll (2004, 2008) alternatively employed the polarization index of Montalvo and Reynal-Querol (2001), calculated using data from Alesina et al. (2003). She also employed the index of cultural fractionalization developed by Fearon (2003) for the ethnic division. The drawback to the former is that it privileges configurations of equally sized groups: according two such groups the highest value, as it does, places it at odds with both the concept of heterogeneity developed in the last chapter and the other components of the heterogeneity index. The drawback to the latter is twofold: first, it is based upon Fearon's (2003) measure of ethnic fractionalization (see note 33); second, it underestimates ethnic diversity by privileging the attribute of language over race, much as the original ELF does (see the following discussion). Nevertheless, generally similar conclusions are drawn if these alternative operationalizations are used in the next chapter's quantitative analyses, although, not surprisingly, less significance is obtained from the index of cultural fractionalization.

[33] Using other measures of ethnic fractionalization, such as that of Alesina et al. (2003) and the original ELF (taking data from Fearon and Laitin 2003), yields similar results in the subsequent chapter's quantitative analyses. The one prominent measure that is not used is Fearon's (2003). This is because it is explicitly not a measure of *latent* ethnic diversity. For more information,

3. Describing Social Heterogeneity: Measures and Testable Hypotheses

For religion, all existing measurements have unfortunately been constructed more recently: the earliest—that of Annett (2001)—is rooted in data from the 1980s. In contrast to the approach taken for the ethnic division, I eschew this data for a slightly later set of measurements: that of Alesina and colleagues (2003), which is based on data from the 1990s.[34] This is because the earliest data from Annett is not available for a large number of countries and has a list of groups that is not allowed to vary from country to country, in contrast to all other existing lists of ethnic and religious groups. These drawbacks outweigh the small exogeneity gain of drawing data from the 1980s instead of from the 1990s.

The remaining four lines of division have received less empirical attention in the quantitative literature. This means that there is less consensus about how to measure a country's heterogeneity with respect to these divisions. I discuss the approach that I have taken for each in turn.

First is the urban–rural division. Agrarian, farmers' or peasants' parties historically emerged to represent the inhabitants of rural areas in their power struggle with the inhabitants of urban areas in some Western European countries during the period of industrialization (Lipset and Rokkan 1967). They have also emerged in several Eastern European countries (e.g., Poland) since the fall of communism and have made sporadic appearances in various Latin American countries (e.g., Chile) since the late 1800s. The two historically relevant latent categories are therefore urban and rural. Because large rural populations should make both the formation and success of agrarian parties more likely, more rural countries are viewed as more heterogeneous. Even today's predominantly rural societies, homogeneous from one perspective, might still give rise to successful agrarian parties because urban groups have been politically and economically dominant there.[35] Hence, urban–rural heterogeneity is operationalized as the percentage of a country's population that is rural (e.g., Powell 1982; Stoll 2004).[36] Data is taken

---

see the discussion in Stoll (2008).

[34] However, substituting either Annett's (2001) or Fearon and Laitin's (2003) measure of religious fractionalization, where available, for Alesina et al.'s (2003) does not alter the conclusions of the next chapter's quantitative analyses.

[35] Of the countries studied, the African countries and India have the largest rural populations by far. For example, even in 2007, Malawi's population was over 80 percent rural (World Bank Group DDG 2009). While successful agrarian parties have not in fact emerged in these developing democracies to date, their absence has been a great puzzle to scholars, a symptom of the powerlessness of farmers (peasants) specifically and the countryside more generally. What makes this political quiescence so surprising is precisely the numeric clout of the rural sector, as well as its legitimate grievances resulting from long-standing political and economic biases in favor of the urban sector. See, for example, Varshney (1998).

[36] Stoll (2004) proposed two alternatives that focused on the economic as opposed to the numeric clout of the rural sector: the percentage of employment in agriculture and agriculture's value added as a percent of gross domestic product (GDP). Similarly, Powell (1982) constructed an ordinal index based on the proportion of adult males engaged in agriculture. However, given the theory developed in the prior chapter, the best approach is to focus on the relative numbers of citizens in the rural and urban categories. A third alternative is a rurality fractionalization index, calculated in the usual way for the two groups of urban and rural individuals. This yields

from the World Development Indicators Online (World Bank Group DDG 2009). As with the ethnic division, data from the earliest year available for each country is used in order to maximize the exogeneity.[37]

Second, the socioeconomic or class division. Heterogeneity in the class structure of the citizenry has historically been a potent springboard for sectarian political parties. For example, the working class, a product of the Industrial Revolution, was particized in many Western Europe countries by socialist and communist parties (Lipset and Rokkan 1967). The most general historically important categories into which individuals have been grouped are the haves and have-nots (originally, the bourgeoisie and the workers). With large lower classes (have-nots) making successful sectarian lower-class parties more likely, the larger the lower class, the more heterogeneous the country. The best proxy for this heterogeneity in the class structure that I am aware of is the Gini coefficient, which measures the inequality of income (Stoll 2004).[38] Large Gini coefficients, which occur when income is unequally concentrated in the hands of the privileged few, accordingly indicate heterogeneity. Data for this operationalization is again taken from the World Development Indicators Online (World Bank Group DDG 2009). As before, the earliest data available is used. The exception is Eastern European countries, for which the earliest data available after their independence or democratization is used instead.[39] However, one might legitimately question the inclusion of this division in the index: as Lipset and Rokkan famously observed in Western Europe, class-based parties have emerged almost ev-

---

similar if less significant results for the next chapter's quantitative analysis. The drawback to this operationalization is that it treats as equivalent a large rural and a large urban population, even though agrarian parties are likely only when there is a large rural population. Hence, my preference is for the simpler percent rural operationalization.

[37]This is usually 1960. The subsequent chapter's conclusions are not altered by either of the following alternatives: (i) averaging over the period of the analysis for which data is available (generally, 1960–2000); (ii) for either newly independent or newly democratic states (e.g., Malawi and Russia), taking data for the year preceding their first appearance in my data set, and for all other states, taking data from 1960 (or the earliest year available).

[38]This operationalization has also been employed to capture the potential for socioeconomic conflict in other literatures. See, for example, Fearon and Laitin (2003). One alternative is to tap heterogeneity in the occupational structure—for example, categorizing workers by their employment in either the industrial, service, or agricultural sector (e.g., Bartolini 2000). However, this approach has the drawbacks of not capturing differences in wealth; of being of limited utility outside of the early Industrial Revolution period, given that left-wing parties have reduced their ties to industrial workers and trade unions over time; and of overlapping with some of the other divisions, such as the urban–rural.

[39]This is due to the jump in inequality that most of these countries experienced as part of the transition to a market economy. Using data on income inequality from the communist era would underestimate the likelihood of class-based sectarian parties forming. The earliest year for which data is usually available is 1980. Alternative approaches again do not alter the conclusions drawn from the next chapter's quantitative analysis. These alternative approaches include: (i) averaging over the period of the analysis for which data is available (1980–2000); (ii) employing the earliest data available for all countries; and (iii) taking the earliest data available, except for either newly independent or newly democratic countries (e.g., Malawi and Russia), for which data is taken from the year closest to their first appearance in the data set (privileging prior years over following years).

3. Describing Social Heterogeneity: Measures and Testable Hypotheses

erywhere. In other words, this division has had a homogenizing effect on party systems because there is little variance from country to country in the basic (conceptualized in terms of haves and have-nots) latent class structure. This is particularly true in the post–World War II era. By way of contrast, great variance in latent structures is observed from country to country with respect to the other divisions.[40] Yet estimating an alternative version of the index that excludes this division does not alter the conclusions of the next chapter's quantitative analysis.

Third, the post-materialist division. This division was initially popularized by Inglehart (1984), but it is closely related to what other scholars have called the authoritarian–libertarian (Kitschelt 1997) and "new politics" (Dalton 1996) divisions. The argument of these scholars is that economic development has had a dramatic impact upon the values and preferences of citizens. Once incomes become high enough, quality-of-life concerns, most prominently concern for the environment, come to replace material concerns. Wealthy societies accordingly contain an additional latent fault line in that their citizens can be divided into groups of post-materialists (those who have embraced post-materialist values) and materialists (those who have not), whereas poorer countries possess only materialists.[41] Greens (such as *Les Verts* in France) are the most prominent example of political parties that have emerged to represent the groups belonging to this division in many advanced industrial democracies; radical right parties in Western Europe (such as the French *Front National*) are arguably another example. Hence, wealthy countries are more heterogeneous than nonwealthy countries, which is operationalized by a dummy variable for countries that the World Bank classifies as high-income (Stoll 2004).[42]

Fourth and finally, the nonsociological division of foreign policy. There are many facets of a country's relations with the outside world that have the potential to divide its citizenry into latent groups that may or may not be particized. Because many are too region- or country-specific to capture in a large-N study like this one—for example, membership in the European Union—here the focus is upon what is arguably the most potentially polariz-

---

[40] For example, Caramani (2004) found that Western European party systems were most differentiated by the religious and ethnic divisions. Socioeconomics (class), by way of contrast, was a politically relevant division almost everywhere. This is precisely why Jones (2004) tapped socioeconomics for his measure of social heterogeneity.

[41] While post-materialist values may in turn be rooted in individuals' sociological attributes such as their income, education, and occupation—for example, if the sector in which they are employed is exposed to international competition (e.g., Kitschelt 1997)—the focus here is simply upon the existence of a reasonable number of post-materialists.

[42] These are countries that had a 2008 gross national income per capita of $11,906 or more. While this ignores differences between wealthy democracies in the extent to which their citizens have embraced post-materialist values, it draws the critical distinction between wealthy (heterogeneous in that at least some citizens have post-materialist values) and nonwealthy (homogeneous in that all citizens have materialist values) democracies. Future work might explore more finely grained operationalizations as alternatives, such as using survey data to calculate the percentage of post-materialists, in a manner akin to the approach taken for the urban–rural division.

83

ing facet of a country's foreign relations: armed conflict between it and other states. In the same way that the existence of more than one ethnic group in a country makes possible the formation of a successful sectarian ethnic party, a country's involvement in an armed conflict makes it possible that sectarian foreign policy parties will form around issues related to that conflict. The most basic of these issues is the conflict's continuance, which might see pro-war and antiwar groups particized. Consider, for example, anti–Vietnam War third-party presidential candidates such as Benjamin Spock in the United States; the Kadima party in Israel, formed to push through an Israeli withdrawal from the Gaza Strip (territory occupied by Israel during the 1967 Six Day War); and de Gaulle's reentry into French politics on the crest of the Algerian War, along with the presidential candidacies of *Algérie Française* figures such as Jean-Louis Tixier-Viganancour. Hence, states that are involved in more armed conflicts with other states are viewed as more heterogeneous. Following Stoll (2004), armed conflictualness is operationalized as the percentage of the post–World War II period during which a state was engaged in international armed conflicts. This data is taken from World Bank Group HSRP (2008).[43]

3.2.3 The Resulting Index

Table 3.2 reports the values of the social heterogeneity index for the fifty-six minimally democratic countries for which data was collected. Descriptive statistics for the overall index, as well as for each component, appear in Table 3.3. Combined, these two tables reveal that the minimum overall index value is taken by Poland; the first quartile by Costa Rica; the median by Peru; the third quartile by Colombia; and the maximum by the United States.

To illustrate the interpretation of this index of social heterogeneity, consider the polar opposites that are Poland and the United States. Ethnically, religiously and socioeconomically homogeneous Poland, not yet rich enough for its citizens' values to have shifted much in a post-materialist direction and with little involvement in international armed conflicts, is heterogeneous only with respect to the urban–rural division: its reasonably large rural population constitutes the sole historically important latent group ripe for particization by sectarian parties. Its small index value reflects this social homogeneity. By way of contrast, the ethnically, religiously,

---

[43]International armed conflicts include interstate conflicts, extra-state conflicts (largely colonial), and civil wars with external military involvement. Purely intrastate conflicts (civil wars) and nonstate conflicts are not included because they are usually related to one of the other lines of division. Specifically, the number of years a state spent in conflict between 1946 and 2005 is divided by the number of years of its existence as a state during this same period. Alternatives include a simple count of the number of conflicts in which a state has engaged and the number of battle deaths. However, the only systematic data on the latter at the state level of which I am aware (also World Bank Group HSRP 2008) is home soil battle deaths, which greatly underestimates the conflictualness of countries that have fought many extra-state conflicts (e.g., the United States and France). The drawback to the simple count is that it will underestimate the conflictualness of newer states relative to older ones.

3. Describing Social Heterogeneity: Measures and Testable Hypotheses

Country	Index	Country	Index
Argentina	1.4	Lithuania	1.9
Armenia	1.7	Macedonia	2.2
Austria	2.2	Madagascar	2.8
Benin	2.5	Malawi	2.9
Brazil	2.3	Mali	2.5
Bulgaria	1.7	Mexico	1.5
Cape Verde	1.9	Moldova	2.4
Central African Republic	3.0	Mongolia	1.5
Chile	1.4	Namibia	3.2
Colombia	2.6	Nicaragua	2.2
Republic of Congo	2.7	Niger	2.4
Costa Rica	1.8	Nigeria	3.0
Croatia	3.1	Panama	1.9
Dominican Republic	2.0	Peru	2.1
Ecuador	2.0	Philippines	3.1
El Salvador	2.0	Poland	1.1
Finland	2.3	Portugal	2.5
France	2.8	Romania	1.5
Ghana	2.9	Russia	2.5
Guatemala	2.8	Sierra Leone	3.0
Haiti	2.0	Slovakia	2.9
Honduras	1.8	Slovenia	2.5
Iceland	1.8	Sri Lanka	2.5
Ireland	2.1	Ukraine	2.0
Israel	3.2	United States	3.6
South Korea	3.0	Venezuela	1.5
Kyrghzstan	2.4	Zambia	3.0

Table 3.2: Values of the social heterogeneity index for the fifty-six minimally democratic countries that popularly elected a chief executive (president) in the post–World War II era.

and socioeconomically heterogeneous United States is rich enough for post-materialist values to have taken root among its citizenry. Moreover, it has engaged in international armed conflicts for a significant portion of the post–World War II era. The United States is reasonably homogeneous only with respect to the urban–rural division, given the relatively small rural population it has had in the post–World War II era. In other words, there are many historically important latent groups that could be particized in the United States. This is reflected in its high index value.

Not surprisingly, the Pearson correlation between my index of social heterogeneity and the quantitative literature's conventional measure of social

	Minimum	First Quartile	Median	Third Quartile	Maximum
Social Heterogeneity Index	1.1	1.8	2.1	2.6	3.6
Ethnic Fractionalization	0.0030	0.16	0.41	0.59	0.88
Religious Fractionalization	0.077	0.19	0.31	0.45	0.82
Population, Percent Rural	0.20	0.38	0.59	0.66	0.96
Gini Coefficient	0.23	0.33	0.45	0.51	0.74
High Income	0.0	0.0	0.0	1.0	1.0
Percent Post–WWII Period in Armed Conflict	0.0	0.017	0.047	0.31	1.0

Table 3.3: Descriptive statistics for the social heterogeneity index. Definitions and sources are as given in the text.

heterogeneity, ethnic fractionalization, is not high. For example, using the Roeder (2001) variant of ELF as the measure of ethnic fractionalization, the correlation is only 0.45. I say "not surprisingly" because there is little theoretical reason to expect ethnic heterogeneity to correlate highly with the other types of heterogeneity tapped by the index, and indeed, empirically, the various components of the index do not in fact correlate highly. To elaborate, of the interval-scale measures of heterogeneity that serve as the components of the index (that is, leaving aside the dichotomous high-income dummy variable), the highest observed correlation between two index components, 0.49, is between the Gini coefficient and ethnic fractionalization. The second-highest correlation, 0.48, is between the percentage of the population that is rural and ethnic fractionalization. The third-highest correlation, a much smaller 0.36, is between the percentage of the post–World War II period during which a country was engaged in armed conflict and ethnic fractionalization.

A prime example of the differences between the two measures of social heterogeneity is provided by Israel. While Israel has the third-highest score on the overall index of social heterogeneity, it has a low value of ethnic fractionalization, 0.20, which is only slightly more than the first quartile of the observed data.[44] Sole reliance upon ethnic heterogeneity as a measure of social heterogeneity would accordingly lead to Israel being classified as a relatively homogeneous country. However, once other historically important

---

[44] However, this measure of ethnic fractionalization, like all others, fails to take into account ethnic divisions within the Jewish community in Israel, the subject of a later chapter. Similarly, existing measures of religious fractionalization do not take into account religious divisions within the Jewish community, such as those between secular and Orthodox Jews. Existing measures of both ethnic and religious fractionalization accordingly underestimate the heterogeneity of Israel relative to other countries. As a result, so too does my index of social heterogeneity.

divisions are taken into account, particularly foreign policy and religion, Israel is instead classified as a relatively heterogeneous country—a portrait much more in keeping with the views of political scientists and sociologists who study Israel, as I will discuss in a later chapter.

3.3 CONCLUSION

Social heterogeneity is not an easy concept to measure. The fundamental problem is that there are infinitely many potential (or latent) divisions, as well as infinitely many potential groups associated with those divisions. Which ones should count when it comes to assessing a polity's heterogeneity? Qualitative studies have narrowed down this crippling infinity of possibilities by using knowledge of specific places and times. Quantitative studies have, with rare exceptions, coped by solely assessing a polity's ethnic heterogeneity at a single point in time. In this chapter, I developed two alternative measurement strategies, each of which produces better (if still historically constrained) measures for a broad sample of countries.

The first of these strategies was to develop longitudinal measures of social heterogeneity for the advanced industrial democracies. Specifically, I identified three key historical processes that have shaped the heterogeneity of the advanced industrial democracies' electorates since the early nineteenth century: changes in the franchise, territory, and volume of net immigration. Even more specifically, the franchise was operationalized in two ways: as the electorate as a percentage of the adult population, and as periods of universal socioeconomic, gender, and ethnic franchises. Territory was operationalized as the net cumulative territorial gain, and the volume of net immigration was operationalized as the percentage of the population that was foreign-born. I then constructed measures by gathering historical data from a variety of primary and secondary sources.

Longitudinal measures of social heterogeneity like these dovetail better with the previous chapter's causal story. There, I argued that social heterogeneity increases when new latent social groups appear *over time* within a polity due to historical processes such as immigration. These new social groups may or may not go on to form their own sectarian political parties. Accordingly, measuring social heterogeneity cross-sectionally only by comparing one country to another, as existing quantitative studies have done, does not allow for a test of this causal story. Moreover, it begs the question of what it means to compare a socially heterogeneous country such as the United States to a socially homogeneous country such as Poland. The United States and Poland are different in many ways that cannot practically be captured by conventional statistical models; comparing them is arguably like comparing apples and oranges. So how reasonable is it to pose the counterfactual that Poland becomes as heterogeneous as the United States, all else being equal? If we admit to the plausibility of such a consequential change in Polish society, which we might justifiably be reluctant to do, we would probably expect many other things about Poland to change at the same time. Yet when a statistical model employs this kind of cross-sectional measure, empirical evidence about how an increase in social heterogeneity affects the number of electoral parties is predicated upon the plausibility of just this sort of implausible counterfactual. This is the well-known problem of omitted variable bias or ignorability, which undermines the causal inferences drawn using such a research design.

Another advantage of these longitudinal measures of social heterogeneity is that they are not solely focused upon ethnic heterogeneity. For example, they allow us to explore how the increased socioeconomic diversity of the citizenry that resulted from the extension of the franchise to lower-class individuals has shaped the number of electoral parties. By way of contrast, as noted earlier, existing quantitative studies have almost exclusively operationalized social heterogeneity as ethnic heterogeneity. Even recent qualitative studies have primarily focused upon ethnic heterogeneity. While new latent ethnic groups may be particularly primed for particization, as I argued in the last chapter, groups defined by nonethnic attributes such as class and gender may also be particized. Ethnic heterogeneity, in other words, is only one dimension of social heterogeneity; measures that tap more than this single dimension will be of greater validity. The problem with focusing solely upon a polity's latent ethnic structure is that one misses other changes in its citizenry that alter its heterogeneity. The likely result will be conclusions about the relationship between social heterogeneity and the number of electoral parties that are off of the mark. Also, a focus upon a polity's ethnic structure obviously precludes the testing of the last chapter's hypotheses about the differential impact of different types of heterogeneity.

Yet as useful as these longitudinal measures are, they still do not capture the heterogeneity of a polity's citizenry with respect to many historically important divisions, such as religion. This is either because these divisions effectively have not evolved since the early nineteenth century in the advanced industrial democracies or because longitudinal data did not exist for them. Moreover, a single measure that simultaneously captures several dimensions of social heterogeneity, in contrast to the four individual longitudinal measures, can be more straightforwardly employed in interaction models to test my hypotheses about the factors that condition the effect of social heterogeneity.

For these reasons, I also developed a second, more holistic measurement strategy in this chapter. Six historically important divisions, as well as the historically important groups associated with those divisions, were identified for a broader sample of minimally democratic countries in the post–World War II era. These divisions were the ethnic; religious; socioeconomic; urban–rural; post-materialist; and foreign policy. Measures of a country's heterogeneity with respect to each of these divisions were then developed. Finally, these indicators were combined into an overall index of social heterogeneity. While solely cross-sectional owing to the limited availability of

3. Describing Social Heterogeneity: Measures and Testable Hypotheses

data, and hence subject to the same critique of existing studies' measures offered here, this measure nevertheless allows me to test hypotheses that cannot easily be tested using the longitudinal measures, and to do so with greater confidence than if only a measure of ethnic heterogeneity was employed.

In summation, then, the two sets of measures of social heterogeneity that I developed in this chapter complement one another. Collectively, they allow me to conduct empirical tests of many of the prior chapter's hypotheses, ones that will have greater internal and external validity than if I were to use only one of these measures or the measure of choice of existing studies, ethnic fractionalization. It is to the task of conducting these empirical tests that I turn in the next chapter.

4 Social Heterogeneity and Party System Fragmentation: Empirical Evidence across Space and Time

Having developed new measures of social heterogeneity, it is time to begin testing my theory about how a democracy's social heterogeneity shapes the fragmentation of its party system. One of the core arguments I advanced in Chapter 2 was that a group of individuals newly added to a democracy's citizenry is likely to successfully form its own sectarian political party, increasing the fragmentation of the party system, when the characteristics of the group and systemic features of the polity take certain favorable forms. That is, I argued that several factors besides the electoral system indirectly condition the effect of social heterogeneity on party system fragmentation. I also argued that the polity's prior social heterogeneity directly conditions this relationship. The question now is whether the empirical evidence supports these arguments.

In this chapter, I provide some answers to this question by conducting a quantitative empirical analysis that assesses the evidence across both space and time. My dependent variable in this analysis is party system fragmentation. I use linear regression to analyze the relationship between this dependent variable, the independent variable of social heterogeneity, and some of the hypothesized conditioning variables. I say "some" because not all of my hypotheses could be tested in this manner due to the difficulty of developing cross-national measures of the variables. Later chapters will turn the empirical lens on the key mechanism of interest, sectarian party success, and subject the remaining hypotheses to empirical scrutiny using case studies of Israel and the United States. The case studies will also provide additional tests of the hypotheses tested here, a triangulation designed to increase the study's internal validity.

The quantitative analysis of the present chapter proceeds in two parts.

4. Empirical Evidence across Space and Time

Each has its own unit of analysis and unique data set that contains one of the original measures of social heterogeneity that I developed in the previous chapter. Commensurate with the discussion thus far, in the first part of this chapter, I empirically analyze the relationship between legislative party system fragmentation and social heterogeneity in legislative elections: specifically, in all minimally democratic and partisan legislative elections in the advanced industrial democracies from the nineteenth century to the present day. In the second part of the chapter, I conversely analyze the relationship between presidential party system fragmentation and social heterogeneity in presidential elections: specifically, in all minimally democratic presidential elections in the post–World War II era. Switching the unit of analysis from legislative to presidential elections is possible because the hypotheses developed earlier generalize to presidential elections, as I will argue.

These two analyses are complimentary in that they jointly test many of the hypotheses developed in the prior chapter, but also in that the strengths of one compensate for the weaknesses of the other. A study of presidential elections has the benefit of sidestepping some of the problematic disjunctures between theory and measures that emerge when studying legislative elections. However, the downside is that it explores the relationship between presidential party system fragmentation and the time-invariant measure of social heterogeneity developed in the second half of the last chapter. By way of contrast, the legislative election analysis assesses how actual historical changes in the heterogeneity of the citizenry relate to legislative party system fragmentation, using the time series cross-sectional measures of social heterogeneity developed in the first part of the last chapter. This analysis accordingly has a quasi-experimental flavor, which provides a better empirical test of the hypothesized causal mechanism. Given the complexity of these measures, however, the legislative elections analysis focuses on testing the hypotheses about how group characteristics condition the effect of social heterogeneity on party system fragmentation. The presidential elections analysis, conversely, focuses on testing for the hypothesized conditioning effect of systemic factors.

Overall, I find that across space and time, social heterogeneity has shaped the fragmentation of the party system in democracies, as hypothesized. However, I also find empirical evidence that several factors besides the electoral system have conditioned this effect, also as hypothesized. Specifically, I find support for my hypotheses that group characteristics; the prior social heterogeneity of the polity; and the regime type are conditioning factors. Conversely, I do not find empirical support for my hypothesis about the conditioning effect of party system openness.

4.1 CHANGING SOCIETIES, CHANGING PARTY SYSTEM FRAGMENTATION IN LEGISLATIVE ELECTIONS?

In this section, I explore how the heterogeneity of the citizenry relates to the fragmentation of the party system in legislative elections. I do so by analyzing a pooled historical time series of legislative elections in twenty-two advanced industrial democracies. In contrast to existing quantitative studies, this empirical analysis employs an operationalization of social heterogeneity that goes beyond ethnicity *and* that varies over time.

The goal of the analysis is to investigate whether some types of new latent groups, and hence some latent divisions, have historically been more successfully particized than others. Accordingly, for the world's oldest contemporary democracies, I study how the fragmentation of their party systems has historically been shaped by the different ways in which their citizenries have changed. This means that I focus on testing the hypotheses I developed in Chapter 2 about the group characteristics that condition the effect of social heterogeneity. My hypotheses about the systemic conditioning factors are momentarily set aside, with the exception of the restrictiveness of the electoral system. This variable has received so much attention in the literature that it is included in this analysis.

4.1.1 Variable Measures and Testable Hypotheses

The dependent variable, party system fragmentation, is operationalized as the effective number of electoral parties (Laakso and Taagepera 1979). This operationalization takes into account both the elite-level supply of political parties and the mass-level dispersion of votes. For example, if three parties compete in an election but one party receives half as many votes as the other two (that is, if the vote shares are 40%, 40%, and 20%), the effective number of electoral parties will be two and a half. To deal with the unfortunate fact that many election returns lump small parties together in one "other" category, the operationalization is even more specifically a modified version of the effective number: that of Taagepera's (1997) method of bounds.[1] For elections held prior to 1946, I used election results reported in Mackie and Rose (1991) to generate the data. For elections from 1946 to 2000, I took data from Golder (2005). For the most recent elections from 2001 to 2005, I used either each country's official election returns if they were available or results reported by the Inter-parliamentary Union if they were not.[2]

---

[1] If v_i is a party's vote share in the ith country–election, the effective number of electoral parties is calculated as follows: ENEP $= \frac{1}{\sum_{i=1}^{n} v_i^2}$. Taagepera's (1997) method of bounds averages between two versions of this statistic: one calculated by treating the residual "others" category as one political party, and one calculated by omitting the parties in the "others" category (that is, by treating each as a party that failed to receive any votes).

[2] Israel is the one exception. For this country only, all calculations are based upon the complete and official government election returns. The sources of each country's post-2000 election results are available upon request.

The first independent variable is the restrictiveness of the electoral system. This variable is operationalized as a dummy variable coded one if a restrictive electoral system is employed for the legislative election and zero otherwise. The restrictive category includes electoral systems that use plurality rule; absolute and qualified majorities; the limited vote; the alternative vote; the single nontransferable vote; and the modified Borda count. All other electoral systems are placed in the nonrestrictive (permissive) category. While the more conventional operationalization of electoral system restrictiveness is the logged average lower-tier district magnitude (e.g., Clark and Golder 2006), my operationalization yields easy-to-interpret interaction models while still capturing the basic differences between the two major types of electoral systems. Moreover, my operationalization circumvents a major disadvantage of the conventional operationalization: lumping together mixed-member proportional electoral systems, which have an average lower-tier district magnitude of one but which yield very proportional outcomes, with many restrictive systems, which also have an average district magnitude of one but which yield very disproportional outcomes. I obtained data for this variable by extending Golder's (2005) original data for the 1946–2000 period both forwards and backwards in time. To do so, I consulted a variety of primary and secondary sources, such as Mackie and Rose (1991).[3]

The second independent variable is social heterogeneity. In the last chapter, I developed time series cross-sectional measures of the three major historical processes—changes in the franchise, territory, and volume of net immigration—that have shaped the heterogeneity of the advanced industrial democracies' citizenries during the modern era. These measures collectively serve as the measure of social heterogeneity in this analysis. To recap, the franchise is measured by the electorate as a percentage of the adult population in some models and by dummy variables for universal socioeconomic, gender, and ethnic franchises in others; territory is measured by the net cumulative territorial gain; and the volume of net immigration is measured by the foreign-born as a percentage of the population.

Drawing upon the theory I developed in Chapter 2, when the electoral system is permissive, the basic testable hypothesis is that each of these dimensions of social heterogeneity should be related to party system fragmentation (H1). Specifically, under these institutional conditions, increases in the heterogeneity of the citizenry from expansions of the franchise, territorial acquisitions, and immigration should *increase* the effective number of electoral parties, all else being equal.

But the theory also suggests that these different types of changes in the heterogeneity of the citizenry should affect the fragmentation of the party

---

[3]Some electoral systems, particularly early ones, combine majoritarian and proportional elements in a way that makes them difficult to classify. An example is the French system employed for the 1919 and 1924 elections. I chose to err on the side of a narrow definition of majoritarianism by coding these cases as nonmajoritarian; however, alternatively coding them as majoritarian does not alter the conclusions reported here.

system in different ways. Accordingly, more nuanced and specific testable hypotheses can also be developed. First, new citizens with an external origin, that is, from territorial change or immigration, should be less likely to be successfully particized than new citizens with an internal origin, that is, from expansions of the franchise. This means that the effective number of electoral parties should have a weaker relationship with the former dimensions of social heterogeneity than with the latter dimensions (H1a). Second, of the two groups of new citizens originating externally, immigrants should be less likely to be successfully particized than the residents of newly acquired territories.[4] Accordingly, the effective number of electoral parties should have a weaker relationship with immigration than with territorial change (H1b). Third, previously disenfranchised ethnic minorities, the inhabitants of newly acquired territories, and immigrants are all new latent groups that have usually been defined by ethnic types of attributes such as skin color and language. This suggests that they should be more likely to be successfully particized than the other new latent social groups studied, even those defined by other relatively sticky types of attributes such as gender (women). The former should therefore have a stronger relationship with the effective number of electoral parties (H1c). However, because this testable hypothesis contradicts the previous one for some groups, it is an empirical question whether the advantage of being ethnically defined outweighs the disadvantage of an external origin.

Finally, there is the hypothesized constraint imposed by restrictive electoral systems. The basic testable hypothesis is that when the electoral system is restrictive, the relationship between each dimension of social heterogeneity and the effective number of electoral parties should be weaker than when the electoral system is permissive (H2). But again, more nuanced testable hypotheses identifying exceptions can be developed. First, because the inhabitants of newly acquired territories are by definition maximally territorially concentrated, a restrictive electoral system should not constrain their successful particization. This means that we should not observe a difference in the relationship between the effective number of electoral parties and territorial change under restrictive versus permissive electoral systems (H2a). Second, women alone of the previously disenfranchised groups stud-

---

[4]Even leaving aside the greater difficulties that immigrants have historically had in obtaining citizenship in many countries relative to the residents of newly acquired territories, an issue touched upon in the last chapter, there are many reasons to believe that immigrants will be at a collective action disadvantage, particularly in the short run. For example, the communal infrastructure of newly acquired territories is usually intact. By way of contrast, because immigrants have been uprooted from their home communities, they must build communal institutions from scratch in their new countries of residence, making their politicization less likely—at least for a number of years. For a recent general overview of the factors shaping immigrant political incorporation, which highlights the generally low level of incorporation in many countries but also recognizes the variation in this incorporation across groups, countries, and time periods, see Hochschild and Mollenkopf (2009). See also Portes, Escobar, and Arana (2009) on the strong positive relationship between the length of time Latin American immigrants to the United States have been resident there and their political activism.

ied have not been territorially concentrated in any way. But because they are such a large group, constituting approximately one-half of both the national electorate and the electorate in each electoral district, a restrictive electoral system should also not constrain their successful particization. As before, this dimension of social heterogeneity should therefore have a similar relationship to the effective number of electoral parties under restrictive and permissive electoral systems (H2b).

4.1.2 MODEL SPECIFICATIONS AND DATA

To test these hypotheses, I first estimate the following model, which is labeled Model 1:

$$\begin{aligned} \text{ENEP}_{i,t} = \beta_0 &+ \beta_1 \text{ELECTORATE}_{i,t} + \beta_2 \text{TERRITORY}_{i,t} \\ &+ \beta_3 \text{FOREIGN}_{i,t} + \beta_4 \text{MAJORITARIAN}_{i,t} \\ &+ \beta_5 \text{ELECTORATE}_{i,t} \times \text{MAJORITARIAN}_{i,t} \\ &+ \beta_6 \text{TERRITORY}_{i,t} \times \text{MAJORITARIAN}_{i,t} \\ &+ \beta_7 \text{FOREIGN}_{i,t} \times \text{MAJORITARIAN}_{i,t} + \epsilon_{i,t} \end{aligned} \quad (4.1)$$

In Equation 4.1, ENEP is the effective number of electoral parties; ELECTORATE is the electorate as a percentage of the twenty-and-over population; TERRITORY is the net cumulative territorial gain in square kilometers; FOREIGN is the foreign-born as a percentage of the population; and MAJORITARIAN is a dummy variable for a majoritarian electoral system. Cross-sections (countries) are indexed by i and time periods (elections) by t. Although they are not shown for reasons of space, country fixed effects are included in the model to control for the many other unmodeled and relatively stable features of countries (e.g., political culture) that might shape fragmentation.[5]

I then estimate a second model, labeled Model 2, that alters Model 1 by employing my alternative operationalization of internal change in the citizenry:

$$\begin{aligned} \text{ENEP}_{i,t} = \beta_0 &+ \beta_1 \text{ECONOMIC}_{i,t} + \beta_2 \text{GENDER}_{i,t} + \beta_3 \text{ETHNIC} \\ &+ \beta_4 \text{TERRITORY}_{i,t} + \beta_5 \text{FOREIGN}_{i,t} + \beta_6 \text{MAJORITARIAN}_{i,t} \\ &+ \beta_7 \text{ECONOMIC}_{i,t} \times \text{MAJORITARIAN}_{i,t} \\ &+ \beta_8 \text{GENDER}_{i,t} \times \text{MAJORITARIAN}_{i,t} \\ &+ \beta_9 \text{ETHNIC}_{i,t} \times \text{MAJORITARIAN}_{i,t} \\ &+ \beta_{10} \text{TERRITORY}_{i,t} \times \text{MAJORITARIAN}_{i,t} \\ &+ \beta_{11} \text{FOREIGN}_{i,t} \times \text{MAJORITARIAN}_{i,t} + \epsilon_{i,t} \end{aligned} \quad (4.2)$$

---

[5] F-tests for the joint significance of the $C-1$ country dummies, where C is the number of countries, supports their inclusion, and many of the dummies individually attain conventional levels of significance.

Everything is as before, bar the substitution of dummy variables for elections conducted under universal socioeconomic (ECONOMIC), gender (GENDER), and ethnic (ETHNIC) franchises for the electorate as a percentage of the adult population.

The cases used to estimate these two models are elections for the lower or only legislative chamber in the twenty-two advanced industrial democracies with populations greater than one million.[6] As discussed in the last chapter, the first election included in the analysis for each country is the earliest procedurally democratic election in which the great majority of seats were contested; reasonably nationalized party labels existed; and for which historical data on the national distribution of votes over party labels exists. All subsequent procedurally democratic elections are then included through 2005, after which it became problematic to obtain more recent data. Note that elections held prior to a country's formal independence but at a time when it was reasonably self-governing are included in the analysis.[7] After list-wise deleting the few cases with missing data, the data set used to estimate Model 1 consists of 639 elections in 21 countries, while the data set used to estimate Model 2 consists of 733 elections in 22 countries. The difference between the two data sets is eighty-nine elections in the United States and five early Greek elections.[8]

4.1.3 RESULTS AND DISCUSSION

To estimate Models 1 and 2, I use ordinary least squares (OLS) regression. The resulting coefficient estimates are shown below in Table 4.1. This same table also presents the robust standard errors of the coefficients in parentheses.[9]

---

[6]Confining the analysis to the advanced industrial democracies ensures that the countries in the sample are largely equal in their degree of democratic consolidation at any one point in time. Nevertheless, differences over time that might be consequential do exist, given my hypothesis about party system openness. One potential solution is to control for elections that were the first since either independence or a transition to democracy. Another potential solution is to control for elections that were the first held under a new electoral system, interacting this dummy variable with the dummy variable for a restrictive electoral system in order to allow the effect to differ depending on whether the electoral system had become more restrictive or permissive. However, both approaches left the conclusions substantively unaltered.

[7]This includes Finland as a Russian Grand Duchy (prior to the 1919 election); New Zealand when it had not yet become a Dominion (prior to the 1908 election); Austria in 1907 and 1911; Ireland in 1918; and Norway prior to the 1906 election. Eliminating all twenty-five of these elections, that is, the elections held prior to formal independence, does not substantively alter the conclusions.

[8]For these elections, data on the electorate as a percentage of the twenty-and-over population was not available. Chapter 3 discussed why this is so for the United States.

[9]Specifically, the table reports Newey-West (Newey and West 1987) standard errors, which are robust to both autocorrelation and heteroskedasticity. A popular alternative is the robust country–clustered estimator. However, it is not appropriate for Models 1 and 2 because the number of clusters (countries) is less than fifty (Kezdi 2004). While Beck and Katz (1995) also raised the issue of cross-country contemporaneous correlation in the context of time series cross-sectional (TSCS) models, there is little theoretical reason to expect it in the kind of electoral data used here. Moreover, it is difficult to obtain a good estimate of the contemporaneous

	Model 1	Model 2
Intercept	2.0***	0.78
	(0.446)	(0.76)
Electorate (%)	0.015***	
	(0.0049)	
Majoritarian	−0.10	1.3*
	(0.43)	(0.72)
Territory	0.000014***	0.000013***
	(0.0000017)	(0.0000017)
Foreign (%)	0.044**	0.062***
	(0.017)	(0.018)
Electorate (%) × Majoritarian	−0.0030***	
	(0.0052)	
Territory × Majoritarian	−0.000014***	−0.000013***
	(0.0000017)	(0.0000017)
Foreign (%) × Majoritarian	−0.046***	−0.047***
	(0.015)	(0.016)
Economic		0.57
		(0.54)
Gender		0.054
		(0.32)
Ethnic		1.6***
		(0.51)
Economic × Majoritarian		−0.21
		(0.55)
Gender × Majoritarian		0.19
		(0.34)
Ethnic × Majoritarian		−1.7***
		(0.53)
N	639	733
Root MSE	1.0	0.99
R^2	0.54	0.57

Table 4.1: Coefficients and robust (Newey-West) standard errors for Models 1 and 2 of the legislative elections analysis. The dependent variable is the effective number of electoral parties. Country fixed effects are not shown. Significance codes are for two-sided tests: 0.001, ***; 0.05, **; 0.10, *.

Permissive Electoral Systems

I begin with elections conducted under permissive electoral systems. For this institutional configuration, the relationship between each dimension of social heterogeneity and the effective number of electoral parties is given by the main effect term in the model, such as the coefficient on "FOREIGN." In both models, all of these terms are positively signed and almost all are statistically significant using either a two-sided or the more appropriate one-sided test. This means that increases in most dimensions of social heterogeneity are found to have significantly increased the fragmentation of the party system, providing support for the basic testable hypothesis (H1).

To elaborate, first consider external changes in the citizenry. Table 4.1 shows that in both models, an increase in a country's territory is predicted to increase its effective number of electoral parties, in accordance with the basic hypothesis. So, too, is an increase in the proportion of a country's population that is foreign-born. Moreover, both of these effects are statistically significant at conventional levels. However, the substantive significances differ. For territorial change, a realistic change in territory, given the skew in the distribution introduced by Canada, is the interquartile range. When confining the sample to those elections where the country experienced some territorial change, this is 17,660 square kilometers, roughly the territorial gain experienced by Italy in the immediate aftermath of World War I. Such a territorial gain is predicted to increase the effective number of electoral parties by at most approximately one-quarter (0.24), ceteris paribus. For immigration, the interquartile range of approximately ten percentage points is again a realistic yardstick of change. For such a change in the foreign-born as a share of the population, the predicted increase in the effective number of electoral parties is at most a little more than one-half (0.64), ceteris paribus.[10] Hence, of the two external dimensions of social heterogeneity, immigration is typically found to have had the largest substantive effect on party system fragmentation when the electoral system is permissive, contrary to H1b.

But what about internal changes in the citizenry? Here, too, the hypothesized positive relationship can be seen. First take the electorate as a percentage of the twenty-and-over population as the operationalization of the franchise (Model 1). Both a statistically and substantively significant relationship is found between this variable and the effective number of electoral parties. Increasing the electorate's share of the adult population by approximately thirty-three percentage points, the interquartile range, yields

---

correlation when there are hardly any common time periods across countries, as is the case in this data set. Their panel corrected standard errors (PCSE) are accordingly also not appropriate for these models.

[10] Interestingly, an increase of this magnitude approximately describes the situation of many Western European countries over the past few decades (the second category of countries identified in the prior chapter). The prediction is accordingly that these countries' party systems should have fragmented by this amount. And indeed, a comparison of the early 2000s to the early 1980s largely bears out this prediction.

a predicted increase in the effective number of electoral parties of one-half (0.49), ceteris paribus. But when considering the larger historical picture, the expansion of the electorate in the advanced industrial democracies from a very small percentage of the adult population in the late 1800s to the entire adult population today is predicted to have increased the effective number of electoral parties by about one and a half, ceteris paribus.[11] Accordingly, internal increases in the heterogeneity of the citizenry resulting from expansion of the franchise seem to have historically had a larger substantive effect upon the number of electoral parties than external increases have had, in accordance with H1a.

Second, when the operationalization of the franchise instead contrasts periods of universal and restricted suffrage according to the different criteria (Model 2), interesting substantive and statistical differences emerge. Only the universal ethnic franchise has a statistically significant effect upon the effective number of electoral parties,[12] ceteris paribus, one that is also substantively significant (an increase in the effective number of electoral parties of more than one and a half). However, as noted in the prior chapter, this finding is based on contrasting a small number of Israeli elections with all other elections. It should accordingly be taken with a grain of salt. What is more interesting is the comparison between the effect of a universal gender franchise and the effect of a universal socioeconomic franchise. The former is found to have little substantive effect, whereas the latter is predicted to increase the effective number of electoral parties by more than one-half, ceteris paribus, even if it narrowly falls short of attaining conventional levels of statistical significance. Accordingly, if the findings regarding the universal ethnic franchise are discounted, the largest impact comes from increasing the socioeconomic heterogeneity of the electorate.

All in all, then, mixed evidence is found about the collective action advantages of a group being ethnically defined. Based on the experiences of disenfranchised ethnic minorities, immigrants, and the residents of newly acquired territories, increasing the ethnic diversity of the citizenry does not, contrary to H1c, seem to have had a *measurably* greater impact on the fragmentation of the party system than increasing other types of diversity have had. Of course, these findings may be explained by the counterbalancing external origin of some of these groups. To definitively untangle the effect of being ethnically defined from the effect of an external origin, we would need historical examples of reasonably large and internally originating eth-

---

[11] An example is Belgium, whose electorate's share of the adult population increased from a minimum of 3.1% in 1848 to a maximum of 97.1% in 1981. Model 1 predicts that this expansion of the franchise should have increased the country's effective number of electoral parties by 1.4—which, in fact, approximately describes the observed change in the number of electoral parties in Belgium from the 1800s to the 1960s, prior to the institutional reforms that fragmented the Belgian party system.

[12] The reduced statistical and substantive significance of this operationalization may be explained by the fact that many elections conducted under a nonuniversal franchise nevertheless had a fairly extensive franchise, blurring the differences between the two periods.

nic groups being added to the citizenry, which—as noted earlier—we simply do not have. Yet there is still another perspective from which the glass is half-full instead of half-empty. Because immigration and territorial acquisitions have both been associated with the fragmentation of the party system, the advantage of being ethnically defined (H1c) does seem to outweigh the disadvantage of an external origin (H1a).

Restrictive Electoral Systems

This brings me to restrictive electoral systems. For these electoral systems, the relationship between each dimension of social heterogeneity and the effective number of electoral parties is the sum of the main effect and interaction terms in the model, for example, the sum of the coefficients on "FOREIGN" and "FOREIGN × MAJORITARIAN". It is the interaction term, in other words, that captures the difference in social heterogeneity's effect between the two types of electoral systems.

On balance, the empirical evidence supports the basic hypothesis about the conditioning effect of restrictive electoral systems (H2). First, the interaction terms in Table 4.1 are statistically significant for all dimensions of social heterogeneity except for the universal socioeconomic and gender franchises. This means that a statistically significant difference between restrictive and permissive electoral systems is found for most dimensions of social heterogeneity. Second, the main effect terms are all positively signed, as previously discussed, and the interaction terms are all negatively signed and of approximately similar magnitudes, with the single exception of women's suffrage (to be discussed below). This means that for most dimensions of social heterogeneity, increasing social heterogeneity is found to have had a *smaller* effect on party system fragmentation when the electoral system is restrictive than when it is permissive. For example, a ten percentage point increase in the foreign-born share of the population is predicted to increase the effective number of electoral parties by at most just shy of one-fifth (0.18)—a substantive effect that is less than a third of that found when the electoral system is permissive.[13]

The exception is the extension of the franchise to women. In accordance with H2b, for this dimension of social heterogeneity, a restrictive electoral system is not found to act as a constraint. Rather, the substantive magnitude of women's suffrage is larger under a restrictive than a permissive electoral system. This can be explained by women's large share of the electorate. Yet somewhat contrary to H2b, although perhaps in keeping with H1c, extending the franchise to women when the electoral system is restrictive is predicted to have a moderate effect on party system fragmentation, at best: an increase in the effective number of electoral parties of only one-quarter (0.25).

---

[13] To illustrate, the calculation of this marginal effect for the foreign-born as a percentage of the population in Model 2 is as follows: it is the sum of $\hat{\beta}_5$ and $\hat{\beta}_{11}$ from Equation 4.2, or $0.064 + -0.046 = 0.017$.

On a similar note, while a restrictive electoral system is predicted to act as a constraint on increases in the socioeconomic heterogeneity of the citizenry from extensions of the franchise, this effect is not statistically significant. An explanation for this finding is that the lower classes have historically been somewhat territorially concentrated and have constituted a large group relative to the total electorate (a large minority to a majority, depending on how the lower classes are defined), making them a large share of the electorate in many electoral districts. Given the hypotheses I developed earlier, the finding that the electoral system has acted as only a limited constraint on this group's successful particization is sensible.

The only truly surprising finding concerns the effect of territorial gains. Contrary to H2a, a restrictive electoral system is found to constrain the effect of increases in social heterogeneity resulting from territorial acquisitions. However, if the settler states of the United States and Canada are treated as if their electorates had not increased through territorial expansion—arguably the more appropriate approach for the reasons discussed earlier—results supportive of the hypothesis are obtained. In other words, alternative measures of territorial gain do not find that restrictive electoral systems have constrained the effect of increases in social heterogeneity resulting from territorial acquisitions; rather, territorial gains are predicted to have had a larger impact upon the fragmentation of the party system when the electoral system is restrictive, as hypothesized.[14]

4.2   SOCIAL HETEROGENEITY AND PRESIDENTIAL PARTY SYSTEM FRAGMENTATION

In this section of the chapter, I turn the empirical lens from legislative to presidential elections. Most quantitative studies have used legislative elections to empirically explore the hypothesized relationship between social heterogeneity and party system fragmentation, as I did in the previous section. Most have also, with rare exceptions, exclusively measured social heterogeneity at the national or aggregate level, again as I did in the previous section.[15] But this is problematic. If there is not a single nationwide electoral district, which there is not in most countries, this approach effectively assumes that the heterogeneity of each electoral district perfectly mirrors

---

[14]See notes 17 and 19 in Chapter 3 for more details on this and other alternative measures of this dimension of social heterogeneity. These models are presented in Appendix A.

[15]For example, Singer and Stephenson (2009) recently tested Duverger's hypotheses regarding the relationship between the effective number of electoral parties and the restrictiveness of the electoral system at the district level, but they employed national (aggregate) measures of social, and specifically ethnic, heterogeneity. For many years, the only study incorporating district-level measures of social heterogeneity was that of Jones (1997), who analyzed the relationship between racial heterogeneity in Louisiana electoral districts and the effective number of electoral candidates for the state legislature in those districts. However, this design obviously holds the electoral system restrictiveness constant. A welcome recent addition on the comparative front is provided by Moser and Scheiner (2012), who have compiled district-level data on ethnic heterogeneity for five countries.

that of the national electorate—an assumption that is usually not valid. At the present time, however, district-level measures of social heterogeneity do not exist for enough countries, let alone for enough time periods, to conduct the much-needed multilevel analysis of legislative elections (Stoll 2008).[16]

Fortunately, there is an alternative research design that enables me to work around this problem: switching the unit of analysis from legislative to presidential elections. The hypotheses developed in Chapter 2 about social heterogeneity's effect on party system fragmentation in legislative elections readily generalize to presidential elections, with a minor exception to be discussed. For example, instead of the dependent variable being the effective number of electoral parties in legislative elections, the dependent variable is the effective number of electoral candidates or party labels in presidential elections. This is why several studies do exist that have used presidential elections as the unit of analysis.[17] And with the exception of the United States, presidential elections take place in single nationwide electoral districts. The only level at which heterogeneity matters in presidential elections, in other words, is the national or aggregate level—the level for which data happens to be most widely available. Presidential elections accordingly better match the measure to the mechanism, to paraphrase Posner (2004a, 852), than legislative elections do.

It is worth noting that using presidential elections as the unit of analysis serves as a hard case for the basic hypothesis. All presidential electoral systems are reasonably restrictive relative to most legislative electoral systems. Given the constraint that restrictive electoral systems are hypothesized to impose upon the successful particization of new latent social groups, I accordingly expect to find a weaker relationship between social heterogeneity and party system fragmentation in presidential elections. To the extent that I do observe a relationship, however, the basic hypothesis will have passed with flying colors. Moreover, because there is little meaningful variation in the restrictiveness of presidential electoral systems, at least relative to the observed variation in the restrictiveness of legislative electoral systems, I do not expect to observe the effect of social heterogeneity differing much from one presidential electoral system to another. This is the exception to the generalizability of the hypotheses mentioned earlier.

Accordingly, in this section, I explore the relationship between social heterogeneity and presidential party system fragmentation by analyzing a time series cross-sectional data set of minimally democratic presidential elections

---

[16]Even district-level data on the dependent variable in legislative elections analyses, the effective number of electoral parties, has only recently become available for a reasonable number of countries and time periods. Examples of district-level analyses, which are increasing with the availability of district-level data, include Reed (1990),Chhibber and Kollman (1998, 2004), Caramani (2004), Hicken and Stoll (2011), and Moser and Scheiner (2012).

[17]See, for example, Amorim Neto and Cox (1997); Cox (1997); Jones (1999); Jones (2004); Stoll (2004); Golder (2006); and Hicken and Stoll (2008). I can also identify many anecdotes that seem to support the applicability of the hypothesis. An example is Bolivia, where indigenous party labels (with presidential candidates such as Evo Morales) have appeared following this group's relatively recent enfranchisement.

4. Empirical Evidence across Space and Time

in the post–World War II era. The goal is to test all save one of my hypotheses about the conditioning effects of a polity's systemic features. These systemic features are the prior heterogeneity of the polity; the regime type; the electoral system; and party system openness. (The omitted systemic factor is the strategies of existing parties, which does not lend itself well to cross-national measurement.) Because this analysis makes use of the holistic measure of social heterogeneity I developed in the last chapter, it is not possible to test my hypotheses about the conditioning effects of group characteristics.

4.2.1 VARIABLE MEASURES AND TESTABLE HYPOTHESES

The dependent variable, the fragmentation of the presidential party system, is operationalized as is conventional: as the size-weighted or effective number of presidential candidates. In a manner comparable to the way in which the effective number of electoral parties is calculated, this statistic weighs each candidate by his or her vote share (Laakso and Taagepera 1979).[18] Accordingly, it takes into account both the elite-level supply of presidential candidates and the mass-level support those presidential candidates receive on election day. I take data for this variable from Golder (2005).

There are two political institutional independent variables. The first is the restrictiveness of the electoral system. This variable is operationalized as a dummy variable coded one for presidential elections conducted using a simple plurality electoral formula, the most restrictive presidential electoral system, and zero otherwise (see, for example, Hicken and Stoll 2008).[19] The less restrictive category includes elections for which there are provisions for a runoff election (that is, a dual-ballot formula of some sort); where the electoral formula is the more permissive single transferable vote (Cox 1997, 144); or where the voters select an electoral college.[20] I also take data for this variable from Golder (2005).

The second political institutional variable is the size of the presidential

---

[18]Letting v_i represent each candidate's vote share in a given country–election, the effective number of presidential candidates (ENPRES) is calculated as follows: ENPRES $= \frac{1}{\sum_{i=1}^{n} v_i^2}$.

[19]Work previous to Hicken and Stoll (2008) compared elections conducted under pure plurality rule to those conducted under pure dual-ballot rules (e.g., Jones 1999, 2004; Golder 2006). As in Hicken and Stoll, presidential elections that do not fall into one of these two categories are still of interest to me because my focus is on a variable other than the electoral system.

[20]I am aware of no extant predictions regarding the relative amounts of coordination in elections with and without electoral colleges. The United States, Finland, and Argentina are the three countries included in this study that have employed an electoral college. While the United States largely selects electors using a plurality formula, the now-defunct electoral colleges of Finland and Argentina were selected using permissive electoral formulas. It is for this reason that Hicken and Stoll (2008) classified the former but not the latter as employing a restrictive electoral system. By way of contrast, I also place the United States in the less restrictive category because of the boost its decentralized, state-based electoral college districts arguably provide to geographically concentrated groups. Note, however, that instead classifying it as restrictive does not alter the conclusions reported here. Further, eliminating all presidential college elections from the analysis also leaves the conclusions substantively unaltered.

prize. My focus here is upon one of the two dimensions of the regime type discussed in Chapter 2: the extent to which policy-making authority is horizontally centralized in the office of the presidency vis-à-vis the legislature. The second dimension, the extent to which policy-making authority is vertically centralized at the national level of government vis-à-vis the subnational level, does also contribute to the size of the presidential prize. However, there are two reasons for focusing solely upon the horizontal dimension. First, in the sample of post–World War II elections that constitutes the set of cases for this analysis, there is only minimal variation in the vertical dimension: the national level of government is important everywhere, even if it is somewhat more important in some countries and elections than in others. By way of contrast, there is great variation in the horizontal dimension: compare, for example, the figurehead Irish president to the imperial Brazilian president. Because the size of the prize can effectively be viewed as an additive function of horizontal and vertical centralization, this means that little is lost by focusing upon horizontal centralization alone, given the little observed variation in vertical centralization.[21] Second, several recent studies have produced weak and contradictory findings regarding the vertical dimension (e.g., Cox and Knoll 2003; Brancati 2008; Hicken and Stoll 2008, 2009, 2011).[22] Accordingly, because the empirically consequential variation in the size of the presidential prize comes from the horizontal dimension of the regime type, I take the "size of the presidential prize" as meaning the horizontal centralization of policy-making authority in the presidency vis-à-vis the legislature in what follows.[23]

Building upon the work of Hicken and Stoll (2008), I operationalize the horizontal centralization of authority in the presidency in two ways. The first is as an index of de jure presidential powers. This index relies upon a coding scheme first developed by Shugart and Carey (1992) and later refined by Frye, Hellman, and Tucker (2000). In total, it measures ten dimensions

---

[21] The only situations in which horizontal and vertical centralization obviously interact in determining the size of the presidential prize are when either the national level of government or the president exercise little policy-making authority. Because there are countries whose presidents exercise virtually no authority in the sample of cases used here, the horizontal dimension will constrain the vertical dimension: in this situation, the size of the presidential prize is zero regardless of how much policy-making authority is vested in the national level of government. However, because the national level of government always exercises substantial authority in the post–World War II era, the vertical dimension will not empirically constrain the horizontal dimension.

[22] The obvious explanation for the discrepancy between the findings from these studies, which used sets of cases similar to the one employed here, and Chhibber and Kollman's (1998, 2004) findings is precisely the limited post-1945 variation in the policy-making authority of national governments. Chhibber and Kollman observed much greater variation in the authority of national governments in their longer historical time series, which reached back into the eighteenth century.

[23] Future research should nevertheless take up the empirical issue of how the vertical centralization of policy-making authority at the national level of government conditions the relationship between social heterogeneity and the number of presidential candidates, either separately or in combination with horizontal centralization.

of presidential power. The first six dimensions relate to the president's legislative powers, ranging from the package veto to budgetary powers. The remaining four dimensions relate to the nonlegislative powers of the president, such as dissolution of the assembly. For a given election, a country is assigned a score ranging from zero (minimal presidential authority) to four (maximal presidential authority) on each dimension, based on the constitution in effect at that time. An overall index of presidential powers is then created by adding the scores on the ten dimensions. This index ranges from a minimum of zero, a value taken by Ireland throughout the post-World War II period, to a maximum of twenty-four, a value taken by Chile under its 1969 constitution.[24] I take data for this variable from Hicken and Stoll (2008), who obtained copies of countries' constitutions from a variety of sources and used the coding scheme just described to code them.[25]

Although a recent survey of different ways of measuring presidential power found the Shugart and Carey (1992) approach upon which this index is based to be the most useful (Metcalf 2000), the index of presidential powers is not without its flaws.[26] Accordingly, I also employ an alternative operationalization of horizontal centralization: an ordinal typology of the regime type in effect at the time of an election. Each country is classified as taking one of three regime types that capture basic differences in presidential authority: the parliamentary, the mixed, or the true presidential.[27] This typology is a version of Shugart and Carey's: as is conventional, their rare president-parliamentary regime and the more common premier-presidential or semi-presidential regime have been combined in one "mixed" category. To illustrate, using this schema, Ireland is coded as a parliamentary regime; France is coded as a mixed regime; and both the United States and Colombia are coded as true presidential regimes. To reflect the ordinal nature of the categories, scores of zero, one, and two are then assigned to countries with parliamentary, mixed, and true presidential regimes, respectively.[28]

---

[24] The theoretical maximum of the index is forty, but twenty-four is the highest observed score.

[25] For the few cases for which Hicken and Stoll (2008) were not themselves able to code the appropriate constitution (such as the 1925 Chilean constitution), they either took data from extant codings, where available, or extrapolated backwards their codings of later constitutions. Confining the analysis to the cases that they themselves coded, that is, list-wise deleting the fifty-one cases for which they either drew upon extant codings or extrapolated, does not substantively alter the conclusions reported here. Similar findings are also obtained when substituting extant values of the index (e.g., from Shugart and Carey 1992) for theirs if there was disagreement (usually minor), as well as when eliminating the twenty-three more problematic cases for which they extrapolated the values of the presidential powers index.

[26] See Hicken and Stoll (2008) for more information about this index, including a discussion of its strengths and weaknesses.

[27] Following Shugart and Carey (1992), the third of these regime types is referred to as "true" or "pure" presidential to distinguish it from the broader category of "presidential" regime (a country possessing a popularly elected chief executive-cum-head of state) that serves as the subject of this analysis.

[28] The conclusions reported here are not sensitive to the use of alternate values for the ordinal scale.

Changing Societies, Changing Party Systems

	Minimum	First Quartile	Median	Mean	Third Quartile	Maximum
Parliamentary	0.0	0.0	4.0	4.3	7.0	10
Mixed	2.0	6.0	8.5	9.1	11	20
True Presidential	8.0	13	14	15	18	24
All Cases	0.0	8.0	13	12	15	24

Table 4.2: Descriptive statistics for the index of presidential powers by regime type. Cases are those used to estimate Model 3 of the presidential elections analysis.

My source of countries' classifications at the time of each election is Golder (2005).

Table 4.2 shows that, not surprisingly, the presidential powers index varies predictably with the three basic ordinal regime types for my set of cases (see also Hicken and Stoll 2008). Presidents in true presidential regimes typically wield more powers than presidents in mixed regimes, just as presidents in mixed regimes typically wield more powers than presidents in parliamentary regimes. However, the index reveals variation within each type of regime that the simple ordered trichotomy obscures. An example is that both Colombia and the United States are always classified as true presidential regimes, despite the Colombian president receiving a much higher index score until 1991.

Turning away from political institutions to the other systemic features of a polity, the third independent variable is that of party system openness. This variable is operationalized in two ways. The first is by a categorical variable for region, following Hicken and Stoll (2008). Countries are classified as belonging to one of six regions that are not necessarily geographically defined: the advanced industrial democracies; Asia; Latin America; Eastern Europe; Africa; and "Other" (the Pacific and Caribbean islands). The "advanced industrial democracies" category serves as the baseline. This enables me to compare the less democratically consolidated countries that have more open party systems, subdivided into geographic groupings, to the more democratically consolidated advanced industrial democracies that have less open party systems. Controlling for region in this way also removes other potentially confounding regional effects, from the cultural to the political institutional. The second operationalization is a dummy variable for elections that are the first since either independence or a transition to democracy. The party system should obviously be more open at moments of great change like these. I take data for both operationalizations from Hicken and Stoll (2008). Other processes that scholars have identified as opening the party system, such as dealignment in Western Europe (Dalton, Flanagan, and Beck 1984) and the decline of leftist parties in Latin America (Van Cott 2005), are too region- or country-specific to capture in this large-N study.

The fourth and final independent variable is obviously social heterogeneity. This variable is measured using the index of social heterogeneity I developed in the second half of Chapter 3. To recap, theoretically ranging from zero to six, although actually ranging from approximately one to four, this index assesses a country's heterogeneity with respect to six historically important latent divisions: the ethnic; the religious; the socioeconomic; the urban–rural; the post-materialist; and the foreign policy. Higher values denote greater social heterogeneity. For comparison, I employ as an alternative the more conventional operationalization of social heterogeneity featured in existing quantitative studies: ethnic fractionalization. I calculate this measure using data compiled by Roeder (2001). Note that this measure also serves as one of the components of my index.[29]

The most general testable hypothesis suggested by the theory I developed in Chapter 2 is that the index of social heterogeneity is positively related to the effective number of presidential candidates. However, I also argued that the prior or initial social heterogeneity of a polity should condition this effect. Specifically, I argued that an increase in social heterogeneity will *not* have a significant and positive effect on the effective number of presidential candidates in two situations: when a polity is initially very homogeneous, or when it is initially very heterogeneous. In these situations, an increase in social heterogeneity is instead hypothesized to have either an insignificant or a significantly negative effect on the fragmentation of the presidential party system. Accordingly, the ultimate testable hypothesis is that the effective number of presidential candidates is a nonlinear function of the index of social heterogeneity. Even more specifically, this nonlinear relationship is hypothesized to change directions twice and hence to take a third-degree polynomial form like that shown in Figure 2.2 (H3).

Further testable hypotheses address the hypothesized conditioning effects of the other systemic variables. Beginning with political institutions, the first of these testable hypotheses is that there is little relationship between social heterogeneity and the effective number of presidential candidates when a restrictive (as opposed to a non-restrictive) electoral system is employed, ceteris paribus (H4a). However, an alternative testable hypothesis is that a restrictive electoral system will not provide as much of a constraint in presidential elections as it does in legislative elections. As I argued briefly earlier, there is simply not much observed variation in the restrictiveness of presidential electoral systems: all are restrictive in that they impose similarly low upper bounds, usually ranging from two to three.[30] By way of contrast,

---

[29]Most studies technically employ the effective number of ethnic groups as their operationalization of heterogeneity (e.g., Clark and Golder 2006). Because this is a simple transformation of the index of ethnic fractionalization that conveys the same information, the index of fractionalization is used instead, for the reasons laid out in the prior chapter.

[30]For example, compare a simple-plurality presidential electoral system, which has a single

in the legislative realm, the upper bound has a much larger range: it varies from two in single-member district systems such as the United States to 151 in the Netherlands, even though the upper bound ceases to bite when the district magnitude reaches five. Hence, a more restrictive presidential electoral system might in fact not significantly constrain the effect of social heterogeneity in presidential elections relative to a less restrictive presidential electoral system (H4b).

A second political institutional hypothesis concerns the regime type. This hypothesis is that the greater the size of the presidential prize, the less effect social heterogeneity should have on the fragmentation of the presidential party system. Specifically, when policy-making authority is horizontally centralized in the office of the presidency, as measured by either the index of presidential powers or the ordinal regime typology, social heterogeneity will have little relationship with the effective number of presidential candidates, all else being equal (H5).

Turning to the remaining hypothesized conditioning variable, the third and final additional testable hypothesis is that the more open (unconsolidated) the party system, the stronger the relationship between social heterogeneity and the effective number of presidential candidates should be, ceteris paribus (H6).

4.2.2 Model Specifications and Data

To test these hypotheses, I estimate the following linear-in-variables model, an extension of the model originally developed by Hicken and Stoll (2008):

$$\begin{aligned} \text{ENPRES}_{i,t} = {} & \beta_0 + \beta_1 \text{SOCHET}_{i,t} + \beta_2 \text{SOCHET}^2_{i,t} + \beta_3 \text{SOCHET}^3_{i,t} \\ & + \beta_4 \text{PRESPOWER}_{i,t} + \beta_5 \text{PRESPOWER}^2_{i,t} + \beta_6 \text{PRESPOWER}^3_{i,t} \\ & + \beta_7 \text{PRESPOWER}_{i,t} \times \text{SOCHET}_{i,t} \\ & + \beta_8 \text{PRESPOWER}_{i,t} \times \text{SOCHET}^2_{i,t} \\ & + \beta_9 \text{PRESPOWER}_{i,t} \times \text{SOCHET}^3_{i,t} + \beta_{10} \text{PLURALITY}_{i,t} \\ & + \beta_{11} \text{ASIA}_i + \beta_{12} \text{LAMER}_i + \beta_{13} \text{EEUR}_i + \beta_{14} \text{AFRICA}_i \\ & + \beta_{15} \text{OTHER}_i + \epsilon_{i,t} \end{aligned} \quad (4.3)$$

This model is labeled Model 3. ENPRES is the effective number of presidential candidates; SOCHET is the index of social heterogeneity; PRESPOWER is the index of presidential powers;[31] PLURALITY is a dummy variable for restrictive (simple-plurality) electoral systems; ASIA is a dummy variable for

---

winner in the first and only round of the election, to a French-style runoff or majoritarian system, where the top two vote getters proceed to a second round if, as is frequently the case, no candidate obtains a majority of the vote in the first round. The former has an upper bound of two, the most restrictive electoral system possible, while the latter is conventionally viewed as having an upper bound of three, a more permissive electoral system.

[31] By interacting the presidential powers index with both of the higher-order social heterogeneity terms, the higher-order partial derivatives with respect to social heterogeneity are al-

4. Empirical Evidence across Space and Time

ASIA; LAMER is a dummy variable for Latin America; EEUR is a dummy variable for Eastern Europe; AFRICA is a dummy variable for Africa; and OTHER is a dummy variable for the Pacific and Caribbean islands. As before, *i* indexes cross-sections (countries), and *t* indexes time periods (elections). Country fixed effects are not included because the index of social heterogeneity is time invariant.

One question that might be asked about this model is why, given H4a and H4b, it does not contain an interaction between the index of social heterogeneity and the dummy variable for restrictive electoral systems. I initially estimated a version of Model 3 that interacted this dummy variable with every term involving the index of social heterogeneity.[32] These results are presented in Appendix A. However, contrary to H4a but in keeping with H4b, none of these interaction terms attained conventional levels of significance. This suggests that presidential electoral systems are all too restrictive for those that are more restrictive to significantly constrain the effect of social heterogeneity, in accordance with H4b. Yet contrary to both hypotheses, social heterogeneity was counterintuitively found to have a larger effect when the electoral system is more restrictive.[33] Accordingly, to simplify what is already a complicated model, Model 3 only controls for (as opposed to conditions on) electoral system restrictiveness.

Another question that might be asked about this model concerns the absence of interactions between the measures of party system openness and the index of social heterogeneity, given H6. The reason for not estimating an interaction model involving the regional dummy variables is the unmanageably large number of interaction terms that such a model would require.[34] An interaction model involving the transitional elections dummy variable is more manageable. Yet contrary to H6, none of the interaction terms achieved conventional levels of significance. These results are accordingly presented in Appendix A, as before, to simplify the presentation and discussion. Moreover, also contrary to the hypothesis, social heterogeneity was found to have a smaller impact in elections that were the first since either independence or a transition to democracy.[35] Hence, little support is forthcoming for H6. I nevertheless control for region in this and the subsequent model, for consis-

---

lowed to vary with presidential powers, in addition to the first-order partial derivative—a more general (i.e, a less restricted) model. Second- and third-order presidential powers terms are included in light of Hicken and Stoll's (2008) argument that the effective number of presidential candidates is a nonlinear (and specifically at least a third-order) function of presidential powers. Omitting these higher-order terms does not alter the conclusions.

[32] Model 4 (to be discussed) cannot be estimated in this way due to the perfect collinearity of some of the interaction terms.

[33] Hicken and Stoll (2008) obtained similarly counterintuitive findings regarding the interaction between a specific type of social heterogeneity, ethnic heterogeneity, and the restrictiveness of the electoral system.

[34] An alternative is to interact the dummy variable for advanced industrial democracies with the social heterogeneity terms. But even this much simpler model cannot be estimated due to the perfect collinearity of some of its terms.

[35] However, some of the interaction terms achieved significance in Model 4 (see the following discussion).

tency with the existing literature.

I also estimate a version of Model 3 that substitutes the ordinal regime typology for the index of presidential powers. This model is as follows:

$$\begin{aligned}
\text{ENPRES}_{i,t} = {} & \beta_0 + \beta_1\text{SOCHET}_{i,t} + \beta_2\text{SOCHET}^2_{i,t} + \beta_3\text{SOCHET}^3_{i,t} \\
& + \beta_4\text{REGIME}_{i,t} + \beta_5\text{REGIME}_{i,t} \times \text{SOCHET}_{i,t} \\
& + \beta_6\text{REGIME}_{i,t} \times \text{SOCHET}^2_{i,t} \\
& + \beta_7\text{REGIME}_{i,t} \times \text{SOCHET}^3_{i,t} + \beta_8\text{PLURALITY}_{i,t} \\
& + \beta_9\text{ASIA}_i + \beta_{10}\text{LAMER}_i + \beta_{11}\text{EEUR}_i \\
& + \beta_{12}\text{AFRICA}_i + \beta_{13}\text{OTHER}_i + \epsilon_{i,t}
\end{aligned} \qquad (4.4)$$

In Equation 4.4, which I label Model 4, REGIME is the ordinal regime type and all other variables are as before. The regime type enters the model only as a first-order term, in contrast to the index of presidential powers in Model 3, because of its less precise (ordinal) scale of measurement.

The cases used to estimate Models 3 and 4 are all popular elections for chief executives (usually but not always known as presidents) that took place under minimally democratic conditions in the post–World War II era, specifically between 1946 and 2000. "Minimally democratic" means democratic according to the minimalist definition of democracy developed by Alvarez and colleagues (1996), as originally coded by Alvarez and colleagues (1999) and updated by Golder (2005).[36] "Popular" denotes elections where voters are *directly* involved in the selection of the president—even if it is to choose an electoral college, as in the United States. Hence, I exclude elections of a president by the legislature, as in Turkey. Beginning with the set of cases compiled by Golder (2005), which satisfies these criteria, elections held under fused electoral systems and elections in Kiribati are eliminated (e.g., Golder 2006; Hicken and Stoll 2008).[37] Then the 1996 and 1999 Israeli direct prime ministerial elections are added (e.g., Hicken and Stoll).[38] Finally, the

---

[36]Using such a minimalist definition means that the countries in the sample vary in the degree to which they are democratically consolidated. While arguments have been made that social heterogeneity (as hypothesized here) and political institutions (see, for example, Shugart 1999 and Hartlyn, McCoy, and Mustillo 2008) might not have the same effects in both consolidated and unconsolidated democracies, dropping elections in African and Pacific/Caribbean countries (generally the least consolidated democracies in the sample) does not alter the conclusions. Neither does dropping the eight (nine for Model 4) countries that held only a single democratic election during the time period analyzed: Ghana, Honduras, Madagascar, Mexico, Moldova, Niger, Sierra Leone, Slovakia, and Comoros (the latter for Model 4 only).

[37]Golder (2006) excluded Kiribatian elections because the number of presidential candidates is constitutionally limited. Elections conducted under a fused electoral system are conventionally excluded by scholars working in this literature (see, for example, Cox 1997) because it is not clear to which electoral system's incentives voters and elites respond: that of the legislature or that of the presidency. Since the 1980s, Bolivia is an example of a presidential regime that has employed a fused electoral system.

[38]From 1996 to 2001, Israel had a popularly elected chief executive and a president-parliamentary (that is, mixed) regime (Hazan 1996). The 1996 and 1999 Israeli elections are accordingly included in analysis; however, their exclusion does not affect my conclusions.

few cases with missing data, generally the very small and less stable democracies, are list-wise deleted. The resulting data set consists of 242 elections in 54 countries for Model 3 and 245 elections in 56 countries for Model 4.[39] A list of these countries and elections is found in Appendix A.

4.2.3 RESULTS AND DISCUSSION

I use ordinary least squares (OLS) to estimate Models 3 and 4. The resulting coefficient estimates are shown in Table 4.3. This same table also presents the robust standard errors of the coefficients in parentheses.[40]

To begin, Table 4.3 shows that in both models, all three individual social heterogeneity terms (the main effect, squared, and cubed terms) achieve conventional levels of significance using two-sided tests. This lends support to H3's claim that the effective number of presidential candidates is non-linearly related to social heterogeneity. In other words, the effect of social heterogeneity is predicted to be conditional upon the prior heterogeneity of the polity. More specifically, the significance of the two higher-order terms suggests that the direction of the relationship changes twice, and hence that the number of presidential candidates is a third-order polynomial of social heterogeneity, as this hypothesis also claims.

Additionally, Table 4.3 shows that all of the interactions between these terms and either the index of presidential powers (Model 3) or the ordinal regime typology (Model 4) achieve conventional levels of significance using two-sided tests. Hence, in accordance with H5, social heterogeneity's effect on the effective number of presidential candidates is found to be conditional on the size of the presidential prize. Moreover, the signs on the interaction terms are the opposite of those on the individual social heterogeneity terms, which suggests that the effect of social heterogeneity decreases as the size of the presidential prize increases, again as hypothesized.

The most direct test of the hypotheses comes not from these coefficients, however, but from a quantity derived from them: the marginal effect of social heterogeneity. For Model 3, this is the partial derivative of Equation 4.3 with respect to social heterogeneity (Brambor, Clark, and Golder 2006); for Model 4, it is the partial derivative of Equation 4.4. Figure 4.1 graphs these marginal effects for Model 3 over the observed range of the social heterogeneity index for four different values of the index of presidential powers: zero (the minimum), a very weak president such as Ireland's; six, a moderately powerful president such as the French Fifth Republic's; thir-

---

[39]The difference is two elections in Guyana and one election in Comoros. For these three cases, data on the index of presidential powers is missing, but data on the regime type is not. Excluding these elections from Model 4 so that the two models are estimated on exactly the same set of cases does not alter the conclusions reported here.

[40]It is again Newey-West (1987) standard errors, robust to both autocorrelation and heteroskedasticity, that are reported. Note, however, that using country-clustered robust standard errors—which is possible in these models because there are more than fifty clusters—does not substantively alter the conclusions. See note 9 for a discussion of why panel corrected standard errors are not appropriate here.

Changing Societies, Changing Party Systems

	Model 3	Model 4
Intercept	47***	44***
	(13)	(9.3)
Social Heterogeneity	−69***	−62***
	(19)	(14)
Social Heterogeneity^2	34***	29***
	(8.8)	(6.6)
Social Heterogeneity^3	−5.3***	−4.4***
	(1.4)	(1.0)
Presidential Powers/Regime Type	−3.2***	−22***
	(1.1)	(5.6)
Presidential Powers^2	−0.030***	
	(0.011)	
Presidential Powers^3	0.00087***	
	(0.00033)	
Social Heterogeneity × Presidential Powers/Regime Type	5.3***	33***
	(1.6)	(8.1)
Social Heterogeneity^2 × Presidential Powers/Regime Type	−2.5***	−15***
	(0.74)	(3.7)
Social Heterogeneity^3 × Presidential Powers/Regime Type	0.39***	2.2***
	(0.11)	(0.56)
Plurality	−0.59***	−0.56***
	(0.17)	(0.15)
Asia	−0.098	0.022
	(0.32)	(0.38)
Latin America	0.67***	−0.11
	(0.24)	(0.35)
Eastern Europe	0.23	−0.0038
	(0.27)	(0.30)
Africa	0.17	0.15
	(0.35)	(0.38)
Other (Pacific/Caribbean Islands)	−0.80***	−1.0***
	(0.22)	(0.31)
N	242	245
Root MSE	1.1	1.1
R^2	0.21	0.19

Table 4.3: Coefficients and robust (Newey-West) standard errors for Models 3 and 4 of the presidential elections analysis. The dependent variable is the effective number of presidential candidates. Horizontal centralization is the presidential powers index in Model 3 and the ordinal regime typology in Model 4. The baseline region is the advanced industrial democracies. Significance codes are for two-sided tests: 0.001, ***; 0.05, **; 0.10, *.

4. Empirical Evidence across Space and Time

teen, a powerful president such as the United States'; and twenty-four (the maximum), an extremely powerful president such as Chile's under its 1969 constitution. Figure 4.2 does the same for Model 4 for the three different ordinal regime types: the parliamentary; the mixed; and the true presidential. Ninety-five percent one-sided confidence intervals band the estimated marginal effects, given my directional hypotheses.[41]

First take the case when the size of the presidential prize is either small or moderate. This corresponds to the index of presidential powers taking values such as zero or six in Model 3, respectively, and to the ordinal regime type being parliamentary or mixed in Model 4, respectively. These situations are graphed in the upper quadrants of Figures 4.1 and 4.2. The graphs show that the estimated marginal effects form concave parabolas. This means that for initially very homogeneous societies, that is, those with a low score on the index of social heterogeneity, an increase in social heterogeneity is predicted to *decrease* the effective number of presidential candidates. As a society's initial heterogeneity increases, however, this effect diminishes and eventually (when the index of social heterogeneity is approximately 1.7) turns positive. Accordingly, for societies that are initially moderately heterogeneous, an increase in social heterogeneity is predicted to *increase* the effective number of presidential candidates. But as a society's initial heterogeneity continues to increase, the magnitude of the effect begins to diminish, and ultimately (when the index of social heterogeneity is approximately 2.7) it again changes sign. For initially very heterogeneous societies, the prediction is therefore that an increase in social heterogeneity will *decrease* the effective number of presidential candidates. The four graphs further show that the marginal effects are significant over much of their range using the appropriate one- and two-sided tests.[42] These findings are commensurate with H3.[43] Finally, what is also apparent from the graphs is that the magnitudes of the marginal effects are smaller for moderately powerful presidents than for weak, figurehead presidents, a finding commensurate with H5.

Now take the case when the size of the presidential prize is considerable. This corresponds to the index of presidential powers taking a value such as thirteen in Model 3 and the ordinal regime type being true presidential in Model 4. The lower-left quadrants of Figures 4.1 and 4.2, respectively, graph these situations. One obvious difference between these graphs and the ones for weaker presidents is that the marginal effects take the form of negatively sloped and approximately straight lines instead of parabolas. More specifically, for initially very homogeneous societies, social heterogeneity is found to have a statistically insignificant and positive relationship with the effec-

---

[41] These are equivalent to 90 percent two-sided confidence intervals.

[42] While not shown for reasons of space, the marginal effects are also significant at the $\alpha = 0.05$ level using two-sided tests for effectively the same range as they are significant at the $\alpha = 0.10$ level.

[43] The finding for very heterogeneous societies is commensurate with the hypothesis because the prediction was that the marginal effect would either diminish to zero, where it would remain, or turn negative as the prior social heterogeneity became very high.

Changing Societies, Changing Party Systems

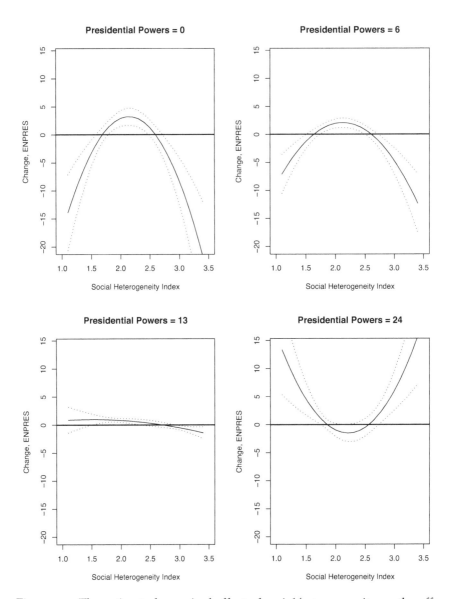

Figure 4.1: The estimated marginal effect of social heterogeneity on the effective number of presidential candidates for regimes with varying degrees of horizontal centralization, operationalized as the index of presidential powers (Model 3). 90% two-sided confidence intervals or 95% one-sided confidence intervals are plotted around the marginal effects.

4. *Empirical Evidence across Space and Time*

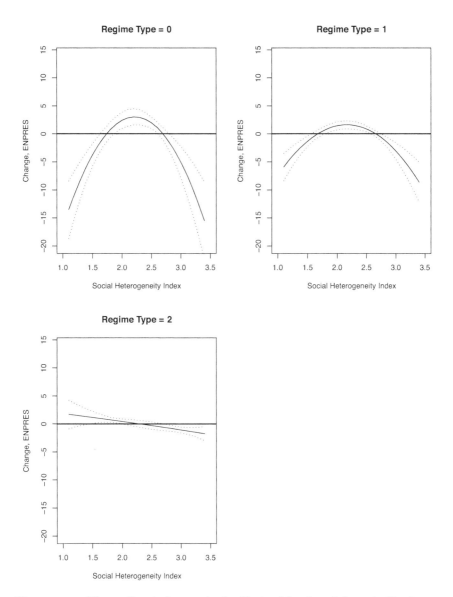

Figure 4.2: The estimated marginal effect of horizontal centralization on the effective number of presidential candidates for regimes with varying degrees of horizontal centralization, operationalized as the ordinal regime type (0 = parliamentary; 1 = mixed; 2 = true presidential) (Model 4). 90% two-sided confidence intervals or 95% one-sided confidence intervals are plotted around the marginal effects.

tive number of presidential candidates, contrary to the findings for weaker presidencies, although consistent with H3. Conversely, as before and as hypothesized, a positive and statistically significant relationship is found for reasonably heterogeneous societies. Also as before and as hypothesized, when a society is initially very heterogeneous (that is, when the index of social heterogeneity is greater than either 2.3 or 2.8, depending on the model), the predicted relationship is both negative and statistically significant. The most striking difference between these and the earlier graphs, however, is the much smaller substantive magnitudes of the marginal effects. To illustrate numerically, when the social heterogeneity index takes the initial value of 2.1 (the median), if the regime is parliamentary, the predicted increase in the effective number of presidential candidates in response to an increase in social heterogeneity is *2.5 times greater than if the regime is true presidential*. Hence, the more powerful the president is, the smaller the effect social heterogeneity is predicted to have on the number of presidential candidates, as posited by H5—at least up to a point (more on this later).

But what about *extremely* powerful presidencies, such as cases where the index of presidential powers takes a value of twenty-four? This situation is broken out from that of powerful presidencies only by Model 3. It is graphed in the lower-right quadrant of Figure 4.1. This graph shows that the marginal effects now take the form of a convex parabola, effectively a reflection around the horizontal axis of the marginal effects for the least powerful presidencies. For initially very homogeneous societies, social heterogeneity is predicted to have a statistically and substantively significant positive effect. By way of contrast, for initially reasonably heterogeneous societies, the predicted effect is negative and both substantively smaller and statistically insignificant. Yet for initially very heterogeneous societies, the predicted effect is again both positive and significant. Accordingly, an increase in social heterogeneity is almost always predicted to *increase* the effective number of presidential candidates, contrary to what H3 claims for initially very homogeneous and heterogeneous societies. Moreover, the rate at which the effective number of presidential candidates changes in response to changes in social heterogeneity approaches that for figurehead presidents who wield little power, contrary to the hypothesis about the conditioning effect of the regime type. As surprising as these counterintuitive results may seem at first blush, they are consistent with those obtained by Hicken and Stoll (2008), who found that electoral coordination breaks down in presidential elections when the size of the presidential prize is extremely large. Because the incentives for coordination are so low, increases in social heterogeneity have the power to substantially boost the number of competitors.[44]

To further illustrate these findings, Figures 4.3 and 4.4 plot the predicted

---

[44] These findings are not sensitive to the inclusion of particular countries with very powerful presidencies in the analysis. The countries with high presidential powers index values (at least seventeen) are Argentina; Benin; Brazil; Chile; Colombia; Ecuador; Ghana; Mexico; Niger; Panama; the Philippines; and Zambia.

relationship between the index of social heterogeneity and the effective number of presidential candidates for the same values of the index of presidential powers (Model 3) and regime types (Model 4) as before, respectively. As is conventional, all other variables are held at their modes.[45] Ninety-five percent confidence intervals band the predicted values. When the size of the presidential prize is not large (that is, a parliamentary or mixed regime, or an Irish- to French-style presidency), these figures show that the effective number of presidential candidates is initially predicted to decrease as social heterogeneity increases; then to increase; and finally to decrease again, with the magnitude of the changes decreasing as the president's policy-making authority increases.[46] By way of contrast, when the size of the presidential prize is large (that is, a true presidential regime or United States–style presidency), the figures show an almost linear positive relationship between social heterogeneity and the effective number of presidential candidates—but one that is so weak as to be substantively uninteresting.[47] Yet when the president is extremely powerful, the effective number of presidential candidates is initially predicted to increase dramatically as social heterogeneity increases; then to decrease slightly; and finally to resume its steep upwards climb.[48]

Finally, I compare the findings using my new measure of social heterogeneity to the findings using the conventional operationalization of social heterogeneity: ethnic fractionalization. For reasons of space, the results obtained from estimating Models 3 and 4 when substituting ethnic fractionalization for the index of social heterogeneity are shown in Appendix A, as are comparable versions of Figures 4.1–4.4. As before, all of the main effect terms for ethnic fractionalization obtain conventional levels of significance in both models, as do all of their interactions with the size of the presidential prize (either the index of presidential powers or the regime type, depending upon the model). Also as before, the signs on the interaction terms are the opposite of the signs on the main effect terms, suggesting that the magnitude and the significance of the effect of ethnic fractionalization diminishes as the size of the presidential prize increases. This is best seen by examining the figures depicting the estimated marginal and conditional effects. The only exception is when the president becomes extremely powerful, in

---

[45] Specifically, the estimated conditional effect of social heterogeneity is shown for elections in Latin American countries with a permissive (non–simple-plurality) electoral system.

[46] With the third quartile of the observed social heterogeneity data equal to 2.5, few countries with weak presidencies will experience the dramatic and eventually nonsensical declines in the number of presidential candidates that are predicted at very high initial levels of social heterogeneity. This dramatic decline is probably in part an artifact of choosing to empirically model the hypothesized relationship using a third-order polynomial. Such functions tend towards either positive or negative infinity, depending upon the sign of the third-order term. I thank Rein Taagepera for this point.

[47] For example, the effective number of presidential candidates increases by a maximum of only one if the regime is true presidential versus a maximum of two if the regime type is mixed.

[48] See note 46 for an explanation for the ultimately nonsensically large predicted increase in the effective number of presidential candidates.

Changing Societies, Changing Party Systems

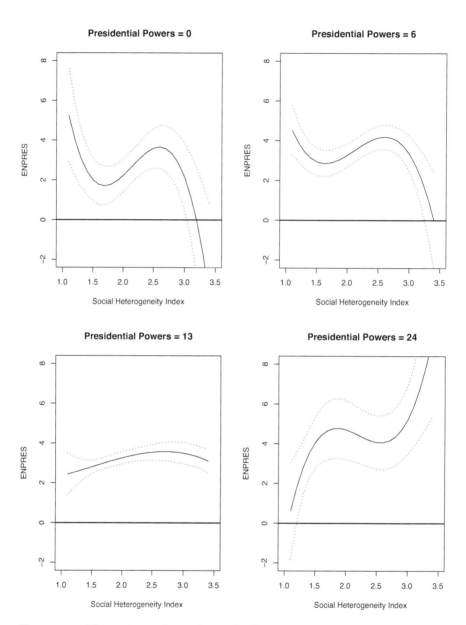

Figure 4.3: The estimated conditional effect of social heterogeneity on the effective number of presidential candidates for regimes with varying degrees of horizontal centralization, operationalized as the index of presidential powers (Model 3). 95% two-sided confidence intervals are plotted around the conditional effects.

4. Empirical Evidence across Space and Time

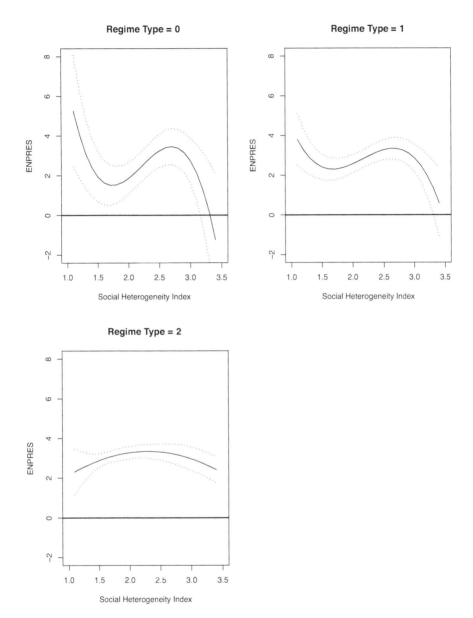

Figure 4.4: The estimated conditional effect of social heterogeneity on the effective number of presidential candidates for regimes with varying degrees of horizontal centralization, operationalized as the ordinal regime type (0 = parliamentary; 1 = mixed; 2 = true presidential) (Model 4). 95% two-sided confidence intervals are plotted around the conditional effects.

which case the magnitude of the effect of ethnic fractionalization is greater than when the president is merely powerful, again as before. Hence, this alternative and less preferred measure of social heterogeneity yields similar conclusions about the hypothesized conditioning effect of the regime type (H5).

Perhaps not surprisingly, however, different conclusions are drawn about the hypothesized conditioning effect of the prior heterogeneity of the polity (H3). This can be seen most clearly in the figures. When the size of the presidential prize is small to moderate, the predicted relationship between ethnic fractionalization and the effective number of presidential candidates resembles that found between the index of social heterogeneity and the effective number of presidential candidates when the president is extremely powerful. This is shown in the lower-right quadrant of Figures 4.1 and 4.3. That is, an increase in ethnic fractionalization is predicted to increase the effective number of presidential candidates except in initially moderately heterogeneous polities, where the predicted relationship is negative.[49] When the size of the presidential prize is large, by way of contrast, the findings are similar to those obtained originally for weaker presidencies. This alternative and more conventional measure accordingly supports portions of H3: for most polities, the effective number of presidential candidates is found initially to increase as heterogeneity increases but then later to decrease, as hypothesized. Less support is forthcoming at the extremes, though: in particular, the addendum about initially very homogeneous polities taken from Dickson and Scheve (2010) only occasionally finds support.

An explanation for these findings is that being ethnically homogeneous is not enough. Only when the polity is also homogeneous with respect to the other historically important latent divisions will the dominant group be large enough to have little incentive to coordinate on a single candidate. Hence, the choice of measure does matter, and it is my preferred measure that yields the theoretically sensible results.

4.3 CONCLUSION

In this chapter, I quantitatively tested several of the hypotheses I developed in Chapter 2 about the relationship between social heterogeneity and the fragmentation of the party system. I did so using two cross-national and longitudinal quantitative analyses: one of all minimally democratic legislative elections in advanced industrial democracies from the nineteenth century to the present day, and one of all minimally democratic presidential elections in the post–World War II era.

Several qualities of this cross-national and quantitative analysis lead to its high internal validity relative to other studies. First, in contrast to most

---

[49]However, with the third quartile of the observed ethnic fractionalization data being 0.60, few countries are ethnically heterogeneous enough to experience the breakdown in electoral coordination that is predicted at very high initial levels of ethnic fractionalization. Again, see note 46.

existing studies, the measures of social heterogeneity I employed in these analyses did not solely tap a polity's ethnic structure. Second, also in contrast to most existing studies, in the presidential elections analysis, I matched national-level or aggregate measures of social heterogeneity with national-level measures of the restrictiveness of the electoral system. Third and finally, again in contrast to most existing studies, in the legislative elections analysis, I observed extensive variation over time within each country, particularly on the independent variable of social heterogeneity.

At the most basic level, my quantitative analysis in this chapter provided empirical support for my core argument that social heterogeneity is related to party system fragmentation. Whether social heterogeneity was dynamically measured as actual historical processes that have altered the heterogeneity of the citizenry, such as immigration, or statically measured as a holistic index, increases in social heterogeneity were often found to have both a statistically and substantively significant positive effect on the effective number of parties or candidates competing in democratic elections. But the operative word here is "often," not always. I also found empirical support for my argument that this relationship is conditional upon several factors besides the electoral system.

The characteristics of a new latent social group serve as the first of these hypothesized conditioning factors. In the legislative elections analysis, I found that different types of social heterogeneity, and hence different new latent social groups, have historically had different effects upon the fragmentation of the party system, as hypothesized. However, because social heterogeneity was measured in terms of distinct historical processes such as territorial change and the expansion of the franchise, this analysis did not enable me to definitively separate out the contributions of a group's politicization, size, and type of attribute, the three key group characteristics about which I earlier developed hypotheses. This is a task that I will take up in future chapters.

To elaborate regarding the effects of these different historical processes, internal increases in the citizenry's heterogeneity resulting from expansions of the franchise were found historically to have had a larger impact on party system fragmentation than external increases from territorial gains and immigration have had. This finding can be attributed to both the smaller sizes of externally originating groups and the disadvantage their external origin poses for their politicization. Second, immigration was found typically to have had a larger substantive effect on party system fragmentation than changes in a country's borders. The tendency for existing citizens to push back against recent waves of immigration by forming anti-immigrant parties may be the best explanation for this finding. Third, women's suffrage was found to have had a relatively minor effect on party system fragmentation. This finding buttresses my earlier observation that women's political parties historically did not emerge in many countries following women's suffrage. But it is nevertheless surprising because women are a large, and specifically a minimally winning, group. Moreover, because gender, like ethnicity, is one of the stickiest of all sociological attributes, it should impart a collective action advantage. It is accordingly a striking historical anachronism that women alone among all the key historically excluded groups have so distinctively settled for representation from existing parties. Fourth and finally, the collective action advantage resulting from a group being ethnically defined was found to outweigh the disadvantage of an external origin.

The second conditioning factor about which I hypothesized was the prior or initial social heterogeneity of the polity. In accordance with this hypothesis, I found a non-linear relationship between social heterogeneity and party system fragmentation in the presidential elections analysis. Specifically, social heterogeneity was found to have either a significant negative or insignificant positive effect on the effective number of presidential candidates in very homogeneous and very heterogeneous countries, and a significant positive effect otherwise. The one exception was when the presidency was extremely powerful. In this case, social heterogeneity was effectively always found to have a positive and significant effect on the number of presidential candidates—an issue that will be revisited later.

A third hypothesis that was tested in this chapter concerned the conditioning effect of a less-studied political institution, the type of regime. In the presidential elections analysis, I also found empirical support for this hypothesis. The larger the size of the presidential prize, measured either as an index of presidential powers or as one of three ordinal regime types where presidential authority varies (parliamentary, mixed, and true presidential), the less impact an increase in social heterogeneity was found to have on the effective number of presidential candidates. The one exception was when the size of the presidential prize was extremely large (that is, when the president was very powerful), in which case the effect of an increase in social heterogeneity was almost always positive, statistically significant, and of a substantively large magnitude. While initially surprising, these findings are commensurate with those of other scholars, who have also found electoral coordination to break down when the size of the prize is substantial.

Less support was obtained for a fourth and less important hypothesis: that party system openness also conditions the effect of social heterogeneity. In both the legislative and presidential elections analysis, a significant difference in social heterogeneity's effect was not usually observed between elections with more or less open party systems. Moreover, to the extent that differences were observed, they usually ran contrary to the hypothesis: for example, in the presidential elections analysis, social heterogeneity was found to have a smaller effect on party system fragmentation in transitional elections when the party system should have been more open. Because this is a very difficult variable to operationalize in a cross-national context, developing better measures is an obvious task for future studies. With better measures, which may need to be regional in nature, the issue of the empirical support for this hypothesis can be revisited.

4. Empirical Evidence across Space and Time

Last and least, given the empirical attention this variable has already received, is the hypothesized conditioning effect of the electoral system. In the legislative elections analysis, restrictive (majoritarian) electoral systems were found to have constrained the effect of those groups that were neither territorially concentrated nor large, as hypothesized. But also as hypothesized, at least some evidence was found that territorially concentrated groups, such as the residents of newly acquired territories, and large if geographically dispersed groups, such as women, were not constrained. By way of contrast, in the presidential elections analysis, the most restrictive presidential electoral system was not found to significantly constrain the effect of social heterogeneity. This finding is not surprising, however, given the small difference in restrictiveness between the various presidential electoral systems. Moreover, my finding that social heterogeneity matters even under restrictive electoral systems is commensurate with the findings of studies operating at the level of the legislative electoral district (e.g., Jones 1997; Moser and Scheiner 2012). Accounting for the disjuncture between the constraints that the electoral system seems to impose at the district and aggregate levels should be a priority for future research.

There is an important caveat regarding the results just discussed, however. Despite being the gold standard measure of party system fragmentation in the quantitative empirical literature, the effective number of either parties or candidates does not measure *only* the fragmentation that results from the successful entry of new sectarian political parties, as I would like it to do. For example, women voting for at least some relatively marginal existing parties is probably what accounts for the finding that women's suffrage is associated with a more fragmented party system. Moreover, to explain why sectarian parties fail to successfully emerge, we must distinguish between situations where elites fail to supply new sectarian parties and situations where elites supply new sectarian parties but voters fail to support them—something that cannot be done with these measures.

One solution is to pursue alternative operationalizations of the dependent variable, such as the number of new sectarian parties. However, while scholars have recently compiled data on the number of new parties in some advanced industrial democracies (e.g., Hug 2001), data specifically on the number of new *sectarian* parties does not currently exist even for these countries. My guess is that this will be difficult data to collect even for the historically important divisions studied here. Accordingly, to obtain better measures, ones that will enable me to investigate the micro-level foundations of the relationship between social heterogeneity and party system fragmentation, the better solution is to turn to case studies. Another reason for conducting case studies is that some of my hypotheses, such as the hypothesis about the strategies played by existing parties, did not lend themselves to testing in these quantitative, cross-national analyses. Hence, I now embark upon case studies of Israel and the United States in an attempt to address these, and other, issues.

5 Israel: New Parties for New Groups?

This chapter begins a case study of Israel, the only Jewish state in the world. A small country with a population of seven and a half million and a land mass the size of New Jersey, Israel has nevertheless been an important actor on the world stage in its sixty years of existence. This has brought it to the attention of historians and scholars of international relations. But Israel has also drawn the attention of political scientists studying comparative politics, both for its plural society and for its political institutions.

Regarding the latter, Israel has been a parliamentary democracy since its founding in 1948. The exception is the period from 1996 to 2001, when it directly elected its prime minister and thus employed an unusual type of regime. However, Israel exhibits less dynamism with respect to the second key political institutional variable: throughout its history, it has had one of the world's most permissive electoral systems. To elaborate, all 120 members of the Knesset, Israel's parliament, are elected in a single nationwide district. A list proportional representation electoral formula, the d'Hondt, is used to translate the votes into seats in the parliamentary elections.[1] This means that voters cast their ballots for a party's list of candidates, and that seats in the parliament are allocated to the parties roughly in proportion to the votes that they receive. Moreover, the threshold for representation in the Knesset has ranged from a low one to two percent of valid votes.[2] Combined, Israel's electoral formula; single nationwide district; and low threshold have generally yielded extremely proportional results.[3] Hence, if electoral system permissiveness is viewed as a continuum, Israel is located at the permissive

---

[1]Technically, it is the Bader-Ofer formula, which is known as the Hagenbach-Bischoff outside of Israel (Lijphart 1994, 192). The more proportional Hare quota with the largest remainder was used between 1949 and 1973.

[2]It was raised from one percent to one and a half percent in 1992, and then to two percent in 2006. The Netherlands, where the threshold is two-thirds of a percent, is one of the few countries with a lower threshold than Israel. At the other end of the continuum are countries such as Germany, where the threshold is five percent.

[3]To illustrate, Lijphart (1999, 162–163) calculates the average Gallagher index, arguably the most common measure of electoral disproportionality, to be 2.3 in Israel through 1996. This is the fourth-best (that is, most proportional) score in his sample of thirty-six democracies.

5. Israel: New Parties for New Groups?

extreme.[4]

Regarding the former, Israeli society is riven by a number of conflicts. Deep divisions around religion; ethnicity; the future of the territories occupied in the 1967 Six Day War; and the role of the state versus the market are just a few of these important fault lines. However, in this chapter, I take a diachronic perspective and focus upon one of the major historical processes identified in a prior chapter as shaping the social heterogeneity of democratic citizenries. This is a process that has radically reshaped Israel's citizenry: immigration. Specifically, two waves of immigration that are unusually large in comparative perspective, as well as one small wave, have introduced two new ethnic groups to Israeli society: Middle Eastern and North African Jews, on the one hand, and Russian Jews, on the other. These increases in Israel's ethnic heterogeneity are specific historical examples of increases in its social heterogeneity.

This combination of political institutional and societal features makes Israel a good case for exploring how changes in society shape party system fragmentation when the electoral system is permissive. Israel in fact serves as a "crucial case," and specifically as a "most likely" case (Eckstein 1975), for the hypothesis that the electoral system alone conditions the relationship between social heterogeneity and the number of electoral parties. As before, the core mechanism of this hypothesis upon which I focus is that of new social groups obtaining political representation by forming and supporting their own sectarian political parties. Why is Israel a crucial case? First, because the electoral system in Israel is effectively held constant over time, as noted earlier. Second, because the Israeli electoral system's extreme permissiveness means that it should not pose a barrier to the successful particization of all but the smallest new social groups, which these new immigrant groups were not, as I later argue. Third, because the new groups introduced to Israeli society by immigration are ethnic in nature, which means that they have collective action advantages that may counterbalance even their external origin. Further, in Israel, in contrast to most democracies, Jewish immigrants are automatically granted Israeli citizenship. This removes one of the largest barriers to the political incorporation of immigrants identified earlier. Hence, either to the extent that new sectarian political parties do *not* successfully emerge to represent these new social groups in Israel, or to the extent that there is variance over either *time* or *groups* in the success of such sectarian parties, empirical support is provided for my argument that factors besides the electoral system determine how social heterogeneity shapes party system fragmentation.

A case study of Israel strengthens the internal validity of my causal inferences in two ways. First, in the quantitative analyses of the previous chap-

---

[4]Returning to Lijphart's (1999) study, the only countries with lower index scores than Israel, and hence even less disproportionality, are the Netherlands (1.3); Denmark (1.8); and Sweden (2.1). To illustrate how far on the proportional and hence permissive side of the continuum Israel falls, compare Israel's score of 2.3 to the mean score of 8.3 and the maximum score of 21 (France).

ter, the variance in social heterogeneity that entered the regression models was observational and also sometimes cross-sectional, which raises the well-known problem of omitted variable bias or ignorability. A within-case analysis of Israel, where social heterogeneity has varied over time, provides a solution to just this problem. As long as the party system fragmentation can be measured both prior to and subsequent to each of the increases in social heterogeneity (which it can be), the increases in social heterogeneity that Israel has experienced approximate experimental treatments that vary certain group characteristics while holding many other factors constant. Hence, by comparing the political trajectories of the different groups of immigrants, the hypotheses regarding these group characteristics can be tested. Similarly, by considering how the success of a single group has varied over time, many group characteristics are held constant while allowing some systemic features to vary. For example, as the next chapter will discuss at greater length, Israel is one of the few democracies in the world to have dramatically altered its type of regime. This allows me to leverage a quasi-experimental design against one of my key hypotheses: that the regime type, like the electoral system, may constrain the successful particization of new latent groups. Further, the case study design allows for process tracing of the causal mechanism.

Second, a case study of Israel also strengthens the study's internal validity by providing a solution to several vexing measurement problems. As I argued earlier, social heterogeneity is a very difficult concept to measure cross-nationally. Yet Israel is one of the few consolidated democracies to have experienced both rapid and large-scale changes in social heterogeneity in the modern era, and it is one of even fewer democracies where these changes are clearly exogenous to the number of parties, as I will argue later. Moreover, these changes have been well documented by the bureaucratic Israeli state. This means that it is possible to validly measure the nature and the magnitude of the exogenous changes in Israel's social heterogeneity. Further, because Israel possesses a single nationwide electoral district, measures of social heterogeneity based on aggregate population data will be district-level measures, removing the problematic disjuncture between the district-level theories about the electoral system and the national-level empirics that plagued the last chapter's quantitative analysis of legislative elections. Last but not least, the operationalization of the dependent variable in the quantitative analyses, the effective number of electoral parties, lumps together party system fragmentation caused by the successful entry of sectarian parties with party system fragmentation caused by other mechanisms. In the context of a single case such as Israel, and for sectarian parties related to a particular line of division such as ethnicity, it is possible to collect the data at both the elite and mass levels that will let me isolate the causal mechanism of interest. This and the subsequent case study, in other words, let me zero in on the causal mechanism—new groups successfully forming new sectarian parties—in a way that I could not do in the quantitative analyses.

Accordingly, in this chapter, I describe the changes in both Israel's social heterogeneity and its party system fragmentation over time. Specifically, focusing upon the causal mechanism of the relationship between these two variables, I ask if new parties have successfully emerged to represent the new ethnic groups that immigration has added to Israeli society. Did Russian political parties form following the waves of Russian immigration, and if so, were they successful in attracting Russian votes? And what about parties to represent Middle Eastern and North African Jews?

To preview the chapter's findings, despite favorable conditions in the form of the permissive electoral system, new parties have emerged to represent the new groups in Israel but have only sometimes been successful. Moreover, despite the lack of change in the electoral system, the political trajectories of the two groups of immigrants to Israel have diverged, with the success of each group's sectarian parties varying over time. Middle Eastern and North African Jewish immigrants have largely failed to successfully form their own sectarian political parties, although they have been more successful in recent years. Russian Jewish immigrants, by way of contrast, have been successful at launching their own sectarian parties from the mid-1990s onwards. Hence, this chapter provides evidence that we must look beyond the electoral system to understand when new social groups will successfully form their own sectarian parties.

5.1 SOCIAL HETEROGENEITY IN ISRAEL

My first task is to describe the social heterogeneity of Israel, the independent variable, at different points in time. As noted earlier, most scholars view Israel as a plural or heterogeneous society (e.g., Smooha 1978; Shuval 1989; Kop and Litan 2002). Yet Israel has not been equally socially heterogeneous throughout its history. In this study, I focus upon the changes in Israeli's citizenry that have resulted from immigration. Specifically, I study how immigration has altered one component of Israel's overall social heterogeneity: its ethnic heterogeneity.

Immigration to Israel is governed by the 1950 Law of Return, which grants every Jew in the world the right to immigrate to Israel.[5] While approximately 20 percent of Israel's population today is Arab (CBS SA, 2011), a fault line that has both ethnic and religious dimensions, effectively no Arab immigration is permitted.[6] This means that the study of immigration to Is-

---

[5]The only exceptions are for security reasons (for example, if the applicant has engaged in activities against the Jewish people or has a criminal past) and for public health. Since 1970, the spouse, child, spouse of child, grandchild, and spouse of grandchild of a Jew also have the right to immigrate to Israel.

[6]At the end of the first Arab-Israeli war in 1949, approximately 160,000 Arabs remained in the territory of the state of Israel (then about 13 percent of the population). Immediate Israeli citizenship was granted to 63,000, while the others were allowed to acquire citizenship under the 1952 Nationality Law (Peled 1992). Today, Israel's Arab citizens and permanent residents number approximately one and a half million (CBS SA, 2011). Their population growth has mostly been due to natural increase (Goldscheider 2002b, 9), because even Arab immigration

rael is the study of *Jewish* immigration to Israel. Hence, to qualify the subject of this section even further, I study how the ethnic heterogeneity of Israel has changed as a result of Jewish immigration. Of course, Israel's ethnic heterogeneity has also increased when the Arab population has increased relative to the Jewish population, which has happened over time. But given my research question, nothing is lost by focusing on how Jewish immigration has increased Israel's ethnic heterogeneity: this is still an increase in ethnic heterogeneity, and an increase in ethnic heterogeneity is also an increase in social heterogeneity writ large.

The details of the Law of Return—such as how to define Jewishness—have been the subject of fierce debate within Israel.[7] The policy itself, however, is viewed as inviolable because it is a powerful expression of Israel's identity as a Jewish state: building a single nation in Israel out of the world's Jews, which naturally requires their ingathering through immigration, is one of the central tenets of Israel's founding ideology (see, for example, Goldscheider 2002a).[8] As a result, changes to the Law of Return have been few and far between. Moreover, Israel's doors have generally been wide open to the world's Jews since its founding, with the volume of immigration largely a function of the usual "push" and "pull" factors (Friedlander and Goldscheider 1979). New political parties, with arguably one or two minor exceptions, have not tried to encourage the immigration of a specific group of eligible individuals with the goal of then representing that group; they have also not tried to expand eligibility. In other words, changes in Jewish Israel's ethnic heterogeneity resulting from immigration, the independent variable, are for all intents and purposes exogenous to changes in the dependent variable, the number of electoral parties.

There is no doubt that Jewish immigration has had a significant impact upon Israel's society. Like the United States, Canada, and Australia, Israel is viewed as a country of immigration. In fact, Goldscheider (2002a, 74) argues that "as for the United States at an earlier point in time, immigration *is* Israeli history" [emphasis in original]. Every year has seen nontrivial numbers of immigrants arrive on Israel's shores, as the second column of Table 5.1 illustrates. All in all, a total of approximately three million persons have immigrated to Israel since its statehood in 1948, relative to a population of approximately seven million in 2006 (CBS SA, 2011). This means that

---

for family reunification, the only kind permitted, has been minimal. For example, the United Nations brokered a family reunion program in 1949 for Arab refugees, in which the return of a mere 3,113 persons was approved (Rouhana 1997, 263–264).

[7]For example, at one extreme, should Orthodox Jewish law (*halacha*) be used to determine who is a Jew and hence who should be allowed to immigrate to Israel, or, at the other extreme, should a person's own honest declaration suffice? Other issues have included which, if any, non-Jewish family members of Jews should be allowed to immigrate—particularly in light of the large numbers of these immigrants in recent years. For a good overview of the "who is a Jew?" debate, see Cohen and Susser (2000, 133–136).

[8]Some have even viewed the Law of Return as having quasi-constitutional status (e.g., Mahler 2011, 104). This is a testament to its importance because Israel lacks a formal constitution.

Years	Immigrants, Total	Immigrants, Percent Sephardi
1948–51	687,624	50
1952–54	54,676	76
1955–57	166,492	68
1958–60	75,970	36
1961–64	228,793	59
1965–68	82,244	50
1969–71	116,791	27
1972–74	142,753	9.2
1975–79	124,827	14
1980–84	83,637	27
1985–89	70,196	20
1990–99	956,319	9.3
2000–04	181,505	21
2005–09	86,858	25
1948–2009	3,058,596	31

Table 5.1: Immigration to Israel by period, 1948 to 2009. Source: based on CBS SA, 2011, Table 4-2.

without immigration, Israel's population would be roughly half its current size. Moreover, 25 percent of Israel's population in 2009 was foreign-born, down from a high of 66 percent in 1951 (CBS SA, 1951/52, 2010). By way of contrast, only 11 percent of the population of the United States, another country of immigration, was foreign-born at the time of the 2000 census (U.S. Census Bureau 2006, Table 1).

It can be seen from Table 5.1 that more than two-thirds of Israel's immigrants arrived in two massive waves, each concentrated in a short ten- to fifteen-year period. The largest of these two waves in relative terms took place in the early years of the state—specifically, in the 1950s and early 1960s. The second occurred in the later years, in the 1990s. What makes both of them important to this study is that each represents a substantial, rapid, and exogenous increase in Israel's social heterogeneity: the first brought Jews of non-European origins to Israel in great numbers, and the second Jews from the former Soviet Union. Also of interest is a small in-gathering of Soviet Jews in the 1970s.

5.1.1 The Early Years: Sephardi Immigration

The state of Israel is a product of Zionism, a political movement of the late nineteenth and early twentieth centuries that sought self-determination for the Jewish people in the ancient biblical land of Israel. The intellectual and organizational backbone of the movement was provided by European Jews such as Theodore Herzl, who drew inspiration from the nationalist movements ascendant in Europe at the time. Moreover, pioneering Jewish settlers who immigrated to what is now Israel in one of the five pre-state waves of immigration (*aliyot*, singular *aliya*) were primarily of European origin, or *Ashkenazi*. The term "Ashkenazi" (plural, Ashkenazim) is used to describe the historically Yiddish-speaking Jews whose origin lies in Central and Eastern Europe, including their descendants such as American, Canadian, and Australian Jews.[9] Yet, as is implied by the existence of this term, not all Jews—and hence not all Israeli Jews—can lay claim to this heritage.

Ethnic divisions began to emerge within world Jewry following its dispersion or diaspora throughout the Middle East and Mediterranean around 70 A.D. as a result of the Roman destruction of the Second Temple. Today, there are many ways of describing Jewish Israel's ethnic landscape. Various sets of ethnic groups may be identified by focusing upon differences in geographic and cultural origin, such as the specific country or even city of birth, as well as upon differences in religious rituals (e.g., Horowitz and Lissak 1989, 64). However, the dominant approach is simple, and it is this approach that I take here: to use geographic origin to distinguish between Ashkenazim or European Jews, on the one hand, and non-European Jews, such as Arabic speakers born in the Muslim lands stretching from North Africa to the Middle East, on the other.[10] I use the Hebrew term "Sephardi" (plural, Sephardim) to refer to the latter ethnic group.[11] In addition to geographic origin, the Ashkenazim and Sephardim are divided by a myriad of factors, including physical appearance; language; liturgy; religious law; and cultural heritage (Smooha 1978, 51–52). Particularly worth noting is the fact that a person's ethnic group is "readily identifiable by physical appearance,

---

[9]"Ashkenaz" is the Hebrew term for Germany, which was the center of the European Jewish community for many years.

[10]In his seminal work, Smooha (1978) initially describes the evolution of *three* ethnic groups in the Jewish community: those who lived in the Middle East and North Africa; those who lived in the Iberian peninsula (particularly, Spain) but were eventually dispersed throughout the Balkans, Turkey, and Palestine; and those who lived elsewhere in Europe (particularly, Germany and Eastern Europe). However, he ultimately combines the two former groups vis-à-vis the latter due to their cultural and religious similarities in addition to the few and dwindling numbers of Iberian Jews.

[11]Another commonly employed term in Israel is "Mizrachi" (plural, Mizrachim). "Mizrach" literally translates as "East." In the older English literature, it was instead often translated as "Oriental" (see, for example, Shama and Iris 1977), although this translation has more recently fallen out of favor following the publication of Said's (1978) *Orientalism*. Technically, "Sephardi" refers only to descendants of the Iberian Jewish community, many of whom were speakers of a dialect of medieval Spanish called Ladino. This arguably makes the Hebrew term "Mizrachi" the better term for describing the broader ethnic group of interest; in fact, it is generally used in Israel to refer to all non-European Jews. Another option is "Arab Jew," which some such as Shenhav (2006) have recently advocated in a surprising throwback to earlier Zionist usage. Here, I opt for the term "Sephardi" despite its flaws because it has become the term of choice for a plurality of scholars, particularly in the English and political science literatures. See Behar (2009) for a recent review of the various terms.

5. Israel: New Parties for New Groups?

accent, surname and by many other signs" (ibid., 72).

This ethnic dichotomization of Jewish Israelis into Ashkenazim and Sephardim has deep roots in history, the academy, and public discourse. It also has roots in the bureaucracy of the state of Israel. Jews are classified by the state as having origins that lie in either Asia or Africa, on the one hand[12]—a group corresponding to the Sephardim—and in either Europe or America, on the other—a group corresponding to the Ashkenazim. More specifically, for first-generation Israelis, "origin" and hence ethnicity is defined by the Israeli Central Bureau of Statistics as the country and continent of birth; for the second generation, it is the place of birth of the father; and for the third generation (the Israeli-born of an Israeli-born father), no official record is kept of ancestry save to classify the individual as having Israeli origin (e.g. Goldscheider 2002a). Government policy in Israel accordingly defines various ethnic groups to which individuals belong. In Israel and in many other countries, these definitions—a form of social policy—then take on a life of their own in that they underpin what come to be viewed as "natural" ethnic divisions.[13]

Accordingly, in what follows, I explore how the numbers of Israelis belonging to the Ashkenazi and Sephardi ethnic groups have changed over time. Two matters deserve elaboration. First, as alluded to earlier, individuals are in reality members of many ascriptive groups (Chandra 2004, 3), some of which are nested within one another. For example, a Jewish Israeli may be Moroccan, but she is also then a North African and, even more broadly, a Sephardi. Similarly, an Israeli Jew from the Ukraine is also a Jew from the former Soviet republics (a "Russian"), as well as an Ashkenazi. While my primary interest lies with the aggregated classification of Jewish Israelis as either Ashkenazi or Sephardi, I also pay attention to the less aggregated ethnic groups that are nested within these aggregated ones, such as subgroups defined by country and region of origin. Of particular interest here are the "Russians," about whom I shall say more later. Second, as discussed in an earlier chapter, membership in a particular ethnic group or "category" is a *latent* component of identity, which may or may not be politicized or particized. Hence, the categories of "Ashkenazi" and "Sephardi" are just that: categories that identify an individual Jew's ancestral place of geographic origin; I imply neither that the Ashkenazi (Sephardi) share a collective identity nor that they are capable of collective action. For now, I simply describe the changing numbers of Israelis in each of these categories.

---

[12] By the Israeli state's reckoning, "Asia" encompasses countries such as Turkey and Iran, while "Africa" encompasses countries such as Morocco and Egypt. In light of the slim numbers of Israeli citizens from Central and East Asian countries such as India, as well as from sub-Saharan African countries, "Asia" largely corresponds to the region that is conventionally called the Middle East, minus Egypt, and "Africa" to the region that is conventionally called North Africa, plus Egypt. See, for example, Cleveland (2000, xiii), who defines the Middle East as "the region from Egypt in the west through Iran in the east, and from Turkey in the north to the Arabian Peninsula in the south."

[13] See Posner (2005) for a theoretical discussion of this issue; Yanow (1999) for an application to Israel; and Goldscheider (2002a) for both.

Later I will turn to the issue of their politicization.

But to return to the categories themselves, still needed is an account of the Sephardi presence in Israel. In spite of the earlier characterization of Israel as a product of Zionism, Jewish settlement in what was to become Israel—the territory then known as Palestine—was never a completely European enterprise. In the late 1800s, just prior to the beginning of Zionist immigration, Sephardim constituted approximately 60 percent of the Jewish population of Palestine (Smooha 1978, 57). Although this share dropped to 23 percent on the eve of Israel's statehood in 1948 as a consequence of the predominantly Ashkenazi Zionist immigration described earlier (ibid.),[14] about 10 percent of pre-state immigration to Palestine was Sephardi,[15] roughly proportional to the Sephardi share of the Jewish population of the world at the time (Shafir and Peled 2002, 74). Nevertheless, large-scale Sephardi immigration, and hence a significant Sephardi presence, is a phenomenon that follows the establishment of the state of Israel. It is to this first wave of mass immigration that I now turn.

Overall, Table 5.1 shows that approximately 1,200,000 immigrants arrived in Israel in the decade and a half following its statehood, that is, between 1948 and 1964. What makes this wave of immigration even more remarkable is that on May 14, 1948, the day on which Israel declared its independence, Israel's Jewish population stood at approximately 650,000 (Friedlander and Goldscheider 1979, 90). With immigration from this date until the end of 1951 alone totaling almost 700,000, the Jewish population of Israel more than *doubled* apart from natural increase in this even shorter period following statehood—a rate unmatched either in other time periods in Israel's history or in other countries in the modern era (e.g., Shama and Iris 1977). It is for this reason that the "unprecedented" three-and-a-half-year stream of immigration following statehood is called "*the* wave of mass migration" (Friedlander and Goldscheider 1979, 25; emphasis added). Most germane for the purposes of this study, however, is the fact that about *half* of the immigrants in both the immediate three and longer fifteen-year periods following statehood were Sephardim. The extent to which Sephardim were encouraged to immigrate to Israel is disputed.[16] Nevertheless, Sephardi im-

---

[14]Smooha (1978, 53) notes that it is "well-established that the Zionist movement was not active among Orientals. It did not set up chapters in lands where Orientals lived, and, with minor exceptions, did not send any emissaries among them until World War II—and very few afterwards." He discusses several reasons for this neglect, but roots it in the "contagious colonial spirit that prevailed in Europe at the time—feelings of superiority and paternalism of Europeans towards Asian and African peoples" (ibid., 55).

[15]Of particular note are two independent waves of Yemenite Jewish immigration during both the first and second *aliyot* (1881 and 1907), and a third wave in 1910 that the Zionists somewhat unusually encouraged. See Smooha (1978, 54–55).

[16]Shafir and Peled (2002, 77), for example, argue that the influx was "orchestrated" by the newly established Israeli state. The long-standing Zionist neglect of the Sephardim (see footnote 14) suggests that this case may be somewhat overstated, however. So too do the selection rules implemented in the mid-1950s, which first implicitly and then explicitly aimed to restrict Sephardi (and especially North African Jewish) immigration, although with limited and

migrants arrived in several distinct subwaves. Sephardim from the Middle East constituted the bulk of the immigrants in the early 1950s, while those hailing from North Africa predominated in the late 1950s and early 1960s (Shafir and Peled 2002, 78).

The first and largest of these subwaves spanned the period from May 15, 1948 to the end of 1951. During this period, a total of 331,303 Sephardi immigrants arrived in Israel, along with 331,926 Ashkenazi immigrants[17] and 24,395 immigrants whose origins were unknown (CBS SA, 2011). Of the Sephardi immigrants, approximately 70 percent hailed from Asia (that is, the Middle East) and 30 percent from North Africa. More specifically, 37 percent came from Iraq; 15 percent from Yemen-Aden; 11 percent from Turkey; 7 percent from Iran; 14 percent from Morocco, Algeria, and Tunisia combined; 9 percent from Libya; and 3 percent from Egypt and the Sudan (calculations based on Friedlander and Goldscheider 1979, 40–41). On the "pull" side, the deep religiosity of the Sephardim—the ability to live a religious life among Jews and in proximity to the Jewish holy places—was the major incentive for their migration. A secondary "pull" factor was their perception that Israel would be a "Land of Milk and Honey," a perception encouraged by Zionist emissaries and the broadcasts of Israeli radio. On the "push" side, the creation of Israel and the defeat of the Arab forces in the first Arab-Israeli war made life difficult for many of the Jews residing in Arab states. However, while anti-Jewish violence produced a greater predisposition to make *aliya*, it was not the most decisive factor (Shama and Iris 1977).

Two smaller subwaves of immigration followed. While immigration had dropped off in late 1951 due to the difficult conditions in Israel (Friedlander and Goldscheider 1979, 86–87, 98–104), it began to pick up again in late 1954. In the three-year period from 1955 to 1957, 166,492 immigrants arrived in Israel, of whom 112,647 were Sephardi (CBS SA, 2011). This came to be viewed as the second of the three subwaves of immigration. The vast majority (90 percent) of these Sephardi immigrants hailed from North Africa, including 63 percent from Morocco; 14 percent from Tunisia; and 12 percent from Egypt and the Sudan (calculations based on Friedlander and Goldscheider 1979, 40–41). In fact, some scholars have collectively called this and the subsequent subwave of immigration the "North African immigration" wave (e.g., Goldscheider 2002b, 52). The major "pull" factor accounting for this rise in immigration was improved economic conditions in Israel, making it a more attractive destination. On the "push" side, the Morocan and Tunisian *aliyot* resulted primarily from the unsettled conditions (including sporadic violence) obtaining as these countries gained independence from France. By contrast, the migration of Egyptian Jews to Israel was primarily a consequence of the 1956 Suez campaign and the military defeat inflicted

---

varying degrees of effectiveness (see Friedlander and Goldscheider 1979, 98–110).

[17]The vast majority of these Ashkenazi immigrants were Holocaust survivors. They poured into Israel from the refugee camps when Israel's provisional government lifted the restrictions on immigration that had been imposed by the British, its first act after declaring independence. See Shama and Iris (1977, 36, 41–44).

upon Egypt by Israel, France and Britain. This made the position of Jews in Egypt as well as elsewhere in North Africa less tenable, a push, while simultaneously making Israel more secure, a pull (Shama and Iris 1977, 74; Friedlander and Goldscheider 1979, 25, 102–105).

After declining during the 1958 to 1960 period, immigration took off yet again in 1961. Between 1961 and 1964, the third and final subwave, a total of 228,793 persons migrated to Israel, 135,401 of whom were Sephardi (CBS SA, 2011). Most (85 percent) were again North African in origin: specifically, 73 percent were from Morocco and 10 percent from Algeria and Tunisia combined (calculations based on Friedlander and Goldscheider 1979, 40–41). As before, improved economic conditions played a large role in "pulling" immigrants to Israel, while continued political unrest elsewhere served as a "push." However, an economic recession in 1965 helped to reduce the stream of immigrants to a trickle, as did the decline of the potential North African immigrant population: almost all of those willing to migrate had already made *aliya* by the mid-1960s (Friedlander and Goldscheider 1979, 25, 109).

Hence, 1965 marks the end of the third and final phase of the first wave of mass immigration to Israel. While Sephardim would continue to immigrate to Israel in subsequent decades, they would do so in much smaller numbers (both relative and absolute), as Table 5.1 makes clear. The most notable stream of Sephardi immigration since 1964 has been the arrival of roughly 85,000 Ethiopian Jews in Israel since the 1980s (CBS SA, 2010).

In conclusion, the number of Sephardim in Israel rose rapidly as a result of the large-scale stream of Sephardi immigration described earlier. Moreover, the relatively high fertility rate of the immigrants subsequently produced a large natural increase (Friedlander and Goldscheider 1979, 26–27). The combined consequence is that from a minority of less than 15 percent of the Jewish population at the end of 1948 (that is, immediately following statehood), the Sephardim are estimated to have attained parity with the Ashkenazim sometime in the 1960s and a slim majority by the early 1970s, as shown in Table 5.2 (see also Table B.1 in Appendix B). However, this table shows that until recently, their share of the electorate has always lagged behind their share of the population, which can be explained by their relative youth.[18] And when Israeli Arabs are taken into account, the Sephardim are never estimated to have attained a majority of the population, let alone of the electorate. I note that these are estimates because of the previously mentioned lack of official data on the origins of third-generation Israelis. Table 5.2 also shows the effective number of ethnic groups in Israel over time. For the Jewish population, this statistic rose from a homogeneous 1.3 in 1948 to a heterogeneous 2.0 as early as 1961. Including Israeli Arabs as a third

---

[18]The exception, according to the table, is 1948. However, the higher Sephardi share of the electorate than of the population in this year is due to the different data sources: data on the electorate is not available from Goldscheider (2002b), so my data, which I believe significantly overestimates the Sephardi share of the population and electorate in Israel's very early years, is used instead.

5. Israel: New Parties for New Groups?

Year	Population, Percent Sephardi	N, Population	Electorate, Percent Sephardi
1948	9.9 (12)	1.8 (1.3)	15 (18)
1961	41 (46)	2.4 (2.0)	35 (38)
1973	44 (52)	2.6 (2.0)	39 (43)
1981	44 (52)	2.7 (2.0)	41 (47)
1992	40 (49)	2.7 (2.0)	40 (47)
2003	36 (44)	2.7 (2.0)	37 (44)

Table 5.2: Estimates of the Sephardi share of Israel's total and Jewish populations; the effective number of ethnic groups (N) in Israel and Jewish Israel; and the Sephardi share of Israel's total and Jewish electorates in selected election years and 1948. Figures for Jewish Israel appear in parentheses. All figures are the best (middle-of-the-road) estimates with the exception of population figures for 1948, which are based upon Goldscheider (2002b, 31). Source: based on CBS (1967); CBS (1969); and CBS SA. See Appendix B for more information.

ethnic group in addition to the Ashkenazim and Sephardim paints a similar picture: the effective number of ethnic groups has risen from 1.8 in 1948 to 2.7 in 2003, an increase of close to one ethnic group.[19]

Accordingly, an entire ethnic group was added to Israeli society by the first wave of mass immigration. Soon I will explore the consequences of this significant increase in social heterogeneity for the number of political parties. First, however, attention must be paid to a later wave of immigration that tipped the scales back in favor of the Ashkenazim in the 1990s. I now turn to this second large-scale wave, which produced Israel's "new masses" (Goldscheider 2002b, 53): the Russians.

5.1.2 THE LATER YEARS: RUSSIAN IMMIGRATION

It is important to begin by noting the misnomer that is the term "Russian." I follow the literature in using this term to refer to all Jewish Israelis[20] whose

---

[19] The effective number of ethnic groups is calculated in a manner similar to that used to calculate the effective number of electoral parties. Here, it is calculated using the population shares of the various ethnic groups. Calculations of this statistic using the groups' shares of the electorate are not presented in light of the reasonable (if certainly not exact) correspondence between the two sets of figures.

[20] However, a large number of Russians are not in fact actually Jewish according to Orthodox law. Cohen and Susser (2000, 113) estimate this proportion to be between 10 and 40 percent of the 1990s immigrants, and Gitelman (2004, 97) puts the number at 250,000 or 25 percent (see also Khanin 2001, 118). For the moment, I gloss over their non-Jewishness because they do still belong in the category of "immigrants from the former USSR," although this is an issue to which I later return.

origin lies in the former Soviet republics—not just in the former *Russian* Soviet Republic. "Russian" is hence an ethnic category like any other, but one that is larger than it prima facie appears to be. Further, I also follow the literature in applying the term pnly to those who immigrated to Israel in the last four decades, as opposed to during the pre-state or early state periods.[21] Finally, I note that while most Russians are Ashkenazi, a strict application of the Ashkenazi and Sephardi categories introduced earlier leads to some Russians—those from the former Soviet republics in Central Asia—being categorized as Sephardi.[22]

Russian immigration to Israel came in two waves. The first and smallest in the 1970s was large in neither absolute nor relative terms. From 1967 to 1980, approximately 160,000 Russians immigrated to Israel, 100,000 of whom arrived during the peak years of 1971–74 (Gitelman 1982, 70–71). Many came from the western periphery of the USSR, such as emigrants from the Baltics and from the republic of Georgia.[23] Improved conditions in Israel from 1968 to 1973, including the greater sense of security engendered by Israel's victory in the 1967 Six Day War, was one general "pull" factor that led to a resurgence of immigration after the drought of the mid-1960s; rapid economic growth was another (Friedlander and Goldscheider 1979, 110–114). More specifically, anti-Semitism combined with events such as the Six Day War to fan the flames of Soviet Jewish nationalism, both pulling and pushing Russian Jews to Israel. Following the internal and external pressure generated by this Jewish nationalist movement, Soviet policy was grudgingly changed in March 1971 to allow for the first mass emigration since the aftermath of World War II. Of those who went to Israel, the peak years of immigration came in 1972 and 1973, after which immigration drastically tapered off as a result of the 1973 Yom Kippur (or October) war (Gitelman 1982, 70–96). Moreover, after 1979, the Soviets began to decrease the number of exit visas, believing that a mass exodus of Soviet Jewry would give the USSR a poor international image. As a result, Jewish emigration from the USSR (and hence Russian immigration to Israel) came to a virtual halt by

---

[21] In particular, the early waves of immigration in the pre-state era were dominated by Eastern Europeans, and specifically by Polish and Russian Jews. However, the common experiences and characteristics of these early Russian immigrants differed so drastically from those of the recent Russian immigrants that both scholars and the immigrants themselves have viewed them as distinct groups. For example, former member of the Knesset Zahava Gal-on, who immigrated to Israel from the former Soviet Union with her family as late as 1960, reported never feeling part of the "Russian" community in Israel despite being fluent in the Russian language (personal communication, July 14, 2008), a sentiment that characterizes the feelings of the majority of pre-1970s Russian immigrants.

[22] The Central Bureau of Statistics classified the Central Asian republics of the former USSR as European until 1995, although they have been classified as Asian from 1996 onwards. All other former Soviet republics are classified as European. The implication for Table 5.2 is that the pre-1996 figures somewhat overestimate the numbers of Ashkenazim.

[23] For example, Gitelman (2004, 98) notes that one-quarter of those arriving between 1968 and 1976 hailed from Georgia, where only less than 3 percent of Soviet Jews lived in 1970; one-third from the Baltic states and other areas annexed by the USSR in 1939–40; and 40 percent from the Slavic heartland of Russia, Belorussia, and Ukraine, home to 80 percent of Soviet Jewry.

5. Israel: New Parties for New Groups?

the mid-1980s (Siegel 1998, 8).

This wave of immigration pales in comparison to the large-scale wave of Russian immigration that began a decade later, however. From 1990 through 2009, 984,136 Russians immigrated to Israel (CBS SA, 2010).[24] This is almost a 30 percent increase in Israel's Jewish population, given that it stood at approximately 3,700,000 in 1989 (ibid.).[25] A large proportion of these Russian immigrants hailed from the Slavic heartland, in contrast to the previous wave.[26] The perestroika and glasnost of 1987 made the wave possible in that the Soviet policies of the earlier 1980s forbidding Jewish emigration were lifted. Yet Russian Jews were "pushed" from the USSR more than they were "pulled" to Israel by factors such as the collapse of the Soviet political system; economic crisis; and rising social and ethnic tensions, particularly an explosion of virulent anti-Semitism (Gitelman 1995, 13). In fact, Gitelman (2004, 96) goes so far as to describe the 1989–1993 wave of immigration as a "panic migration." The United States' sharply limiting its own intake of refugees in 1989 also contributed. Immigration rose again in the late 1990s following the August 1998 collapse of the Russian economy, but fell off in the 2000s as the Russian economy began to improve and the second intifada erupted in Israel. It is for this reason that many place the end date of the wave at 2000.

In summary, these two waves of Russian immigration—and particularly the larger, 1990s wave—substantially increased Israel's ethnic heterogeneity. This can be seen in Table 5.3, which presents estimates of the Russian proportion of Israel's population and electorate. It also presents estimates of the effective number of ethnic groups in Israel when the Russians are treated as a separate ethnic group alongside the non-Russian Ashkenazim, the Sephardim and Israeli Arabs.[27] The Russian ethnic group is defined in two ways in this table. The first considers only those Russians who immigrated after 1990, as well as their children, to be "Russians"; the second additionally considers the approximately 160,000 Russian immigrants of the 1970s to be "Russians."[28]

Depending on the treatment of the 1970s Russians, this table shows that by the early 2000s, Russians are estimated to have constituted between 14

---

[24] Many scholars date the beginning of this wave of immigration to either 1988 or 1989 because of the 1987 change in Soviet policy to again allow for emigration. However, relatively few Russians actually immigrated to Israel in 1988 and 1989—Gitelman (1995, 13) reports 12,000 in the latter year, for example—which is why 1990 is usually viewed as the wave's substantive beginning.

[25] In 1990 alone, the year of the largest Soviet *aliya*, the Jewish population of Israel increased by five percent solely through immigration (Gitelman 2004, 95–96).

[26] As of 1999, Gitelman (2004, 98) reported that one-third came from Russia; one-third from the Ukraine; 8 percent from Belarus; and 13 percent from Central Asia.

[27] To perform this calculation, all Russians are treated as Ashkenazim. As discussed earlier, this is not entirely accurate, but it does not do gross injustice to reality, either, given the small number of Russians from the Central Asian republics.

[28] Data on the latter group's natural increase is not available. This means that the Russian population and electorate is underestimated in Table 5.3, which in turn means that the effective number of ethnic groups in Israel is also underestimated.

Changing Societies, Changing Party Systems

	Russians: Only 1990s			Russians: 1970s and 1990s		
Year	Population, Percent Russian	N, Population	Electorate, Percent Russian	Population, Percent Russian	N, Population	Electorate, Percent Russian
1961	0.0 (0.0)	2.4 (2.0)	0.0 (0.0)	0.0 (0.0)	2.4 (2.0)	0.0 (0.0)
1973	0.0 (0.0)	2.6 (2.0)	0.0 (0.0)	2.5 (2.9)	2.7 (2.1)	3.0 (3.4)
1981	0.0 (0.0)	2.7 (2.0)	0.0 (0.0)	4.0 (4.8)	2.9 (2.2)	5.4 (6.2)
1992	7.3 (8.9)	3.1 (2.3)	8.4 (9.9)	10 (13)	3.2 (2.4)	13 (15)
2003	14 (17)	3.5 (2.7)	16 (18)	16 (20)	3.6 (2.7)	19 (22)

Table 5.3: For selected election years, estimates of the Russian share of Israel's total and Jewish populations; the effective number of ethnic groups (N) in Israel and Jewish Israel when Russians are treated as a separate ethnic group; and the Russian share of Israel's total and Jewish electorates. Jewish figures shown in parentheses. Source: based on CBS SA and Gitelman (1982). See Appendix B for more information.

and 16 percent of the total population and between 16 and 19 percent of the total electorate, with the latter being higher because of their older age distribution. Their estimated share of the Jewish population and electorate is, not surprisingly, higher: by the early 2000s, they made up approximately one-fifth of each. Accordingly, as a result of Russian immigration, the effective number of ethnic groups increased from 2.0 in 1961 to 2.7 in 2003 for Jewish Israel and from 2.4 to approximately 3.5 for Israel as a whole, respectively. This increase in heterogeneity is akin to that experienced by Israel between 1948 and the early 1960s as a result of Sephardi immigration. Moreover, by the late 1990s, Russians had become the largest ethnic group in Jewish Israel when ethnicity is defined by *country* of origin, passing those of Moroccan extraction (Cohen and Susser 2000, 110).

5.2 PARTY SYSTEM FRAGMENTATION IN ISRAEL

My second task is to describe the fragmentation of the party system, the dependent variable, in Israel at different points in time. Israel has had a multiparty system since its founding. Numerous small parties catering to specific constituencies, such as the religious, have existed alongside more broadly based parties. Of the latter, Israeli politics was dominated by the major party of the center-left, Labor, prior to 1977; since 1977 and until the 2006 election, Labor and the major party of the center-right, Likud, have traded off and sometimes shared power. In 2006, a new party, Kadima, positioned itself in the oft-empty center of the political spectrum and emerged as the largest party, drawing support away from both Labor and Likud. On average, approximately five parties have contested Israel's seventeen elections when each party is weighed by its share of the vote,[29] a comparatively large number.[30]

In this section, I ask whether party system fragmentation in Israel has changed over time. More specifically, I ask whether new sectarian political parties did in fact successfully form to represent the new groups that immigration added to Israeli society. The alternative is that the new groups were absorbed by the existing party system. I initially present some quantitative data on the number of parties in Israel, after which I flesh out the picture with a more qualitative brush.

5.2.1 A Quantitative Look: The Effective Number of Electoral Parties

Two operationalizations of the number of electoral parties may help to shed empirical light on the hypothesis. The first is simply the raw number of parties. This operationalization captures elite behavior: how political entrepreneurs and existing party leaders decide to contest elections—for example, deciding whether to form a new party. The second is the effective number of electoral parties in Israel, the same operationalization that was employed in the prior chapter's quantitative analysis of legislative elections. This operationalization additionally captures mass behavior: how voters decide to vote given the field of entrants offered by elites—for example, deciding whether to support a new party. As discussed earlier, studying the elite and mass levels separately will pinpoint exactly where any representational "failures" (in light of the hypothesis) have occurred: on the supply side, that is, at the elite level, or on the demand side, that is, at the mass level. Figure 5.1 plots both operationalizations from 1949, the year of Israel's first legislative election, to 2009, the year of its most recent legislative election.

Beginning with the first, elite-level operationalization, the raw number of parties, the quantitative evidence in support of the hypothesis seems mixed. The general trend evident from the figure is towards a larger number of competing parties, consistent with the increased ethnic heterogeneity in Israel over time. More specifically, upwards spikes have occurred in the late 1950s and late 1990s, somewhat commensurate with the large-scale waves of Sephardi and Russian immigration. However, the uptick in the early 1980s and dramatic drops in the raw number of parties in the early 1960s and

---

[29]This is nothing other than the effective number of electoral parties (Laakso and Taagepera 1979) introduced in the prior chapter. I count *electoral* parties instead of *legislative* parties for the reasons given earlier. However, the high proportionality of the electoral system means that the two measures are quite similar for Israel.

[30]For example, Israel had the sixth-highest average number of parties in Lijphart's (1999, 76–77) sample of thirty-six democracies in the post-war period. Note that Lijphart reports the average effective number of *legislative* parties, where the parties are weighed by their seat shares instead of their vote shares. From 1945 to 1996, he found Israel to have an average of 4.6 effective legislative parties. The countries in his sample with higher averages are Papua New Guinea; Switzerland; Finland; Italy; and the Netherlands.

Changing Societies, Changing Party Systems

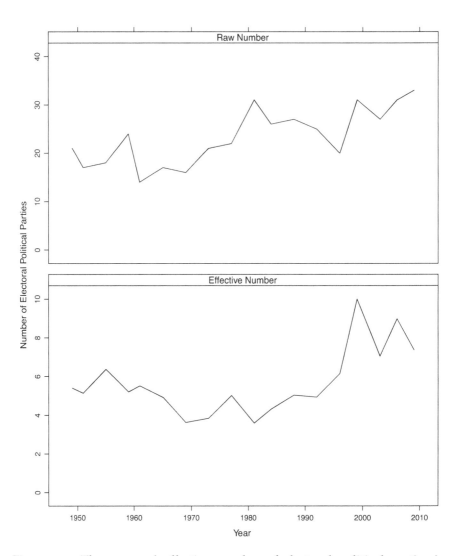

Figure 5.1: The raw and effective number of electoral political parties in Israel. Source: based on CBS (1956); CBS (1961); CBS (1964); CBS (1967–1974); CBS (1981–1997); Knesset (1999); Knesset (2003); Knesset (2006); and Knesset (2009).

5. Israel: New Parties for New Groups?

mid-1990s are less commensurate with the changes in Israel's ethnic heterogeneity described here.

Turning to the second, mass-level operationalization, the effective number of electoral parties, there is also mixed support for the hypothesis. What is most notable from the graph is the dramatic spike in the effective number of electoral parties in the late 1990s, commensurate with the wave of Russian immigration: prior to this point, voters seemed to be consolidating their votes around a smaller number of parties despite both the trend of increasing ethnic heterogeneity and the greater number of parties competing for their votes. There is also an uptick in the effective number of electoral parties, albeit a smaller one, in 1977 on the heels of the smaller wave of Russian immigration of the 1970s. But in Israel's early years, with the exception of a small spike in the mid-1950s, the effective number of electoral parties largely proceeded to decline until 1977, despite Sephardi immigration having greatly increased the ethnic heterogeneity of Israel during this period.

5.2.2 A Qualitative Look: Sephardi and Russian Sectarian Parties

The drawback to this quantitative data, however, is that it does not isolate the changes in Israel's party system fragmentation resulting from the mechanism of interest. As discussed earlier, the effective number of electoral parties can increase when votes become more dispersed over the existing set of political parties, not just when a new party enters and attracts at least some support; moreover, even in the latter case, there is no guarantee that the new entrant is both targeting and drawing support from one of the new ethnic groups introduced to Israeli society by immigration. There are similar difficulties with the raw number of parties. Two key questions remain to be answered. First, did Russian political parties actually enter and attract reasonable numbers of Russian votes following the wave of Russian immigration? Second, did Sephardi political parties appear on the political scene but fail to attract Sephardi votes, or did they not appear at all? Taking a more qualitative approach enables me to answer these questions.

Definitional Matters, and More

Yet there is a critical issue that has been sidestepped until now: how do we know whether a political party is a "Russian" or a "Sephardi" one? More generally, how should the concept of a "group-specific" or "sectarian" political party, that is, a party that primarily represents one particular group in society, be defined and operationalized?[31]

---

[31] Hazan and Rahat (2000) apply the label "sectarian" only to parties that seek exclusively to represent *ascriptive* social groups, such as religious or ethnic categories, although I do not believe that the definition needs to be restricted in this way. Other terms used in the literature to describe this type of party are "confessional" and "communal."

Some scholars such as Horowitz (1985) classify a party as sectarian if the group in question disproportionally supports the party at the polls.[32] A countervailing perspective is offered by Lijphart (1981, 28), who argues that "Ideologies and programmes must be distinguished from the characteristics of the voters that parties represent. For instance, the fact that a party receives unusually strong support from Roman Catholic voters does not automatically make it a Catholic party...." Chandra (2004, 3–6) sides with Lijphart's view that the critical factor is a party's message. Because she is interested in identifying when a particular type of sectarian party, an ethnic party, is able to attract support from voters, she argues that voter support should not be built into the definition.[33] Intermediary positions between these two camps, which take both voting behavior and a party's message into account, can also be identified.[34]

My goal in this section is to identify when group-specific parties compete, as well as when they are electorally successful. Consequently, I side with the second group of scholars in defining a group-specific or sectarian party as one that makes the representation of a particular group its raison d'etre. Like Chandra (2004), I believe that this necessarily means that it must exclude another group from its appeal. For example, an Israeli party that ran on a platform of representing Russian interests, as opposed to the interests of all other groups, would qualify as a sectarian party according to this definition. More specifically, we would classify it as a *Russian* sectarian party. By way of contrast, a party that campaigned to represent Russian, Sephardi, and Ashkenazi interests (that is, all of the ethnic groups in Jewish Israel) would not be classified as a sectarian party. Similarly, while a party that campaigned to jointly represent Russian and Sephardi interests against the Ashkenazim would be sectarian because of the exclusion of the Ashkenazi from its appeal, it would not be a *Russian* sectarian party because it did not primarily seek to represent the Russian community. To reiterate, an exclusionary message is what matters in classifying a party as sectarian, not the support that it is able to attract from its target group.

So how does the support that a party attracts matter? I follow Chandra (2004) in viewing sectarian parties that are able to attract the votes of a ma-

---

[32]This approach has a long and distinguished history in the voting behavior literature, where scholars routinely identify the relevant social divisions or cleavages in a country on the basis of the support political parties receive from different social groups. A good example from the American politics literature is Manza and Brooks (1999), and a good example from the Israeli politics literature is Peres and Shemer (1984).

[33]While Hazan and Rahat (2000) do not clearly spell out the distinguishing characteristics of their sectarian parties, they implicitly place themselves in the latter camp: one of the tasks of their paper is to evaluate the electoral success of these parties during the period in the 1990s when Israel's prime minister was directly elected, and this task requires success at the polls to be evaluated apart from the classification of parties as sectarian or nonsectarian.

[34]In the Israeli context, an example is Shamir and Arian (1983). They argue that although many by the early 1980s began classifying the major parties as "ethnic" based upon the social (ethnic) composition of their voters, the "full" understanding of what constitutes an ethnic party also encompasses its appeal (from the issues it raises to the goals it stakes out) as well as the identity of its personnel.

5. Israel: New Parties for New Groups?

jority or close to a majority of their target group as *successful*. If they are instead able to capture the votes of only a plurality or close to a plurality of the target group, we view them as *moderately successful*. I differ from Chandra, however, in evaluating the collective as well as the individual success of parties. A group's votes may be dispersed so that no individual party is successful, even while a plurality to majority of its votes are collectively directed to parties that seek exclusively to represent it. Such an outcome occurs when both elites and voters fail to coordinate. Underlying this coordination failure may be the fact that some individuals are members of nested ascriptive categories, as I earlier argued. If individuals identify with categories at different levels in the nested hierarchy, differences between individual and collective success are likely to arise. This is an issue to which I will later return. For now, it suffices to argue that if an individual's vote goes to a party representing a lower-order category such as Jewish Israelis of Yemeni origin, she may still be said to be casting a vote for a sectarian and specifically for a *Sephardi* sectarian party, the higher-order (more encompassing) category in which this lower-order category nests. Hence, I evaluate success at these different, nested levels.

This leaves the operational issue of how the group-specific content of a party's message should be identified. For many parties in many countries, this is practically a nonissue: obvious appeals are made to a particular group in venues such as the party's platform. An example is the Scottish National Party in the United Kingdom, which appeals to Scots by calling for Scottish independence. This is the first operational approach I take to identify a party as sectarian: looking for exclusionary appeals in its propaganda.

It is not clear that this operational approach will suffice in Israel, however. For example, Herzog (1983, 1984, 1985a, 1985b, 1986), who has made one of the most extensive studies of ethnic parties in Israel, argues that Sephardi parties have lacked an ethnic ideology. She instead characterizes them as seeking both greater integration and a re-distribution of resources.[35] Yet even such resource-driven and integrationary appeals can be viewed as hallmarks of a sectarian party. For example, resource distributions are generally zero-sum (at least in the short run), which means that directing more resources to one group will mean fewer resources for another group. The operational issue still at hand, though, is to identify which group is being targeted, something that the formal appeal may not (and in Israel, often does not) always convey.

If exclusionary appeals in a party's propaganda do not clearly identify the targeted group, the operational approach that I take in this and subse-

---

[35] For example, she argues that a "content analysis of the platforms and election propaganda of all the ethnic lists... reveals no ethnic ideology whatsoever... [they] did not have a separatist ideology and in most cases did not demand the preservation of ethnic uniqueness" (Herzog 1985a, 47–48). Rather, their goals were "a redivision of economic, political, and prestige assets" (Herzog 1984, 526) and "greater integration into society" (ibid., 523); see also Smooha (1978, 77–78) on the latter point. By way of contrast, Horowitz and Lissak (1989, 68) provide a somewhat less instrumental account of these parties' appeals.

quent chapters identifies a party as group-specific or sectarian on the basis of (i) its name and (ii) the origin of its founders and other leaders. A party's name reflects the way in which the party chooses to represent itself to the public symbolically (Herzog 1985a, 48). For example, a party that names itself the "Yemenite Association" is clearly signaling that it aims to represent Yemenite Jews, not, say, Ashkenazi Jews. However, Herzog notes that while parties' names conveyed the identity of the targeted group during the early years of the state, they became extremely general and ceased to do so as time passed. Herzog's solution is to find another indicator: the origin of the party's founders. When a party's founders and to a lesser extent its other leaders all belong to a particular group, the party can claim to descriptively represent that group, with more ideological representation, such as demands for resource redistribution, likely to follow.[36] Hence, I follow Herzog in viewing such a party as sectarian. This is comparable to the approach taken by Chandra (2004, 82–98), who argues that voters in patronage (limited-information) democracies develop preferences over parties by "counting the heads" of co-ethnics among party personnel.

But a sectarian party is not the only type of party that might come to represent a new social group such as Israel's Sephardi immigrants. What about the alternative type of party, which Hazan and Rahat (2000) call either an "ideological" or a "catch-all" party? The "catch-all" term was coined by Kirchheimer (1966), who traced the origin of this type of party to the early post–World War II period. In contrast to sectarian parties, catch-all parties seek support where it can be found and embrace only the ideology of electoral success (Rose 1980). While they might not appeal to every last voter, they appeal to all voters whose interests do not adamantly conflict. In other words, they cast as wide a net as possible. The result is a social composition that approximates that of the electorate at large (Torgovnik 1986). Relatedly, Chandra (2004) contrasts her type of sectarian party, the ethnic party, with what she calls multiethnic parties, on the one hand, and nonethnic parties, on the other. The former type of party appeals to more than one group relatively equally, the catch-all phenomenon, whereas the latter downplays one division, such as ethnicity, in favor of another division, such as religion, that bisects it. In either of these circumstances, an ethnic group will not have obtained representation *qua* ethnic group, although Chandra's nonethnic type of party may still be sectarian. Accordingly, drawing upon these various

---

[36] For example, MK David Rotem of Israel Beiteinu describes the party as Russian in the sense that the "Russianness" of its key figures is a draw to the Russian immigrant population. Lieberman, the party's founder and leader, is a case in point: he is "apparently forever" Russian to veteran Israelis (and hence to other Russians) because of his accent, in spite of the fact he came to Israel in the 1970s; went to university in Israel; and worked his way up from the bottom (interview, May 27, 2008). Similarly, when asking both politicians and ordinary Israelis whether Israel Beiteinu was a "Russian" party, some pointed to its several non-Russian MKs (such as Rotem) to argue that it was no longer really Russian, while others pointed to the preponderance of Russians in its Knesset contingent to argue that it was Russian. Hence, the identity of party personnel, and particularly the identity of a party's parliamentary contingent, appears to be the major factor driving peoples' perceptions of parties as sectarian or not.

scholars, I define a nonsectarian or catch-all party as one that seeks to represent most if not all social groups (that is, exogenous or latent categories), in contrast to a sectarian party, which seeks primarily to represent a single social group.

Two paths to political representation accordingly faced the Sephardim and Russians in Israel. On the first path, they could obtain representation through sectarian parties that exclusively aimed to represent their communities. On the second path, an existing and catch-all Israeli party, such as the Likud, that already represented a broad constituency could reach out to them, further broadening its base of support; in turn, they could reward this party with their votes. I now turn to the task of exploring which of these two paths each group has taken.

Sephardim

For each Israeli election, Table 5.4 summarizes the appearance and electoral performance of Sephardi sectarian parties, which were identified by drawing upon both popular accounts in the media and the academic literature. The table lists how many Sephardi sectarian parties contested the election; the highest vote share and Knesset seat share obtained by an individual party; and the Sephardi parties' collective vote and seat shares.[37] This table shows that between one and five Sephardi political parties or "lists" have stood for each Israeli election, beginning with the first in 1949. Yet as I will argue later, contrary to theoretical expectations, not a single successful Sephardi party (as defined here) emerged out of the massive wave of Sephardi immigration. In what follows, I initially describe the political developments of the first three decades (through the 1977 election), after which I turn to the more recent decades (1981 onwards).

Between 1949 and 1977, an average of three Sephardi parties contested each election. The Sephardi parties that contested the 1949 election were effectively continuations of Mandatory period parties, which had enjoyed some success in elections to the legislature of the pre-state Jewish community. However, their organizers were the veteran Sephardim.[38] They proceeded "paradoxically" to fade away in the face of post-state Sephardi immigration (Horowitz and Lissak 1989, 68): as early as 1955, they began splitting apart and then dying off, presumably because they were unable to absorb the new immigrants (Herzog 1985a, 45). At about the same time (beginning in 1951), new parties founded after the establishment of the state by recent Sephardi immigrants with a political entrepreneurial bent began to emerge, but none lasted long.[39] The numbers of these parties tapered off

---

[37]Tables C.1–C.3 in Appendix C provide more detail about these parties and their electoral performance.

[38]See Lissak (1972, 264–265), Herzog (1984, 524), and Herzog (1986, 292). To elaborate, Swirski (1989, 45) argues that they were "dismissed as the particularistic representation of the old-time Sephardic elite of Jerusalem."

[39]A vivid illustration is provided by the chart of splits and mergers in Herzog (1986, 292).

Election	Number Contesting	Highest Individual Party Vote Share	Highest Individual Party Seat Share	Collective Vote Share	Collective Seat Share
1949	2	3.5	3.3	4.5	4.2
1951	3	1.7	1.7	3.5	2.5
1955	3	0.82	0.0	1.4	0.0
1959	4	0.85	0.0	1.6	0.0
1961	2	0.32	0.0	0.32	0.0
1965	2	0.93	0.0	1.1	0.0
1969	1	0.15	0.0	0.15	0.0
1973	5	0.85	0.0	2.2	0.0
1977	4	0.83	0.0	1.6	0.0
1981	5	2.3	2.5	2.6	2.5
1984	4	3.1	3.3	4.9	4.2
1988	1	4.7	5.0	4.7	5.0
1992	1	4.9	5.0	4.9	5.0
1996	2	8.5	8.3	8.9	8.3
1999	1	13	14	13	14
2003	2	8.2	9.2	8.4	9.2
2006	2	9.5	10	10	10
2009	1	8.5	9.2	8.5	9.2

Table 5.4: The entry and electoral performance of Sephardi sectarian parties. Source: Tables C.1–C.3 in Appendix C.

in the 1960s but experienced a resurgence beginning in 1973, when five new parties appeared.

While the two parties of the veteran Sephardim won a few Knesset seats in the 1949 and 1951 elections, in the next seven elections Sephardi parties failed to draw significant electoral support (Shafir and Peled 2002, 89). From 1955 through 1977, none managed to get passed the low electoral threshold (at the time, one percent of valid votes) for attaining representation in the Knesset, as shown by Table 5.4. Yet it must be noted that a lack of coordination at the elite level did hinder Sephardi attempts to attain sectarian representation during this period: in all of the early elections except for

---

One potential objection to studying these parties is that not all of them were "real" parties: in the 1950s, some openly announced ties to and received assistance from a broad-based "mother" party (e.g., Smooha 1978, 128), while in later years, some received covert support (e.g., Herzog 1983, 126–127). But this objection has little force. Even if we recognize that these Sephardi parties were affiliates or satellites of catch-all parties, their existence still begs two important questions: (i) why even these semi-independent parties stood for election instead of allowing the Sephardi community to be *directly* represented by a catch-all party, and (ii) what, if any, normative consequences followed from this strategic choice.

those in 1961 and 1969, Sephardi parties collectively received enough votes to scrape over the electoral threshold, if barely, even though individually they fell short.

This failure to obtain Knesset seats does not directly speak to my criteria for evaluating the success of sectarian parties, however: we want to know the extent of *Sephardi* support for these Sephardi parties. That is, the relevant question is whether Sephardi parties managed to capture the votes of a majority of the Sephardim who were eligible to vote; a plurality; or neither. There are two ways to answer this question.

The first and simplest approach is to compare the parties' vote shares to the Sephardi share of Israel's electorate. If we somewhat reasonably assume that only Sephardim voted for Sephardi parties,[40] a rough estimate of the proportion of eligible Sephardi voters who cast their ballots for each Sephardi party, a measure of individual party success, can be obtained by dividing the party's vote share by the Sephardi share of the electorate. Accordingly, for each election year, Table 5.5 presents the most conservative available estimate of the Sephardi proportion of the Israeli electorate, as well as the measure of individual Sephardi party success just described, which is calculated using these estimates and the election results reported in Table 5.4.[41] The table also presents a measure of collective party success: the proportion of the Sephardi electorate that voted for one of these Sephardi parties in each election, calculated using this same data. These statistics appear in the first three columns of the table.

The second and arguably more direct way is to make use of survey data. Sephardi party success can be straightforwardly evaluated by drawing upon surveys that asked Israelis about both their ethnicity (defined as place of birth and father's place of birth, as usual) and their voting intentions. From 1969 onwards, when the Israeli National Election Studies (INES) began, it is possible to take this approach. Prior to 1965, however, systematic survey data is not available, so the simple comparison of vote shares to the relative size of the electorate just described must suffice.[42] The fourth column of Table 5.5 presents this measure of individual Sephardi party success: the percentage of Sephardim out of the total number of Sephardim surveyed who either expressed the intent to vote for or recalled voting for each Sephardi party, depending upon whether the survey was pre- or post-election.[43] For

---

[40]Smooha (1978, 177–178) took a similar approach for the Israeli case, as did Chandra (2004) for the Indian case, although she more crudely compared vote shares to population shares. See Appendix B for evidence as to the reasonableness of this assumption, as well as for more about this approach to measuring party success in general.

[41]I use conservative estimates because this favors the success of Sephardi parties. What makes these estimates conservative is that they do not classify any third-generation Israelis, whose ethnicity is unknown (as discussed in a prior section), as Sephardi. See Appendix B for more information.

[42]Survey data is available for 1965 because the 1969 INES survey respondents were asked about their votes in the 1965 election, although these responses should obviously be taken with a hearty grain of salt.

[43]This means that the total includes those who did not vote, who were undecided, and who

	Election Returns and Demographics			Survey Data	
Election	Electorate, Percent Sephardi	Highest Percent Voting for Individual Sephardi Party	Percent Collectively Voting for Sephardi Parties	Percent Voting for Individual Sephardi Parties	Percent Collectively Voting for Sephardi Parties
1949	16	21	28		
1951	24	7.0	14		
1955	27	3.0	5.1		
1959	30	2.8	5.3		
1961	34	0.96	0.96		
1965	36	2.6	3.0	"An ethnic party": 0.40; "Another party": 2.5	2.9
1969	37	0.41	0.41	"An ethnic party": 1.7	1.7
1973	37	2.3	5.9	"Other": 0.40	0.40
1977	38	2.2	4.2	"Other": 0.60	0.60
1981	39	5.9	6.7	"Abu Hatzira's list" [Tami]: 1.6; "An ethnic party": 0.40; "Other party": 0.40	2.4
1984	38	8.2	13	Agudat Yisrael + Shas: 1.3; Tami: 0.40; "Ethnic party": 0.20; "Other party": 0.60	2.5
1988	40	12	12	Shas: 2.8; "Other": 0.0	2.8

Table 5.5: The success of Sephardi parties in Israel in each election evaluated using two approaches: (i) election results and demographic data (conservative estimates) and (ii) survey data. Continued on next page. Source: demographic data based on CBS (1967), CBS (1969), and CBS SA; success calculated using this data combined with individual and collective party vote shares from Table 5.4; survey data based on INES. See Appendix B for the demographic data and Appendix C for the survey data.

	Election Returns and Demographics			Survey Data	
Election	Electorate, Percent Sephardi	Highest Percent Voting for Individual Sephardi Party	Percent Collectively Voting for Sephardi Parties	Percent Voting for Individual Sephardi Parties	Percent Collectively Voting for Sephardi Parties
1992	37	13	13	Shas: 3.2; "Other party": 0.70	3.9
1996	35	24	26	Shas: 2.5; "Another party": 0.3	2.8
1999	34	39	39	Shas: 5.1; "Another party": 0.0	5.1
2003	31	26	27	Shas: 4.0; Love of Israel: 0.0	4.0
2006	30	32	33	Shas: 14	14
2009	30	29	29	Shas: 7.5	7.5

Table 5.5: Continued from previous page.

years when a specific Sephardi party was not offered as a choice to survey respondents, the proportion of the surveyed Sephardim choosing "an ethnic party" is presented instead; additionally, or for years when even this was not a choice, the proportion of those choosing "other" appears in the table. This expansive definition of Sephardi parties obviously favors their success. To evaluate the collective success of Sephardi parties, the final column of Table 5.5 sums over the individual party percentages for each election. It is important to note that one advantage of the survey data approach is that it allows an evaluation of whether parties were *moderately* successful at both individual and collective levels. However, in the interests of space, the table does not summarize the proportion of Sephardim who reported voting for each non-Sephardi party in the table.

Momentarily focusing upon the pre-1981 portions of Table 5.5, it shows that *not one* of the Sephardi parties competing in Israel's first three decades was individually successful according to my definition. Nor were Sephardi parties collectively successful during this period. The best performance, both individually and collectively, was in 1949, when about 30 percent of the Sephardi electorate collectively voted for Sephardi parties and about a quarter individually voted for the National Union of Sephardis. Yet, as already noted, this success came prior to the real influx of post-state Sephardi immigrants, which began only in 1950. Hence, contrary to the hypothesis, increasing social heterogeneity *reduced* the number of successful Sephardi parties in the young Israel. So for which parties were the Sephardim voting during this period, given that they were not voting for Sephardi parties? Until 1973, an overwhelming plurality voted for the forerunner of today's Labor party, the major party of the center-left and Israel's dominant party until 1977.[44] After 1973, the plurality to majority instead voted for Likud, the major party of the center-right (ibid.).[45] Accordingly, in Israel's early

---

refused to respond. A comparison of the INES data from Table 5.5 to the vote shares of Table 5.4 suggests that the INES tends to underestimate the support of Sephardi parties. This in turn suggests that the undecided and nonresponsive respondents, of which there were often many, may have broken heavily towards Sephardi parties (see, for example, Peres, Yuchtman, and Shafat 1975 for the systematic tendency for respondents to understate support for non-mainstream parties in Israel's early years). The observed underestimation may also be due to the fact that I have again defined "Sephardi" conservatively given the lack of information about the ethnicity of third-generation Israelis. However, instead classifying as Sephardim all third-generation Israelis and others not classified as Ashkenazim (such as those who declared ethnicity irrelevant) generally paints a more unfavorable portrait of Sephardi party success. See Appendix C for details.

[44]Shafir and Peled (2002, 89) go further and argue that it was a majority. For example, of the Sephardim surveyed by the 1969 INES, approximately 40 percent reported voting for the Labor Alignment (that is, Labor "aligned" with a smaller party on the left, Mapam) in both 1965 and 1969.

[45]For example, in 1973, 37 percent of the Sephardim surveyed by the INES reported voting for Likud and 32 percent for the Labor Alignment; in 1977, 49 percent reported voting for Likud and only 16 percent for the Alignment. This swing of Sephardi votes from Labor to Likud was largely responsible for bringing Likud to power for the first time (Shafir and Peled 2002, 89), ushering in the first turnover of government in Israel's history. Swirski (1989, 45) nevertheless argues that the initial "big success" of the Sephardim was the 1981 reelection of the Likud

years, Sephardi voters preferred what I have called broad-based or catch-all parties to sectarian ones (see, for example, Herzog 1995, 88). This means that Sephardi parties did not even attain *moderate* success during this period in that they failed to capture a plurality of Sephardi votes.[46]

But did all of these parties in fact target the Sephardim as a collectivity? The answer is "no." Particularly in the 1950s, some of the parties just described actually aimed only to represent subgroups of the Sephardim. The smaller of these groups was Jewish Israelis with origins in the single country of Yemen, and the larger was those with origins in the multicountry region of North Africa. To fairly assess the success of these parties, their vote shares should be compared to their more narrowly defined target constituencies' shares of the electorate, given the lack of survey data for this time period.[47] First, the Yemeni share of Israel's electorate has conservatively ranged from a high of about five percent in 1949 to a low of about three percent in 2006. None of the parties that sought to represent this group were successful on either the individual or collective level.[48] Like the Sephardim as a whole, their greatest success came in the very early elections and tapered off from there. For example, the Yemeni party contesting Israel's first election in 1949 captured the votes of 22 percent of the Yemeni electorate, but in 1959, only 4 percent of the Yemeni electorate voted for the Yemeni party. Second, the North African share of Israel's electorate conservatively increased from a low of about 4 percent in 1949 to a high of about 21 percent in 1977, after which it declined to about 16 percent in 2006. But once again, the only North African party to contest elections, the Union of Independent North African Immigrants in 1959, was not successful: it captured the votes of only seven percent of the North African electorate.[49] Accordingly, like the Sephardim as a whole, sectarian parties did not successfully emerge to represent these subgroups of Sephardim.

Turning to the more recent period, did political entrepreneurs continue to create Sephardi parties from the 1980s through the present day, and if so, how did these parties fare at the polls? Table 5.4 shows that an average of two and a half Sephardi parties contested elections during these three decades: fewer than in the earlier years, but still a goodly number. How-

---

government, which again owed much to Sephardi votes: this event proved that 1977 had not been an accident, and hence led the Sephardim to recognize their collective political power in a way that 1977 alone had not.

[46]Sephardi lists did achieve greater success in local elections, as well as in elections to the Histradrut (the Jewish Labor Federation), during this period. But here, too, both the number of lists running and their success tapered off over the years, mirroring the national-level trend (Smooha 1978, 128; see also Lissak 1972).

[47]Again, see Appendix B for these estimates.

[48]The following parties are classified as Yemeni: the 1949, 1951, and 1955 Yemenite Association; the 1955 Sons of Yemen Movement; the 1959 Yemenite Faction; the 1961 Yemenite Immigrants List; and the 1973 Yemenis List.

[49]Herzog (1986, 289) also identifies a second North African party garnering 0.2% of the vote in this election (see also many of her other studies), but I can find no other reference to this party, and it is absent from official Israeli election results.

ever, from 1988 onwards, only one or two parties have contested elections, a demonstration of better elite-level coordination over time. The story undergoes a significant twist, however, with regard to the success of these parties. Sephardi parties at long last began to improve their electoral performance. Herzog (1995, 88) has classified two parties that appeared in the 1980s, Tami and Shas, as the only successful "ethnic" (Sephardi) parties in Israel's history; Shafir and Peled (2002, 93), by contrast, believe that Shas alone is deserving of this label. Nevertheless, Sephardi parties remained unsuccessful according to my definition in more recent decades, although in testament to their improved performance, one eventually did become moderately successful.

Tami appeared in 1981 and ran again in 1984. It was the first Sephardi party to break the glass ceiling of obtaining representation in the Knesset since 1955: it won three seats in 1981 and one seat in 1984. However, it was still not a successful party as I have defined it. Table 5.5 shows that it captured the votes of only six percent of the Sephardi electorate in 1981, its peak performance; moreover, this same table reveals that only two percent of the Sephardim surveyed by the INES expressed an intent to vote for it in that election.[50] The clearer success story is Shas, which appeared in 1984. In this election, it won four Knesset seats, individually tying the seat-earning record set by a Sephardi party in the 1949 election, and captured the votes of 12 percent of the Sephardi electorate, although only 3 percent of the surveyed Sephardim expressed an intent to vote for it (see Table 5.5). Shas's peak performance came in 1999, when it captured the votes of almost 40 percent of the Sephardi electorate. Based on analyses of geographic areas with high concentrations of Sephardim, some have argued that in this election, "Likud lost to Shas the status it had enjoyed since 1977, that of the largest Sephardi political party" (Shafir and Peled 2002, 94). However, the survey data from the 1999 INES shows Shas failing to capture even a plurality of the Sephardi vote. Hence, using my criteria, Shas *at best* can be classified as a moderate success because it has taken no more than a plurality of the Sephardi vote.

What complicates any evaluation of the success of both Shas and Tami is that they are not solely Sephardi parties: they are also *religious* parties (e.g., Herzog 1995; Tepe and Baum 2008). For example, Shas is a breakaway from Agudat Israel, the original party of the non-Zionist, ultra-Orthodox (*haredi*, plural *haredim*) Jewish community. Both its spiritual and temporal leaders and, most importantly, its founders have been ultra-Orthodox Sephardim. Further, its claims have been formulated in religious as well as in ethnic terms (ibid).[51] Hence, one possible characterization of Shas is that it targets a religiously defined subgroup of the Sephardim: those Sephardim who are

---

[50] If we more narrowly view Tami as a North African party, as some have suggested (e.g., Shamir and Arian 1983, 99), it fares better but still falls short of success: for example, it captured the votes of 12 percent of the North African electorate in 1981.

[51] However, others have argued that is hard to find political demands that refer specifically to Sephardi culture, that is, to ethnicity, in Shas's official pronouncements (Shafir and Peled 2002, 93). These scholars accordingly paint the party as more religious than ethnic.

5. Israel: New Parties for New Groups?

religious, from the merely traditional to the ultra-Orthodox. From this perspective, it is not a *Sephardi* sectarian party as I have defined it, although it is sectarian; in Chandra's (2004) terms, it is a nonethnic party because of its emphasis on the cross-cutting division of religion. Another possible characterization of Shas is that it does not exclusively seek to represent even this subgroup of the Sephardim. Instead, it is a movement that articulates the interests of the "popular strata" who have been excluded from the center of Israeli society and who seek to transform that society in order to take their rightful place in it; this constituency includes the Sephardim and the ultra-Orthodox, but also national minorities such as Arab Israelis (see, for example, Shafir and Peled 2002, 94).[52] From this perspective, while it may still be a sectarian party, it is not a *Sephardi* sectarian party. If we were to compare Shas's vote share to the size of its more narrowly defined constituency, the religious Sephardi electorate, it would be more successful than in the portrait just painted. Alternatively, if we take into account its broader appeals to groups such as Israeli Arabs, it would be less successful.

What about parties that sought to represent subgroups of the Sephardim during this period? There is really only one example of such a sectarian party: the Ethiopian party "One Future" (Atid Echad) that activist Avraham Neguise organized for the 2006 election. With the Ethiopians constituting a little more than one percent of the Israeli electorate in 2006 (see Appendix B), this party captured about one-third of the Ethiopian vote. This means that it was not successful, even though it fared better at the polls among its target constituency than did any other party attempting to represent a subgroup of the Sephardim since Israel's founding.

Russians

Table 5.6 summarizes the appearance and electoral performance of Russian sectarian parties, which were again identified by drawing upon both the academic literature and popular accounts in the media. This table shows that with the exception of 1988, at least one sectarian political party has sought to represent Russian immigrants in Israel in every election since 1981. Political entrepreneurs have accordingly sought to supply the Russians, like the Sephardim, with sectarian representation. However, in contrast to Israel's Sephardi parties, Russian parties have been both individually and collectively successful.

Prior to the large-scale wave of Russian immigration in the 1990s, only two Russian parties competed in Israeli elections: the List for Russian Immigrants in 1981 and Young and Immigration in 1984. This is a small number of parties over a period of almost two decades (that is, from 1973 to 1988).

---

[52] For example, Willis (1995, 131) describes how Shas appealed to Israeli Arabs in 1992 on the grounds of their religiosity and the discrimination that they, like the Sephardim, have faced, which netted Shas close to 13,000 Arab votes. Further, Tepe and Baum (2008) discuss the increasing prominence of social (class and ethnic) issues in the party's appeals since 1999 under the leadership of Eli Yishai.

Election	Number Contesting	Highest Individual Party Vote Share	Highest Individual Party Seat Share	Collective Vote Share	Collective Seat Share
1981	1	0.36	0.0	0.36	0.0
1984	1	0.28	0.0	0.28	0.0
1988	0	0.0	0.0	0.0	0.0
1992	3	0.45	0.0	0.45	0.0
1996	2	5.7	5.8	6.5	5.8
1999	4	5.2	5.0	8.3	8.3
2003	4	5.5	5.8	7.7	7.5
2006	3	9.0	9.2	9.1	9.2
2009	3	12	13	12	13

Table 5.6: The entry and electoral performance of Russian sectarian parties. Source: Table C.4 in Appendix C.

The literature has had little to say about these parties.[53] Both emerged following the wave of Russian immigration in the 1970s and campaigned to represent this constituency.

Following the wave of Russian immigration that began in 1990, more sectarian parties that targeted the Russian community appeared: between two and four in each subsequent election, with about three Russian parties competing on average. The 1992 election saw the creation of three new Russian parties. Early that year, a party calling itself Democracy and Immigration but known by the acronym "DA" ("yes" in Russian) was formed under the leadership of Yuli Kosharovsky, a well-known Soviet Jewish activist and immigrant of 1989. Largely the creation of earlier (pre-1990) Russian immigrants, it aimed to improve the resettlement or absorption of the newer (post-1989) immigrants (Gitelman 1995). However, the most prominent figure in the Russian community, Natan Sharansky, declined to support the party publicly.[54] The other parties characterized as Russian that were created to contest this election were the Movement for Israel Renewal (Tali), led by 1970s Russian immigrant Robert Golan, and Pensioners and Immigrants (Yad b'Yad).[55] Like DA, both of these parties placed the need for better absorption of Russian immigrants, from employment to economic assistance,

---
[53]See, for example, Khanin (2001, 2004), who notes only their failure—an issue to which I will return.

[54]Sharansky, formerly known as Anatoly Shcharansky, had arrived in Israel in 1986 after his release from a Siberian labor camp. He was a refusenik and the most prominent of the "Prisoners of Zion," a group of Soviet Jews who had been imprisoned for their Zionist beliefs and activities. See, for example, Herzog (1995) and Reich, Wurmser, and Dropkin (1994).

[55]Siegel (1998, 145) alone identifies a fourth Russian party: One Folk (Am Ehad).

5. Israel: New Parties for New Groups?

at the center of their agendas (e.g., Reich, Wurmser, and Dropkin 1994; Bick 1997). However, while Pensioners included two Russian immigrants on its list of candidates, it did not primarily—let alone exclusively—target the Russian community; accordingly, it is not really a Russian sectarian party as per my definition, although I include it here due to its treatment in both the literature and the media.

Two new Russian parties appeared in 1996 to replace the defunct parties from the 1992 election, the most prominent of which was Israel b'Aliya, which translates as both "Israel on the Rise" and "Israel in Immigration." This party emerged out of the Zionist Forum of Soviet Jewry, an umbrella organization founded by ex-Soviet dissidents in 1988 and headed by Natan Sharansk with the goal of aiding the absorption of Russian immigrants. This party aimed to represent the interests of Russian immigrants while positioning itself at the center of the political spectrum. An argument against classifying Israel b'Aliya as a *Russian* sectarian party is that to some extent its appeal was directed to all immigrants, not just to Russians. Particularly, it reached out to the Anglo-Saxon community (see, for example, Siegel 1998; Khanin 2004).[56] However, the substantially greater weight it placed on representing the Russian community, as well as the small roles played by Anglo-Saxons, leads me to concur with the dominant characterization of the party as Russian.[57] Also emerging to compete in this election was the Unity and Aliya (Edinstvo and Aliya) party, led by two Russian immigrants from the 1970s. This short-lived party cultivated the support of Russians from the Central Asian and Caucasus regions (Bick 1997); specifically, it targeted those from Georgia (Khanin 2001).

New sectarian parties competed with Israel b'Aliya to represent the Russian community in the 1999 election. The most important was Israel Beiteinu, which translates as "Israel Our Home." This party was founded in early 1999 by Avigdor Lieberman, who had immigrated from Moldova in 1978. Its core consisted of activists from the "Russian Likud" who disliked Netanyahu's concessions to the Palestinians and felt that their ambitions were being ignored by the Likud leadership (Khanin 2004). This new party was quickly joined by a breakaway faction from Israel b'Aliya (Khanin 2001).[58] Two other new parties challenged the front-runners. The first, Hope

---

[56] For example, Zvi Weinberg, a Canadian who immigrated in 1992, was placed sixth on the party's list. There is some disagreement in the literature about the party's targeting of Ethiopian immigrants, with both Siegel (1998, 161) and Khanin (2004, 162) arguing that it did, but Bick (1997, 134) arguing that it did not.

[57] For one, only once during the election campaign did Sharansky appeal in Hebrew to the Israeli public; in most television appearances and meetings, he spoke Russian (Siegel 1998, 173). For another, the first five places on the party's list all went to Russians who had immigrated in either the 1980s or early 1990s, as did the seventh place. Moreover, the Canadian in the fifth place was fluent in Russian and had been active in the struggle on behalf of Soviet Jews (Bick 1997, 134).

[58] Three months after the election, another faction split away from Israel b'Aliya, although this faction leaned to the left. This faction became the Democratic Choice (Habehira Hademocratit) party. However, because this party never independently contested an election, it does not

(Tikva in Hebrew, Nadezhda in Russian), made the struggle for civil marriage one of the centerpieces of its campaign and was widely viewed as a satellite of Labor (Khanin 2001). The second, Heart of Immigrants (Lev), targeted a subset of the Russian immigrant community: Bukharian, Georgian, and Caucus Jews, who are often viewed as Sephardi; however, many prominent figures in this community instead supported other parties, ranging from the catch-all Likud to the Sephardi Shas (ibid.).

The 2003 election saw the birth of two more small parties: the ephemeral Citizen and the State (Ezrach Umedina) party and the Progressive Liberal Democratic Party (Leeder). Both were founded by 1990s Russian immigrants. The latter sought to represent ethnic Slavs with anti-Jewish sentiments, on the one hand, and to serve as the Israeli branch of the Russian Liberal Democratic party, on the other; the former targeted both Armenian immigrants and non-Jewish Russians with an anticlerical appeal (Khanin 2004). Interestingly, Israel Beiteinu fought the 2003 election as part of a coalition with a hawkish right-wing party, the National Union (Ihud Haleumi). Security and the Israeli-Palestinian conflict dominated the coalition's agenda, as it did the election as a whole (ibid.). For this election, this calls into question the standard classification of Israel Beiteinu as a Russian party.[59] However, for consistency with the literature, and in light of the fact that it parted ways with the National Union for the 2006 election, I nevertheless classify it as a Russian sectarian party in 2003. The other major subsequent elite-level development was that shortly after the 2003 elections, Israel b'Aliya merged with the Likud and thereby passed from the political scene. The most recent elections in 2006 and 2009 were accordingly fought only by a once-more independent Israel Beiteinu; a resuscitated Heart of Immigrants from the 1999 election; and the Leeder party from the 2003 election.

But what degree of support were these Russian sectarian parties able to attract from their target constituency of Russian immigrants? Table 5.7 summarizes their success using the same two approaches that were used to evaluate the success of Sephardi parties: comparing actual election results to demographic data and examining survey data. However, because Russian immigrants can be clearly identified in the Israeli National Election Studies (INES) only from 2003 onwards, and because other surveys of Russian voting behavior, such as exit polls, do exist and appear to have greater external validity, the table presents estimates of voting behavior drawn from sources other than the INES.[60] Even though the latter forms the basis for the following discussion, in the name of consistency, INES data is presented in parentheses for the years for which it is available.

While not shown in Table 5.7, surveys of the first wave of Russian immigrants throughout the 1970s show them with political affiliations similar

---

appear in either Table 5.6 or Appendix C's Table C.4.

[59]For example, of the top seven candidates on the joint list of the National Union–Israel Beiteinu (the candidates who would become its seven MKs), only three were Russian.

[60]This includes exit polls, other surveys, and analyses of votes by geographic areas with varying concentrations of immigrants. See Appendix C for more detail.

	Election Returns and Demographics			Survey Data	
Election	Electorate, Percent Russian	Highest Individual Party Share of Russian Vote	Collective Share of Russian Vote	Percent Voting for Individual Russian Parties	Percent Collectively Voting for Russian Parties
1981	5.4	7.4	7.4		
1984	5.1	5.8	5.8		
1992	13	3.1	5.8	DA: 5.5	5.5
1996	15	39	44	Israel b'Aliya: 38; Unity and Aliya: 5	43
1999	18	30	47	Israel b'Aliya: 35 (13) ; Israel Beiteinu: 17 (1.1)	52 (14)
2003	19	29	41	Israel Beiteinu/National Union: 24 (12); Israel b'Aliya: 16 (4.7); Leeder: (0.0); Citizen and State: (0.0)	40 (17)
2006	18	49	50	Israel Beiteinu: 48 (57); "Other": (0.0)	48 (57)
2009	17	69	69	Israel Beiteinu: 50 (50)	50 (50)

Table 5.7: The success of Russian parties in Israel evaluated using actual election results and demographic data: (i) election results and demographic data and (ii) survey data. Source: demographic data based on CBS SA and Gitelman (1982); success calculated using this data combined with individual and collective party vote shares from Table 5.6; survey data based on INES (in parentheses); Reich, Wurmser, and Dropkin (1994) for 1992; Bick (1997), Horowitz (1999), and Gitelman and Goldstein (2002) for 1996; Gitelman and Goldstein (2002) for 1999; Goldstein and Gitelman (2005) for 2003; Konstantinov (2008) for 2006; and Khanin (2009) for 2009. See Appendix B for the demographic data and Appendix C for the survey data.

to those of the Jewish electorate as a whole (e.g., Gitelman 1995, 21), and, more specifically, show them identifying with the two largest parties, Likud and Labor (Gitelman 1982, 276). This suggests that most voted for catch-all instead of for Russian sectarian parties in the 1981 and 1984 elections. This same pattern was observed in the 1992 election. Specifically, exit polls found that approximately 60 percent of Russians supported Labor and parties to its left, with the plurality of just under 50 percent voting for Labor. By way of contrast, only approximately 6 percent supported DA, the most successful of the three Russian sectarian parties (e.g., Reich, Wurmser, and Dropkin 1994; Gitelman and Goldstein 2002). Table 5.7 also underscores the poor performance of Russian parties in these elections: the share of the Russian electorate casting votes for Russian parties was in the single digits throughout. Hence, Russian parties had not even attained moderate success as of 1992.

This changed in 1996, when Russian parties broke through the glass ceiling and obtained their first Knesset seats. Exit polls showed that a plurality of approximately 40 percent of Russians cast a sectarian vote for Israel b'Aliya (e.g., Bick 1997; Horowitz 1999; Gitelman and Goldstein 2002). This means that in this election, Israel b'Aliya became the first moderately successful Russian party, even though Russian parties still collectively fell short of achieving success—judgments that the comparison of vote shares to shares of the electorate in Table 5.7 confirm. Continuing the trend, the 1999 election saw the first full-fledged collective if not individual Russian party success: exit polls found that slightly more than half of Russian voters cast a sectarian Knesset ballot, and the demographic data for all intents and purposes concurs. The exit polls also show that the plurality again voted for Israel b'Aliya (e.g., Gitelman and Goldstein 2002; Goldstein and Gitelman 2005). This suggests that better elite coordination in this election might have led to an individually successful Russian party. Russian parties were less successful on both the individual and collective levels in 2003. Only approximately 40 percent cast sectarian ballots according to both the survey and demographic approaches, with the plurality narrowly going to Likud over Israel Beiteinu/National Union (e.g., Goldstein and Gitelman 2005). Of note is the eclipse of Israel b'Aliya by Israel Beiteinu/National Union in this election: the former's support fell drastically, while the latter only just fell short of attaining moderate individual success. Russian parties' fortunes again rose in 2006, however, when both the survey and demographic data suggest that between slightly less than half and slightly more than half of Russian voters cast a sectarian ballot for Israel Beiteinu (e.g., Konstantinov 2008; Philippov 2008). Accordingly, I view this as the first individual success of a Russian party, and the second collective Russian success. Israel Beiteinu's star continued to rise in 2009, when it became the third-largest party in the Knesset. This election accordingly again saw both individual and collective success for Russian parties.

For the Russian parties that targeted subgroups of Russians (the 1996

Unity and Aliya and 1999 and 2006 Heart of Immigrants parties), their performance obviously improves when their vote shares are compared to the subgroups' smaller shares of the electorate. However, while it is difficult to say absent hard data, it is doubtful that either of these parties would satisfy my criteria for success even when taking this approach.[61]

5.3 CONCLUSION

Immigration has led to substantial changes in Israel's social heterogeneity. Two large-scale waves of immigration effectively added two new ethnic groups to Israeli society: the Sephardim in the 1950s and 1960s and the Russians in the 1990s, although there was also a smaller wave of Russian immigration in the 1970s.

In this chapter, I explored the implications of these increases in social heterogeneity for the fragmentation of the party system in Israel. These new social groups, like any new social group in a democracy, had to choose between two different ways of obtaining political representation: forming their own sectarian political parties or being absorbed by the existing party system, with representation being supplied by broadly based, catch-all parties. Given the extremely permissive electoral system that Israel has employed throughout its history, the expectation drawn from the existing literature was that the Sephardim and Russians in Israel would choose the former and successfully form sectarian parties to represent themselves in the Knesset, Israel's parliament. Why? As Cox (1997) has influentially argued, when the electoral system poses little of a barrier to the entry of new parties, new groups—particularly new *ethnic* groups—will demand representation, and elites will supply it in the form of new parties. There is little incentive for the masses to engage in strategic voting, and accordingly little incentive for elites to engage in strategic entry.

Yet this is not what happened in Israel. Despite the electoral system being held constant, there has been variation in sectarian party success over both *time* and *groups*. To date, only one of the two groups has eventually followed the predicted path: the Russians. From the 1980s onwards, political entrepreneurial elites attempted to supply the Russian community in Israel with representation in the form of sectarian political parties. While Russians initially tended to support existing catch-all parties, since 1996 they have consistently provided substantial support for their own sectarian parties. Certainly, to date, it is "premature" to conclude that political assimilation for the Russian community is on the horizon (Goldstein and Gitelman 2005, 256–257). By way of contrast, while Sephardi elites have also attempted to supply the Sephardi community with sectarian representation since Israel's first election in 1949, these attempts have largely foundered at the mass level:

---

[61] For example, if the target audience of both is taken to be Central Asian Russians, a rough estimate is that Unity and Aliya captured about 40 percent of the Central Asian Russian vote in 1996, whereas Heart of Immigrant's best performance in 1999 was about 9 percent.

until recently, Sephardi voters have failed to flock to the banners unfurled by these elites. The consequence is that Sephardi parties have yet to capture the votes of a majority of the Sephardim, leaving the Sephardim receiving representation primarily from existing catch-all parties. However, in the late 1990s, what is arguably a Sephardi party did manage to capture a plurality of the Sephardi vote—what I have called a moderate success.

Hence, the Israeli case illustrates that the effect of social heterogeneity upon party system fragmentation depends upon factors other than the electoral system. The overarching question raised by this chapter is accordingly what these other conditioning factors are. That is, what can explain why the Russians but not the Sephardim have managed to successfully launch their own sectarian parties? And what can explain why Shas, the greatest Sephardi success story, took so long to appear, and even longer to attain its moderate success in the late 1990s? Similarly, what can explain why was it only in 1996 that Russian parties began to achieve success? In the next chapter, drawing upon the theory developed in Chapter 2, I will attempt to provide some answers to these questions.

6 Israel: Testing Hypotheses about Sectarian Party Success

The last chapter closed with several puzzles. For one, what can explain the different political trajectories of Sephardi and Russian immigrants in Israel? Specifically, why have the Russians been more successful at forming sectarian political parties than the Sephardim have been? For another, what can explain the specific timing of the success of these new, latent social groups' sectarian parties? At a more general level, then, the puzzle is why increases in social heterogeneity have only *sometimes* increased party system fragmentation in Israel, despite its extremely permissive electoral system.

From the perspective of the existing literature, the failure of some of the new social groups added to Israeli society by immigration to obtain sectarian representation makes Israel a "deviant case" in need of explanation (Lijphart 1971, 692–693; see also Rogowski 2004, 77–83). A within-case analysis of such a case provides an "opportunity to discover the processes that caused the case to diverge from the hypothesized outcome" (Munck 2004, 118). Hence, another reason for conducting a case study of Israel is to fine-tune the argument. By holding constant the political institution upon which the existing literature has focused, the electoral system, I can explore how other factors matter.

These other factors are the focus of this chapter. Using the variation in sectarian party success across both immigrant groups and time in Israel uncovered in the last chapter, I test the theory I developed in Chapter 2 about how factors other than the electoral system shape the likelihood of sectarian party success, the primary mechanism by which social heterogeneity affects party system fragmentation. This allows me to triangulate the results of my two prior quantitative analyses. Of particular importance here, the quantitative empirical analyses found little support for my hypothesis about party system openness. Evidence from the Israeli case can accordingly help to tilt the scale one way or the other. But hypothesis testing using the Israeli case also allows me to bring empirical evidence to bear against my hypotheses that either have not yet been tested, such as that about the strategies played by existing parties, or have been tested only indirectly, such as those about the effects of a new social group's size and politicization.

Specifically, comparing the characteristics of the two immigrant groups studied, the Sephardim and the Russians, at any one point in time holds constant the systemic features of the polity. To the extent that the variation in the outcome of interest, the success of the group's sectarian political parties, corresponds to the variation in the group characteristic (Mill's Method of Difference), the group characteristic can be viewed as an explanatory factor. Similarly, holding constant the group and its characteristics allows one to see how variation in the features of the polity correspond to variation in the success of the group's sectarian parties over time. Of course, some group characteristics have varied over time, and all save one of the systemic features of the polity cannot be held constant simultaneously; this well-known "many variables" (Lijphart 1971) problem of the comparative method means that I cannot come to definite conclusions regarding each variable's causal status. Nevertheless, some variables can be eliminated from consideration, and suggestively supportive evidence in favor of others can be amassed. Moreover, sharp changes in one variable over time, when others are held reasonably constant in the short term, approximates a quasi- or natural experiment (Campbell and Ross 1968), a design that has high internal validity. My analysis of Israel's brief use of a unique type of regime in the late 1990s takes on such a quasi-experimental flavor.

Using this within-case study of Israel, I find that the regime type, party system openness, and the politicization of the new immigrant group are the primary factors that help to explain the variation in sectarian party success over time. The regime type has a particularly important role to play in explaining the marked increase in both Russian and Sephardi sectarian party success in 1996. With respect to the observed variation across new immigrant groups, I find the explanatory factors to be the strategies played by existing parties, party system openness, and group politicization. The factors that do not contribute to an explanation for the outcomes of the Israeli case are the electoral system and the type of the new social group, both of which are held constant by design, as well as the size of the group. However, while group size does not explain the differences in Sephardi and Russian sectarian party success, it does explain why other new immigrant groups in Israel have not been successfully particized.

6.1 NONEXPLANATORY FACTORS

There are three factors that, for the most part, do not contribute to an explanation for the observed variation in sectarian party success over either groups or time in Israel. The first factor is political institutional: the electoral system. The two remaining factors are group characteristics: the type of attribute defining the new latent social group and the group's size. I

6. Israel: Testing Hypotheses about Sectarian Party Success

discuss each in turn.

6.1.1 Electoral System

The first factor that cannot explain the variation in sectarian party success across either groups or time in Israel is the electoral system, the explanatory factor that has been the primary focus of the literature to date.

Israel has always employed one of the world's most permissive electoral systems, as I argued in the previous chapter. Given the low threshold for representation in the Knesset (currently two percent of valid votes); the single nationwide district; and the proportional formula for converting votes into seats, neither the Sephardim nor the Russians should have been constrained in their ability to successfully launch their own political parties by the electoral system. The absence of this important form of constraint can explain the persistent elite attempts to supply sectarian parties to the two groups, as well as the eventual at least moderate support each group's sectarian parties have obtained at the ballot box. However, the effective time invariance of this variable renders it unable to account for either the differential success of the Sephardim and the Russians in obtaining sectarian representation or the specific timing of whatever successes they have achieved.

Moreover, the minor changes to Israel's electoral system that have been made since its founding election in 1949 have *increased* its restrictiveness.[1] Given the theory I developed in Chapter 2, if these minor increases in electoral system restrictiveness were to have any effect at all, it would be to decrease sectarian party success. Yet the evidence does not bear out this prediction: over time, the Sephardim have been more successful at achieving sectarian representation, and the later-arriving Russians, facing a more restrictive electoral system, have achieved even greater success. Hence, the electoral system is not a factor that can explain the outcomes of the Israeli case.

6.1.2 Type of Attribute

Second, by design, I have held constant the type of attribute defining the new latent social groups I study in this within-case analysis of Israel: all are defined by ethnic attributes, the type of attribute deemed most likely to facilitate sectarian party success. Moreover, all have been added to Israeli society by the same historical process: immigration. Because a constant obviously cannot explain variation, this factor does not provide explanatory leverage over the outcomes of the Israeli case.

---

[1] The first of these changes was the replacement of the LR-Hare formula with the d'Hondt in 1973; the second was the raising of the threshold of representation from one to one and a half percent of valid votes in time for the 1992 election; and the third was the threshold's further rise to two percent for the 2006 election. The one exception to this claim of increasing restrictiveness was an initial switch from the d'Hondt formula to the LR-Hare for the 1951 election.

6.1.3 GROUP SIZE

The third and final factor that cannot explain the observed variation in sectarian party success across either groups or, for the most part, time is the size of each group of immigrants. Note that because of Israel's single nationwide electoral district, a group's size is always evaluated relative to that of the entire electorate.

Since Israel's founding, the Sephardim have been large enough both to win seats in the Knesset and to play a governing role. Table 5.2 showed that this group's share of the electorate is estimated to have increased from approximately 20 percent at the end of 1949 to a peak of 43 percent in 1988, after which its share of the electorate fell into the high thirties.[2] Accordingly, a Sephardi sectarian party should have been able to win at least one Knesset seat in all Israeli elections, given a threshold of representation of at most two percent. A Sephardi sectarian party should also have been able to win enough seats in the Knesset to play a governing role, given that the fragmented Israeli party system has allowed parties with as few as two seats to serve as members of the governing coalition.[3] The successful particization of the Sephardim should therefore not have been constrained by their size. Moreover, while the initial growth and later decline in the Sephardi share of the electorate somewhat mirrors the changing success of Sephardi sectarian parties over time, these gradual changes in size seem ill-suited to explaining the more abrupt changes in parties' electoral fortunes.

A similar case can be made about the Russians. Table 5.3 shows that the "mass" wave of Russian immigration took the Russian share of the electorate from between 3 to 5 percent throughout the 1970s and 1980s to 13 percent by the time of the 1992 election, a percentage that then climbed to just shy of 20 by 1999.[4] This is clearly a group that has always been large enough for its sectarian parties to win at least one seat in the Knesset. It is also a group that has been large enough to support sectarian parties capable of playing a governing role, at least since 1992. And indeed, scholars such as Khanin (2001, 107–108) have argued that one of the "internal" factors facilitating Russian party success in the mid-1990s was demographics: that by 1995, Russian immigrants exceeded 10 percent of the population, a "critical mass" for the successful appearance of sectarian immigrant parties.[5] Certainly, the

---

[2] These are the maximum percentages of the electorate that this group would command if all members of the group cast a sectarian ballot. Note that here and in what follows, the figures reported are the *best* estimates of the various groups' shares of the electorate. See also Table B.1 in Appendix B.

[3] For example, Agudat Yisrael served in Israel's third government (1951-1952), despite its having only two seats in the Knesset. Similarly, since 2009, the Jewish Home party has been a member of the current (third-second) government, despite having only three seats. These examples are low outliers, however: most parties joining governing coalitions have had at least four seats, which a Sephardi sectarian party should have easily been able to obtain.

[4] See also Table B.3 in Appendix B.

[5] It is not clear, however, why ten percent of the population (or more appropriately, the electorate) should be the critical threshold, as opposed to either a slightly smaller (say, five) or a slightly larger (say, twelve) percentage.

great increase in the Russian share of the electorate in the 1990s relative to the 1970s and 1980s, when the group was small enough to cast some doubt on the ability of any sectarian party representing it to play a governing role, contributes to an explanation of why it was only in the 1990s that Russian sectarian parties became successful.[6] Yet in light of the small differences in the Russian share of the electorate in these later years, the size of the group does not seem capable of accounting for the more specific timing of this sectarian party's success (that is, why 1996 and not 1992?).

Accordingly, group size does not contribute meaningfully to an explanation for either the differential success of Sephardi and Russian sectarian parties or, with the partial exception of the Russians, the specific timing of each group's success. However, this is not to say that group size does not matter. It *can* explain why some subgroups of the Russians and Sephardim have never been successfully particized. Examples include the 1970s Russians; one prominent subgroup of the Sephardim that elites have supplied with sectarian representation, the Yemenis; and another Sephardi subgroup, the Ethiopians, whose party achieved remarkable, if fleeting, near-success in 2006.[7] Specifically, this within-case analysis of Israel suggests that even when the electoral system is very permissive, a group must command at least approximately five percent of the electorate in order for its members to support elite attempts to supply it with sectarian representation—a low bar, but a bar nonetheless. Yet not all large groups have been successfully particized, the North Africans being a case in point. This shows that while group size may be a necessary factor for sectarian party success, it is not a sufficient one.

6.2 EXPLANATORY FACTORS

This brings me to the factors that do provide explanatory leverage over the Israeli puzzle. Drawing upon the theory I developed in Chapter 2, there are four such factors in total. Three are systemic: the regime type; the strategies

---

[6] A sectarian party representing the 1970s Russians alone would have at most been capable of winning four seats in the Knesset. This falls at the lower end of the spectrum for parties that have historically played a governing role in Israel (see note 3).

[7] For example, as shown by Table B.2 in Appendix B, the Yeminis have been large enough to win a seat in the Knesset but small enough for both elites and voters to doubt the ability of a sectarian party representing the group to play a governing role. However, another Sephardi subgroup, the Ethiopians, has been too small (commanding at most a little more than one percent of the electorate) to even win a seat in the Knesset. This makes both the appearance of a sectarian party to represent this group and the level of mass support that it managed to obtain surprising. Channeling my argument, Kadima MK Shlomo Molla, the second Ethiopian to serve in the Knesset, argued that even if the party could have gotten enough votes to pass the threshold, it would have had a "useless" one or two seats, with which nothing could have been done. Moreover, channeling Duverger, he argued that because it had failed to pass the threshold, the votes of those who had voted for the party were lost. For these reasons, he did not think that Ethiopians would support Ethiopian parties in the future (interview, June 1, 2008). Like Molla, all of the politicians and activists with whom I spoke showed a keen awareness of the size of a group as a key factor; they assessed its size at least relative to the electoral threshold and often also relative to the electorate as a whole.

played by existing parties; and the openness of the party system. One factor, by way of contrast, is a feature of the new latent social groups themselves: their politicization.

6.2.1 REGIME TYPE

Israel has always had a horizontally and vertically centralized type of regime in the tradition of the British Westministerian model, one that has "allowed the executive branch to remain relatively unchecked, and unbalanced, by the other branches of government" (Hazan 1997a, 331).[8] This may contribute to an explanation of why so many Russian and Sephardi sectarian parties have been unsuccessful. Nevertheless, there have been important changes in Israel's regime type over time. The regime type accordingly helps to explain the timing of sectarian party success in Israel, even though it does not help to explain the differences in sectarian party success across groups.

The Size of the Legislative Prize

During the final days of the twelfth Knesset, the most significant political institutional reform in Israel's history was enacted: the introduction of popular and direct elections for the prime minister.[9] The prime minister was to be elected using a majoritarian double-ballot electoral formula, similar to that used to elect the French president.[10] Further, he or she was given the sole power to form and head the cabinet, although the cabinet needed the Knesset's confidence. Finally, the prime minister and the Knesset were given the mutual power of dissolution, whereas prior to the reform only the Knesset could dissolve itself.[11] This reform took effect for the 1996 elections to

---

[8] For a general discussion of the majoritarian (Westministerian) and consensus (proportional) models, see Lijphart (1999) and Powell (2000). One important indicator of the extent to which policy-making authority has been horizontally centralized in the hands of the government is the Knesset's lack of a strong committee system that would allow the opposition to play a substantial policy-making role (e.g., Hazan 1998). Turning to the vertical dimension of the authority distribution, while Israel is formally unitary, a telling indicator of its high vertical centralization is the fiscal dominance of the national level of government. For example, between 1972 and 2000, the central (national) government's share of total government revenue has averaged a comparatively high 94 percent (World Bank Group PSG n.d.).

[9] See Arian and Shamir (1999) for a more detailed but still concise overview of the reform. An extensive literature provides additional background information, from the rationale for to the provisions of the reform. Examples include Diskin and Diskin (1995); Doron and Kay (1995); Hazan (1996, 1997a,b, 1998, 1999a,b,c, 2000); Stellman (1996); Mahler (1997); Susser (1997); Brichta (1998); Diskin (1999); Harris and Doron (1999); Ottolenghi (1999, 2001, 2002, 2004, 2007); Nachmias and Sened (1999); Aronoff (2000); De Mesquita (2000); Hazan and Diskin (2000); Hazan and Rahat (2000); Rahat (2001, 2004); Kenig (2005); and Kenig, Hazan, and Rahat (2005).

[10] This formula specified that a run-off between the two candidates with the highest number of votes would take place if no candidate received a majority in the first round.

[11] Specifically, by a special vote of eighty members, the Knesset could dismiss the prime minister and force a new election for the prime ministership; the prime minister could dissolve the Knesset with the president's approval, forcing new elections for both his or her position and the legislature; and the Knesset could bring about double elections for both itself and the

6. Israel: Testing Hypotheses about Sectarian Party Success

the fourteenth Knesset, and it was repealed in 2001. All in all, two elections for the Knesset (1996 and 1999) were held under these provisions, and three elections for the prime minister (1996, 1999, 2001).

The best way to understand the 1992 reform is that it replaced Israel's parliamentary regime with what Shugart and Carey (1992) have labeled a president–parliamentary regime (Hazan 1996, 1997a), although I note that this characterization is not without controversy.[12] To elaborate, from 1996 to 2001, a popularly elected chief executive, the directly elected prime minister (commonly referred to as a president outside of Israel), existed alongside the popularly elected legislature, the Knesset.[13] The legislature and the directly elected prime minister each had separate sources of origin (that is, were elected in separate popular elections), one of the defining characteristics of presidential regimes (Shugart and Carey 1992, 18–22). Yet at the same time, they did not have separate sources of survival, the other defining characteristic of presidentialism: as described earlier, each had the authority to oust the other in certain circumstances. In contrast to the other hybrid type of regime that combines features of parliamentarism and presidentialism, the semi- or premier-presidential (Duverger 1980), the directly elected chief executive had clear constitutional authority to dismiss the cabinet.[14]

The result was to decrease the horizontal centralization of policy-making authority in the hands of the largest party in the Knesset, which I earlier called the "size of the legislative prize." First, the president-parliamentary regime created an additional political institutional actor with policy-making authority: the directly elected prime minister, an external constraint on the largest party in the legislature's policy-making authority (Hicken and Stoll 2009). Second, the internal constraints on the largest party also increased— and drastically so (ibid.). Most importantly, the reform introduced a disjuncture between being the largest party in the Knesset and government formation: under the parliamentary regime, the largest party in the legislature was

---

prime minister either by a vote of no confidence or by failing to pass the national budget.

[12] Most importantly, Shugart (2005) and Samuels and Shugart (2010) make a compelling argument for viewing the new regime as a unique "elected prime ministerial" regime. I will later return to this classificatory issue. Moreover, some studies such as De Mesquita (2000), Hazan (2001), and Rahat (2001) emphasize the electoral aspect of the reform. While I agree that this is one possible understanding, the change in regime type strikes me as more fundamental. Bolstering this position, several scholars (e.g., Diskin and Diskin 1995; Harris and Doron 1999; Kenig 2005) argue that the reformers ultimately settled upon a reform that was governmental in nature (that is, a change in the type of regime) because opposition from the small political parties made the more direct and hence desirable electoral reform impossible.

[13] I do not adopt the conventional terminology and refer to the directly elected prime minister as a president in what follows solely to avoid confusion with Israel's ceremonial head of state, who is indirectly elected by the Knesset and also called a president.

[14] For an elaboration on the distinction between premier-presidential and president–parliamentary regimes, one that focuses upon the dual accountability of the cabinet to the president and legislature in president–parliamentary regimes, see Shugart (2005). More recently, Samuels and Shugart (2010) have argued for viewing president–parliamentarism as a subtype of premier-presidentialism, with the president's authority to dismiss the premier and cabinet being the defining feature of the subtype.

167

(and is) conventionally given the first opportunity to form a government, but under the president-parliamentary regime, it was the party winning the direct prime ministerial election that would form the government.[15] Because policy-making authority within the Knesset is either constitutionally or de facto concentrated in the hands of the *government*,[16] being the largest party in the legislature accordingly no longer conferred any benefits. Further reducing the strategic incentives for both voters and elites to coordinate in order to become the largest party in the legislature, the Knesset became "weaker" (Hazan 1997a, 344) relative to the government as a result of other aspects of the reform that strengthened the prime minister's hand, "erod[ing] the Knesset's power over governance and policymaking more generally" (Arian 2005, 281).[17]

From the perspective of hypothesis testing, this change in the regime type, and hence in the horizontal centralization of policy-making authority in the largest party in the legislature, can be viewed as a quasi-experiment (Campbell and Ross 1968): the regime type is allowed to vary over time, but most other factors are effectively held constant in the time span immediately preceding and following the reform.[18] Because neither the Sephardim nor the Russians constituted a majority of the electorate, by removing the strategic incentive to cast a legislative ballot for the most preferred of the catch-all parties that could credibly form a government (the center-left Labor or the center-right Likud), both elites and voters from these groups were instead freed to support a smaller sectarian party that they sincerely preferred. The

---

[15] An example is the 1996 legislative and prime ministerial elections: while the largest party in the legislature was the center-left Labor party, Binyamin Netanyahu of the center-right Likud party won the prime ministership and consequently formed a center-right government.

[16] For example, members of the governing coalition hold most committee chairmanships, particularly the important ones such as Foreign Affairs (Hazan 1998, 175–176).

[17] Examples include granting the prime minister the right to dissolve the legislature and instituting a (semi-) constructive vote of no confidence (I thank Matthew Shugart for both this distinction and the term). Moreover, at approximately the same time, many Israeli political parties began employing primaries to select their Knesset candidates—that is, allowing voter input into both who appeared on the party's list of candidates and the order in which those candidates appeared. This strengthened individual legislators vis-à-vis their parties, leading Hazan (1997a, 344–345) to characterize the combined result of the intraparty and political institutional reforms as "a weaker legislature with stronger legislators."

[18] This approximates a quasi-experiment because there is a pre-test (the pre-1996 Israeli party system), an experimental treatment (the 1996 change in Israel's regime type), and a post-test (the post-1996 Israeli party system), leaving aside the second regime change in 2001 for the sake of simplicity. I can attribute changes in Israel's party system between the pre- and post-1996 periods to the experimental treatment, the change in regime type, "provided consideration is given to plausible rival explanations of the differences" (Campbell and Ross 1968, 37). Accordingly, we must ask the following: are there either specific events occurring between 1996 and 2001 or long-running processes in Israel that might alternatively account for the observed changes in sectarian party entry and success? As I will argue, the only such process seems to be the increasing politicization of the Sephardim and the Russians. However, for the Sephardim in particular, this alternative explanation does not seem able to account for the sharp increase in sectarian party success in 1996, something for which the change in regime type can account. See Samuels and Shugart (2010) for a similar quasi-experimental perspective on the Israeli change in regime type.

6. Israel: Testing Hypotheses about Sectarian Party Success

hypothesis is accordingly that sectarian party entry and success should increase from 1996 to 2001, a period when policy-making authority was less concentrated in the hands of the largest party in the Knesset because of the change in regime type, relative to either the preceding or following periods. Interestingly, this hypothesis runs contrary to the reformers' expectations.[19]

And indeed, scholars have exhaustively documented changes in the Israeli party system during this period that seem to confirm the hypothesis: the decimation of Israel's two major parties, Labor and Likud; a massive increase in support for small sectarian parties of all stripes; and hence the fragmentation of the Israeli party system.[20] The evidence most germane to my task in this chapter, however, is presented in Figure 6.1, which graphically summarizes the information from the last chapter's Tables 5.4–5.7. The top half of the figure deals with Sephardi and Russian sectarian party entry: shown is the raw number of Sephardi and Russian sectarian political parties contesting each Israeli election from 1949 through 2009. The bottom half of the figure addresses Sephardi and Russian sectarian party success: shown are the collective vote shares of each group's sectarian parties as a percentage of the group's share of the electorate (that is, my measure of success, based on demographic data) in these same elections. Grey vertical lines bound the period of the president–parliamentary regime.

With respect to the supply of sectarian parties, this figure shows that entry does not appear to have greatly increased in 1996 and 1999 relative to either prior or subsequent years. For the Sephardim, the peak elite supply of sectarian parties came in the 1970s and 1980s; since 1988, elites have been fluctuating between supplying one and two sectarian parties in each election. For the Russians, while the elite supply of sectarian parties did peak in 1999 (but again in 2003), a substantial increase had already taken place prior to the change in regime. While the number of cases (elections) is too small for a conventional statistical analysis, the evidence suggests that the change in regime type did not, contrary to the hypothesis, affect sectarian party entry.

The real story is at the mass level and hence with respect to sectarian party success. Both Sephardi and Russian sectarian parties experienced a substantial surge in support in the 1996 and 1999 elections. Support for Russian sectarian parties had been negligible prior to 1996, after which the percentage of Russians voting for Sephardi parties increased more than tenfold. While support for Sephardi parties had been trending upwards since

---

[19]The ostensible goal of the reformers was to weaken the influence of small parties and ultimately to arrive at a more majoritarian policy process (e.g., Doron and Kay 1995). Opinion amongst academic commentators, however, was divided as to whether this (e.g., Bogdanor 1993); the opposite effect, that is, the strengthening of small parties and reduced governability (e.g., Diskin and Diskin 1995; Sartori 1997); or something in between (e.g., Lijphart 1993) would occur.

[20]See note 9 for an extensive, if not a comprehensive, list of the studies making these points. The contrary position is staked out only by Ottolenghi (2007). He instead argues that the ultimate cause of Israel's party system fragmentation is a long-term erosion of support for Labor and Likud, although he concedes that the regime change likely accelerated this trend.

Changing Societies, Changing Party Systems

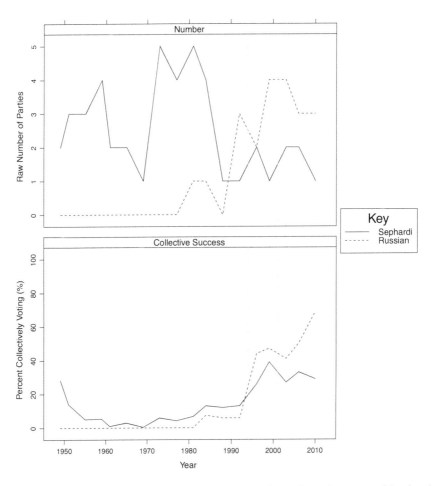

Figure 6.1: The number and collective success (based on demographic data) of Sephardi and Russian sectarian parties in Israeli elections, 1949–2009. Source: Tables 5.4–5.7.

6. Israel: Testing Hypotheses about Sectarian Party Success

its nadir in the 1969 election, this support seems to have stabilized at around 13 percent of Sephardim voting for Sephardi sectarian parties prior to 1996, when the percentage suddenly doubled.[21] The number of cases is again too small for a conventional statistical analysis, but the evidence nevertheless suggests that one plausible explanation for the dramatic increase in the electoral fortunes of both Sephardi and Russian sectarian parties in 1996 is the change in the regime type. As hypothesized, the reduced horizontal centralization of policy-making authority in the hands of the largest party in the legislature seems to have encouraged members of these immigrant groups to cast a sincere sectarian ballot in the legislative race.[22] Strategic considerations about who would govern instead surfaced in the direct prime ministerial election—an issue to which I will return later.

However, Israel's post-reform experience in the 2000s provides some evidence contradicting the hypothesis that the change in regime type is responsible for the change in voting behavior, and hence in sectarian party success, just described.[23] Figure 6.1 shows that Sephardi support for Sephardi sectarian parties dropped substantially in 2003 relative to 1999, as hypothesized. However, contrary to the hypothesis, since then it seems to have stabilized, with minor fluctuations, at more than twice its level prior to the original change in regime type. More damning is the performance of the Russian sectarian parties. While Russian support for Russian sectarian parties also decreased in 2003 relative to its peak under the president–parliamentary regime in 1999, this support—and hence Russian party success—resumed its upwards trajectory in 2006. In fact, new records were set in both 2006 and 2009, when Avigdor Lieberman's Israel Beiteinu obtained almost 70 percent of the Russian vote, making it the third-largest party in the Knesset. This evidence is problematic for the hypothesis because the switch back to a parliamentary regime in 2001 once again horizontally centralized policy-making authority in the hands of the largest party in the Knesset, which should have decreased sectarian party entry and success.

One explanation for these findings suggested by both Kenig (2005) and Kenig, Hazan, and Rahat (2005) is that it takes time for elites and voters to adjust to new institutions.[24] However, three elections have now occurred under the parliamentary regime with little sign of sectarian party success

---

[21] These findings hold regardless of whether one assesses sectarian party success using demographic data, as in Figure 6.1, or survey data, as discussed in Chapter 5.

[22] This perspective is shared by those on the ground: every politician and activist I spoke with mentioned the direct prime ministerial elections as a key factor behind the success of sectarian parties in the 1990s. See also note 27.

[23] One of the few scholarly voices to dissent from the orthodox position that the regime change was responsible for the increased fragmentation of the Israeli party system in the late 1990s points to just this fact (Ottolenghi 2007).

[24] As discussed in Chapter 2, my argument about the constraint imposed by horizontal and vertical centralization is at heart an equilibrium argument (see Cox 1997). Unfortunately, to date, we know little about how and why rates of learning about optimal strategic behavior differ under various electoral systems and regime types (see, for example, Reed and Thies 2001).

returning to the original, pre–regime change levels. Moreover, this explanation does not account for the differential trajectories of Sephardi and Russian sectarian parties since the restoration of the parliamentary regime. The best explanation may simply be that sectarian party success under the president–parliamentary regime altered other variables and hence both elite and voter behavior in future elections—an issue to which I will return.

The Presidential Coattails

But there is one additional matter that needs to be considered. A large literature in comparative politics has observed that presidential elections held concurrently or otherwise in close temporal proximity to legislative elections cast a shadow over the party system (e.g., Shugart and Carey 1992; Jones 1994; Shugart 1995; Amorim Neto and Cox 1997; Cox 1997; Golder 2006; Hicken 2009; Hicken and Stoll 2011, 2013). Specifically, when there are few viable presidential candidates, as is usually the case, this shadow or coattails effect takes the form of fewer legislative parties, which means a less fragmented party system. This is referred to as the deflationary effect of presidential elections. The mechanism underlying the presidential coattails is the attention that presidential campaigns draw from the national media; legislative candidates and parties; donors and other political elites; and, ultimately, voters.[25]

The hypothesis is accordingly that the presidential coattails should reduce the entry and success of sectarian parties whose groups are not large enough to mount a viable campaign for the presidency, such as the Sephardim and the Russians. That is, Sephardi and Russian sectarian parties should have fared less well in the 1996 and 1996 Knesset elections, which were held concurrently with elections for the directly elected prime minister, than in other elections. Reformers in Israel were banking on just this kind of deflationary shadow being cast over the legislative elections by the introduction of popular elections for a "president." The hope was that the two major parties (Labor and Likud) would be the only ones fielding candidates in the direct prime ministerial election, and that straight-ticket voting would be encouraged, reducing the electoral support for smaller parties in the Knesset (e.g., Hazan and Rahat 2000, 1318).

Yet as I argued earlier, the evidence does not bear out this hypothesis. To the contrary, Sephardi and Russian sectarian parties were *more* successful in the 1996 and 1999 elections. As Table 6.1 illustrates, the direct prime ministerial elections, somewhat surprisingly, did come down to a race between the Labor and Likud candidates, as the reformers expected.[26] However, con-

---

[25]For more on this mechanism, see Shugart (1995), Cox (1997), Golder (2006), and Hicken and Stoll (2011).

[26]Hazan and Rahat (2000, 1318) point out the absurdity of this expectation: dual ballot systems are viewed by most political scientists as less restrictive than simple plurality because they tend not to constrain the competition to two candidates (e.g., Cox 1997; Golder 2006). The fact that the race always did come down to two candidates in Israel is likely a testament to the large

6. Israel: Testing Hypotheses about Sectarian Party Success

Percent of Valid Votes in First Round				
1996		1999	
Netanyahu (Likud)	50.5	Netanyahu (Likud)	43.9
Peres (Labor)	49.5	Barak (Labor)	56.1

Table 6.1: Results of the 1996 and 1999 Israeli direct prime ministerial elections. Source: CBS (1981–1997) and Knesset (1999).

trary both to their expectations and to the predictions of the scholarly literature on presidential coattails, it was split rather than straight-ticket voting that prevailed in 1996 and 1999. Voters cast a strategic ballot in the direct prime ministerial race to determine which of the two major parties, and hence which bloc in Israel's bipolar system, would govern. Yet, relieved of these strategic considerations in their Knesset ballot, many then voted sincerely for a minor party (e.g., De Mesquita 2000).[27] It is this ballot splitting in favor of a *minor* party in the legislative race that is so anomalous from the perspective of the scholarly literature.[28]

This begs the question: why were there no presidential coattails in Israel under the president–parliamentary regime? While the existing Israeli politics literature provides convincing explanations in the context of the Israeli case along the lines of that offered in the prior paragraph, it does not link Israel's experiences back to the comparative literature on presidential coattails. Yet an analysis of deviant cases allows us to refine and sharpen the original hypothesis—for example, by establishing scope conditions or by uncovering additional relevant variables (Lijphart 1971).

One possible explanation for the deviance of the Israeli case is that the directly elected Israeli prime minister was not a large enough prize to cast a shadow (Hicken and Stoll 2013). However, this explanation can quickly be rejected: when using conventional measures of presidential power, such as the index developed by Shugart and Carey (1992), the directly elected prime minister is classified as wielding power of a similar magnitude to that wielded by the president of the United States—powerful enough, in other

---

size of the "presidential" prize, an argument I will later develop further.

[27] For example, Russian parties in 1999 either informally (Sharansky of Israel b'Aliya) or formally (Lieberman of Israel Beiteinu) endorsed one of the two major parties in the prime ministerial race, encouraging Russians to vote "ethnically" on one level and as "statespersons" on the other (Gitelman and Goldstein 2002, 156). Arguments along with more abundant evidence to this effect may be found in many of the studies referenced in note 9.

[28] Splitting ballots to vote for one major party in the prime ministerial race and the other major party in the legislative race is a time-honed practice that is both commensurate with the literature's predictions and strategically sensible for policy-oriented voters (see, for example, Kedar 2006).

words, to have possessed coattails.[29] This quantitative assessment dovetails with the qualitative assessment offered earlier: that policy-making authority was centralized in the hands of the Israeli government, and specifically in the hands of the directly elected prime minister, under the president–parliamentary regime.

A better explanation is that the directly elected Israeli prime minister was *too* large a prize for the race to cast a deflationary shadow (Hicken and Stoll 2013). In president–parliamentary regimes, the president is the dominant institutional actor, arguably having even greater authority than presidents in true presidential regimes (e.g., Samuels and Shugart 2010). For example, she has direct authority over the legislature through her ability to dissolve it, and indirect authority through her control of the prime minister and cabinet (she both appoints and dismisses them). Conventional measures such as the index of presidential power may accordingly underestimate presidential authority in these regimes.[30] The result is that this type of regime provides the fewest incentives out of all of the regimes with popularly elected chief executives (presidents) for actors to ride the presidential coattails in a bid to become the largest legislative party.[31] My earlier argument that there was little incentive to be the largest party in the Israeli Knesset from 1996 to 2001 showcases this dynamic. Unfortunately, however, a paucity of data makes it difficult to assess empirically the extent to which concurrent presidential elections in president–parliamentary regimes other than Israel's have lacked a deflationary shadow.[32]

---

[29]For more about this measure, see either Chapter 4 or Hicken and Stoll (2008, 2013). Israel's directly elected prime minister is coded as scoring twelve on this index, whereas the president of the United States scores thirteen.

[30]For example, of the thirteen post–World War II regimes identified by Samuels and Shugart (2010, Table 2.1) as being president–parliamentary, the legislatures of all save two were found to exercise fewer powers than the legislature of the United States (Fish and Kroenig 2009). One of the few president–parliamentary regimes with a weak president is that of Austria, where convention has established an almost purely parliamentary regime despite its de jure president–parliamentarism (Shugart 2005, 342).

[31]In semi- (premier-) presidential regimes, it is the largest party in the legislature that usually holds the prime ministership and hence forms the government, even where the president has the constitutional initiative to name a prime minister. For example, in France, the archetypical premier-presidential regime, the French president has named a prime minister who was not from the largest party in the legislature on only two occasions. With the government responsible only to the legislature for its survival and most lawmaking powers in the hands of the legislature (Shugart 2005, 341–342), there is still an incentive to ride the presidential coattails in order to become the largest party in the legislature. And in true presidential regimes, the largest party is often advantaged in a variety of ways that also make it worthwhile to ride the presidential coattails, such as the majority party's control of committee chairmanships in the United States Congress—at least, that is, in the typical true presidential regime where the president does not wield near-imperial powers.

[32]There are few real-world examples of this type of regime, a matter exacerbated by disagreements over the classification of cases: compare, for example, the Samuels and Shugart (2010) list of president–parliamentary regimes to that of Shugart (2005). Moreover, of those few examples, most either have not held concurrent (or even reasonably temporally proximate) presidential and legislative elections, or have had presidential races with too many presidential candidates for a deflationary shadow to be cast. Where there have been concurrent elections

6. Israel: Testing Hypotheses about Sectarian Party Success

Moreover, problematizing the enterprise of generalizing from Israel's experience, Israel's regime stands out from other president–parliamentary regimes due to its single executive: all others have dual executives in the form of a prime minister (sometimes called a chancellor or premier) in addition to a president. For this reason, Shugart (2005) and Samuels and Shugart (2010) even go so far as to characterize it as a unique type of regime, which they call the "elected prime ministerial," of which Israel is the only real-world example.[33] This regime fuses executive and legislative survival to an even greater extent than do dual executive president–parliamentary regimes. The consequence is that if the prime minister's party does not win a legislative majority (as has always been the case in Israel), the elected prime ministerial regime uniquely gives small parties bargaining power: the directly elected prime minister is dependent upon the legislature, which means her party's coalition partners, to remain in office (Samuels and Shugart 2010). Accordingly, voters and elites who do not sincerely prefer the parties of the presidential front-runners have no incentive to ride their coattails into the legislature. Rather, the incentive is to jump *off* of the presidential coattails. Existing theories of presidential coattails fail to account for the Israeli case because they are both theoretically and empirically rooted in the more popular true presidential and semi-presidential regimes, where there are usually incentives to ride the presidential coattails to become the largest party in the legislature.

6.2.2 Existing Party Strategy

A second explanatory factor is the strategy existing parties have played towards the new immigrant groups. Because existing parties have responded differently to the Sephardim and Russians, this factor helps to explain the differences in sectarian party success across groups. To a lesser extent, the variance in these strategies over time also helps to explain the timing of sectarian party success.

The hypothesis is that existing parties playing any combination of accommodative or dismissive strategies towards the Russians and the Sephardim should both deter the entry and reduce the success of new sectarian parties seeking to represent these groups. A dismissive strategy involves downplaying the existence of a new social group *qua* group, whereas an accommodative strategy acknowledges the new group and seeks to meet its demands. By way of contrast, one or more existing parties playing an adversarial strategy, where the new group is acknowledged *qua* group but its demands are opposed, is hypothesized to increase both sectarian party entry and success. Here, I initially paint qualitative portraits of the strategies played by exist-

---

with few presidential candidates, it has been in new and unconsolidated democracies, which are of limited comparative value. An example is Namibia in 1994.

[33]Note, however, that the dual-executive criterion was absent from Shugart and Carey's (1992, 24–25) original definition of president–parliamentarism, which is why most scholars have classified the Israeli regime from 1996 to 2001 as president-parliamentary.

ing parties towards the Sephardim, after which I present some quantitative data. I then do the same for the Russians.

Sephardim

The existing parties' initial responses to the Sephardim might best be called a dismissive strategy. What Smooha (1978, 76–77) describes as the "triple ideology" of Zionism (nationalism), socialism, and modernization led Ashkenazi elites to reject ethnic pluralism early on. State policies were aimed at assimilating Sephardi immigrants into Israeli (meaning Ashkenazi) culture and society, the "melting pot" model (e.g., Goldscheider 2002b, 24–26; see also Shafir and Peled 2002, 87–88). Organizing around ethnicity was even painted as a danger to the nation (Herzog 1986, 299). Hence, the existing Ashkenazi-dominated political parties ideologically dismissed both ethnicity as a line of division suitable for political organization and ethnic political organizations themselves (Shafir and Peled 2002, 89; see also Herzog 1986). The full flowering of this dismissive strategy, which at times verged upon the adversarial, came as the massive post-state wave of immigration peaked: Ashkenazi fears of the Sephardi threat increased as the number of Sephardim grew.[34]

Yet at the same time that existing parties were ideologically delegitimizing the ethnic identity of the Sephardim, they gave organizational support to Sephardi political entrepreneurs. They supported Sephardi political activities within their own organizations (for example, by encouraging the formation of internal Sephardi sections), as well as pseudo-independent Sephardi satellite parties that were deliberately kept weak. The fact that they later frequently co-opted the leaders of these parties by offering them positions on their own lists can be explained by the tension between their vote-seeking desire to accommodate and the almost adversarial desire to dismiss just described (Herzog 1986, 296–297). Regardless, this facilitation of Sephardi political entrepreneurship and representation, with direct, internal representation increasing over time, can be characterized as an accommodative strategy. However, as I will argue more fully later, this accommodation has been only partial, leaving open the door to a sectarian path to political representation for the Sephardim. Not surprisingly, it also eventually undermined the strategy of ideological dismissiveness (ibid., 299).

An exception to the argument that existing parties played at least a partially accommodative strategy vis-à-vis the Sephardim concerns the religious parties. Here I refer to both the National Religious Party, the party of the religious Zionists and long an important junior coalition partner of the major parties, and the various forerunners of today's United Torah Judaism, the party of the ultra-Orthodox. Both the short-lived Tami, the first Sephardi

---

[34]To capture this adversarial tone, consider the following quote from the most revered of Israel's founding fathers, David Ben-Gurion, in the mid-1960s (Smooha 1978, 88): "The Moroccan Jew took a lot from the Moroccan Arabs. The culture of Morocco I would not like to have here. And I don't see what contribution present Persians have to make."

6. Israel: Testing Hypotheses about Sectarian Party Success

party to obtain Knesset representation since the 1950s, and Shas, the only Sephardi party to attain even moderate success as I have defined it, started out as protests by ambitious political leaders against the underrepresentation of the Sephardim in the existing religious parties (e.g., Bick 1997).[35] Hence, the more religious Sephardim are the subgroup of the Sephardi community that has been most successfully particized because it is they who were the least accommodated by existing parties.

But it is possible to be more precise about exactly how accommodative the major existing parties have been to the Sephardim: the prior qualitative portrait can be supplemented by a "head count" of Sephardim as a proportion of party personnel (Chandra 2004). The more accommodative a party's strategy, the more Sephardim will be found in its ranks. The testable hypothesis predicts greater Sephardi voter support for parties that provide relatively greater representation to Sephardim.[36] More specifically, the testable hypothesis is that Sephardi sectarian parties will succeed electorally to the extent that existing catch-all parties do not adopt a fully accommodative strategy, as indicated by the Sephardi share of their party personnel being less than the Sephardi share of the electorate. Because Knesset members (MKs) are highly visible to the public in their capacity as the parliamentary wing of a party, I operationally focus upon the proportion of a party's MKs who are Sephardi, although I also present some data on the composition of a party's extra-parliamentary wing.[37] I collected information about the ethnicity of MKs from a variety of primary and secondary sources, such as the Knesset's website, for the foreign-born, and major Israeli newspapers' political coverage of elections, for the Israeli-born.[38] The top half of Figure 6.2

---

[35] For example, for the 1981 election, Tami's founder, Aharon Abuhatzeira, had been denied a high place on the National Religious Party's list, and only two of the party's top ten candidates were Sephardi. Abuhatzeira eventually demanded that half of the first ten positions be given to Sephardim and that he be named party leader; when the National Religious Party turned him down, he quit the party and formed Tami (Peretz and Smooha 1981, 513–514).

[36] On the general point, former Russian MK Victor Brailovsky, for example, pointed out that he was put on Shinui's list (a now-defunct secular party of the center) for the 1999 election precisely because it was believed that this would bring the party Russian votes (interview, May 18, 2008). The belief that votes follow descriptive representation is widespread in Israel, from the media to politicians.

[37] I would also have liked to collect information about the Sephardi proportion of candidate lists, but this data was too difficult to come by in historical perspective for many parties.

[38] For the eighteenth Knesset elected in 2009, data is through April of 2012. Each party's Knesset contingent is determined by an individual's party affiliation at the time he or she entered the Knesset. Replacement MKs are included instead of confining the analysis solely to those initially entering the Knesset on a party's slate because replacements also send a signal about the group specificity of a party's message. Ethnicity is defined as usual here: by country (and hence continent) of origin for the foreign-born, and for the Israeli-born, by father's origin. My numbers closely resemble Smooha's (1978, 333–335; but see 311 for somewhat different ones) for the first through the most recent Knesset included in his study, the eighth (elected in 1973). A minor difference is that he seems to rely upon the more traditional definition of the Sephardi category—those of Iberian ancestry—because his figures include the few European-born Sephardim, e.g., Mapam's Victor Shem-Tov, a Bulgarian immigrant. I, by contrast, do not count these individuals as Sephardi given my definition of the category. The only other

displays these proportions over time (by Knesset, displayed by the election year for convenience) for Sephardi sectarian parties and the following major parties: Labor and its forerunner; Likud and its forerunner; Kadima (from 2006 onwards); and the religious parties.[39] Also displayed is the proportion of a party's MKs that would need to be Sephardi in order to attain parity with the Sephardi share of the electorate.[40]

This figure shows that the Sephardi sectarian parties that have attained Knesset representation have almost exclusively sent their own to the Knesset.[41] By way of contrast, the existing parties have provided much lower levels of representation to the Sephardim. Yet these parties have always offered them at least some representation, and this representation has generally increased over time.[42] For example, the forerunner of the Labor party, which has generally placed relatively more Sephardim in the Knesset than the other major parties, averaged a Knesset contingent that was 9 percent Sephardi in the 1950s; 22 percent in the 1970s; and 36 percent in the 1990s. While even today the Sephardim are still slightly underrepresented relative

---

quantitative time series data of which I am aware, that of Brichta (2001, 77), is not broken down by party. Moreover, he reports surprisingly low numbers of Sephardim in the early years relative to both my and Smooha's numbers, as well as surprisingly high numbers in more recent years relative to mine. My numbers for very recent elections are commensurate with those reported by newspapers such as *The Jerusalem Post* in their post-election coverage.

[39] For Labor, this means Mapai prior to 1965; the Alignment between Ahdut Ha'avoda and Mapai for the 1965 election; and the Alignment between the newly formed Labor party and Mapam from 1969 to 1984. For Likud, this means Herut prior to 1965 and Gahal from 1965 to 1969. Calculating the proportions for Mapai and its closely related allies on the left (Ahdut Ha'avoda, Mapam, and Rafi), as well as for Herut and its closely-related allies on the right (the General Zionists, Liberals, and the Free Center) yields similar results. In the category of religious parties is the National Religious Party and its forerunners, Mizrachi and Hapoel HaMizrachi (including the National Religious Party–National Union electoral alliance for the 2006 election), and United Torah Judaism and its forerunners, Agudat Israel, Poalei Agudat Israel, and Degel HaTorah. Note that Shas is not included in this category. All parties identified in the prior chapter as Sephardi parties are grouped together in the Sephardi sectarian category.

[40] This is my best estimate of the Sephardi (or Russian, for the Russians) share of the *total* electorate in the given year. See Appendix B for this data. Note that any underrepresentation is greater if only the *Jewish* electorate is considered, that is, if the major parties are viewed as catch-all solely with respect to the Jewish citizenry.

[41] The lower proportions of Sephardim (85 to 92 percent) in the three most recent Knessets comes from Shas's MKs including one or two Russians from the former Asian republics of the Soviet Union. Strict adherence to the definitions of the latent Russian and Sephardi categories that I offered in the prior chapter, for consistency with other data, requires me to treat these MKs as non-Sephardi. However, this subgroup of Russians is more properly viewed as Sephardi than as Ashkenazi, as I acknowledged in the last chapter; if they are instead classified as Sephardi, all Sephardi parties' MKs are Sephardi for each Knesset. While not shown in this figure, the many Sephardi parties that failed to pass the threshold for representation in Israel's first few decades also populated their list of Knesset candidates primarily with Sephardim.

[42] An interesting partial exception is the religious parties. The figure shows a sharp increase in the Sephardi share of the religious parties' (and specifically, the National Religious Party's) MKs following the success of Tami and Shas in the early 1980s. This suggests that their initial nonaccommodative (perhaps even adversarial) stance gave way to a more accommodative one at this point in time. However, in the late 1990s, the Sephardi share of their MKs fell back to the level of the 1970s, a reversal of this accommodative stance. These are all issues to which I return in a later chapter.

6. Israel: Testing Hypotheses about Sectarian Party Success

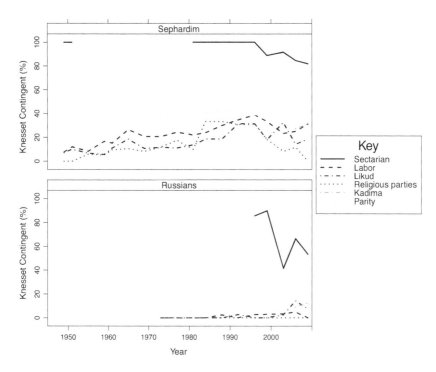

Figure 6.2: The percentage of Sephardi and Russian Members of the Knesset (MKs), by Knesset (election year) and political party. Note that all sectarian parties for each group are considered collectively. The line labeled "parity" is the proportion of a party's MKs needed to attain parity with the group's share of the electorate. Source: see text.

to their share of the electorate, the situation has greatly improved since the first few decades,[43] when the Sephardi share of most parliamentary parties would have had to more than double in order for their representation to be proportional to their share of the electorate.

---

[43] A comparable increase over time can be observed in Smooha's (1978, 321–330) data on the ethnic composition of the governing bodies of the major parties (that is, their extra-parliamentary wings) through 1973. However, in general, extra-parliamentary Sephardi representation during this early period decreased with the rank of the governing body and position (ibid., 167). While Labor and its forerunners seem to have offered the Sephardim extra-parliamentary representation comparable to that offered by Likud and its forerunners, they both, surprisingly (relative to the parliamentary representation offered), usually lagged behind the National Religious Party at this less visible level. Moreover, Peretz and Smooha (1981, 513) note that Labor had amended its constitution prior to the 1981 election to require that a minimum of one-third of all political posts be staffed by non-Ashkenazim, while the Likud remained officially color-blind.

Changing Societies, Changing Party Systems

This accommodatory strategy combined with my finding, as summarized in Figure 6.1, that Sephardi parties have achieved only modest success in Israel provides suggestive support for the hypothesis. Moreover, the greater accommodation the Sephardim have been offered by existing parties over time does seem to correspond to diminished new Sephardi party entry, at least since the 1980s. Yet the fact that this accommodation has been far from complete, particularly in the first few decades, has allowed for some Sephardi sectarian party entry and success, also as hypothesized. However, existing parties' strategies cannot account for the specific timing of Sephardi party success, such as the surge in support they enjoyed in 1996. Further, the growing success of Sephardi sectarian parties over time is not consistent with existing parties having generally become more accommodative towards the Sephardim as the years have passed.

One possible explanation for the latter is that head counts may matter less in Israel than in other countries because it has only some of the characteristics of a patronage democracy as Chandra (2004) defines it. Ethnicity is therefore less valuable as an information shortcut. This is plausible: counterbalancing the relative head count are more ideological factors, such as a paternalistic establishment associated with the existing parties that had treated the Sephardim so poorly for so long.[44]

Another response might be that the *quality* of representation that a party provides to a group matters as much if not more than the *quantity*. The top half of Figure 6.3 displays the proportion of a party's cabinet ministers who were Sephardi over time (by government, displayed by the date of the government's taking office, for convenience) for the thirty-two Israeli governments that have held office to date. To construct this data, I drew upon and extended data about the ethnicity of Israeli cabinet members collected by Kenig and Barnea (2009).[45] This figure again shows that existing parties have offered representation to the Sephardim, but that there is a marked contrast between this representation, which today still falls short of demo-

---

[44] This may also help to explain the Sephardi revolution of 1977, when Sephardi voters switched their support from Labor to Likud despite Labor's head count advantage. Labor was particularly identified with the establishment's paternalism, and the opposition Likud made important moves to symbolically accommodate the Sephardim during this period. For example, the Likud campaigns of the period attacked Labor for its discrimination against the Sephardim (Peretz and Smooha 1981, 513). Further, the more religiously traditional Sephardim placed great importance on the religious symbolism projected by long-time Likud leader and later prime minister Menachem Begin, who was personally observant. In fact, Begin is frequently called Israel's first Jewish prime minister (Aronoff 1993, 187), a marked contrast to the largely secular leaders of the Labor party.

[45] I thank Ofer Kenig for sharing this data (through the thirty-first government) with me. Comparable to my data on the ethnic composition of parties' Knesset contingents, a cabinet minister's party affiliation is determined at the time she entered the government. Ministers who were not MKs are counted as a member of a party if they had a clear affiliation with it at that time. Also as before, I include ministers added later in the government's tenure. Only full, not deputy, ministers are included. The unit is the individual, meaning that individuals who have held more than one portfolio during a government's tenure are counted only once. Data for the thirty-second government is through April of 2012.

6. Israel: Testing Hypotheses about Sectarian Party Success

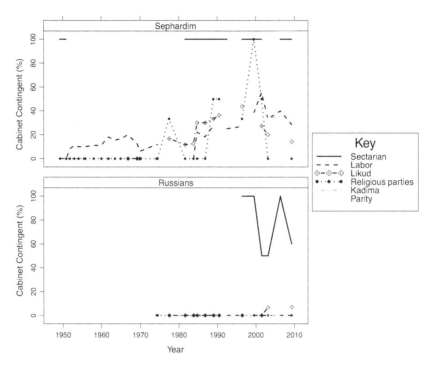

Figure 6.3: The percentage of Sephardi and Russian cabinet ministers, by government (year taking office) and political party. Note that all sectarian parties for each group are considered collectively. The line labeled "parity" is the proportion of a party's ministers needed to attain parity with the group's share of the electorate. Source: see text.

graphic parity, if barely, and that offered by the Sephardi sectarian parties, which have exclusively put their own in the cabinet.[46] As before, this is consistent with the moderate success attained by Sephardi sectarian parties overall. Yet also as before, the time trend of greater accommodation runs contrary to the increased success of Sephardi sectarian parties over time.

Russians

But what about the Russians? To date, existing parties have played a less accommodative strategy towards this group. This is particularly true of

---

[46] One also sees from this figure that until recently, when the Likud has been in government, it has offered the Sephardim relatively more important policy-making roles in the form of cabinet ministerships than has Labor. This factor may also help to counterbalance Labor's advantage in the realm of the less important MKs and hence to explain the swing from Labor to Likud.

the religious parties, which is not surprising given the predominantly secular character of both waves of Russian immigration.[47] The story is more mixed for the other major existing parties. Likud and Labor began organizing internal Russian departments in the early 1990s, and some Russians were reasonably well placed within the party hierarchies. However, by the late 1990s, this extra-parliamentary organizational accommodation had been hamstrung by the departure of key activists (Khanin 2001, 102–107). Yet at the same time, both parties have been reluctant to offer representation to Russians in their parliamentary wings. For example, neither initially included even a single Russian in a realistic place on their candidate lists for the 1996 election (Siegel 1998, 170), and the launch of Israel Beiteinu in the 1999 elections is commonly attributed in part to the Likud leadership's ignoring the demands and ambitions of the "Russian Likud" for too long (Khanin 2001, 114). At the ideological level, existing parties have made only short-lived attempts to accommodate the Russians.[48]

There have been moments, however, when existing party strategies have verged upon the adversarial, something akin to their strategies towards the Sephardim. For example, Khanin (2001, 109) argues that one external factor leading to the success of Russian parties in the 1996 election was the "blackening" of the community by Labor.[49] The religious, and particularly the ultra-Orthodox, parties have been especially virulent in staking out opposition to the secular Russians and their demands, such as those for instituting civil marriage in Israel and allowing the sale of pork.[50]

This extremely minimal accommodation on the part of the major existing parties can be seen more precisely in the bottom half of Figure 6.2, which presents the percentage of Russians in a party's Knesset contingent over time, beginning with the first election (1973) following the start of the 1970s wave of immigration. Prior to 1996, Labor and Likud each sent 1970s immigrant Ephraim Gur to the Knesset for one term apiece. Matters have

---

[47] The exception is Shas's strategy with respect to a subgroup of the Russians. As discussed earlier, it has incorporated members of the Bukharian and Caucasian communities into its parliamentary wing since the late 1990s. These Russian immigrants, more properly classed as Sephardi than Ashkenazi, are by far the most religiously traditional of the Russians.

[48] For example, Labor made a strenuous accommodative effort for the 1999 election by campaigning against religious coercion (Khanin 2004, 148). In other campaigns, major parties have played to Russians' desire for assistance as new immigrants (encouraging them to cast a protest vote against the incumbents), as well as for a hawkish security policy (e.g., Fein 1995, 168–173).

[49] Ora Namir and Moshe Shahal, Labor cabinet ministers at the time, famously launched an unprecedented media campaign that slandered Russian immigrants: the former claimed that one-third of the Russian immigrants were prostitutes, one-third were "social cases," and the remaining third were single-mother families, while the latter called the wave of Russian immigration the *aliya* of Mafioso (Khanin 2001, 109).

[50] With respect to the exception noted earlier, Shas's outreach to religious Russians from the Asian republics of the former USSR, the spiritual leader of Shas, Rabbi Ovadia Yosef, has in recent years attacked both Russian immigrants and Russian parties. For example, in 1999, he talked about "the Russians that [had] cropped up from the netherworld" (*Haaretz*, February 11, 2009), and in a 2009 campaign rally that was also attended by the heads of the Ashkenazi United Torah Judaism, he said that "whoever votes for Lieberman gives strength to Satan" (*Haaretz*, February 9, 2009).

6. Israel: Testing Hypotheses about Sectarian Party Success

not improved much since: from 1996 through 2006, Labor included only one Russian in each of its Knesset contingents, and none in 2009, while the Likud included only one in 2003 and two in both 2006 and 2009. The apparent increase in Russian Knesset representation in the figure is accordingly mostly an artifact of the dramatic electoral declines of these two parties during this period. Kadima has made a slightly greater effort to woo the Russian vote, placing three Russians in the Knesset in 2006 and four in 2009. The religious parties, by contrast, have not sent any Russians to the Knesset, as expected. Moreover, this low level of representation has not meaningfully improved over time. Russians remain substantially underrepresented in existing parties' parliamentary wings relative to their share of the electorate today, just as they were in the mid-1990s. By way of contrast, like their Sephardi counterparts, Russian sectarian parties have primarily sent their own to the Knesset, although they have reached out to others to a greater extent.[51]

A similar if even less accommodative pattern emerges with respect to higher-quality cabinet representation. With two exceptions—Likud including Natan Sharansky in the thirtieth government and Yuli-Yoel Edelstein in the thirty-second (the former following Israel b'Aliya's absorption into Likud on the heels of the 2003 elections)—the lower portion of Figure 6.3 shows that only Russian sectarian parties have supplied Russian cabinet ministers.[52] These nonaccommodative strategies adopted by the existing major parties vis-à-vis the Russians with respect to the plummest political positions, cabinet ministerships, are particularly surprising when one considers their strategies towards the Sephardim. Within two years of the state's founding, that is, by the end of the first subwave of Sephardi immigration, the Labor party had co-opted Bechor-Shalom Sheetrit from one of the soon-to-be-defunct "old-time" Sephardi sectarian parties and put him both in the Knesset and in the cabinet on its slate. By way of contrast, more than a decade after the end of the bulk of Russian immigration in the 1990s, no major existing party except Likud has made a comparably accommodative gesture to the Russians, and Likud's gesture has been a fleeting one.

Accordingly, Russian sectarian parties have offered Russians a substantially greater quantity and quality of representation than the major existing parties have. And as hypothesized, Russian sectarian parties have both contested elections and enjoyed electoral success.[53] Existing parties having

---

[51] The low percentage of Russians in the Knesset contingent of Russian sectarian parties for the sixteenth Knesset (2003) is due to the short-lived electoral alliance between Israel Beiteinu and the non-Russian National Union. I argued in the last chapter that this "party" technically failed to meet my criteria for a Russian sectarian party, although I treated it as one for consistency with the literature.

[52] I compiled this data using primary sources such as the Knesset's website. Comparable to the data on the ethnic composition of Knesset contingents, the first data point in the figure is the first government that took office following the beginning of the 1970s wave of Russian immigration. This is the sixteenth government, which was invested in March 1974.

[53] As an aside, the effectively similar nonaccommodative strategies played by both Labor and Likud can also explain why Russians have generally split evenly between these two parties in

played a much less accommodative strategy towards the Russians than the Sephardim helps to explain the greater success of Russian sectarian parties. Moreover, accommodation has certainly not improved—if anything, it has worsened—over time, which is at least minimally consistent with the increased Russian sectarian party entry and success over the years.

6.2.3 Party System Openness

The third explanatory factor is the openness of the party system, which is the final systemic factor that plays an explanatory role. This variable helps to explain differences in sectarian party success over both time and groups.

The Israeli party system has become more open over the years. During the pre-state (Mandatory) era and in the early years of statehood, the Labor party (initially in the form of its precursor, Mapai) dominated the Israeli political scene: it was always the largest party in the Knesset, and it always formed the government with the support of a few smaller parties, particularly the National Religious Party. In addition, it dominated a host of quasi-state institutions that provided important services to Israel's citizens.[54] Yet by the late 1960s, Labor and the left were in decline, as was made brutally apparent by the 1977 "revolution" that brought the Likud to power and excluded Labor from government for the first time. Even prior to its loss of political power, gradual structural changes in the economy and a program of liberalization had reduced the extensive patronage formerly dispensed by Labor, leaving it less able to socialize new generations.[55] The hypothesis is accordingly that new latent groups should have been more successfully particized in recent years, when the party system became more open.

Looking at the Sephardim, the longitudinal evidence is consistent with

---

their Knesset ballots, sometimes tipping in favor of one and sometimes the other; the greater Russian support for Kadima in the 2006 election is also consistent with the hypothesized effects of its more accommodative stance relative to Labor and Likud.

[54] One prominent example is the Histradrut, the Federation (Association) of Jewish Laborers in Palestine: far more than just a trade union, the Histadrut owned many enterprises and supplied a variety of social services, particularly health care. Another is the Jewish Agency, the quasi-state organization in the Mandatory period that remained active in the economy, immigrant settlement, and education after statehood. Shafir and Peled (2002) go so far as to describe the Labor party during this period as sitting at the apex of a labor-cum-colonial movement that exercised both ideological hegemony and political dominance via an impressive bureaucratic apparatus, which they term the "Labor Settlement Movement."

[55] An early and particularly important blow came in the form of the nationalization of the education system. In the Mandatory and early state periods, the education system was divided into different "trends," each of which was affiliated with an ideological strand of Zionism and hence with a particular political party (e.g., the "Labor Trend"). This affiliation went beyond ideology in that the schools were consciously employed as instruments of political socialization. After several government crises around who would educate immigrant children, the curriculum was standardized into two tracks (religious and nonreligious), and schools were placed under the national government's supervision by the 1953 State Education Law. Hence, Labor was the biggest loser, given that its trend alone was eliminated (see, for example, Hacohen 2003, 162–176).

6. Israel: Testing Hypotheses about Sectarian Party Success

this hypothesis. As discussed earlier here and in the prior chapter, it was not until the 1980s, after the opening of the party system, that post-state Sephardi sectarian parties attained the representation in the Knesset that was eventually leveraged into moderate success. Moreover, scholars have indeed linked the Sephardi political shift away from Labor (initially to Likud and later to Sephardi sectarian parties) to Labor's decline: specifically, to the reduced dependence of the Sephardim upon Labor-dominated institutions for employment and social services (e.g., Shafir and Peled 2002, 89; see also Smooha 1978, 128). My focus here is upon the Sephardim because the Russians, having arrived on the political scene only after the opening of the party system, do not provide longitudinal explanatory leverage. However, from a cross-sectional perspective, the greater success of the later-arriving Russians is also evidence consistent with the hypothesis.

Yet there are limits to this factor's explanatory contribution. With respect to the timing of Sephardi sectarian party success, while the bulk of Labor's decline had occurred by the late 1970s, support for Sephardi sectarian parties reached reasonable levels only in the late 1990s—coincident with the change in regime type. With respect to the different political trajectories of the two groups, Russian and Sephardi sectarian parties have experienced differential success in recent decades, yet both have faced the same relatively open party system.

This begs the question of why this variable has mattered at all in Israel. I earlier hypothesized that the constraint imposed by less open party systems should diminish when the new latent social group originates from outside of the polity, as is the case for both the Sephardim and the Russians. Accordingly, the expectation is that this variable should not provide explanatory leverage here. The explanation for why it does seems to lie in the unique characteristics of the Sephardi wave of mass immigration: most came virtually destitute to a country struggling to build the necessary infrastructure to accommodate them (including the basics such as housing) while it simultaneously grappled with economic privation, war, and state building.[56] Relative to both later immigrants to Israel such as the Russians and immigrants to other countries, the confluence of these factors led the Sephardim to become unusually and immediately dependent upon Israeli state institutions. In turn, this left them unusually prone to capture by the parties that controlled those institutions.

---

[56] By the end of 1949, Israel's immigrant absorption network was on the brink of collapse due to the unexpected volume of immigration. Immigrants were housed in temporary camps called *ma'abarot*, which consisted of collections of tents and wooden shacks that were scattered around the country. With the economy in crisis and jobs scarce, immigrants found themselves trapped in these camps for years, humiliated by their dependence upon the Israeli absorption authorities for their basic sustenance—and Sephardi immigrants more than most, for reasons that will be discussed later. See, for example, Smooha (1978, 95–95) and Hacohen (2003, 84–94, 134–137, 148–161).

6.2.4 GROUP POLITICIZATION

The final factor that can help to account for the variance in sectarian party success over both time and groups is group politicization. I first explore the groups' organizational resources before turning to their collective identities, factors that together shape the capacity for collective action in the political realm—that is, their politicization.

Organization and Leadership

To begin, the Russians have enjoyed a clear organizational advantage relative to the Sephardim. In fact, organizational and leadership failure is an oft-heard explanation for the Sephardi parties' lack of electoral success in Israel's first few decades (see, for example, the review in Herzog 1985b, 160–161).

First consider leadership. Both groups had a small advance contingent that, by virtue of their experiences with Israeli society and its democratic politics, might have provided the groups with skilled leadership in the early years. For the Russians, this was the 1970s Russian immigrants. For the Sephardim, this was the Sephardim who had immigrated to Palestine in the pre-state era, as well as those Sephardim who had long been resident in the biblical land of Israel (the "Old Yishuv"). Yet in both groups there has been friction between the early and late arrivals. In the case of the Sephardim, the late arrivals were reluctant to view the early arrivals as authentic members of their community.[57] And in the case of the Russians, the early arrivals were for the most part either not interested in playing a sectarian leadership role[58] or were viewed skeptically by the latecomers.[59]

But there the resemblance ends. The post-state Sephardi immigrants had low levels of both income and education and included few entrepreneurs with experience in community organization.[60] Specifically, this wave of

---

[57]They were mere "tokens" viewed as hand-picked and co-opted by the Ashkenazi establishment. See, for example, Peretz and Smooha (1981, 511–512, 515) and Chapter 5's note 38. As discussed in the last chapter, an indicator of this schism is the failure of the "old-time" Sephardi parties from the Mandatory period within a few elections of statehood. These charges of tokenism or co-option were also directed against the few post-state Sephardi elites who were allowed to rise in the political ranks of existing parties early on (Smooha 1978, 222).

[58]For example, Khanin (2001, 108) argues that many prominent figures who immigrated in the 1970s and very early in the 1990s wave found the idea of an ethnic party unacceptable.

[59]Siegel (1998, 41, 153–155) describes how the 1990s immigrants viewed the older 1970s immigrants as part of the Israeli establishment and hence were reluctant to follow their lead. In the 1992 elections, this "generational" schism was arguably a factor contributing to the failure of the Russian parties, which the last chapter argued were primarily the creation of the earlier Russian immigrants. Even in 1996, the Unity and Immigration list of 1970s immigrant Ephraim Gur failed because Gur was viewed as a man of little authority within the new immigrant community (Bick 1997, 139).

[60]Of course, this characterization elides important differences within the Sephardi community by country of origin. Iraqi and Egyptian Jewish immigrants, for example, had much higher levels of education than other Sephardi immigrants (e.g., Cohen 2002, 45). Further, leaders of the Iraqi Jewish community had both extensively engaged in Zionist activities in the pre-state

6. Israel: Testing Hypotheses about Sectarian Party Success

immigration disproportionally consisted of lower-class individuals such as nonprofessional shopkeepers and craftsmen (Shama and Iris 1977, 37–39). The wealthier and better educated had instead chosen to emigrate elsewhere (to France, for example, in the case of the Moroccan Jews), stripping the group of its entrepreneurs, intelligentsia, and social and political leadership (ibid., 73–74, 115; see also Hacohen 2003, 234). Many accordingly lacked the skills that would facilitate their political organization (Smooha 1978, 130).[61] This situation was exacerbated both by their difficult reception in Israel and by the ways in which existing parties responded to them.[62]

By way of contrast, the Russian Jewish immigrants of the 1990s were highly educated, including many doctors, engineers, scientists and other technologically skilled white-collar professionals such as writers and teachers in their ranks.[63] Further, many had experience in community organization: they had either led or participated in the revival of Eastern European Jewry's infrastructure in the USSR from the 1970s onwards, which ranged from the creation of Jewish schools to the formation of community associations. In contrast to the "underground" generation of the 1970s immigrants, the explosion of political ethnicity that the more recent immigrants had witnessed in the USSR led prominent figures among them to be more accepting of political ethnicity and its most obvious manifestation, ethnic parties (Khanin 2001, 108).

Second, consider the organizational (institutional) infrastructure of the community, at least in part a function of the human capital just described. By the time of the 1996 election, a very strong institutional infrastructure had developed in the Russian community. This included clubs; interest group–type associations, particularly the umbrella organization that was the Forum of Soviet Jewry; educational institutions; cultural and youth groups; student unions; professional workers' unions; and newspapers and other mass me-

---

era (Smooha 1978, 54) and played important political roles in their wider society (Simon 2003), giving them entrepreneurial, community-building experience. At the other end of the spectrum were the Ethiopians, who had mostly been engaged in agriculture and living in pastoral villages prior to their immigration to Israel (e.g., Hacohen 2003, 259).

[61] For example, the failure of the Black Panther social protest movement, about which more will be said later, to successfully transform itself into a political party in the 1970s is commonly attributed at least in part to the founders' lack of organizational and administrative skills. This in turn is attributed to their deficient formal education and marginal position in society (e.g., Shama and Iris 1977, 148–155).

[62] More will be said on the circumstances of their reception later. For now, I note the difficulty the various Sephardi Jewish communities had in maintaining their traditional communal organizations due to their dispersal throughout the country; the trying personal conditions they faced, such as exhausting work and poor housing; and their dependence upon the new authorities (Swirski 1989, 46–47).

[63] For example, 61 percent of the recent arrivals had thirteen or more years of education, and 42 percent had scientific and academic training, a figure four times the average in Israel (Bick 1997, 121). Nevertheless, Cohen (2002, 50) does note that Russian Jews who emigrated to countries such as the United States and Canada had slightly higher levels of schooling, meaning that the best and brightest among Soviet Jewry also elected to immigrate to countries other than Israel, even if the gap between those emigrating to Israel and those emigrating elsewhere was less than that observed for the Sephardim.

dia, from TV to the internet (e.g., Khanin 2001, 108–109). The vibrancy of the Russian media deserves special attention: by the mid-1990s, there were more than twenty daily newspapers, weekly magazines, and monthly journals published in Israel in Russian. Not surprisingly, the Russian media played a critical role in enabling Russian elites to communicate with their public, facilitating both the creation of a collective Russian identity and mass support for the Russian sectarian parties (Bick 1997, 141).

This can be contrasted with the Sephardi community. A few Sephardi newspapers had been published by elites of the "old-time" Sephardi community during the Mandatory period, but all had shut down by 1951 (Kark and Glass 2003, 343). Following statehood, immigrant associations were developed. However, they were fragmented by either country or region of origin.[64] Moreover, instead of being independent organizations, they were largely satellites of either particular political parties or the Israeli state (Smooha 1978, 209).[65] An exception to this characterization is that over the last two decades, Shas has been at the forefront of building an array of institutions for the Sephardi community, from an educational system to day care centers (Shafir and Peled 2002, 95). However, this institution building has been made possible by the state largesse Shas has received as a result of its growing political clout. In other words, the recent organizational growth of the Sephardi community is a consequence rather than the cause of the group's (reasonably) successful particization. This may in turn lay the groundwork for even greater sectarian party success in the future.

Identity and Politicization

Russians have also enjoyed a slight advantage relative to the Sephardim with respect to their sense of a group identity: their consciousness of themselves *qua* Russians. However, arguably the larger variance in identity can be observed over time in each group.

Thus far I have studied *latent* ethnic groups in Israel, where membership is defined by paternal country of origin. But does membership in such a latent group entail participation in a common identity, meaning that members share at least some beliefs and interests? This is a critical question because, as I argued in an earlier chapter, a shared identity as well as an organizational life (my definition of a *politicized* group) facilitates a latent group's collective action in the political realm. The hypothesis is accordingly that more politicized groups will be more likely to obtain sectarian political representation.

Yet self-conscious groups do not simply spring forth fully formed; they

---

[64] An example is the Association of Immigrants from North African and French-Speaking Countries. This follows the pattern established during the Mandatory period for Sephardi community infrastructure. For example, each Sephardi subgroup (e.g., the North Africans) had its own religious institutions (Kark and Glass 2003, 340–341).

[65] See also Tsur (2007) for more on the early North African immigrant associations and their links with Ashkenazi institutions.

must be constructed or "politically forged" (Laitin 1986, 159–160), as I also argued earlier. Individuals have to choose to identify with a category, a choice that can change over time. Complicating these choices and hence the construction of group identities is an individual's membership in multiple, often nested categories. For example, is someone holding an Israeli passport an Israeli, a Jew, a Sephardi, or a Yemeni? Another complicating factor is the often contested definition of categories. An example here is an Israeli child of mixed ethnic parentage who might identify with the ethnicity of the mother instead of the father, contrary to the way in which both the Israeli government and I have defined the latent ethnic categories in Israel.[66] Moreover, political entrepreneurs complicate matters further by attempting to manipulate individuals' choices using what Chandra (2004, 287) calls "heresthetical maneuvers" (see also Riker 1986; Posner 2005). Take as an example Shas's outreach to Russian immigrants from the Central Asian republics of the former USSR. As a result, the story of the growth of Sephardi and Russian identities is the story of how individuals choose to both redefine and identify with the menu of latent categories available to them, as well as how political entrepreneurs influence this process.

Unfortunately, extensive longitudinal data on the extent to which members of the latent social groups of Sephardim and Russians identify with or "attach to" those groups (Brady and Kaplan 2009) does not exist. The only time series data is found in the Israeli National Election Studies (INES), but even this is limited in time and effectively confined to the Sephardim. The most useful of the two questions that touch upon ethnic identity appears in the 1984 through 1996 surveys and asks if the respondent defines himself as Ashkenazi, Sephardi, or neither.[67] Of the Sephardim, a latent group that I define as usual, 72 percent identify as Sephardi on average, with the percentage ranging from 67 to 79 over time. Of those of "Israeli origin," that

---

[66]For example, in a recent interview in *Haaretz* (September 3, 2009, "Mama's Boy"), longtime Labor party MK and cabinet minister Uzi Baram, born to a politically prominent Ashkenazi father and a Sephardi mother, describes his personal vacillation between the two ethnic categories: "I was much closer to my mother's family than to my father's...I look Ashkenazi but have a Mizrachi [Sephardi] attitude. I prefer Mizrachi food and listen to Mediterranean music on the plane but I cannot say I'm a full-fledged Mizrachi. I was surrounded by Ashkenazim."

[67]Sometimes "both" is included as an option. Nominal measures of ethnic identification (salience) like this one do not work well for those for whom ethnic identity is not already highly salient (Brady and Kaplan 2000). Because the salience of the identity is precisely the empirical question here, a graded measure would be preferable. However, the only measures available in the INES are nominal. The other question measuring ethnic identification appears in the 1996, 1999, and 2006 INES surveys. It asks respondents to choose which of the following best (and second-best, third-best, and, for 1999 and 2006, fourth-best) describes their identity: "Israeli," "Jewish," "ethnic group" (in 1999 and 2006, further labeled Ashkenazi/Sephardi), or "secular/religious." In 2006 alone, "Russian" was included as an additional choice, but only for the first- and second-best identifications. Not surprisingly in light of Russian immigrants' attachment to Israel and their fellow Jews (discussed later), few chose this as their primary or secondary identity; where I might have expected it to appear would be as a tertiary identity, but it was not an option there. Regardless, the responses are commensurate with the portrait painted here: for the Sephardim, the primary to secondary identifications tend to be Israeli and Jewish, and the secondary to tertiary tend to be ethnic and religious.

is, those born in Israel to an Israeli-born father, an average of 32 percent identify as Sephardi, with the proportions ranging from 29 to 34.[68] Hence, since the mid-1980s, a significant proportion of the members of the latent Sephardi group have identified as Sephardim.

But to test the hypothesis about politicization and to help fill in the final piece of the puzzle about the differential Russian and Sephardi political trajectories, data is needed both for earlier years and for the Russians. Accordingly, I will now paint a more qualitative portrait of Sephardi collective identity over time before doing the same for the Russians. This portrait makes use of several of the methods and sources discussed by Brady and Kaplan (2009) for measuring the properties of ethnicity, such as historical inquiry and evaluation through surveys.

The obvious obstacle to the development of a Sephardi collective identity is the many countries from which the Sephardim have come. Country of origin serves as a competing lower-level category nested within the higher-level Sephardi category. In order for a Sephardi identity to develop, individuals must begin to identify with immigrants from other Asian or African countries instead of just with their fellow countrymen. Standing in the way of this identification are different languages (e.g., Persian for Iranian Jewish immigrants, Arabic for others), including different dialects (e.g., the Egyptian dialect of Arabic versus the Tunisian); different historical communal experiences; different religious and cultural traditions; and different socioeconomic characteristics (see, for example, note 60), to name just a few of the attributes associated with an individual's country of origin. In fact, one of the very terms often used to refer to the group that I have labeled the Sephardim is *Edot HaMizrach*. Usually translated as the Oriental or Eastern communities (in the plural), it evokes a sense of plurality and variety (Swirski 1989, 1).

Despite this latent plurality, the "social reality has been for all Mizrachim [Sephardim] to crystallize into one group, in socio-economic terms as well as in the public consciousness, both their own and the Ashkenazim's" (Shafir and Peled 2002, 88). A Sephardi collective identity emerged because Jewish immigrants from Asian and African countries underwent a "common social experience" after making *aliya* (Swirski 1989, 1; see also Shenhav 2006, 15). Discrimination was the predominant common experience.[69] It began even before they set foot in Israel: many Sephardi immigrants, in contrast to their European brethren, received no advance preparation for their immigration and traveled under worse conditions. Upon arrival, they were paid lower (Arab-style) wages. Moreover, somewhat by happenstance and somewhat

---

[68]It is also worth noting that a nontrivial percentage of the latent Ashkenazim often identify as Sephardi: an average of 20 percent, with a range of between 7 and 35 percent. These are likely children of mixed marriages with a Sephardi mother and an Ashkenazi father (see note 66). The percentage of Sephardim who identify as Ashkenazi is smaller: on average three percent.

[69]Many poignant first-person accounts can be found in Segev (1998, 155–194).

6. Israel: Testing Hypotheses about Sectarian Party Success

by design, the best housing predominantly went to European immigrants.[70] The consequence of these discriminatory policies combined with the lower Sephardi human capital described earlier has been a persistent socioeconomic gap. Other sociodemographic traits marking the common Sephardi experience were their greater religiosity (e.g., Smooha 1978, 101); their inability to speak either Hebrew or Yiddish; their larger family sizes; and their darker complexions (earning them the label "schvartz," Yiddish for "black"; see Shama and Iris 1977, 54).[71] Accordingly, the Sephardim have been spatially, economically, culturally, and educationally segregated from the Ashkenazi mainstream of Israeli society (Shafir and Peled 2002, 94).

In Israel's first decade, active Sephardi identification with this higher-level, pan-Sephardi category was blunted by the dismissive strategy played by the existing Ashkenazi establishment vis-à-vis the Sephardim, which encouraged the Sephardim on the one hand to identify with the even broader group of Jewish Israelis, and on the other hand to identify with their subgroup by country or region of origin.[72] By the end of the 1960s, however, a "Sephardi Awakening" (e.g., Shama and Iris 1977, 134) was under way. Identification with the pan-Sephardi category was ironically (albeit somewhat inadvertently) facilitated by the Ashkenazi establishment via the support existing parties gave to Sephardi political entrepreneurs, as already discussed. Even the ultimately unsuccessful Sephardi sectarian parties of the 1960s and 1970s served to raise the salience of the broader Ashkenazi–Sephardi ethnic division (e.g., Herzog 1986), one of several possible objectives that protest parties like these might have. Moreover, at this same time, funds began to be allocated for research into Sephardi traditions and curricula exploring these traditions were introduced into the schools, legitimizing the broader Sephardi cultural heritage (Herzog 1985b, 173–174). Similarly, extensive Sephardi service in the military blurred the differences by country of origin while increasing pride in Sephardi culture and identity (Shama and Iris 1977, 134–136). An equally important role in increasing Sephardi group consciousness was played by a series of public disturbances and other extra-parliamentary protests that drew attention to existing ethnic discrim-

---

[70] The Sephardi immigrants, particularly the later-coming North Africans, languished in camps and temporary settlements (*ma'abarot*; see note 56) before eventually being transferred to newly founded small urban settlements ("development towns") in peripheral areas of the country with both limited employment opportunities and poor agricultural prospects. The happenstance has to do with timing: the first immigrants were predominantly European, and to a large extent, housing was allocated on a first-come, first-serve basis. However, beyond timing, later groups of European immigrants such as the Poles were blatantly given special privileges. See, for example, Hacohen (2003).

[71] For example, Danny Adamasu, executive director of the Israel Association for Ethiopian Jews, noted that Ethiopians are made Ethiopian by Israelis; despite being born in Israel, they are Ethiopian because of their skin color (interview, June 1, 2008).

[72] Exemplifying the effort to prevent the formation of a pan-Sephardi coalition are the many satellite Sephardi parties supported by the existing parties during this period that targeted subgroups of Sephardim, such as the Yemenites and the North Africans. The also reflects the unwillingness of the different subgroups of Sephardi immigrants to cooperate in these early years (Lissak 1972, 269).

ination, such as the 1959 Wadi Salib riots in Haifa and the Black Panther demonstrations of the early 1970s.[73]

Accordingly, tension between identifying with the larger group of Jewish Israelis, fellow Sephardi immigrants, and the smaller group of immigrants sharing a country of origin has been present for the Sephardim since Israel's early years. Pan-Sephardi identification has been waxing, however, while country-of-origin identification has been waning.[74] While this has given rise to somewhat conflicting quantitative evidence regarding the extent of identification with the broader Sephardi group at any given point in time,[75] the evidence suggests that by the 1980s, the vast majority of Sephardim identified as Sephardim. This collective identity entails both the recognition and the rejection of their second-class status, as well as (increasingly) a repudiation of the melting pot model of assimilation in favor of maintaining aspects of Sephardi culture, especially its greater religiosity.

Growing Sephardi identification with a Sephardi identity since the 1960s is consistent with the greater success of Sephardi sectarian parties from the 1980s on, as hypothesized. It is difficult, however, to discount the possibility that some of the recent growth in a Sephardi identity is an effect instead of a cause of Sephardi sectarian party success: that Sephardi parties such as Shas have used their political resources, facilitated in turn by other factors such as the type of regime, to herestheticly encourage the growth of this group consciousness.[76] Reaching beyond its North African roots enables Shas to forge a larger coalition that will bring it greater political power in the longer term, the dynamic interplay between particization and politicization discussed in an earlier chapter.[77] Moreover, the competing identification of many Sephardim with the cross-cutting, lower-level category of country

---

[73] The Wadi Salib riots were triggered by a policeman's shooting of a Moroccan drunkard in a Haifa slum. Sympathy demonstrations appeared in various development towns; a government commission was formed; and there was extensive media coverage of the fallout. The Black Panthers were a street gang-cum-protest movement that borrowed imagery (such as their name) from the American Black Panthers, and whose activities also received much public attention. See, for example, Smooha (1978, 209–212).

[74] The Ethiopians are the group that has most remained outside of the pan-Sephardi fold. While they have many commonalities with the Sephardim, such as dark skin, other things such as their much later arrival in Israel (in the 1980s and 1990s) have set them apart.

[75] For example, somewhat contrary to the INES results reported earlier, Herzog (1985a, 50–51) points to a 1982 study of upwardly mobile Israelis of Yemenite and Moroccan origin that found a much stronger identification with fellow country-of-origin immigrants than with the broader group of Sephardim. More consistent with the INES data are recent studies such as Yiftachel and Tzfadia's (2004) 1998 survey of individuals in six representative development towns, which found that respondents felt closer to other Sephardim than to all other groups, including subgroups such as North African immigrants.

[76] In other words, the president–parliamentary regime facilitated the politicization of the ethnic cleavage in Israel (Kenig, Hazan, and Rahat 2005, 53).

[77] For example, Willis (1995, 136) argues that "Shas has been innovative, forging a generic Sephardic identity, which even mixes Ashkenazi styles, rather than arguing for a return to particularistic regional customs. The values and traditions that Shas has utilized to build a more general Sephardic identity play on the common experiences of these many constituent ethnicities vis-à-vis the dominant Ashkenazi 'other'."

6. Israel: Testing Hypotheses about Sectarian Party Success

of origin, exacerbated by their low level of institutionalization, is consistent with the limited success Sephardi sectarian parties have enjoyed to date, both absolutely and relative to the Russians. Overall, the Sephardim do not seem to satisfy my definition of a fully politicized group, at least not until recently.

Like the Sephardim, the Russian immigrants of the 1990s face conflicting pulls between identifying with their fellow Russian immigrants and the larger group of Jewish Israelis. The only study I know of that explores their identification with these categories shows that while a high percentage (78 percent) identify as Jewish, only slightly lower percentages also identify as Russians, that is, as "an immigrant from the former Soviet Union" (69 percent) and as "a Jew from the former Soviet Union" (66 percent) (Al-haj 2002, 55). These figures are similar to those obtained from the INES for the Sephardim for the 1980s and 1990s. In general, surveys show that the Russians have a strong desire to maintain their cultural uniqueness through autonomous educational, cultural, and political institutions, such as Russian-language schools (e.g., Al-haj 2004, 687–688). This strong dual identification with Jewish Israelis and fellow Russians has been described by scholars using terms ranging from a "cultural enclave" to a "Russian bubble" (ibid., 686).

By way of contrast with the Sephardim, however, most Russians do not feel a competing pull to identify with a nested, lower-level category. In other words, they are a more internally homogeneous group, complementing their advantages in the realm of organization and leadership. Most importantly, they share the historical communal experience of life in the former USSR; the Russian language (even though they may also speak other languages); Russian cultural traditions; and a secular orientation that sets them at odds with the Jewish character of the Israeli state.

This is not to say that the Russians completely lack internally crosscutting divisions, however. The most significant is the division between Sephardi Russians from the Central Asian and Caucasus republics and Ashkenazi Russians from the European republics. This ethnic division is reinforced by an overlapping division of religion, because the former are more traditionally religious than the latter. Indeed, Sephardi Russians have identified more strongly with the Sephardi than with the Russian category. An indicator of this is the electoral support they have given to Shas (Khanin 2001, 120)—one fruit of Shas's campaign to build a pan-Sephardi identity, which led it to include Central Asian Russians in its last few Knesset contingents (see note 41). Another internal division is between the subgroups of Russian immigrants who are not Jewish according to Orthodox Jewish law and those who are. However, the majority of experts consider these non-Jewish Russians to be "socially still a part of the Jewish community of the country" (Khanin 2001, 120). Moreover, because of their alienation from the dominant Orthodox Jewish aspects of Israeli society, they identify even more strongly as Russians than do Jewish Russian immigrants (Al-haj 2002,

56).

The 1996 election campaign is often pointed to as the event that spurred the growth in the Russian collective identity. Specifically, Khanin (2001, 109) discusses the "unprecedented campaign of blackening the [Russian] aliya... in Israeli mass-media and government structures in 1992–96," part of the adversarial strategy towards the Russians adopted by existing parties such as Labor, as described earlier. For example, references to criminal activities on the part of Russian immigrants, from the existence of a Russian mafia to prostitution rings, abounded in the press. The newly founded Israel b'Aliya accordingly made the cornerstone of its campaign a call for community pride, respect, and recognition (Bick 1997, 129–133). The ultimate effect of the "blackening" was to bring Russians together, including the two separate waves of Russian immigrants. While most of the 1970s Russian immigrants had originally identified with the Jewish Israeli community and not as Russians, they, too, began to identify as Russians at this point.[78]

When coupled with the group's institutional development, this increased and broadened Russian group consciousness suggests that by 1996, the Russians had come to satisfy my definition of a politicized group. In contrast to the Sephardim, political entrepreneurs seeking to supply the Russians with sectarian representation accordingly enjoyed many advantages.[79] As hypothesized, this is consistent with the greater success of Russian sectarian parties in 1996 relative to 1992, as well as relative to the Sephardim overall. Of course, the change to a president–parliamentary regime for the 1996 election is almost certainly another contributory factor, as argued earlier, one that in turn is likely to have boosted elite efforts to both broaden and deepen a Russian collective identity at this time. This may account for the continued Russian sectarian party success subsequent to the switch back to the parliamentary regime in 2001.

6.3 CONCLUSION

In this chapter, I sought explanations for the variation in the success of Sephardi and Russian sectarian political parties in Israel. In the last chapter, I traced this variation back to immigration and the resulting changes in Israel's social heterogeneity. But that still left the puzzle of why Sephardi and Russian immigrants to Israel had taken different political representational

---

[78] For example, Gitelman (1982, 239–241) presents evidence that by 1975, most 1970s Russian immigrants (65 percent) had "never" felt Russian. Moreover, although most (62 percent) perceived other Israelis as identifying them as Russians, almost none (2 percent) desired to be identified in that way. Yet during the 1996 campaign, Yuri Stern, who made *aliya* in 1981 at the tail end of the 1970s wave of immigration and who was fourth on Israel b'Aliya's list, said that "I have never felt so 'Russian' as in the last few years..." (Bick 1997, 130).

[79] Russian MK Ze'ev Elkin (then of Kadima, now of Likud), like other politicians I interviewed, voiced just these sentiments—pointing to the two groups' relative levels of education and abilities to organize politically—in offering an explanation for the different political trajectories (interview, June 2, 2008).

paths, and why those paths had diverged (and at other times, converged) at particular moments in time. Why, in other words, have only some increases in Israel's social heterogeneity led to the successful emergence of new sectarian parties to represent the new social groups, the primary mechanism through which I have linked social heterogeneity to party system fragmentation?

Drawing upon the theory I developed in Chapter 2, the within-case, qualitative analysis I undertook here identified four factors as explanatory. Notably, the electoral system, the focus of the existing literature, is not one of them. With respect to the specific timing of sectarian party success, I presented evidence that Israel's mid-1990s change in regime type and the increasing politicization of both the Sephardim and Russians are the primary explanatory factors. With respect to the greater success of Russian sectarian parties, I argued that the explanatory factors are the less accommodative strategies existing parties have adopted towards the Russians vis-à-vis the Sephardim and the relatively greater politicization of the Russians. The opening of the party system by the 1970s also seems to have contributed to the explanation of both puzzles, but this variable should be viewed as less important, for reasons I will discuss. While group size was not relevant for explaining these puzzles because both immigrant groups were always large enough for their sectarian parties to play a governing role, group size did explain why some smaller immigrant groups, such as the Ethiopians, were not successfully particized.

To elaborate regarding the explanatory factors, first and of particular importance is the regime type. Israel's 1996 switch to a regime that reduced the policy-making authority in the hands of the largest party in the legislature provides an explanation for one key piece of the puzzle: why in 1996 both the Sephardim and the Russians began to provide significant support to sectarian parties, whereas prior to 1996, immigrants to Israel had generally been absorbed into the existing party system (e.g., Horowitz 1999). This suggests that, as hypothesized, the regime type is usually a necessary if not a sufficient condition for successful particization. For example, can we really imagine Russian sectarian parties having achieved such success under the resuscitated parliamentary regime had not the president–parliamentary regime initially facilitated their sectarian political representation, providing incentives for elites to hone, and for voters to embrace, a distinctive Russian collective identity? This use of the Israeli case to leverage a quasi-experimental design against my hypothesis about the regime type deserves special note. Quasi-experimental designs are largely absent from the literature because in the postwar period, few countries have embarked upon the kind of radical, far-reaching reforms of their regime types that Israel embarked upon in 1996. It is for this reason that the Israeli experiment with its unique president-parliamentary regime is a social scientific gold mine.

Second is existing party strategy, a hypothesis that was tested here for the first time. The failure of the existing parties in Israel to adopt a fully accommodative strategy towards either group explains why both have been at least somewhat successful at obtaining sectarian representation. However, the fact that more accommodation has been offered to the Sephardim helps to explain the Russians' greater success. Overall, the Israeli case suggests that playing a dismissive strategy is dangerous because it easily becomes adversarial. Likewise, the case suggests that existing parties adopting a partially but not fully accommodative strategy may facilitate sectarian party success almost as much as an adversarial one does. To head off both the entry and success of sectarian parties, existing parties need to either fully accommodate new latent social groups or carefully work to dismiss them without prejudice.

Third is the politicization of a new latent social group. The politicization of both immigrant groups has grown over time, increasing their capacity for collective action and facilitating the success of their sectarian parties. Nevertheless, the Russians have always held the edge over the Sephardim, particularly in the organizational realm. The Israeli case accordingly confirms my hypothesis that politicized groups are more likely to be successfully particized.

Fourth and finally is party system openness. The opening of the Israeli party system in the past few decades has facilitated the recent success of Sephardi sectarian parties. It has also provided an advantage to the later-arriving Russians. This case study accordingly suggests that the openness of the party system does matter, contrary to the null-to-contradictory findings about this hypothesis obtained from the quantitative analyses. However, the case-specific nature of the process of opening, not directly tied to a cross-national phenomenon such as dealignment, supports my arguments in earlier chapters that this is a less important variable that will be very difficult to operationalize in a cross-national context.

Of course, the "many variables, few cases" problem means that I cannot definitively isolate the independent effects of each of these variables using this within-case analysis of Israel. I also cannot rule out, and have in fact explicitly recognized, that there may be feedback effects. An example is sectarian party success facilitating the institutionalization and hence the politicization of the Sephardim. Nevertheless, the analysis of the Israeli case in this chapter supports my overarching argument that factors other than the electoral system play a critical role in shaping sectarian party success. More specifically, this chapter enabled me to triangulate some of the conclusions drawn on the basis of the quantitative analyses, particularly for my key hypothesis regarding the type of regime. This chapter also enabled me to provide at least suggestive evidence in support of some hypotheses that the quantitative analyses did not test, such as that regarding existing party strategies. Moreover, the better measures that I was able to construct and the process tracing that I was able to undertake, including my finding that many of these variables actually seemed to matter to the actors on the ground, all raise the internal validity of the study as a whole.

6. Israel: Testing Hypotheses about Sectarian Party Success

In a future chapter, I will turn to the democratic consequences of the different paths to political representation taken by new social groups such as the Sephardi and Russian immigrants to Israel. My immediate task, however, is to undertake a within-case analysis of the United States.

7 The United States: New Parties for New Groups? Testing Hypotheses

In this chapter, I conduct a within-case analysis of the United States. Unlike Israel, the United States has never been a parliamentary democracy. Instead, it has employed a presidential system of government since its founding. Also in marked contrast to Israel, its electoral system falls on the extremely restrictive end of the continuum: with minor exceptions since the mid-1800s, the electoral system used by the United States at the federal or national level has consisted of single-member districts and a plurality formula, otherwise known as "first past the post." This makes the United States a good case with which to explore how changes in society have shaped the fragmentation of the party system when the electoral system is majoritarian, this chapter's goal.

What the United States and Israel do have in common, however, is that both have experienced rapid, fairly large-scale change in the composition of their citizenries. Like Israel, the United States is a country of immigration. But immigration has not been the only historical process to increase the social, and specifically the ethnic, heterogeneity of the United States' citizenry: the extension of the franchise to African Americans is another. While immigration has introduced numerous social groups differentiated by various attributes, from language to religion, to the United States, African American enfranchisement has introduced a single social group with an accordingly greater latent capacity for collective action. This is why I turn my lens from the historical process of immigration to the franchise in this within-case analysis of the United States. First emancipated from slavery and then enfranchised in the late 1860s and early 1870s following a civil war between the northern and southern states, African Americans were subsequently disenfranchised in large parts of the country by the turn of the last century and finally re-enfranchised only in the 1960s, almost one hundred years later. Many also migrated from southern to northern and western states in the mid-twentieth century.

7. The United States: New Parties for New Groups? Testing Hypotheses

The obvious question raised by these changes in social heterogeneity concerns their effect upon party system fragmentation in the United States. As noted earlier, the federal electoral system of the United States has been effectively held constant over the period I study. Accordingly, to the extent to which African American sectarian parties have successfully emerged to contest some federal elections but not others, empirical support is provided for my argument that factors other than the electoral system help to determine sectarian party success, thereby conditioning the relationship between social heterogeneity and party system fragmentation. Any appearance and success of African American sectarian parties also suggests that we need to think carefully about how majoritarian electoral systems do (or do not) act as a constraint on the particization of new latent social groups.

Moreover, because social heterogeneity has varied over time and space in the United States owing to African American enfranchisement and internal migration, this within-case study is well suited to testing my hypotheses about why some new social groups are likely to be more successful than others at forming their own sectarian parties. As in the Israeli case, the addition of this new social group to the electorate can be viewed as a quasi-experiment. Many factors are held constant while allowing for variance in some of the factors that were hypothesized to shape the likelihood of a new latent group's successful particization. For example, with respect to the factor of group size, while African Americans have never been a large share of the United States' national electorate, they have sometimes constituted a large share of the electorates of some states. Specifically, they have been a majority of some states' electorates at some points in time (e.g., Mississippi until the early 1900s) and an extreme minority of others' (e.g., Vermont). By seeing how variation in the emergence and success of African American sectarian parties empirically relates to variation in the hypothesized independent variables, I can draw conclusions about which factors do shape sectarian party success. Further, by taking advantage of the United States' longer history and its federal structure, I can conduct a rigorous quantitative empirical analysis, in contrast to the Israeli case study.

As I will argue, there has been great empirical variation in both the entry and success of African American sectarian parties at the federal level. The case of African Americans in the United States accordingly bolsters my argument that factors other than the electoral system shape the success of sectarian parties that aim to represent new social groups—just as the case of the Sephardim and Russians in Israel did. Further, I find that group size, group politicization, and the strategies played by existing catch-all parties are the factors that empirically account for the observed variation in African American sectarian party entry and success. The findings of this chapter accordingly either triangulate or supplement the findings of the earlier empirical chapters. Last but not least, I argue that the appearance but ultimately limited success of African American sectarian parties in the United States is best not laid at the altar of the United States' restrictive electoral system, as we might erroneously be tempted to assume.

7.1 SOCIAL HETEROGENEITY IN THE UNITED STATES

In 1867, in the aftermath of the bloody four year Civil War that pitted northern states against southern ones, the United States embarked upon a remarkable experiment in biracial democracy (Valelly 2004, 73). The Civil War saw the emancipation of African Americans from slavery.[1] But an equally momentous sea change in race relations followed on emancipation's heels. From 1867 to 1877, the victorious northern states attempted to both rebuild the rebellious southern states and reintegrate them into the federal union, a period known as Reconstruction.[2] During this period, African Americans were enfranchised, an exceptional event that radically reshaped the electorate.[3]

Once the Civil War guns fell silent, African Americans began pressing for the right to vote. They were supported by many northern whites, particularly those in the Radical wing of the Republican Party. The June 1866 passage of the Fourteenth Amendment to the Constitution of the United States was Congress's first national sally in this direction. This amendment affirmed African American citizenship and challenged legal discrimination on racial grounds by guaranteeing all citizens equal protection under the law. It fell short of African American enfranchisement, however (Foner 2002, 254–258). At the same time, a campaign of violence was unleashed against both African Americans and white Republicans in the South, while the newly formed southern state governments legally codified racial discrimination. Beginning in early 1866, Congress accordingly embarked upon a variety of measures that expanded federal oversight of the franchise with the goal of securing the civil and political liberties of African Americans.

These Congressional actions cumulated in the Reconstruction Act of

---

[1] In the former Confederate states of the South, home to the vast majority of slaves, emancipation was enacted by the two executive orders that constituted the Emancipation Proclamation (1862 and 1863). The Thirteenth Amendment to the United States Constitution later (in 1865) ended slavery throughout the country.

[2] Much has been written on this chapter of American history. To provide just a few examples, see Kousser (1975), Keyssar (2001), Perman (2001), Valelly (2004), and the modern classic of Foner (2002).

[3] This exceptionalism becomes apparent when one considers the history of the franchise in the first half of the nineteenth century, when most states had retracted suffrage for free African Americans while simultaneously broadening the franchise to lower-class white males (Keyssar 2001, 43–47). Slaves had always been ineligible to vote, but free African Americans had intially been granted the franchise if they met property and taxpaying restrictions in all states except Virginia, Georgia, and South Carolina. However, as more free African Americans became eligible to vote with the broadening of the economic franchise; the free African American population grew; and what Keyssar (2001, 45) describes as an "efflorescence" of racism swept over the land, a cascade of racial suffrage exclusions were enacted either in constitutional conventions or through popular referenda. By the 1850s, only Massachusetts, Vermont, New Hampshire, Maine, and Rhode Island did *not* deny African Americans the vote on racial grounds, even though they collectively contained less than five percent of the nation's free African American population (ibid.).

7. The United States: New Parties for New Groups? Testing Hypotheses

March 1867, which enfranchised African Americans in the former Confederate states. Existing southern state governments were denied recognition and continued military rule was authorized. To be readmitted to the Union, each southern state was required to ratify the Fourteenth Amendment and to approve by universal male suffrage a constitution permitting African Americans the vote on the same terms as whites. The effect was a wholesale transformation of Southern politics.

Republicans then turned their attention to granting African Americans voting rights in the North while simultaneously securing them more permanently in the South via a constitutional amendment. The Fifteenth Amendment to the United States Constitution, the subject of a dramatic and partisan debate, was passed in February 1869 and eventually ratified in February 1870. This amendment forbade the denial of the vote on account of race, color or previous condition of servitude. While African American men were accordingly granted the vote on the same terms as white men, the amendment fell short of establishing universal male suffrage, opening the door to poll taxes, literacy tests and property qualifications in the South, and failed to guarantee African Americans' right to hold office (Foner 2002, 446–447). Nevertheless, it was a "landmark in the history of the right to vote" (Keyssar 2001, 82).

Yet biracial politics in the South did not last. Direct northern enforcement of the Fourteenth and Fifteenth Amendments, and hence Reconstruction, came to an end following the 1876 presidential election and the removal of the last federal soldiers from the South. The ebbing of the "high tide of faith in democracy" reached at midcentury left an "increasingly heterogeneous society contending awkwardly with its own professed political values" (Keyssar 2001, 63). Women's suffrage aside, the period from the 1850s through World War I was generally characterized by a narrowing of the franchise. African Americans were to prove no exception.

In this vacuum, white Southern Democrats launched an two-phase assault on African American voting rights, the key both to driving Republican governments from power and to maintaining white control of black labor.[4] The first phase, a period labeled "Redemption" by Perman (2001), lasted from 1877 through the mid-1890s. It was characterized by hotly contested elections marked by efforts at de facto disenfranchisement of African Americans and opposition whites through fraud and violence. The second phase, labeled "Restoration" (ibid.), followed on the heels of the first. It was characterized by systematic campaigns to disenfranchise African Americans legally through the use of poll taxes, literacy tests, secret-ballot laws, gerrymandering, a statewide white Democratic primary, and lengthy residence requirements, among other devices. The less well-known result of these

---

[4] Valelly (2004, 1-2) draws attention to the exceptionalism of this assault by arguing that no other social group has ever entered the electorate of an established democracy only to then be "extruded" by nominally democratic means—another little-recognized facet of American exceptionalism. See also the discussion in Chapter 3 for more on this point.

campaigns was to additionally disenfranchise a wide swathe of lower-class white voters (Kousser 1975, 238, 250–257). By 1910, the process of disenfranchisement was complete (ibid., 224), and the solidly Democratic South, with its strikingly low levels of electoral participation overall and particularly for African Americans, was born.[5]

Reconstruction seemed a failure. Yet its "unfinished revolution" (Foner 2002) planted the seeds for eventual more far-reaching changes in America's citizenry. In the Restored South, what came to be called Jim Crow laws mandated supposedly separate but equal racial segregation, which in reality translated into second-class status for African Americans. Denied a vote at the ballot box, African Americans began to vote with their feet around the time of World War I, forsaking the South for greater opportunities in northern and western cities. World War II then drew millions into the army and the booming factories outside of the rural South, intensifying the exodus. The most obvious consequence of this "Great Migration" was demographic: by the 1970s, approximately half of all African Americans had come to live outside of the South, as compared to 10 percent in 1915 when the migration had begun (Wilkerson 2010, 10). Another consequence was to arguably push the country toward the Civil Rights movement of the 1960s (ibid., 9)—a "second reconstruction" that would take America down a more egalitarian and democratic path (Woodward 1960).

Beginning in the 1950s, African Americans began to push back against their second-class status. They were aided by a host of national and regional organizations such as the Southern Christian Leadership Conference; by a string of Supreme Court decisions that chipped away at both segregation (such as *Brown v. Board of Education*) and the legal disenfranchisement apparatus (such as *Smith v. Allwright*); by the growing electoral clout of African Americans in the North; and by shifts in public opinion away from racial discrimination rooted in the ideological battles fought against both fascism and communism. Growing violence in the South in response to a more activist African American Civil Rights movement finally prompted the federal government to intervene. First came the modest civil rights acts of the late 1950s and early 1960s and then finally the ground-breaking Voting Rights Act of 1965. The latter tore down the last legal barriers to voting and authorized federal oversight to protect African American political rights. The impact was dramatic: in the South as a whole, roughly one million new voters were registered within a few years after the bill became law, bringing African American registration to a record 62 percent (Keyssar 2001, 212). The Civil Rights movement of the 1960s accordingly saw African Americans brought into the American electorate for good.

These changes in the social, and specifically in the ethnic, heterogeneity of the United States' citizenry are summarized in Table 7.1 and shown graphically in Figure 7.1. Both the table and the figure provide estimates

---

[5]To illustrate how complete this disenfranchisement was, by 1940 only three percent of southern African Americans were registered to vote (Keyssar 2001, 199).

7. The United States: New Parties for New Groups? Testing Hypotheses

Year	Population, Percent African American	Electorate, Percent African American	N
1860	14	0.055	1.0
1870	12	11	1.2
1910	11	2.3	1.0
1960	10	4.9	1.1
1970	11	9.5	1.2
2006	13	12	1.3

Table 7.1: For selected election years, estimates of the African American share of the United States' population and of the theoretical electorate (that is, the voting-age, race, and gendered population), as well as the effective number of ethnic groups in the United States' theoretical electorate (N). Source: estimates based on U.S. Census Bureau (1860–1960, 1965, 1966–2006, 2000b, 2008, 2009a); Gibson and Jung (2002); and Carter et al. (2006). See Appendix D for more details.

of the African American share of the country's population and of the theoretical electorate (that is, the voting-age, race, and gendered population) for all federal election years from 1860 to 2006.[6] Figure 7.1 additionally shows estimates of the African American share of the actual electorate (that is, of registered voters) from 1966 onwards, the only years for which this data is available.[7]

This table and figure show that the African American share of the American population attained an all-time high of 14 percent in 1860; dropped (albeit temporarily) with the secession of the southern states; and then eventually gradually climbed back up to about 13 percent today. More importantly, however, the table and figure show that African Americans' share

---

[6]The theoretical electorate consists of the population that is of the age, race, and gender granted the franchise at the time of each election. For example, in 1870, this was all males of age twenty-one and over. By way of contrast, in 1910, it was all white males of age twenty-one and over and all black males of age twenty-one and over who resided outside of the South. Economic characteristics are not used to define the theoretical electorate because economic restrictions on the franchise had effectively been removed by the 1860s, as discussed in Chapter 3 (see, for example, Keyssar 2001, 29). See Appendix D for more information about these estimates.

[7]The United States is the only advanced industrial democracy to require individuals to actively register to vote to join the electorate. This is accordingly the root of the distinction unique to the United States between what I have called the theoretical electorate, all those granted the franchise and hence eligible to vote (who would constitute the electorate in all other advanced industrial democracies), and what I have called the actual electorate, a subset of the theoretical electorate consisting of those eligible individuals who have actually registered (the electorate in the United States). Unfortunately, data on the actual electorate (that is, registered voters) is available only since the Civil Rights movement.

Changing Societies, Changing Party Systems

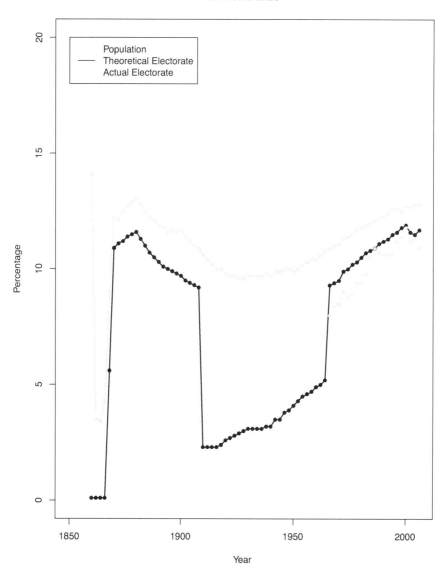

Figure 7.1: For the United States as a whole, the African American proportion of the population and of the theoretical electorate (that is, the voting-age, race, and gendered population) from 1860 through 2006. The African American proportion of the *actual* electorate (that is, registered voters) is also shown for the years for which it is available (1966 onwards). Source: see Table 7.1.

7. The United States: New Parties for New Groups? Testing Hypotheses

of the national theoretical electorate has always lagged behind their share of the population, often quite significantly so. Prior to 1868, for example, when African Americans were enfranchised only in five northern states, they made up less than one-tenth of one percent of the American electorate. And while their share of the national electorate peaked at approximately 11 percent at the height of Reconstruction, a time when they were enfranchised everywhere, by 1910 it is estimated to have dropped to a mere 2 percent as a result of their effective disenfranchisement in the former Confederate states. Even with the exodus of African Americans from the South to the North and hence from states where they were disenfranchised to states where they were enfranchised during the Great Migration, their share of the national electorate is estimated not to have exceeded 6 percent prior to the passage of the Voting Rights Act in 1965. Further, from the figure, it is clear that African Americans have made up an even smaller percentage of registered voters, that is, of the actual electorate, in recent decades than would be expected based upon their share of the theoretical electorate.

A final statistic presented in Table 7.1 also captures these changes in the social heterogeneity of the United States: estimates of the effective number of ethnic groups in the theoretical electorate for the same election years, which is calculated by including all non–African Americans in a single ethnic group.[8] This statistic shows that when African Americans have been *disenfranchised* in the South, the United States has had effectively one (white) ethnic group. Conversely, when African Americans have been *enfranchised* in the South, the effective number of ethnic groups in the United States has increased, but only to a maximum of 1.3. The increase is far less than one whole ethnic group because of the small number of African Americans relative to non–African Americans at the national level.

But this aggregate story masks remarkable variation in ethnic heterogeneity at the subnational level. I specifically focus upon one subnational unit, the state. Table 7.2 presents the African American share of the population and of the theoretical electorate for each of the fifty states for four selected election years. Moreover, for a selection of states that collectively represent the variation in the states' ethnic demographics, Figure 7.2 graphs both of these statistics for each election year from 1860 through 2006.[9]

What this table and figure show is that while African Americans have

---

[8] While this simple approach has obvious drawbacks, as recently as 2000, 81 percent of the American population was classified as being racially white. With African Americans, the second-largest racial group, making up approximately 12 percent of the population, only approximately 7 percent of the population belonged to other racial groups. Even if Hispanics are broken out from the white population and treated as a separate ethnic group, non-Hispanic whites still make up the vast majority of the population: approximately 70 percent. In the country's earlier years, non-Hispanic whites made up an even larger share of the population, increasing the attractiveness of this approach.

[9] The effective number of ethnic groups is not shown at the state level for reasons of space, but interested readers can easily calculate it from the data presented in Table 7.2. Time series data for all states can be found in Appendix D. This appendix also contains more information about the construction of these estimates.

Changing Societies, Changing Party Systems

State	Population (%) 1860	1870	1960	2006	Theoretical Electorate (%) 1860	1870	1960	2006
Alabama	45	48	30	26	0.0	48	2.0	24
Alaska	NA	NA	3.0	4.1	NA	NA	5.4	3.0
Arizona	NA	NA	3.3	4.0	NA	NA	3.4	3.5
Arkansas	26	25	22	16	0.0	26	2.0	14
California	1.1	0.76	5.6	6.7	0.0	0.76	5.8	6.3
Colorado	NA	NA	2.3	4.3	NA	NA	2.4	3.7
Connecticut	1.9	1.8	4.2	10	0.0	1.8	3.8	9.2
Delaware	19	18	14	21	0.0	17	13	19
Florida	45	49	18	16	0.0	47	2.0	14
Georgia	44	46	28	30	0.0	45	2.0	28
Hawaii	NA	NA	0.77	2.9	NA	NA	0.91	1.6
Idaho	NA	NA	0.22	0.85	NA	NA	0.26	0.66
Illinois	0.45	1.1	10	15	0.0	1.2	9.4	14
Indiana	0.85	1.5	5.8	9.0	0.0	1.6	5.4	8.2
Iowa	0.16	0.48	0.92	2.5	0.0	0.53	0.84	2.2
Kansas	NA	4.7	4.2	6.0	NA	3.8	3.9	4.9
Kentucky	20	17	7.1	7.7	0.0	15	6.8	6.2
Louisiana	50	50	32	31	0.0	50	2.0	29
Maine	0.21	0.26	0.34	1.0	0.22	0.29	0.34	0.48
Maryland	25	22	17	29	0.0	21	16	28
Massachusetts	0.78	0.96	2.2	6.9	0.76	0.98	2.0	6.0
Michigan	0.91	1.0	9.2	14	0.0	0.99	8.9	13
Minnesota	0.15	0.17	0.65	4.5	0.0	0.21	0.63	3.5
Mississippi	55	54	42	37	0.0	46	2.0	34
Missouri	10	6.9	9.0	11	0.0	5.9	8.4	10
Montana	NA	NA	0.22	0.29	NA	NA	0.24	0.27
Nebraska	NA	0.64	2.1	4.5	NA	0.74	1.9	4.4
Nevada	NA	0.83	4.6	7.9	NA	0.75	4.3	7.5
New Hampshire	0.15	0.18	0.31	1.2	0.15	0.19	0.33	0.99
New Jersey	3.8	3.4	8.4	14	0.0	3.4	11	13
New Mexico	NA	NA	1.8	2.8	NA	NA	1.9	2.5
New York	1.3	1.2	8.4	17	0.0	1.3	8.1	16

Table 7.2: For selected election years, estimates of the African American share of each state's population and of the theoretical electorate (that is, the voting-age, race, and gendered population), all rounded to two significant digits. "NA" indicates election years for which the state was not yet a state. Continued on next page. Source: estimates based on U.S. Census Bureau (1860–1960, 1948, 1954–1962, 1966–2006, 1968–2000, 1970, 1990, 2000c, 2009c) and Carter et al. (2006).

7. The United States: New Parties for New Groups? Testing Hypotheses

State	Population (%) 1860	1870	1960	2006	Theoretical Electorate (%) 1860	1870	1960	2006
North Carolina	36	37	24	22	0.0	36	2.0	20
North Dakota	NA	NA	0.12	1.0	NA	NA	0.16	0.21
Ohio	1.6	2.4	8.1	12	0.0	2.4	7.7	11
Oklahoma	NA	NA	6.6	8.0	NA	NA	6.0	7.2
Oregon	0.24	0.38	1.0	1.9	0.0	0.50	0.91	1.4
Pennsylvania	2.0	1.9	7.2	11	0.0	2.0	7.1	9.5
Rhode Island	2.3	2.3	2.1	6.3	2.2	2.4	1.8	5.0
South Carolina	59	59	35	29	0.0	58	2.0	27
South Dakota	NA	NA	0.16	1.0	NA	NA	0.19	0.69
Tennessee	26	26	16	17	0.0	24	2.0	15
Texas	30	31	12	11	0.0	28	2.0	11
Utah	NA	NA	0.46	1.2	NA	NA	0.51	0.86
Vermont	0.23	0.28	0.13	0.81	0.22	0.31	0.17	0.61
Virginia	43	42	20	20	0.0	40	2.0	18
Washington	NA	NA	1.7	3.7	NA	NA	1.6	3.0
West Virginia	NA	4.1	4.8	3.4	NA	4.2	4.5	3.2
Wisconsin	0.15	0.20	1.9	6.0	0.0	0.25	1.6	4.8
Wyoming	NA	NA	0.66	1.2	NA	NA	0.66	0.77

Table 7.2: Continued from previous page.

been a negligible minority throughout the United States' history in some states, such as Vermont, they have at times actually been a *majority* in other states, such as South Carolina. For example, with their 1867 enfranchisement, African Americans went from zero to almost 60 percent of the theoretical electorate in South Carolina, their maximum share of a state electorate to date. They also constituted a majority of the theoretical electorate in both Louisiana and Mississippi during the Reconstruction era, and had the Jim Crow system not begun to disenfranchise them in its aftermath, they would have remained a majority in South Carolina until the 1920s and in Mississippi until the 1940s. Additionally, African Americans have in the past constituted close to a majority (more than 40 percent) of the theoretical electorate in other southern states such as Alabama, Florida, Georgia, and Virginia when they have been enfranchised. And at the time of their Civil Rights–era re-enfranchisement in 1966, almost one-third of the theoretical electorates of states such as South Carolina and Mississippi were African American—a significant minority within striking distance of a plurality. Last but not least is today's small but certainly not negligible African American minority in many northern states such as Michigan. The Great Migration is responsible for the growth in these states' African American electorates and the concomitant decline of the southern states'.

Changing Societies, Changing Party Systems

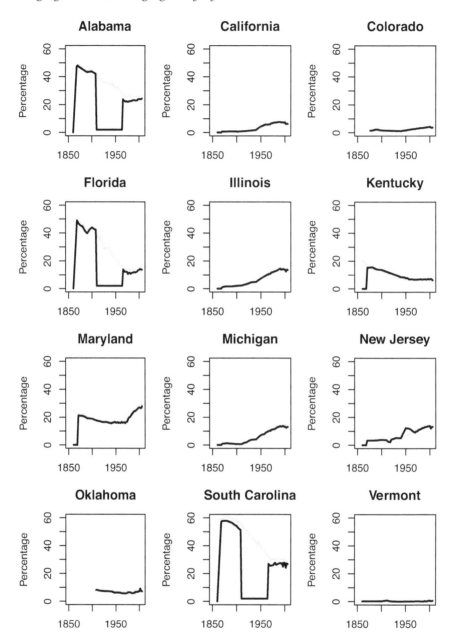

Figure 7.2: The African American proportion of the population [gray line] and of the theoretical electorate (that is, the voting-age, race, and gendered population) [black line] for selected states from 1860 through 2006. Source: see Table 7.2.

7. *The United States: New Parties for New Groups? Testing Hypotheses*

Hence, at the state level, there is substantial variation in ethnic heterogeneity both cross-sectionally (from state to state) and longitudinally (over time within many states).

7.2 PARTY SYSTEM FRAGMENTATION IN THE UNITED STATES

I now turn to the dependent variable, the fragmentation of the party system. I first examine data for the conventional quantitative operationalization of this variable, the effective number of electoral political parties, in federal legislative elections in the United States. However, the drawbacks to this operationalization, which were discussed at length in prior chapters, justify the brevity of my look at this data. More directly on point, I then identify the African American sectarian parties that have emerged to contest federal elections and evaluate the success of these parties.

7.2.1 The Effective Number of Electoral Parties

Figure 7.3 plots the effective number of electoral parties for the United States' lower legislative chamber (the House of Representatives) from 1860 to 2006. This is the same time period for which I explored changes in the ethnic heterogeneity of the United States' electorate. As before, referring to the number of parties as "effective" and "electoral" indicates that parties are weighed by their vote shares when counting.

This figure shows sharp increases in the effective number of electoral parties from the late 1870s through 1900, commensurate with the increase in ethnic heterogeneity resulting from African American enfranchisement during Reconstruction. However, there is no comparable increase in party system fragmentation following the Civil Rights–era re-enfranchisement of African Americans. Also puzzling is the increase, instead of the expected decrease, in party system fragmentation after 1910, given the decrease in ethnic heterogeneity resulting from African American disenfranchisement in the post-Reconstruction South. Empirical support for the hypothesis accordingly appears mixed. However, as I have argued in earlier chapters, the effective number of electoral parties does not capture only the changes in party system fragmentation that result from the successful entry or exit of African American sectarian parties, the mechanism of interest to this study.[10]

7.2.2 African American Sectarian Parties

As before, an African American sectarian party is operationally defined as a political party that either (i) has an exclusionary message, that is, a party

---

[10]For example, as students of American politics are well aware, the explanation for the record-setting number of parties in 1912 is *not* an African American party both entering the race and performing well at the ballot box; rather, it is the electoral success of Theodore Roosevelt's new Progressive Party.

209

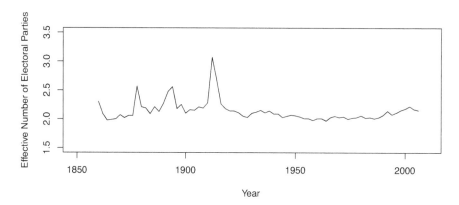

Figure 7.3: The effective number of electoral political parties in the United States, 1860–2006. Source: based on U.S. House (1920–2006); Mackie and Rose (1991); and Golder (2005).

that targets African Americans to the exclusion of other groups in its propaganda; (ii) identifies itself with African Americans by its name; or (iii) has predominately African American leadership and/or personnel. Further, also as before, I define such a party as successful if it managed to attract a majority or close to a majority of African American votes, and as moderately successful if it attracted only a plurality or close to a plurality of the group's votes.

So did African American sectarian parties successfully emerge to contest federal elections in the United States? To answer this question, Table 7.3 lists all African American sectarian parties that participated in at least one federal election, whether presidential or congressional, from 1860 through 2006. These parties were identified through searches of the secondary literature, election returns, and media accounts.[11] This table makes it clear that

---

[11]Not included in the table is the National Liberty Party, which nominated George E. Taylor for president in 1904. This party is omitted because Taylor's name did not appear on any state's ballot, and no other candidates were nominated (Kruschke 1991). Two other coding decisions are worth elaborating upon. One is to include the Peace and Freedom party through 1974. Even in 1968, this party was not clearly an African American party. This is reflected in its astronomical success figures for congressional races from 1970–1974 in Table 7.3 (to be discussed), a function of the party's best electoral performances coming from districts with miniscule African American electorates. I nevertheless chose to include it here given its appearance in prominent studies such as that of Walton (1969, 82–83). The second is the inclusion of the Black and Tans. These were African American factions of the Republican party in the former Confederate states that emerged in the post-Reconstruction era and lasted until the 1960s in some states. They supported African American suffrage and equality more generally, in opposition to the exclusively white (dubbed "Lily White") Republican factions. However, the Republican party ceased to be

7. The United States: New Parties for New Groups? Testing Hypotheses

African American parties have entered the political fray at the national level from the 1870s through the 1980s. Interestingly, only one emerged during Reconstruction on the heels of African American enfranchisement, making African Americans a case in point for Ciment's (2000, 22) argument that the Civil War and Reconstruction eras had the least third-party activity of all major periods of American politics since the 1820s.[12] More African American parties emerged in the aftermath of Reconstruction, including the period subsequent to the southern disenfranchisement of most African Americans. However, the numbers were still not large: an average of 0.55 parties per election in the eighty-year period from 1878 through 1958. By way of contrast, a particularly large number appeared in the 1960s and 1970s during the period known as the Second Reconstruction, following African American re-enfranchisement: an average of 1.4 parties per election for the twenty-year period from 1960 to 1980. Of course, these and other African American parties also participated in state and local elections, where their electoral performance was often even better.[13] However, both in the interest of space and because of the difficulty in assembling historical state-level electoral returns, I do not provide equivalent information about state-level elections here.

One general observation about African American party entry at the federal level is that the vast majority have contested elections only in a single state (e.g., the Alabama Colored Republicans), as opposed to running a multistate, that is, truly national, campaign (e.g., the Peace and Freedom party in 1968). Second, the states where the vast majority of these parties have appeared are southern. Third, African American parties have been more likely to contest a federal legislative race than the presidency, the problematic Peace and Freedom Party aside. Fourth and finally, these parties have all been short-lived: leaving aside the Black and Tan factions, which existed

---

a competitive force in southern politics around the turn of the last century, given the disenfranchisement programs of the Redeemers. One influential view of these political organizations is accordingly that they were essentially "patronage farmers and [national] convention functionaries" (Walton 2000c, 189). Most problematic from this perspective is their participation in presidential elections: they ran separate slates of electors but endorsed the national Republican candidates. Another view, however, is that they did play electoral politics, just as any other political party did, running candidates in opposition to other parties, from the Lily Whites to the Democrats (ibid.). I again err on the side of inclusion and opt to treat the Black and Tans as independent political parties. Note that their electoral prominence is likely underestimated in Table 7.3 because their candidates were not always clearly labeled as such. For example, Walton (1975, 77–78) reports that the Black and Tans ran their own congressional slate of candidates in both 1886 and 1890 in Alabama, but these candidates are not identified in the election results reported by either CQ (1987) or Dubin (1998).

[12] Ciment's (2000, 21) explanation for this is the fact that with the two main parties so ideologically divided over the central issue of American political life, third parties seemed irrelevant.

[13] The National Democratic Party of Alabama is a case in point: many of its candidates were successful at the local level in the early 1970s, and it placed one of the first two African Americans since Reconstruction in the state legislature in 1970 (see, for example, Frye 1980). Other African American parties existed solely at the state and/or local level, including the Black Panther Party; the Lowndes Freedom Association; and the Loyal Democrats of Mississippi. For an overview of these parties, see Kruschke (1991) and Ness and Ciment (2000).

		Presidential			Congressional		
Year	Party	% Votes	% Seats	Success	% Votes	% Seats	Success
1876	Alabama Colored Republicans	–	–	–	28 (H 4)	0.0	48
1888	Alabama Colored Republicans	–	–	–	38 (H 1)	0.0	69
1898	Alabama Colored Republicans	NA	NA	NA	15 (H 1)	0.0	27
1898	Mississippi Colored Republicans	NA	NA	NA	15 (H 3)	0.0	18
1898	Virginia Colored Republicans	NA	NA	NA	1.3 (H 4)	0.0	2.1
1906	Virginia Black and Tans	NA	NA	NA	4.1 (H 3)	0.0	9.5
1920	Florida Black and Tans	19	0.0	55	26 (S)	0.0	76
1920	Texas Black and Tans	5.6	0.0	36	17 (H 8)	0.0	[a]
1920	Virginia Colored Republicans	–	–	–	9.7 (H 3)	0.0	[a]
1928	Mississippi Black and Tans	0.53	0.0	1.1	–	–	–
1932	Mississippi Black and Tans	1.3	0.0	2.5	2.5 (H 3)	0.0	[a]
1936	Mississippi Black and Tans	1.7	0.0	3.4	–	–	–
1936	South Carolina Black and Tans	–	–	–	0.83 (S)	0.0	1.8

Table 7.3: Vote and seat shares for African American parties active at the federal level (both presidential and congressional). The state abbreviation is given in parentheses for single-state parties if the state is not obvious from the name. The nature of the congressional race is denoted by "S" for Senate and "H" for House (district in parentheses). For a party participating in more than one congressional race, statistics are for the race in which it performed the best. Success is the party's vote share as a proportion of the relevant African American electorate (population for 1910–1964 for southern states). A dash indicates that a party did not contest a race, and "NA" indicates that there was not a presidential election for it to contest. Continued on next page. Source: election results, U.S. House (1920–2006), CQ (1987), and Dubin (1998); national and state demographic data, my data described earlier; Congressional district demographic data, Parsons, Beach, and Dubin (1986), Parsons, Dubin, and Toombs Parsons (1990), and Lublin (1997).

[a]Congressional district demographic data unavailable.

		Presidential			Congressional		
Year	Party	% Votes	% Seats	Success	% Votes	% Seats	Success
1940	Mississippi Black and Tans	1.6	0.0	3.2	—	—	—
1944	Mississippi Black and Tans	2.1	0.0	4.4	—	—	—
1944	South Carolina Black and Tans	0.061	0.0	0.13	—	—	—
1944	South Carolina Progressive Democrats	—	—	—	3.2 (S)	0.0	7.6
1946	South Carolina Progressive Democrats	NA	NA	NA	2.4 (H 6)	0.0	[a]
1948	Mississippi Black and Tans	2.6	0.0	5.4	—	—	—
1948	South Carolina Progressive Democrats	0.11	0.0	0.23	—	—	—
1952	Mississippi Black and Tans	1.0	0.0	2.2	—	—	—
1952	South Carolina Black and Tans	2.9	0.0	7.7	—	—	—
1956	Mississippi Black and Tans	1.7	0.0	3.8	—	—	—
1960	Independent Afro-Americans (AL)	0.26	0.0	0.87	—	—	—
1964	Freedom Now (MI)	—	—	—	0.91 (H 1)	0.0	1.9
1966	Mississippi Freedom Democrats	NA	NA	NA	24 (H 3)	0.0	60
1968	National Democratic (AL)	5.2	0.0	23	23 (H 5)	0.0	62
1968	Peace and Freedom[b]	0.10	0.0	1.2	7.5 (CA H 7)	0.0	42

Table 7.3: Continued from previous page.

[a] Congressional district demographic data unavailable.

[b] Official election results seem to include votes for the splinter Freedom and Peace party headed by Richard Gregory. Other sources such as CQ (1987, 139) report the two factions separately. In addition to California, the party contested congressional races in Hawaii, New York, and Washington in 1968 and in Rhode Island in 1970. It appeared on the presidential ballot in twelve states in 1968: Arizona; California; Colorado; Iowa; Minnesota; New Jersey; New York; Ohio; Pennsylvania; Utah; Virginia; and Washington. The vote share in the table is its aggregate national performance; its best performance in a single state was in California, where is received 0.38% of the popular presidential vote.

		Presidential			Congressional		
Year	Party	% Votes	% Seats	Success	% Votes	% Seats	Success
1970	National Democratic (AL)	NA	NA	NA	24 (H 5)	0.0	66
1970	Peace and Freedom	NA	NA	NA	2.8 (CA H 36)	0.0	240[a]
1972	National Democratic (AL)	3.8	0.0	17	14 (H 7)	0.0	43
1972	Peace and Freedom (CA)	0.65	0.0	10	4.9 (H 19)	0.0	1900[a]
1972	United Citizens (SC)	0.34	0.0	1.3	–	–	–
1974	National Democratic (AL)	NA	NA	NA	3.6 (H 1)	0.0	13
1974	Peace and Freedom (CA)	NA	NA	NA	4.3 (H 2)	0.0	650[a]
1974	United Citizens (SC)	NA	NA	NA	0.61 (H 1)[b]	0.0	2.1
1976	National Democratic (AL)	–	–	–	0.63 (H 6)	0.0	2.3
1980	National Democratic (AL)	–	–	–	0.93 (H 6)	0.0	3.4

Table 7.3: Continued from previous page.

---

[a] For an explanation for this astronomically large statistic, see footnote 11 in the main text.
[b] In an April 1971 special election for this seat resulting from the death of longtime representative L. Mendel Rivers, the United Citizens' candidate Victoria DeLee garnered 10% of the vote (Walton 2000a), approximately 30% of the African American vote in the district.

7. The United States: New Parties for New Groups? Testing Hypotheses

for decades in most states but only sporadically contested federal elections, the longest-lived party has been the National Democratic Party of Alabama, which contested six federal elections from 1968 through 1980.

Turning from the elite to the mass level, this table also provides information about how successful these African American parties have been at attracting the support of African American voters. As with the Israeli case, the simplest approach is to compare the parties' vote shares to the African American share of the relevant (that is, district, state, or national) theoretical electorate. Specifically, success is operationalized by dividing a party's vote share by the African American share of the relevant electorate, yielding the proportion of African Americans casting a ballot for the party in question.[14] This approach also yields the most extensive historical measure of success, given that survey data is not available for much of the period studied.[15] While the resulting estimates are just estimates, they paint a suggestive enough picture to allow us to draw some conclusions about how African American parties fared at the polls among their target constituencies.

What these statistics show is that at times, some African American political parties have been successful at the national level, even though most have not been. It should be noted that this claim rests upon my definition of success, to which some may object: no African American party has ever managed to place its candidate in either the presidency or Congress, a con-

---

[14] As in the Israeli case, this approach rests on the assumption that only African Americans voted for African American parties—an assumption that is generally reasonable, although certainly not always accurate (see, for example, footnote 11). The key here is to define the (theoretical) electorate. In races for the House, this is naturally defined to be the electorate of the congressional district; in races for the Senate, it is the state's electorate. In the presidential race, if the party contested more than one state, the national electorate is the benchmark, but if it contested only a single state, the state's electorate serves as the benchmark instead. There are two exceptions. First, if the African American share of the theoretical electorate is not available, the African American share of the population is used instead (e.g., for Congressional districts prior to the 1940s; the Alabama 5th district in 1970; the California 7th district in 1968; and the California 36th district in 1970). Second, the African American share of the population is also used for southern states from 1910 to 1964, when most but not all African Americans were disenfranchised. This obviously overestimates the African American electorate and hence underestimates the success of African American parties. For example, if the success of the Independent Afro-American party in 1960 is instead calculated using data in Walton (2000b) on the actual African American electorate in Alabama in 1960 (66,000 African Americans registered to vote relative to a white voting-age population of 1.85 million, for an electorate that was approximately 3.4 percent African American), the party attracted 7.5% of African American votes instead of less than 1 percent. Unfortunately, data such as this on the exact number of registered African American voters exists for only a few elections and states. The alternative, using my estimate of 2 percent as the African American share of the electorate (see Appendix D), would so grossly overestimate sectarian party success, however, that I opt for the underestimate. Mitigating this underestimation is the fact that some of the elections where African American parties did appear were accompanied by registration drives that (temporarily) led to a reasonable numbers of African Americans registering, such as the 1920 election in Florida.

[15] For example, the American National Election Study began only in 1948, meaning that survey data is available for an even smaller portion of the total period studied than in the Israeli case.

ventional understanding of success. Nevertheless, even if African American parties have never won political office at the national level, some have managed to attract a majority of African American votes, an achievement that deserves recognition.

To elaborate, just as more African American parties emerged to contest elections in the Civil Rights era, it is during this same period that African American parties have been the most successful. In the pre–Civil Rights era, only two African American parties have been successful as I have defined it.[16] One was the Alabama Colored Republicans in the 1888 House race for the Alabama 1st district. The second, more successful party was the Florida Black and Tans in 1920. They captured an estimated 55 percent of the African American vote in the Florida presidential ballot and a whopping 75 percent of the group's vote in the senatorial race.[17] In the Civil Rights era, two parties have again been successful, but one has been successful in multiple elections. The Mississippi Freedom Democrats and the National Democratic Party of Alabama both attained success in their House races in the late 1960s and early 1970s: the former earned 60 percent of the African American vote in the 1966 Mississippi House 3rd district race, while the latter had its best showing in the 1970 Alabama House 5th district race, when it obtained two-thirds of the African American vote. Moreover, with the caveats noted earlier (see footnote 11), a third party, Peace and Freedom, was also successful in that it came within striking distance of capturing a majority of African American votes in the 1968 California House 7th district race.

Overall, African American parties have been more successful in legislative than presidential races. For example, the National Democratic party attracted 62 percent of the African American vote in the 1968 Alabama House 5th district race, but only 23 percent of the African American popular presidential vote in Alabama. Also, these parties have been successful for very short periods, usually just one or two elections, even relative to their short life spans.

7.3 EXPLAINING SECTARIAN PARTY (UN)SUCCESS

The data just presented raises two obvious questions. First, why have African American parties appeared to contest federal elections in some states and years but not in others? Second, how can the appearance and success of African American sectarian parties be reconciled with the United States'

---

[16]However, success is likely underestimated during this period: in Southern elections between 1910 and 1964, the relevant African American theoretical electorate is overestimated for the purposes of calculating success (see note 14). If the theoretical electorate for these states and elections is instead taken to be only two percent African American as a result of disenfranchisement, as is assumed in Table 7.2 and Figure 7.2, then most of the African American parties appearing in this period were successful. The truth probably lies somewhere in between.

[17]For more on this episode in Florida's history, known as the "Bloody Election," see Ortiz (2005).

7. The United States: New Parties for New Groups? Testing Hypotheses

majoritarian electoral system? I tackle each question in turn.

7.3.1 WHY SOME STATES AND ELECTIONS BUT NOT OTHERS?

Let me begin by noting which factors *cannot* explain the observed variation across space and time in the fortunes of African American sectarian parties at the federal level.

As with the Israeli case, one such factor is the political institution that has been the primary focus of the literature to date: the electoral system. This factor can be ruled out as an explanation for why some states and years have seen African American parties contest elections but others have not, because effectively equivalent electoral systems have been used by all states throughout the period studied. Obviously, a constant cannot explain variance. For example, all states have selected their electors for the United States' indirect presidential election by winner-take-all popular vote during this period, with two relatively recent exceptions: Maine (since 1972) and Nebraska (since 1992). And further, single-member districts and a plurality formula have been used by all states to elect their members of Congress, with minor exceptions.[18]

In contrast to the Israeli case, a second such factor is the other political institution upon which this study has focused: the regime type, or the centralization of policy-making authority. As Chhibber and Kollman (2004) argue with respect to the vertical distribution of authority in the United States, the major contrast to be drawn is between the decentralized early years of the republic and the more centralized later years, with 1854 being the dividing line. This leaves the size of the federal prize effectively constant throughout the period I study.[19] Further, turning to the horizontal

---

[18] The most consequential of these exceptions is the dual-ballot electoral system that Louisiana has employed since 1978 (1975 for the state legislature), where a second-round election consisting of the top two candidates is held if no candidate receives a majority in the first round. Other exceptions are the use of additional ballots until one candidate achieved a majority in Vermont until 1878 and Rhode Island until 1893, and the election of some representatives at large until 1970. All of these minor electoral system features unfortunately perfectly predict the absence of African American parties at the federal level, so they are not included in the quantitative analyses reported here. Of course, prior to 1870 and from the 1930s through the 1960s, states did not redistrict to ensure that congressional districts were composed of roughly equivalent populations, but this is another kettle of fish that will be dealt with later. To find greater variation in the electoral systems for the presidency and the legislature, one must look to practices from earlier in the United States' history, such as to the use of some multimember districts to elect early Congresses. See Dubin (1998) for a good historical overview. There both was and is greater variation in the electoral systems governing the election of *state* legislatures.

[19] Chhibber and Kollman (2004, 156) do identify an "ambiguous" period sandwiched between the two major centralizing eras of the Civil War/Reconstruction and the New Deal (that is, 1876-1932), however. Including a dummy variable for this period in the models discussed here yields an incorrectly signed coefficient that is significant in some models and insignificant in others. The insignificance is a testament to the small substantive difference in the overall size of the federal prize from the 1860s onwards. The incorrect sign may reflect the disenfranchisement of African Americans that was also in progress during this period, which should deter entry, and

distribution of authority among the various institutional actors within the federal level of government, there have also been no significant formal (that is, constitutional) changes in how authority is distributed since the 1860s. A reflection of this is the constancy of the index of presidential powers discussed in Chapter 4 for the United States in the nineteenth and twentieth centuries.[20] In other words, the incentives to become the largest party in each house of the federal legislature, as well as to gain control of the presidency, have not substantially changed during the period studied; they have also been the same from state to state.

There is one exception to the argument that the regime type cannot explain when African American sectarian parties have appeared and when they have been successful, however. This exception concerns the coattails of the president. Because the electoral district in the restrictive presidential electoral system is ultimately the entire country, both voters and elites should be less likely to support the sectarian presidential candidates of groups that do not command at least close to a plurality of the national electorate. In turn, when legislative elections are held concurrently with presidential elections, the presidential race will cast a shadow over the legislative race, which will disadvantage the sectarian parties of such groups (e.g., Cox 1997; Golder 2006; Hicken and Stoll 2011). And African Americans are such a group, as the data presented earlier demonstrates. Hence, the hypothesis is that African American sectarian parties should both more frequently enter and be more successful at contesting *nonconcurrent* legislative races (that is, those held at the presidential midterm). This proposition is tested here.

The third nonfactor is party system openness. Throughout the period of this study, the Democratic and Republican parties have dominated electoral politics in the United States at the federal level.[21] For example, the largest share of the vote going to other parties in House elections (the lower legislative chamber) was 24 percent in 1912, but this is an extreme outlier: the median share is only 3 percent.[22] While dealignment has occurred in the United States, as it has in all advanced industrial democracies, it has not yet blunted the dominance of the two major parties at the polls. Moreover, the periods of the most extensive third-party activity at the congressional level, which might indicate a more open party system, do not closely correspond

---

which is not adequately captured by my data on the theoretical electorate.

[20] There have been informal changes, however, as discussed in Hicken and Stoll (2008). But quantifying these changes is beyond the scope of this project.

[21] This aggregate situation masks variation at the state level, however: some states have experienced substantial periods of one-party dominance. The solidly Democratic southern states in the first half of the twentieth century serve as the quintessential example. Such extremely noncompetitive (that is, closed) settings might facilitate sectarian party success in the same way that conventionally open party systems do; however, one could also make a compelling argument to the contrary. Future work should certainly explore this issue, both theoretically and empirically.

[22] These statistics are based on data in U.S. House (1920–2006) and Mackie and Rose (1991).

7. The United States: New Parties for New Groups? Testing Hypotheses

to periods of African American sectarian party activity.[23]

Fourth and finally, turning from the systemic to the group level, the type of attribute defining the new social group is held constant by design in this within-case study: in every state, the object of study is a racial (ethnic) latent group. Accordingly, this factor also cannot play a role in explaining the observed variance.

So which factors should play a role, given the hypotheses I developed in Chapter 2? The first and most obvious factor is the size of the new social group in the electoral districts. The data presented in an earlier section of this chapter showed that the African American share of the states' theoretical electorates has varied greatly, both from state to state and over time. With the electoral district for both a state's presidential electors and its senators being the state itself, and given the majoritarian electoral systems employed for the United States' federal elections, African American parties are more likely both to appear and to be successful in a state's presidential and senatorial elections when African Americans constitute a large share of the state's electorate in that year. Similarly, the larger the African American share of a state's theoretical electorate, the larger the African American share of the theoretical electorates of at least some House electoral districts, and hence the more likely the entry and the success of African American parties in the state's House elections. Specifically, African Americans' constituting approximately a plurality of a state's electorate makes it possible that an African American party could win federal elections in that state. This in turn makes it more likely that voters will support and that elites will supply such a party.[24]

Yet at the same time, as scholars such as Posner (2005) have argued, po-

---

[23] Indeed, if either the lagged or contemporary national third-party vote share in House races is included in the models discussed here, the coefficient is incorrectly signed and statistically significant. This means that third-party challenges to Republican and Democratic dominance are found to have counterintuitively *discouraged* African American party entry. While the national third-party vote in House races seems the most straightforward way of operationalizing party system openness, future research might explore alternatives, including disaggregating the third-party vote by state, in light of these findings.

[24] Exactly what share of the electorate constitutes a plurality will depend upon which, if any, divisions there are in the non–African American community, that is, if African Americans face a monolithic white community or one divided by cross-cutting internal cleavages. In the former case (exemplified by the old "Solid South"), African Americans would need to constitute an outright majority of the electorate, although in the latter case, constituting as little as 35 percent of the electorate might ensure victory at the polls. Given the lower rate at which African Americans have historically both registered and turned out to vote relative to white Americans, however, a higher share of the electorate might be necessary for an African American party to be competitive at the polls. For example, in adjudicating redistricting cases under the Voting Rights Act, courts and the Justice Department have at times made the case for African Americans constituting 65 percent of the theoretical electorate instead of merely a majority. Conversely, others such as Grofman and Handley (1989) have argued that a mere majority suffices. Siding with the latter scholars, Lublin (1997) additionally provides empirical evidence that a sizeable Latino presence substantially lowers the minimal proportion of African Americans required, although it should be noted that his study, like most in the literature, focuses upon African American descriptive representation instead of African American sectarian parties.

litical entrepreneurs should have an interest in politicizing minimum winning groups, that is, groups that are not larger than needed to win. This logic suggests that when African Americans constitute a super-majority of a state's electorate (e.g., in excess of 60 or 70 percent), both elites and voters should be less likely to support an African American party. Combining these two arguments, I accordingly hypothesize that the African American share of the theoretical electorate is nonlinearly related to the probability of both the entry and the success of African American sectarian parties. Specifically, the relationship should be concave parabolic. The larger the African American share of a state's theoretical electorate, the greater the probability of an African American party both entering and being successful, although once African Americans constitute substantially more than a majority of the theoretical electorate, this probability should decrease.

And indeed, there is impressionistic evidence in support of this hypothesis from Tables 7.2 and 7.3. These tables illustrate that almost all African American parties have appeared in southern states, as was noted earlier, which is where African Americans have constituted the largest share of the theoretical electorate. Similarly, all African American parties' successes have also been in southern states save one, the exception being the Peace and Freedom party in California's 1968 federal election.[25] And for the few African American parties that have contested elections in northern and western states, all of these appearances have been subsequent to the Great Migration, which increased these states' African American electorates. Further, these tables illustrate that the bulk of elections contested by African American parties have been in those southern states with the *largest* African American populations, such as Alabama, Mississippi, and South Carolina. For example, the average African American share of the theoretical electorate was 25 percent in states where an African American party was successful in a federal election (as I have defined success), compared to an average of 7 percent in states where one was not. Finally, providing suggestive support for the hypothesized nonlinearity, an African American party has only once contested a federal election in a state where African Americans constituted more than a majority of the theoretical electorate.

A second explanatory factor at the group level is the new social group's politicization. For African Americans, this factor has varied over time, and to a lesser extent from state to state. Take first the issue of collective identity, one of the two dimensions of politicization that shape a group's capacity for collective action in the political realm. There have always been internal divisions within the African American community along a variety of lines. Nevertheless, a substantial body of evidence points to a strong African American group consciousness. Slavery, Jim Crow, and contemporary racism have combined to create what Dawson (1994) famously described as a belief in

---

[25] In making this claim, I ignore the problematic cases of the Peace and Freedom party's successes in elections in California after 1968, as well as in other states, for the reasons discussed in footnote 11.

7. The United States: New Parties for New Groups? Testing Hypotheses

a linked fate. Survey evidence of this group consciousness exists only for the last few decades, but scholars have identified many indirect pieces of evidence pointing to its existence as early as Reconstruction (e.g., Valelly 2004). Hence, while there no doubt has been some increase in group consciousness over time, this component of politicization has always been at least minimally present.

Now take the issue of organizational resources and leadership, the second dimension of politicization that shapes the capacity for collective action. Here there has been substantial change over time. Reconstruction allowed for the development of political skills, while also establishing a basic system of public education in the South (Johnson 2010, 15). In the Restored South, the struggle for and the growth of African American educational institutions combined with the managed race relations of the Jim Crow system to gradually create and sustain a dense network of African American organizations and institutions, ranging from civic groups to voter leagues (ibid., 16). For example, scholars have pointed to the central role in the Civil Rights movement played by African American churches, African American colleges, and chapters of the National Association for the Advancement of Colored People (NAACP) (e.g., McAdam 1982)—institutions that either did not exist at the time of emancipation or existed on a much smaller scale. Further, the Great Migration out of the South and the urbanization of the South itself brought greater economic resources. Accordingly, African American organizational resources and hence politicization have greatly increased over time. While there has also been variation from state to state, these differences have been dwarfed by the longitudinal variation just described.[26]

As politicization increases, political entrepreneurs come to expect both greater support at the polls from the masses and greater support prior to election day from other elites. This makes it more likely that they will supply the African American community with a sectarian political party. Accordingly, the hypothesis is that greater politicization will increase the likelihood of an African American sectarian party contesting federal elections. It is also hypothesized to increase the success of these parties.

Last but not least is a systemic factor: the strategy adopted by existing catch-all political parties towards African Americans. This factor has also varied greatly over both states and time. In the South, the Republican party initially played an accommodative strategy. To court the votes of this newly enfranchised group during Reconstruction, African Americans were incorporated into the party rank and file and even, if to a far lesser extent, into the party leadership. They also received party nominations for both state and federal office and accordingly made up a significant share of

---

[26]See, for example, Johnson (2010, 216–218) on the intraregional variation in the growth of the NAACP in the South. However, despite this variation, her data shows substantial growth in both chapters and membership over time, even in the most hostile states such as Mississippi; moreover, to a large extent, African American associational life simply took other forms in the states with the smallest NAACP presence.

the party's parliamentary wing.[27] But this accommodative strategy faded into a dismissive-to-adversarial strategy resembling that of the Democrats as Reconstruction ended and disenfranchisement progressed.[28] This status quo largely persisted until the Second Reconstruction, when the Democratic party began to play an accommodative strategy in the South. The New Deal and the national Democratic party's volte-face on civil rights, particularly under Truman, were key girders of this new strategy, one that gradually wooed African Americans from the "party of Lincoln" (e.g., Walton 1972). However, the individual southern state Democratic parties differed in exactly when and to what extent they chose to accommodate; many remained obdurate until the 1960s or 1970s. By way of contrast, outside of the South, the Republican party remained minimally accommodationist for much longer. Yet in northern and western states, a similar shift in party strategies was under way by the late 1940s (e.g., Feinstein and Schickler 2008), which would ultimately leave only the Democrats practicing accommodation.

Figure 7.4 bolsters this qualitative portrait with quantitative data. As in the Israeli case study, I measure the extent of accommodation by the descriptive representation offered to African Americans. For selected states and for all federal election years from 1860 to 2006, this figure shows African American representatives from the two major parties (the Democrats and the Republicans) as a percentage of the total number of lower chamber representatives at both the state and federal levels. This data was collected from a variety of primary and secondary sources.[29] An example of the state-level variation in accommodation that can be seen from this data is that while African Americans were accommodated by the Florida Democratic party as early as 1968 at the state level, it took until 1975 for the Mississippi Democratic party to abandon its dismissive-to-adversarial stance.

The hypothesis is accordingly that the greater the responsiveness of the

---

[27]For example, in 1872, 65 percent of South Carolina's state representatives were African American, all of whom were Republican. See any of the state-specific historical accounts of Reconstruction, such as Uzee (1950) for Louisiana, as well as multistate studies such as that of Foner (1993).

[28]Elements of dismissiveness can be found in both white Republican factions and Democrats appealing to African Americans' shared interests with "white folks" (see, for example Uzee 1950, 134), and ultimately (arguably) in their push to disenfranchise African Americans. Elements of adversity can be found in campaigns denouncing "Negro domination" and advocating either white supremacy or a white color line, such as the 1898 Democratic "white supremacy" campaign in North Carolina (see, for example, Edmonds 1973, 136–157).

[29]Given how few third parties have obtained seats in state legislatures, let alone the federal legislature, during the period of study, these figures are effectively equivalent to the African American share of the major parties' parliamentary wings—equivalent measures to those employed in the previous Israeli case study. When possible, replacements for originally elected members were not counted, but the available data did not always allow for this distinction to be made. The focus is upon the lower chambers of the federal and state legislatures because African American representation in the upper chambers has always, with the exception of Georgia during the Second Reconstruction, either mirrored or lagged behind it. Data for all fifty states can be found in Appendix E, which also contains more information about the data collection process.

7. The United States: New Parties for New Groups? Testing Hypotheses

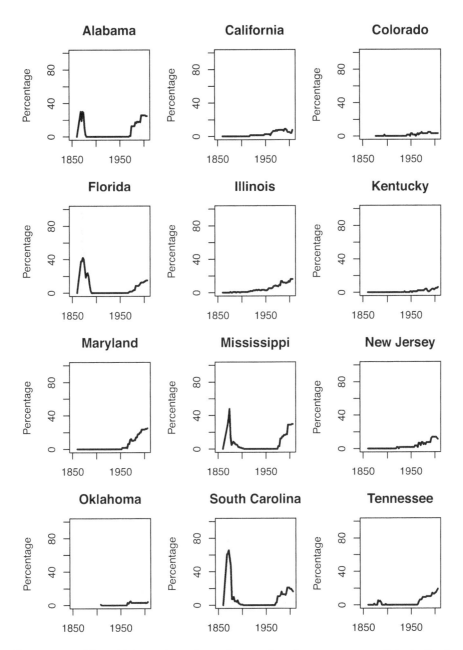

Figure 7.4: The African American share of major party state [black line] and federal [grey line] representatives (that is, lower house legislators) for selected states from 1860 through 2006. Source: see text.

major existing parties, that is, the more accommodative their strategies vis-à-vis African Americans, the less likely the entry and the success of African American sectarian parties. Table 7.3 and Figure 7.4 together provide impressionistic support for this hypothesis. Only one African American party contested a federal election during Reconstruction, and then only at its very end, just as no African American parties have contested federal elections since 1980. In both of these periods, at least one of the major existing parties has played an exceedingly accommodative strategy towards African Americans, in accordance with the hypothesis. Conversely, the period during which most African American parties have both appeared and been successful is the years between the two Reconstructions. And it is during this period that neither of the two major parties was accommodative towards the group, particularly in the South, again in accordance with the hypothesis.

A formal statistical analysis will enable me to shed even greater empirical light upon the hypotheses. Accordingly, I first conduct a logistic regression analysis of African American party entry. It is possible to conduct such an analysis for this within-case study, unlike the Israeli one, because of the United States' federal structure. The unit of analysis is the federal election at the level of the state. The cases are all federal elections in which each state participated during the period from 1860 or statehood, whichever is earliest, to 2006. The dependent variable, African American party entry, is a dummy variable. It is coded one if an African American party contested a federal election (whether for the presidency, the Senate, or the House) in a given state and election and zero if one did not. The coding of this variable is based upon Table 7.3.

In accordance with the hypotheses just developed, there are three independent variables. The first is the African American share of the theoretical electorate for the state and election. To test for the hypothesized nonlinearity, the square of this term is also included in the model. The data is as described earlier. The second is African American politicization. Lacking alternative measures, I operationalize this variable by the election year, given the hypothesis that politicization has increased over time.[30] The third and final independent variable is the lag of African American major party state representatives as a proportion of total state representatives, where "lagged" means the proportion following the previous election. This data is also as described earlier. I take the lagged instead of the contemporary proportion because elites' decisions about entry must, by necessity, be made in advance

---

[30]This is obviously a rough proxy for politicization, and particularly for its key organizational dimension. Alternative measures that would also pick up state-to-state variation range from membership in African American community institutions such as churches (e.g., Jenkins, Jacobs, and Agnone 2003) to either the number of NAACP branches or NAACP membership (e.g., Johnson 2010). Unfortunately, historical data of this sort does not exist at the national level for the long time period that I study, let alone at the state level. For example, the most extensive state-level time series data I have found on the NAACP is that of Johnson (2010), whose data extends from 1940 to 1952 for the eleven former Confederate states. While collecting this data will be no easy task, hopefully scholars will do so in the future, enabling a more nuanced empirical assessment of the effect of African American politicization.

7. The United States: New Parties for New Groups? Testing Hypotheses

of an election, and the best information they have about the strategies of the existing major parties at the beginning of the current round of competition is what those parties did in the previous round.[31] Further, accommodation is measured at the state instead of the federal level for two reasons.[32] First, accommodation in the federal legislature has always either lagged behind or occurred simultaneously with accommodation in the state legislature, and accommodation in the state legislature *is* accommodation.[33] Second, because of many states' small numbers of federal representatives, the coarseness of the federal data results in some extreme and unrepresentative values.[34]

The results of this analysis are reported in the second column of Table 7.4. Robust (state-clustered) standard errors appear in parentheses.[35] In this table, all variables have the hypothesized signs. Moreover, all of the terms are statistically significant at conventional or close to conventional levels, with the exception of the square of the African American proportion of the electorate. I now discuss each variable in turn.

First, the African American proportion of the theoretical electorate. This variable is estimated to be positively signed, and its square is estimated to be negatively signed. Accordingly, as hypothesized, increasing the African American proportion of a state's electorate is predicted to increase the probability of an African American party contesting a federal election in that state, although only up to a point: after the African American share of the

---

[31] Using the contemporary proportion instead yields substantively similar and even more significant results. Another alternative is a dummy variable for an African American party having contested a state election within the past decade. Here, too, the sign of the coefficient is as predicted, and even this substantially less precise measure attains close to conventional levels of significance.

[32] If African American major party federal representatives as a proportion of total federal representatives is employed as an alternative operationalization, however, it yields a substantively similar if less statistically significant coefficient. The reduction in significance is not surprising in light of the coarseness of the federal-level data (to be discussed in the main text).

[33] An example is that Kentucky has never sent an African American to the federal House, yet both the Kentucky Republican and Democratic parties have sent African Americans to the lower chamber of the Kentucky state legislature—and approximately in proportion to their share of the theoretical electorate. The federal-level data accordingly greatly underestimates the accommodation that African Americans have been offered by the two major parties in Kentucky.

[34] For example, in the 1870 election, Florida's single representative was an African American Republican, resulting in a federal percentage of one hundred. By way of contrast, only 38 percent of state representatives from one of the two major parties were African Americans. Accordingly, the federal-level data clearly overstates the extent of accommodation that the major parties were offering African Americans in Florida in 1870.

[35] The use of this robust estimator reflects my belief that correlation from election to election within a state is most likely. However, it is also possible that what happens in one state at a given time influences what happens in another. When alternatively clustering on the election year, all coefficients remain significant at conventional levels, although their significance is reduced. Further, a conditional logistic regression version of the model (that is, fixed effects logit) yields similar results with one exception: the proportion of the electorate that is African American is no longer statistically significant at conventional levels, although it only narrowly falls short. Finally, correcting for rare-events bias in this and the remaining models (King and Zeng 2001; Imai, King, and Lau 2007) yields coefficients with similar substantive and statistical significance, although both are sometimes somewhat counterintuitively reduced in Models 2 and 3.

Changing Societies, Changing Party Systems

	Model			
	1: Entry	2: Success	3: House Entry	4: State Entry
Intercept	−32***	−31**	−30**	−31**
	(3.8)	(14)	(6.6)	(13)
Electorate (%)	0.090*	0.25**	0.14**	0.23***
	(0.050)	(0.098)	(0.059)	(0.083)
Square of	−0.00079	−0.0030**	−0.0015	−0.0025**
Electorate (%)	(0.00085)	(0.0014)	(0.00095)	(0.0012)
Lagged Repre-	−0.097**	−0.078*	−0.079**	−0.16***
sentatives (%)	(0.041)	(0.046)	(0.032)	(0.060)
Year	0.015***	0.012*	0.012***	0.013*
	(0.0019)	(0.0067)	(0.0033)	(0.0064)
Concurrent Presidential Election			0.37 (0.29)	
N	3348	3346	3348	3478
Log Likelihood	−249	−48	−152	−133

Table 7.4: Logistic regression analysis of African American party entry (Models 1 and 3) and success (Model 2) in federal elections (House elections only for Model 3), as well as entry in state elections (Model 4). Significance codes are for two-sided tests: 0.01, ***; 0.05, **; 0.10, *.

state's electorate reaches approximately 56 percent, further increases in the size of the group are predicted to decrease the probability, ceteris paribus. Specifically, for example, for the mean year (1938) and degree of major party accommodation of African Americans (just over 2 percent of state representatives being both from a major party and African American), increasing a state's theoretical electorate from zero to 56 percent African American is predicted to increase the probability of an African American party contesting the state's federal election from less than 1 percent (0.73%) to 8.5 percent. This is a substantial elevenfold increase. Increasing the African American share of the theoretical electorate further to 58 percent, the maximum observed, is then predicted to slightly (imperceptibly to two significant digits) decrease the probability of African American party entry. Hence, over the observed range of data, the relationship between the probability of African American party entry and the African American share of the theoretical electorate is both substantively significant and effectively linear. The insignificance of the coefficient on the model's squared electorate term reflects this linearity.[36]

---

[36] As another reflection of this, omitting the square of the African American proportion of the

7. The United States: New Parties for New Groups? Testing Hypotheses

Second, African American politicization. The coefficient on this variable is estimated to be both positive and statistically significant. This means that in accordance with the hypothesis, the passing of time, which has increased the politicization of the African American community, is found to have increased the probability of African American party entry. To be precise, holding the other variables at their means,[37] the probability of African American party entry is predicted to have risen from 0.5 percent in 1870 to slightly more than 3 percent in 2006—a more than sixfold increase. To further illustrate, consider a state with the optimum African American share of the electorate of 56 percent and where existing parties are not playing an accommodatory strategy (that is, they sent no African Americans to the state legislature in the previous election). In 1870, the predicted probability of an African American party contesting such a state's federal election is just over 4 percent, whereas in 2006, the predicted probability is 23 percent.

Third and finally, the responsiveness of the existing major parties. For this variable, the coefficient is estimated to be both negative and statistically significant. Hence, as hypothesized, the more accommodation offered to African Americans by the two existing major parties, the less likely it is that an African American party will emerge to contest a federal election in a state. For example, again holding other variables at their means, when the lagged proportion of a state's representatives who are both African American and from one of the two existing major parties rises from zero (the observed minimum, a completely nonaccommodative strategy) to 65 (the observed maximum, a very accommodative strategy), the predicted probability of African American party entry declines from slightly more than 1.5 percent to effectively zero percent. But a better illustration of the substantive significance of this variable comes from holding other variables at the observed values most favorable to African American party entry.[38] In this situation, when the two existing major parties adopt a completely nonaccommodative strategy (that is, none of their state representatives from the previous election are African American), the probability of African American party entry is 23 percent—a nontrivial probability. By way of contrast, playing the observed maximally accommodative strategy (65 percent African American) is predicted to effectively eliminate the probability of African American party entry. Accordingly, the responsiveness of the existing major parties to African

---

electorate from the model yields a positive and statistically significant coefficient on the remaining first-order term. Specifically, a one percentage point increase in the African American share of the theoretical electorate is predicted to multiply the odds of African American party entry by slightly more than one (1.1). To illustrate further, again holding all other variables at their means, increasing the proportion of African Americans in a state's theoretical electorate from zero (the observed minimum) to fifty-eight (the observed maximum) is predicted to increase the probability of African American party entry from less than 1 percent (0.84%) to 15 percent.

[37] That is, the probabilities are calculated for a state with an electorate that is 7.1% African American and where 2.3% of state representatives had been both African American and from a major party after the previous election.

[38] As alluded to in the earlier discussion, this is when African Americans constitute 56 percent of a state's theoretical electorate and the election year is 2006.

Americans clearly has a substantively large impact upon African American party entry—in fact, the largest impact of the three variables.

But what about the success of African American parties, as opposed solely to their entry? To quantitatively test the hypotheses regarding this dependent variable, I estimate a model similar to the one just described. The only difference is that the dependent variable is now a dummy variable for an African American party being successful, as I have defined it, in a state's federal election. That is, the dependent variable is coded one if an African American party managed to attract close to a majority of the votes of the African American electorate in one of the federal races it contested and zero otherwise.[39] These codings are based upon Table 7.3.

The third column of Table 7.4 presents the results for this model. Given the rarity of African American party success, too much should not be made of these results.[40] Yet they provide at least suggestive support for the hypothesis that the same factors that shape sectarian party entry also shape sectarian party success. Specifically, the table shows that all variables again have the hypothesized signs. Moreover, they have either equal or greater significance, both statistically and substantively, as in the model of African American party entry. The one difference is that the square of the African American proportion of the electorate is now statistically significant at conventional levels. Accordingly, as hypothesized, the same three factors—the African American share of the theoretical electorate, African American politicization, and existing parties' accommodation of African Americans—appear to shape the success of African American sectarian political parties.

Last and least, I test for the coattails of presidential elections, the one way in which I hypothesized that the regime type might affect the likelihood of African American sectarian party entry and success. To do so, I reestimate the model of African American party entry described earlier with two changes. First, I include a dummy variable for presidential election years as an additional covariate. Second, the dependent variable of entry is redefined to include only African American parties that contested elections for the lower legislative chamber (that is, the House): including entry in presidential but not legislative elections would, by definition, bias the results

---

[39] Specifically, an African American party is deemed successful if it managed to attract more than 40 percent of the votes of the electoral district's African American electorate. This slightly lower bar (40 as opposed to 50 percent) in the quantitative analysis is designed to at least partially compensate for the likely underestimation of African American sectarian party success (see notes 14 and 16). However, for the reasons discussed in footnote 11, the Peace and Freedom party is not classified as successful except in California in 1968. Note that two cases are listwise deleted due to missing data on the success of African American parties: 1920 Virginia and 1946 South Carolina. While data is also missing on the success of African American parties in House elections in 1920 Texas and 1932 Mississippi, I base my coding of success for these states and years on the parties' performances in the presidential race, for which I do have data.

[40] There are only eight cases of success so defined, whereas there are fifty cases of entry. Nevertheless, see footnote 35 for the basic insensitivity of the results to rare-events bias. Note that because of the few cases of African American party success, I do not estimate a conditional logistic version of this model.

towards finding a coattails effect.

The results of this model are presented in the fourth column of Table 7.4. The estimated coefficients on the original variables all have the hypothesized signs, as before, and they attain both similar magnitudes and similar levels of statistical significance. My conclusions about these variables are accordingly not sensitive to whether entry encompasses all federal races or simply races for the lower legislative chamber, the latter being the approach taken elsewhere in this study. Turning to the presidential coattails variable, the table shows that, contrary to the hypothesis, a presidential election being held concurrently with a federal legislative election does not decrease the probability of African American sectarian party entry—rather, it increases it. However, this effect is not statistically significant.

7.3.2 How Does the Electoral System Matter? Or Putting the Case of the United States in Comparative Perspective

This brings me to the issue of how, if at all, the electoral system matters, given that it cannot explain why African American sectarian parties have contested national elections in the United States in some states and years but not in others. A casual reading of the literature suggests that restrictive electoral systems, like those employed for both the United States' legislature and presidency, should reduce the likelihood that new latent social groups will be successfully particized. In other words, conventional wisdom holds that restrictive electoral systems constrain the effect of social heterogeneity upon party system fragmentation. Yet the appearance and success of African American sectarian parties seems to provide empirical evidence against this hypothesis. We accordingly need to think carefully about how restrictive electoral systems actually exert their effect.

In Chapter 2, I argued for a more nuanced hypothesis: that restrictive electoral systems constrain the effect of social heterogeneity only when *new social groups are small in the electoral districts*. In this light, we should *not* expect the United States' majoritarian electoral system to serve as a constraint on African Americans' successful particization in all federal elections. It is true that African Americans have always been a small minority of the national electorate, the ultimate electoral district for the presidency. Yet the uneven geographic distribution of African Americans from state and to state and within states has meant that they have been a large group in some legislative electoral districts. As I demonstrated earlier, African Americans have at times been at least a plurality of the theoretical electorates of some states, which serve as the electoral districts for the Senate. The same is true of some House districts. For example, African Americans constituted either a majority or close to a majority of the theoretical electorate in 17 percent of House districts in 1870 and 11 percent of House districts in 2006.[41] This means that

---

[41] By close to a majority, I mean more than 30 and less than 50 percent. See Appendix D

African Americans have had the capacity to send their sectarian parties to the House and Senate. Hence, the United States' restrictive electoral system does not preclude the equilibrium success of African American sectarian parties in some legislative races, contrary to the conventional wisdom.

Accordingly, the electoral system in combination with group size can explain the puzzle of why African American sectarian parties have been more likely to successfully contest some federal political offices than others. Specifically, these parties should more frequently contest and enjoy success in elections for the federal legislature than for the presidency, given African Americans' shares of the respective theoretical electorates. And that is what Table 7.3 empirically demonstrates. If the problematic Peace and Freedom Party is excluded, legislative races have been strongly favored for contestation: 50 percent of African American sectarian party appearances have been solely to contest a congressional race; 35 percent solely to contest the presidency; and 15 percent to contest both. Regarding success, all instances of success have come in congressional races, save one: the Florida Black and Tans were also successful in their presidential run in 1920.

Yet the electoral system cannot explain the arguably more important puzzle of why African Americans have failed to be successfully particized in equilibrium at the congressional level. So why have African Americans only sporadically and usually unsuccessfully contested congressional elections? The answer, I believe, lies in another political institution: the regime type. As I also argued in Chapter 2, in order for a new social group's sectarian party to experience success at the ballot box in equilibrium, the group must also be large enough for its party to win enough seats in the legislature to play a governing role. While policy-making authority is not overly centralized in the United States, it is centralized enough that there is still an incentive to be the largest party in each chamber of the national legislature. Yet this is something that an African American sectarian party could never be, given demographic realities. Moreover, with one of the two major parties (first the Democrats and later the Republicans) often playing a dismissive-to-adversarial strategy towards African Americans, both African American political elites and ordinary voters have instead had an incentive to strategically support the more accommodative of the two existing major parties, even if they sincerely preferred to support a party of their own.

A different level of analysis, state elections, may allow us to further explore the impact of the size of a group as compared to a polity's entire electorate. While state legislatures in the United States exercise less policy-making authority than the federal legislature does, they still do exercise policy-making authority. Further, their internal legislative structures are borrowed from the federal legislature.[42] There is consequently an incen-

---

for this data. The 1870 election for the 42nd Congress was the first federal election in which African Americans were enfranchised in all states, and the 2006 election for the 110th Congress is the most recent federal election included in this study.

[42] The one exception is Nebraska, which has had a unicameral legislature since 1936.

7. The United States: New Parties for New Groups? Testing Hypotheses

tive to become the largest party in both chambers of a state's legislature, just as there is in the federal legislature. But in contrast to the situation at the federal level, African Americans have constituted a significant share (sometimes even a majority) of some states' electorates, as discussed earlier. It is therefore possible that an African American party could become the largest party in a one or both of a state's legislative chambers, although this possibility was greater in the past than it is today. Similarly, state governorships, the state-level equivalent of the presidency, are valuable prizes that African Americans have had a shot at controlling. Accordingly, African American sectarian parties should be more likely both to enter and to enjoy success at the state than at the federal level.

To empirically test this hypothesis, I used a dummy variable for African American sectarian party entry in a state election as the dependent variable in a version of the federal elections logit model presented in the second column of Table 7.4.[43] This state elections model is shown in the fifth column of this table. In accordance with the hypothesis, all of the coefficients in this model save that on the year are of larger substantive magnitude and of greater statistical significance than those in the federal model. Even more telling, while the maximum predicted probability of African American party entry at the federal level is 23 percent, at the state level it is a much greater 38 percent. Anecdotal evidence also supports the hypothesis with respect to success. For example, as was noted earlier, African American parties have on a few occasions managed to place their candidates in state legislatures, something that they have never managed to do at the federal level. Hence, as hypothesized, African American sectarian parties have been more likely both to enter state elections and to be successful in them.

Yet even at the state level, African American sectarian parties have not been an equilibrium phenomenon. The best explanation for this state of affairs is the relatively short time period during which African Americans commanded a plurality to a majority of some states' theoretical electorates. The disappearance of their numerical advantage has largely, although not exclusively, been a consequence of their dispersion throughout the country in the Great Migration, making this seminal event a double-edged sword. Other factors can contribute to the explanation, however, including the accommodative strategy played by at least one of the two existing parties for significant periods of time (e.g., since the 1970s); the dominance of these major parties; and the impact of African Americans' lower socioeconomic status upon their capacity for collective action.

---

[43] I identified all of the state elections that African American parties have contested by combing through a variety of secondary sources such as Walton (1972, 1985). Contestation could be for the governorship or for either chamber of the state legislature. I do not estimate a model of state-level African American sectarian party success due to the difficulty of obtaining the relevant historical data (e.g., complete state election returns), which makes it impossible to quantify success using my definition of it. Note that this state elections model ignores differences in state electoral systems, which do exist (see note 18).

7.4 CONCLUSION

In this chapter, I asked how changes in the social heterogeneity of the United States resulting from the enfranchisement and disenfranchisement of African Americans have shaped party system fragmentation in American elections. More specifically, in keeping with the book's focus, I tackled the question of why African American sectarian political parties have emerged to contest federal elections, albeit with varying degrees of success, in some states and election years but not in others.

I argued that four factors—two group-specific and two systemic—should explain this within-case variation. These factors are the size of the group; the group's politicization; the strategy played by existing catch-all parties towards the group; and the presidential system of government, that is, the presidential coattails. I also argued that all of the other explanatory factors I identified in Chapter 2, from the restrictiveness of the electoral system to the ethnic nature of the group, could not contribute to the explanation because these factors were effectively held constant by the within-case, quasi-experimental research design. This chapter accordingly supplements the prior cross-national quantitative analyses and triangulates the Israeli case study. Using a logistic regression analysis of both African American party entry and success in a state's federal elections from 1860 through 2006, empirical support was found for three of the four hypotheses. Each is now discussed in turn.

First, empirical support was found for the hypothesis that larger new social groups in the electoral districts are more likely to be successfully particized than smaller groups. As long as African Americans did not constitute more than a comfortable majority of a state's theoretical electorate, I found that the greater the African American share of a state's electorate, the more likely it was that an African American party would contest and be successful in a federal election there, ceteris paribus. Hence, this is an explanation for why African American sectarian parties have overwhelmingly emerged and been successful in southern states: African Americans have often constituted at least a plurality of these state's electorates, even though their presence in this region has declined over time. However, only limited support was found for the hypothesis that larger than minimal winning groups in the electoral districts will not be successfully particized. Once African Americans constituted more than a comfortable majority of a state's electorate, the probability of African American party entry and success were both found to decrease. Yet this decrease was found to be substantively small as well as statistically insignificant, contrary to the hypothesis. Because African Americans have at most constituted just shy of 60 percent of a state's theoretical electorate, a better test would come from a group that is observed to constitute at least a super-majority of the electorate in some electoral districts. This suggests that future research might fruitfully either use a different level of analysis (such as the local level) for the case of African Americans or study a different new social group entirely.

7. The United States: New Parties for New Groups? Testing Hypotheses

Second, contrary to the hypothesis about the presidential coattails effect, holding presidential elections concurrently with legislative elections was found to increase the probability of the successful particization of African Americans, although the effect was not statistically significant. This finding might reflect the unique orientation of many African American political parties towards presidential elections because of the federal patronage at stake. The Black and Tans, Republican party factions-cum-sectarian political parties, are a case in point: disenfranchised in southern states by the early twentieth century, southern African Americans' only effective means of political participation during the first few decades of that century was to trade their votes for the spoils of office during Republican presidential nominating conventions, a bizarre situation made possible by the United States' federal structure. In light of the substantial evidence the literature has assembled that points towards the existence of presidential coattails, African American sectarian parties seem best viewed as an exceptional case rather than as the rule.

Third, I found empirical support for the hypothesis that the politicization of a new social group increases the likelihood of its successful particization. Over time, African Americans' organizational capacity for collective action has increased. And controlling for other factors, African American parties were more likely both to appear and to be successful with the passing of time. This can help to explain why fewer African American parties successfully emerged during Reconstruction, immediately on the heels of African Americans' emancipation from slavery, than in the Civil Rights era, when African Americans had spent 100 years accumulating economic, educational, and institutional resources.

Last but not least, empirical support was also found for the hypothesis that the strategy existing parties adopt towards a new social group shapes the likelihood of the group's successful particization. When at least one of the two existing major parties played an accommodative strategy towards African Americans, African American sectarian political parties were unlikely to form, and even less likely to be successful. Specifically, the accommodative strategy played by the Republican party during Reconstruction and in its immediate aftermath helps to explain the failure of African Americans to pursue sectarian representation during this period—despite their majority or near-majority status in many southern states. By way of contrast, the door to African American sectarian party entry was left open for the first half of the twentieth century by both the Democratic and Republican parties choosing to adopt effectively nonaccommodative strategies, even though African Americans were fleeing the South in the Great Migration. Later, the specific timing of the Democratic party's postwar accommodative volte-face with respect to African Americans explains why African American sectarian parties died out when they did by the 1980s.

In this chapter, I also took a closer look at the role played by the United States' restrictive electoral system. I argued that given demographic realities, this factor can explain why African American sectarian parties have more frequently contested and been successful in elections for some political offices (e.g., the House) than others (e.g., the presidency). However, it *cannot* explain the overall failure of African Americans to be successfully particized in equilibrium in the United States. African Americans have constituted a plurality to a majority of many federal legislative electoral districts, and hence could have sent African American sectarian parties to Washington if they had chosen to do so. Why did they not choose to do so? I argued that the best explanation is the combination of the minority status of African Americans in the national electorate and the fact that policy-making authority is reasonably centralized in the United States. Under these circumstances, neither strategically minded elites nor strategically minded voters would support an African American sectarian party in equilibrium. They might nevertheless have an incentive to support one in the short run—an issue that I will explore in the next and final chapter.

Hence, in this chapter, I have again both argued and provided evidence that understanding how social heterogeneity shapes the fragmentation of the party system in democracies requires us to look at factors other than the electoral system. New social groups may successfully form their own sectarian parties even when the electoral system is restrictive. They may also fail to do so for reasons unrelated to the electoral system. Particularly, the size of a new social group in the polity as a whole, not just in the electoral districts, must be considered. All in all, the case of African Americans in the United States illustrates how misleading a focus on the electoral system alone can be: the electoral system lets us explain neither the short-term success of African American sectarian parties nor their equilibrium failure.

8 Conclusion: Party System Fragmentation and Beyond

Democratic societies change. Historically, processes such as immigration, changes in the territory of a state, and changes in the franchise, among others, have added new groups of individuals to and subtracted existing groups of individuals from a democratic state's citizenry. Over time, countries have become more or less socially heterogeneous as a result, and at any one given time, some countries have been more socially heterogeneous than others. A natural question to ask is how these changes in social heterogeneity have shaped the democratic party system. This is the overarching research question with which I have been concerned in this book.

In this chapter, I offer final thoughts about the effect of social heterogeneity upon party system fragmentation, the dimension of the party system and hence the specific research question that has been my primary focus. Based on the arguments I have developed and the empirical analyses I have undertaken in the preceding chapters, what can we say about how social heterogeneity shapes this dimension of the party system? Even more specifically, what can we say about when new latent social groups will successfully manage to form their own sectarian political parties? This is the key mechanism by which, I have argued, social heterogeneity shapes party system fragmentation and the second and arguably more fundamental research question with which I have been concerned. The answer in a nutshell is that we can say a fair amount: several systemic factors explicitly not limited to the electoral system combine with features of the new social groups themselves to determine the likelihood that these groups will succeed at forming sectarian parties, and hence to determine what the effect of increases in social heterogeneity upon party system fragmentation will be. However, there are still areas in need of attention from future researchers.

Yet there are dimensions of the party system other than fragmentation that we should care about, for both practical and normative reasons. My final task in this chapter is to turn to these other dimensions, sketching out preliminary hypotheses and presenting some preliminary empirical evidence about these hypotheses. My argument is that, perhaps not surprisingly, social heterogeneity has also shaped other dimensions of the party system. But perhaps more surprisingly, I argue that it may have an even larger effect upon these other dimensions than it does upon party system fragmentation. Focusing on descriptive representation, the last component of my argument concerns the role played by sectarian parties. I argue that they have been important in linking changes in society to changes in these other dimensions of the party system, an argument that has implications for constitutional engineers. However, there is much work for future researchers to do on this topic at both the theoretical and empirical levels.

8.1 SOCIAL HETEROGENEITY AND PARTY SYSTEM FRAGMENTATION

A large literature in comparative politics has studied how political institutions shape the number of political parties competing in democratic elections, a concept that is usually called the fragmentation of the democratic party system. However, less attention has been paid to the countervailing variable of the heterogeneity of society. In this book, I have sought to begin redressing the imbalance by turning my lens upon the relatively neglected societal variable. Because social heterogeneity varies extensively from country to country as well as over time within most countries, bringing it into the equation—linking this variation to variation in party system fragmentation—allows us to greatly increase our explanatory leverage over this both normatively and practically important dimension of the party system. In short, in this book, I have tried to take the first steps towards doing for social heterogeneity what the new institutionalism has done for political institutions.

In the realm of theory, I initially argued that social heterogeneity does shape party system fragmentation. I then argued, however, that this relationship is a contingent one and identified the factors that both directly and indirectly condition it. Turning to empirics, I developed both longitudinal and cross-sectional measures of social heterogeneity that encompassed more than a society's ethnic structure. Finally, I developed testable hypotheses drawn from my theory and tested them using my new measures and a multi-method research design. Specifically, time series cross-sectional analyses of both all minimally democratic and partisan legislative elections in the advanced industrial democracies and all minimally democratic post–World War II presidential elections were coupled with case studies of Israel (Sephardi and Russian Jewish immigration) and the United States (African American enfranchisement).

In contrast to the existing literature, which has focused almost exclusively upon the electoral system, I argued that seven other factors also condition the effect of social heterogeneity. These factors were divided into two types: characteristics of a new latent social group itself and systemic features of the polity. The former included the size of the group; the type of attribute defining it; and its politicization. The latter included the openness of the party system; the strategies played by existing parties towards the group; and another political institution, the regime type. I argued that along with the electoral system, these six factors shape the likelihood of a new social group successfully forming its own sectarian political party in equilibrium, that is, being successfully particized, instead of obtaining representation from an existing party. Because this is the most prominent mechanism by which an increase in social heterogeneity shapes the fragmentation of the party system, these factors indirectly condition the effect of social heterogeneity. I also argued that a seventh and systemic factor, the prior social heterogeneity of the polity, directly conditions the relationship between social heterogeneity and the fragmentation of the party system.

In the empirical analyses, I found that increases in social heterogeneity did often, if not always, translate into increases in party system fragmentation. The book's primary take-away message is accordingly that society does matter. Moreover, I found at least some support for the hypothesized effects of all of the conditioning variables. The book's secondary take-away message is therefore that if we wish to understand which new latent social groups are likely to successfully form their own sectarian political parties, and when, which in turn enables us to understand when increases in social heterogeneity shape party system fragmentation, we must take into account factors other than the electoral system. Whether we look at actual examples of new groups being added to the citizenry, such as African American enfranchisement in the United States, or at cross-national quantitative analyses, the answer is the same: the electoral system provides only limited explanatory leverage over how changes in society shape party system fragmentation. While parsimony is desirable, the better strategy is to maximize leverage: to explain as much as possible with as little as possible (King, Keohane, and Verba 1994). Given the explanatory payoffs from broadening our theories beyond the electoral system, it would be foolish not to do so. I will now elaborate.

At the level of the new social groups, my theoretical arguments and empirical analyses identified a group's size and politicization as the most important variables. First, up to a point, larger groups were more likely to be successfully particized than smaller groups. Second, more politicized groups were more likely to be successfully particized than less politicized groups. Third, among other findings regarding the type of attribute defining the group, different historical processes that have altered the social heterogeneity of today's advanced industrial democracies, from territorial change to expansions of the franchise, have had different effects upon party system fragmentation. For example, internal increases in a polity's heterogeneity, such as those resulting from expansions of the franchise, were found to have had a more substantial effect on party system fragmentation than external increases, such as those resulting from immigration. However, I argued that the type of attribute was not a necessary factor in a group's successful particization.

Turning to the systemic level, in addition to the electoral system, I identified existing party strategies and the regime type as the key variables. First, existing political parties adopting an accommodative strategy towards a new group was found to decrease the likelihood of the group's successful particization. Second, of particular importance, the less the regime type centralized policy-making authority in an elected office, the more likely new social groups were to succeed in forming a sectarian party to contest that office. Third, social heterogeneity was found to be nonlinearly related to fragmentation: when a polity is initially either very homogeneous or very heterogeneous, an increase in social heterogeneity does not lead to an increase in fragmentation, as it does when the polity is initially of moderate heterogeneity. However, I argued that this variable was also not a necessary factor. Fourth, more limited empirical support was found for the final factor of party system openness, another variable that I argued was theoretically less important: in some analyses, closed party systems did seem to constrain the successful particization of new latent social groups, but in others they did not.

The conditioning effect of political institutions deserves special attention. Seemingly contrary to the literature's hypothesis, a restrictive electoral system was not consistently found to discourage the successful particization of new latent social groups. These findings underscore the importance of moving beyond aggregate, national-level analyses of the party system, as well as the importance of taking into account group-level factors such as a new latent social group's size. As I have argued at length in this book, group size and political institutions interact in a more complicated way than is usually recognized to condition the effect of social heterogeneity on party system fragmentation. Restrictive electoral systems actually act as a constraint only on the successful particization of small groups at the level of the electoral district. The regime type, by way of contrast, acts as a constraint on the successful particization of small groups at the aggregate (national) level. This is why aggregate-level predictions based on the electoral system will often be in error. For example, a group that is large in many electoral districts but small relative to the national electorate, like African Americans in the United States, will be constrained in successfully forming its own sectarian parties by a type of regime that reasonably centralizes policy-making authority, not by a restrictive electoral system. For these reasons, the regime type is as important a political institution as the electoral system in conditioning the effect of social heterogeneity. And in fact, over the course of the empirical analyses, I provided examples of the regime type having a *more* important effect.

Accordingly, in this book, I identified conditions under which new social groups are likely to successfully strike out on their own politically, and conditions under which they are not. Armed with this knowledge, we can answer questions about the political trajectories of particular new social groups

8. Conclusion: Party System Fragmentation and Beyond

in particular countries and at particular moments of time. Examples of such questions posed in the introductory chapter and grappled with elsewhere in this book include why Sephardi Jews have generally been less successful than Russian Jews at forming their own political parties in Israel, and why African Americans were more successful at forming their own political parties during the Civil Rights era than during Reconstruction. More generally, by identifying the conditions under which social heterogeneity is likely to shape the fragmentation of the party system, policy makers and activists alike will be better positioned to predict the political consequences of social changes. They will also be better able to predict the impact of institutional reforms, such as Israel's experiment with a unique president–parliamentary regime in the late 1990s. To reiterate, the case I have made in this book is that society matters, but in determining *how* society matters, the electoral system alone does not give us sufficient explanatory leverage. It is therefore time for the electoral system to share the stage, both with other political institutions and with non-institutions.

8.2 SOCIAL HETEROGENEITY AND OTHER DIMENSIONS OF THE PARTY SYSTEM

Yet, as I noted in the first chapter of this book, fragmentation is but one dimension of the party system. There are a myriad ways of thinking about, and hence characterizing, this multidimensional concept. For example, in a recent textbook on Israeli politics, the second section of the chapter on political parties discusses the salient ideological dimensions of political competition in Israel, such as private enterprise versus socialism and a Torah-oriented life versus secularism (Mahler 2011). Fragmentation is relegated to a later section. For yet another example, commentary on the contemporary American party system usually ranges from noting the dominance of the Democratic and Republican parties (and hence the persistent two-party system) to pointing out the catch-all, historically inclusive nature and relative ideological moderation of these parties (see, for example Hetherington and Larson 2009). Accordingly, my task in this final portion of this final chapter of the book is to touch briefly upon these other dimensions.

Without attempting an exhaustive enumeration, three other dimensions of the party system have garnered substantial attention from political scientists. First is the political agenda, which consists of the salient issues or underlying ideological dimensions that structure political competition.[1]

---

[1] For example, scholars have explored to what extent elections are fought over the proportion of economic activity left to the private sector as opposed to other types of issues, ranging from social control (e.g., abortion and religious education) to foreign policy (e.g., membership in the European Union and involvement in foreign wars). Studies in this vein have drawn upon a variety of data sources, from expert surveys to the Comparative Manifestos Project's content analysis of political party election manifestos. They also range from the cross-national to the case study in design. Examples include Lijphart (1999); Caramani (2004); Monroe and Maeda (2004); Stoll (2004, 2010); Posner (2005); and Benoit and Laver (2006).

Second is the positions that political parties take on these dimensions. This includes characteristics of the parties' collective positions such as how centripetal or centrifugal they are.[2] Last but not least is the sociodemographic characteristics of political parties' personnel.[3] While the number of political parties is important for all of the practical and normative reasons I laid out in the introductory chapter, there are nevertheless compelling reasons for broadening the scope of the inquiry.

One such reason is that from the perspective of democratic theory, many of these other dimensions are arguably of greater normative importance (Stoll 2004). Consider the positions that parties take on particular issue or ideological dimensions. Comparing these positions to the positions that citizens take on the same dimensions at any given time reveals the degree of ideological congruence between representatives and citizens.[4] This speaks directly to the quality of a democracy's static substantive representation. Similarly, comparing changes in parties' positions to changes in citizens' positions reveals the responsiveness of parties to public opinion, the quality of the democracy's dynamic substantive representation.[5] Finally, consider the sociodemographic characteristics of political parties' personnel, particularly in their parliamentary wings. Comparing these characteristics to the sociodemographic characteristics of the citizens reveals the degree of physical congruence between representatives and citizens. This speaks directly to the quality of the democracy's descriptive representation and indirectly to the quality of its substantive representation.[6]

This naturally raises the question of how changes in democratic societies have shaped these other dimensions of the party system. The obvious hypothesis is that social heterogeneity will have an effect here, too. However, because social heterogeneity's effect upon party system fragmentation may be constrained by the setting, and particularly by the political institutional setting, it is likely to have a *larger* effect upon these other dimensions, as suggested by Stoll (2004, 2011). This should be especially likely in countries with restrictive electoral systems and political regimes that concentrate policy-making authority. In other words, in such countries, while an in-

---

[2]Of particular note here is the literature exploring political parties' positions on the left–right dimension. This ideological dimension subsumes many specific issues and is predominant in most democracies. Moreover, based on parties' positions on the different salient dimensions, some scholars have explored the relationship between the dimensions (the extent to which they are cross-cutting versus overlapping), and hence the dimensionality of the political space. See, for example, Downs (1957); Kitschelt (1997); Budge et al. (2001); Adams et al. (2004); McDonald and Budge (2005); Benoit and Laver (2006); Hooghe et al. (2004); and Stoll (2010, 2011).

[3]Most cross-national work has focused upon the descriptive representation of either lower-class individuals or women. Case studies have explored the descriptive representation of ethnic minorities. Examples here include Rule and Zimmerman (1994), Jones (2009), and Moser and Scheiner (2012).

[4]See, for example, Powell (2000), Powell (2004), McDonald and Budge (2005), Blais and Bodet (2006), and Golder and Stramski (2010).

[5]Examples here include Stimson, MacKuen, and Erikson (1995), and Adams et al. (2004).

[6]For some prominent examples, see Pitkin (1967); Phillips (1995); Mansbridge (1999); Carroll (2001); Menifield and Shaffer (2005); and Caul (2008).

crease in social heterogeneity will probably not lead to an increase in the effective number of political parties in equilibrium, it may lead political parties to alter their positions, pay attention to different issues, or change the sociodemographic characteristics of their personnel. These are all open empirical questions. With the exception of Stoll's (2004) work on the political agenda, scholars have tackled these questions only indirectly or piecemeal.[7]

In the remainder of this chapter, I delve into these matters further in the context of one of the other dimensions of the party system just discussed. Specifically, I explore how social heterogeneity shapes descriptive representation, arguably the most important of these other dimensions. The goal is not to provide a definitive answer to this research question. Rather, I aim to sketch preliminary answers, provide preliminary evidence, and suggest directions for future research.

8.3 DESCRIPTIVE REPRESENTATION: CHANGING THE SOCIODEMOGRAPHIC FACE OF POLITICS?

Scholars of democratic representation, from political theorists to empiricists, have naturally concerned themselves with the composition of representative bodies such as legislatures. In the words of John Adams, one of the founding fathers of the United States, a representative legislature "should be an exact portrait, in miniature, of the people at large, as it should think, feel, reason and act like them" (Adams 1852–1865). This influential conception of representation, usually called descriptive representation, views representatives as "standing for" others by virtue of being like them in certain characteristics (Pitkin 1967, 60–61). While these shared characteristics may be ideational, that is, concerning opinions and beliefs, an increasingly influential perspective holds that they should also be sociodemographic. That is, in order for representatives to act in the interests of and be responsive to the represented (ibid., 209), they must come from the diverse social groups that make up the citizenry, and they must do so in numbers that mirror the citizenry's composition. Phillips (1995) calls this the politics of presence, in contrast to the politics of ideas.

If *who* politicians are is indeed as important as *what* (ideas, policies) they represent (Phillips 1995, 4), either prima facie or because descriptive representation facilitates substantive representation,[8] then the relationship be-

---

[7]To provide just one example, while there is a large literature studying how shifts in voters' policy positions shape parties' policy positions (see note 2), these changes in voters' preferences have not been endogenized. In other words, shifts in voters' policy positions have not been linked to changes in social heterogeneity due to historical processes such as franchise reform.

[8]The literature on women in politics demonstrates the link between descriptive and substantive representation most conclusively (e.g., Norris and Lovenduski 1995; Swers 2002; Caul 2008; Reingold 2008).However, contrary to the findings of Norris and Lovenduski (1995) regarding social class and race in the United Kingdom, the literature on minority politics in the United States also provides evidence of a link. For example, most if not all studies find that the race of members of Congress does affect legislative behavior, ranging from the type of legislation sponsored to roll call votes (e.g., Canon 2002).

tween this dimension of the party system and social heterogeneity is worthy of study. As argued earlier, the empirical question is whether or not increases in social heterogeneity have changed the sociodemographic characteristics of politicians—that is, the sociodemographic "face" of politics. To what extent have new latent social groups obtained a presence in the policymaking class? In other words, are there politicians who are members of the new groups, and are the relative numbers of these politicians proportional to the groups' shares of the electorate? The obvious hypothesis is that a change in social heterogeneity will change the sociodemographic face of politics. A more specific hypothesis capturing the normative democratic ideal is that a new group's share of the political class will come to mirror its share of the electorate.

Accordingly, I present some preliminary evidence regarding changes in the sociodemographic characteristics of politicians. Because of their central roles in policy making, I focus upon elected officials. Even more specifically, I focus upon legislators (parliamentarians), commensurate with the literature, although some attention is also paid to the executive (e.g., cabinet members, presidents, and prime ministers). Broadly cross-national evidence is presented before turning to the two case studies.

8.3.1 Cross-National Evidence

There are many different possible dimensions of societal change. Hence, there are many different new groups that, historically, have been added to democratic citizenries, as I have discussed in earlier chapters. It accordingly does not seem possible to conduct a cross-national analysis assessing how the sociodemographic face of politics has changed in response to *all* of these different societal changes simultaneously. Indeed, to date, I am aware of no study that attempts such a heroic feat.

An alternative cross-national approach is to assess changes in descriptive representation from a single dimension of societal change, such as immigration (are new immigrants represented in the halls of power?) or women's suffrage (do women rub shoulders with men in the legislature?). However, the appropriate data on descriptive representation can be straightforwardly gathered across countries and time for only a few of the relevant social divisions, such as gender and socioeconomics, and hence for only a few of the relevant dimensions of societal change. For example, for the gender division, the same two categories of "man" and "woman" are found in each country across time, and specifically both prior and subsequent to the increased heterogeneity of the citizenry that resulted from women's suffrage. By way of contrast, the menu of categories for other divisions such as the ethnic must be determined on a case-by-case basis: by country, time, and dimension of change. For example, the ethnic category sets relevant for extensions of the ethnic franchise will differ from those relevant for territorial changes.

8. Conclusion: Party System Fragmentation and Beyond

This is the likely reason that cross-national empirical studies of descriptive representation have focused upon the internal dimension of societal change, that is, change in the franchise, and specifically on *women's* representation.[9] In keeping with the hypothesis that changes in the electorate should lead to changes in the sociological characteristics of elected officials, studies have documented an increase in the number of elected offices held by women since women's suffrage (e.g., Paxton and Hughes 2007). Table 8.1 provides some illustrative statistics for a few of the advanced industrial democracies studied. An example is Switzerland, which—following universal women's suffrage in 1971—saw female parliamentarians' share of its lower house immediately increase from zero to almost 6 percent, and gradually increase from there to almost 30 percent in 2009 (Paxton, Hughes, and Greene 2008; IPU 2009). However, from a starting point of legislatures consisting solely of men prior to women's suffrage,[10] in no country has the share of elected offices held by women come to equal their share of the electorate. Moreover, there is great variation even within the advanced industrial democracies as to how close to parity women have come. For example, the share of seats in the national legislature held by women in October 2009 ranges from a low of 11 percent in Japan to a high of 47 percent in Sweden (IPU 2009).

The dimension of societal change that has received the second-most attention with respect to descriptive representation is the extension of the socioeconomic franchise. Here the empirical findings are even less commensurate with the democratic ideal: everywhere, elected officials today are overwhelmingly drawn from the upper socioeconomic strata. This state of affairs is similar to, if less extreme than, that prior to the extension of the socioeconomic franchise. It is true that over time, the membership of legislatures has become less aristocratic and more middle-class in composition. Yet while legislators are no longer primarily drawn from the nobility as they were prior to the late 1800s, they are now primarily drawn from the professions and white-collar occupations—that is, still from the better-educated and higher-status socioeconomic groups (e.g., Loewenberg and Patterson 1979; Norris and Lovenduski 1995). For example, while the lower-middle and working classes increased their share of the French parliament from 10 percent in 1871 to 30 percent in 1945, this means that 70 percent of the parliament remained in the hands of the upper classes even after universal socioeconomic enfranchisement (Loewenberg and Patterson 1979, 73). While there is variation from country to country, there are no advanced industrial

---

[9]See, for example, Rule and Zimmerman (1994): minority (meaning ethnic or religious minority) representation is explored in the case study chapters of this edited volume, but the only cross-national data and analyses concern the representation of women.

[10]In a few countries, women were allowed to stand for national legislative office prior to universal women's suffrage. A prominent example is the United States: Jeanette Rankin, known as the "Lady of the House," became the first woman elected to the House as well as to Congress in 1917, preceding the ratification of the Nineteenth Amendment (which enfranchised women) by three years.

243

Changing Societies, Changing Party Systems

	Year of Universal Woman's Suffrage	Year Women Allowed to Stand for Election	Year First Woman Elected to Legislature	Percent Women Legislators, 1945	Percent Women Legislators, 2009
Israel	Always	Always	1949	11	18
Japan	1946	1946	1946	8.4	11
New Zealand	1893	1919	1933	2.5	34
Sweden	1921	1921	1921	7.8	47
Switzerland	1971	1971	1971	0.0	29
United States	1920	Always	1917	2.5	17

Table 8.1: The representation of women in the lower or single legislative chamber for selected advanced industrial democracies. Years refer to election years; "always" means that the right to either vote or stand for election was never constrained for the years for which the country is included in my study (see Table 3.1). Source: for columns 2–5, Table 3.1 in Chapter 3 and Paxton, Hughes, and Greene (2008), supplemented by other secondary and primary sources; for column 6, IPU (2009).

democracies where the socioeconomic characteristics of the legislature come close to mirroring those of the citizenry today, in contrast to the situation regarding gender.[11]

Not surprisingly, in light of how few countries have employed ethnic restrictions on the franchise, there is no cross-national work tackling changes in descriptive representation in this area. Nevertheless, for most countries that have employed ethnic restrictions on the franchise, a pattern emerges comparable to that described earlier for gender and socioeconomics: the ethnic diversity of elected officials has increased following expansions of the ethnic franchise, but while parity has nowhere been attained, there is variation in the extent of the shortfall. For example, in Australia, the only two aborigines to serve in parliament were elected subsequent to their 1962 enfranchisement (Australia EC 2006). In Israel, Arabs did hold seats in the first two parliaments, when only some Arabs were enfranchised, but their representation has increased over time while still falling short of parity following their full enfranchisement (Knesset 2009). Last but not least, in Canada, the first parliamentarians of Chinese, South Asian, and First Nation ances-

---

[11]To illustrate, in their study of six Western democracies in the early 1970s, Aberbach, Putnam, and Rockman (1981, 53–55) found that the legislators with the *lowest* social origins hailed from Italy, yet only 23 percent had fathers whose occupations were semiskilled or unskilled, in contrast to 58 percent of the Italian electorate (technically, population) at large—a substantial discrepancy.

8. Conclusion: Party System Fragmentation and Beyond

try were all elected subsequent to their enfranchisement but have yet to attain parity (Canada EC 2006; Canada OCEO 2007). By way of contrast, the United States is a prominent exception in the extent to which parity has been attained between a formerly disenfranchised ethnic group's share of the electorate and its share of elected offices. I will present evidence to this effect in the following section.

8.3.2 CASE STUDY EVIDENCE

Future research might fruitfully attempt a more systematic exploration of this research question in a cross-national setting. However, given the difficulty of the enterprise, for the purposes of this preliminary study the primary empirical evidence is drawn from my two case studies: Israel and the United States. This allows an in-depth look at ethnic descriptive representation over time, one of the most systematic such looks to date, even if the generalizability of the findings is limited. Accordingly, the empirical questions I ask in what follows are: have the sociodemographic characteristics, and specifically the ethnicity, of elected officials in Israel changed as society has grown more ethnically heterogeneous following the immigration of Sephardi and Russian Jews? What about the situation in the United States following the enfranchisement of African Americans?

Israel

To empirically weigh in on this issue using the Israeli case, the top half of Figure 8.1 displays for each Knesset the percentage of Knesset members who are Sephardi, while the bottom half displays the percentage of Knesset members who are Russian. Similarly, the top half of Figure 8.2 displays for each government the percentage of cabinet ministers who are Sephardi, while the bottom half displays the percentage of cabinet members who are Russian.[12] For the moment, my interest lies in the total percentages of Sephardim and Russians over time (that is, from all political parties, not just from sectarian parties), which are shown by the dark grey bars in the two figures.

Perhaps not surprisingly, these figures for the most part show what Herzog (1995, 85) calls a "politics of inclusion" in Israel. Beginning with the Sephardim, the general trend over time is for an increase in Sephardi representation and hence a reduction in the disparity between the Sephardi shares of the electorate and the policy-making class. Specifically, after fluctuating around 10 percent from 1949 to 1965, Sephardi legislative representation increased monotonically from 14 percent of the Knesset in 1969 to 32 percent in 1996. After 1996, however, it begin decreasing from this high to the slightly lower levels of the late 1980s. Turning the lens on Sephardi executive representation, the Sephardi proportion of cabinet ministers has also exhibited an upward trend, but with greater fluctuations over time. Specifically, it jumped back and forth between 7 and 12 percent in Israel's first seven-

---

[12]See Chapter 6 for more information about this data.

Changing Societies, Changing Party Systems

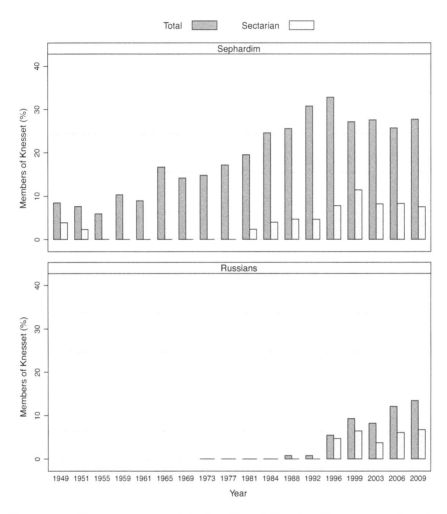

Figure 8.1: The percentage of Sephardi and Russian Knesset members by Knesset, both in total (for all parties) and for sectarian parties. Note that sectarian parties for each group are considered collectively. Source: see Chapter 6.

8. Conclusion: Party System Fragmentation and Beyond

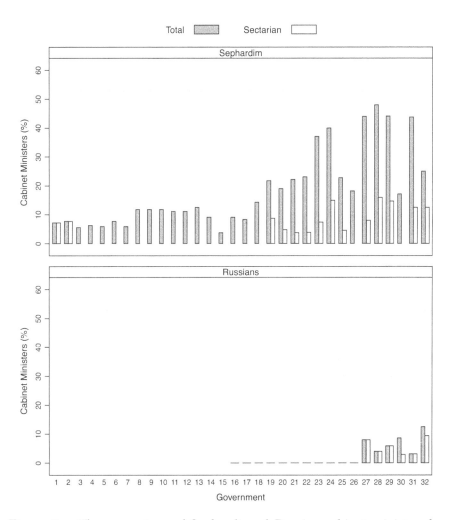

Figure 8.2: The percentage of Sephardi and Russian cabinet ministers by government (numbered), both in total (for all parties) and for sectarian parties. Note that sectarian parties for each group are considered collectively. Source: see Chapter 6.

teen governments, after which it began climbing but has still ranged widely, from a low of 17 percent in the thirtieth government (2003–2006) to a high of 48 percent in the twenty-eighth government (1999–2001). At the executive level, the Sephardim have accordingly sometimes been overrepresented and sometimes even more severely underrepresented than they have been at the legislative level. Yet looking even more specifically at the most consequential ministerial portfolios, that is, defense, foreign affairs, and finance, they have been held by Sephardim only a handful of times.[13] Moreover, there has never been a Sephardi prime minister.

When compared to my best estimates of the Sephardi share of the electorate,[14] this data leads to the conclusion that while the Sephardim have made substantial inroads into the political class over time, as hypothesized, their presence usually still falls short of parity with their share of the electorate, contrary to the hypothesis. For example, in 2009, the Sephardi share of the Knesset was only 74 percent of the Sephardi share of the electorate. Chapter 6 made a similar argument in the context of Sephardi representation in Israel's individual catch-all political parties.

Moving on to the Russians, a similarly positive trend of increasing representation over time is seen at the legislative level: Russians have almost monotonically increased their share of the Knesset from no representation prior to 1988 to 13 percent of MKs in 2009. However, the same cannot be said of their presence at the executive level. From 8 percent of cabinet ministers in the twenty-seventh government (1996–1999), their share fell to a mere 3 percent in the thirty-first government (2006–2009) before rebounding to a record high of 13 percent in the thirty-second government (2009 onwards). Moreover, even relative to the Sephardim, they suffer from an extremely minimal presence at the highest executive levels. Tellingly, a Russian has never held one of the key ministerial portfolios during the period studied here, with the sole exception of Avigdor Lieberman serving as minister of foreign affairs in the current (thirty-second) government. A Russian has also never served as prime minister.

These figures tell us that compared to their share of the electorate,[15] the Russians, like the Sephardim, are underrepresented in the Israeli political class. For example, their share of the Knesset in 2009—their best performance to date—was 74 percent of their share of the electorate, the same as the Sephardim's. Accordingly, as hypothesized, the ethnic composition of

---

[13] The defense ministry was held by Binyamin Ben-Eliezer in the twenty-ninth government (partial tenure); by Shaul Mofaz in the twenty-ninth (partial tenure) and thirtieth governments; and by Amir Peretz in the thirty-first (partial tenure) government. The finance portfolio was held by Moshe Nissam in the twenty-first (partial tenure) and twenty-second governments; by Meir Sheetrit in the twenty-seventh, and thirtieth governments; and by Silvan Shalom in the twenty-ninth government. The foreign affairs portfolio was held by David Levy in the twenty-fourth, twenty-seventh, and twenty-eighth (partial tenure) governments; by Shlomo Ben-Ami in the twenty-eighth (partial tenure) government; and by Silvan Shalom in the thirtieth government.

[14] See either Figures 6.2 and 6.3 or Appendix B.

[15] As before, see either Figures 6.2 and 6.3 or Appendix B.

8. Conclusion: Party System Fragmentation and Beyond

Israel's political class has changed to reflect the Russian presence in Israeli society, but, contrary to the hypothesis, normative parity has yet to be attained. Moreover, as compared to the portrait of the Russian presence in catch-all parties painted in Chapter 6, when looking at the *overall* Russian political presence in Israel, the Russians seem to have closed the representational gap with the Sephardim. The discrepancy between the two portraits has to do with the role of sectarian parties in supplying representation to these new social groups, an issue to which I will return.

United States

To empirically weigh in on this issue using the case of African Americans in the United States, the top half of Figure 8.3 displays the percentage of African American members of the federal House, while the bottom half displays the percentage of African American members of the federal Senate. Similarly, for the two states where African American parties have successfully placed candidates in the lower house of the state legislature, Mississippi and Alabama, Figure 8.4 displays the percentage of African American state representatives.[16] As before, the focus here is on the total percentage of African American legislators over time (that is, from all political parties, not just from sectarian parties), which is shown by the dark grey bars in the two figures.

These figures show that at the national (federal) level, African Americans have always been grossly underrepresented in the Senate, contrary to the hypothesis. However, as hypothesized, in the periods during which they were enfranchised (Reconstruction and post-1965), they have achieved at least some representation in this legislative chamber (a high of one and a half percent following the 1868 election), in contrast to the periods of their disenfranchisement, when the Senate has been exclusively white. They have had a larger presence in the House. During Reconstruction, a maximum of 2.5 percent of representatives were African American. This is greater than their share of the Senate but still falls far short of parity with their share of the electorate at the time. By the turn of the century, the percentage of African Americans in the House had fallen to zero with disenfranchisement in the South. In was not until 1928, in the wake of the Great Migration to the North and West, that an African American was again to sit in the House. It then took until the 1970 elections, a good five years after the passage of the Voting Rights Act, to break the record set during Reconstruction. But from there, the African American share of the House hardly budged: it did not exceed 6 percent, less than half of the African American share of the electorate, until the early 1990s, when it jumped to nine percent.[17] It has

---

[16] See Chapter 7 for more information about this data. In the interests of space, the focus at the state level is upon the lower house, where African Americans have been more successful at obtaining representation.

[17] This substantial increase in African American representation is attributed by most scholars to the 1990 round of redistricting. See, for example, Grofman (1998).

Changing Societies, Changing Party Systems

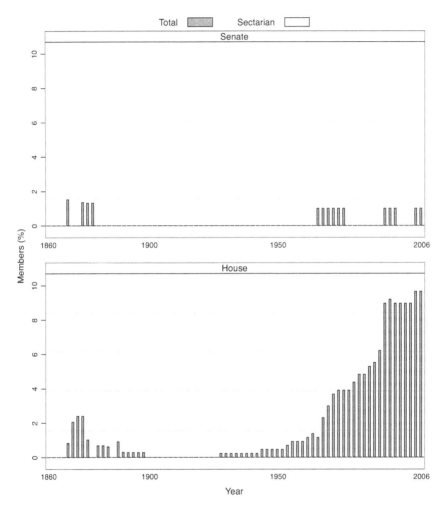

Figure 8.3: The percentage of African American members, in total and for African American sectarian political parties, at the federal level for both the House and the Senate. Source: see Chapter 7.

8. Conclusion: Party System Fragmentation and Beyond

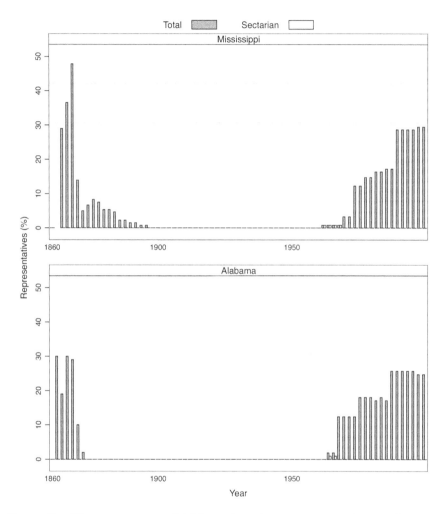

Figure 8.4: The percentage of African American representatives at the state level (lower house), in total and for African American sectarian political parties, for the two states of Mississippi and Alabama. Source: see Chapter 7.

since crept up to slightly less than 10 percent, which is just shy of parity, largely in keeping with the hypothesis. A similar story can be told at the state level.

In the interests of space, comparable data is not presented regarding the presence of African Americans in the executive branch of the United States. Nevertheless, it is worth noting that the descriptive representation of African Americans at this higher political level, not surprisingly, falls short of their descriptive representation at the legislative level, as was also usually the case for Sephardi and Russian Jews in Israel. For example, the first African American to be appointed to a Cabinet post was Robert Weaver in 1966, on the heels of the Voting Rights Act. Fewer than twenty African Americans have served in Cabinet posts since. The election of Barack Obama as the first African American president in 2008 was obviously a notable historical milestone.

8.4 THE ROLE OF SECTARIAN PARTIES

This discussion of the descriptive representation obtained by new latent social groups begs an important question, however: what role do sectarian political parties play in securing a group's presence in the policy-making class? In other words, with respect to this one normative dimension of democratic representation, descriptive representation, does it matter if new latent social groups are successful at forming their own sectarian political parties?

8.4.1 THE DEBATE

Optimists have answered "yes" to this question, viewing the role of sectarian parties positively. They argue that sectarian parties provide a group with descriptive representation that it would not otherwise have, and that this in turn leads to both substantive representation and a host of other beneficial outcomes, ranging from a stable regime to a legitimate government. This is the view taken by the influential advocates of the consensual (e.g., Lijphart 1984) or proportional (e.g., Powell 2000) type of democracy, who stand in opposition to advocates of majoritarianism. In addition to its symbolic importance, sectarian representation is viewed by these scholars as substantively important because many groups have proven unable in practice to "stand for" others, even if in principle they should be able to do so (Phillips 1995, 15). Moreover, the spatial literature that builds upon the work of Downs (1957) argues that sectarian parties, even when they take the form of unsuccessful protest parties or are successful only fleetingly, may pressure existing catch-all parties into adopting an accommodative stance towards the new group.[18] Hence, sectarian parties are believed by many to play a critical role in empirically ensuring presence.

---

[18]See, for example, work by scholars such as Meguid (2005, 2008). Outside of the spatial literature, see Krupavicius and Matonyte (2003) for arguments and some evidence to this effect with respect to women's representation.

8. Conclusion: Party System Fragmentation and Beyond

Pessimists, however, have taken a negative view of the role of sectarian parties. One argument is that they lead mainstream catch-all parties to write off a new group's members as potential supporters, discouraging these parties from accommodating the group in the long run. The resulting political segregation of the new social group in turn prevents its integration into the citizenry and impedes it from attaining its policy goals. This case has been made most vigorously by scholars of women's representation (e.g., Moser 2003; Matland 2003).[19] Another argument falling in this camp is that some groups are unlikely to successfully form sectarian political parties. Marginalized groups outside of the dominant norm frequently fall into this category (Phillips 1995, 14–15). So, too, are groups faced with unfavorable conditions, whether pertaining to their own characteristics or to the settings in which they must operate, as I have argued in earlier chapters. In these all-too-common circumstances, it seems difficult to view sectarian political parties as a credible means of securing representation. Accordingly, there are good theoretical reasons to believe that successful sectarian parties are at minimum not necessary to secure descriptive representation for a group, and that they may in fact be counterproductive.

With both optimists and pessimists making plausible theoretical arguments in support of their positions, I argue that the role sectarian parties play in securing descriptive representation for a new latent social group is best viewed as an *empirical* question. This is particularly the case in polities where political institutional conditions are favorable for the group's successful particization. Where political institutional conditions are not favorable, sectarian parties should not be expected to play an equilibrium role in directly securing descriptive representation for the group. However, as noted earlier, they might in the short run spur existing parties to adopt an accommodative stance, an indirect contribution.

Moreover, the role sectarian parties play in securing descriptive representation is an *open* empirical question. As with descriptive representation in general, the most extensive empirical analyses to date have been with respect to women's representation, but even this has been piecemeal: particular countries have been studied at particular moments in time, yielding mixed results (some favorable, some not).[20] While some attention has been drawn to the role of socioeconomic sectarian parties, that is, working-class (socialist and communist) parties, in placing individuals of lower socioeconomic status in political office,[21] even less systematic evidence has been

---

[19]But see also scholars such as Birnir (2007, 12-15) regarding ethnic representation. Birnir, for example, argues that ethnic representation through sectarian parties may be a second-best solution for two reasons: excessive legislative fractionalization impedes successful coalition building and hampers government; and larger, broad-based parties representing a variety of ethnic interests may on average have greater access to government, ensuring better ethnic representation.

[20]See, for example, the country studies of post-Communist Europe in Matland and Montgomery (2003).

[21]For evidence to this effect, see Loewenberg and Patterson (1979), Aberbach, Putnam, and

Changing Societies, Changing Party Systems

assembled for this division.

8.4.2 EMPIRICAL EVIDENCE

To weigh in on the role sectarian parties have played in securing descriptive representation for new latent social groups, I again present empirical evidence from my two case studies, the United States and Israel. This turns the lens on ethnic sectarian parties for the first time. Generalizability is still limited as a result of the comparative case study design confining the analysis to two countries, but by varying the appearance and success of sectarian parties, as is done both across and within the cases, relatively systematic conclusions about the role of sectarian parties can nevertheless be drawn.

Israel

Within Israel, political entrepreneurs and other elites in the Sephardi and Russian communities have been very conscious of the debate just discussed: some have argued in favor of launching and supporting sectarian parties, while others have argued against it.[22] Figure 8.1 provides some evidence as to the actual empirical role sectarian parties have played in securing descriptive representation for the two communities since Israel's founding. The light grey bars show the Sephardi and Russian MKs supplied by Sephardi and Russian sectarian parties as a percentage of the total number of MKs, respectively. By comparing this percentage to the total percentage of Sephardi and Russian MKs—the dark grey bars discussed in the previous section—I can assess the representational importance of sectarian parties. Figure 8.2 does the same for cabinet ministers.

As before, I begin with the Sephardim. Figure 8.1 shows that in Israel's first two Knessets, Sephardi sectarian parties supplied approximately half of the Sephardi legislators. When these parties failed to cross the electoral threshold in the third election (1955), however, mainstream catch-all parties took over the supply of Sephardi MKs, a situation that would continue for the next three decades. The Sephardi legislative contingent from the mainstream parties initially stood at around 5 percent of the Knesset before jumping to 10 percent in the fourth election; from there, with some exceptions, it slowly increased to 17 percent by the end of the 1970s. The 1981 election saw the mainstream parties sweeten their offering of Sephardi representatives slightly to approximately 20 percent, but with the exceptions of the

---

Rockman (1981), and Norris and Lovenduski (1995), among others.

[22]For example, in the 1992 Israeli elections, no Russian parties were able to obtain representation in the Knesset, and no Russians from the 1990s wave of immigration were placed highly enough on existing parties' lists to earn a seat. Siegel (1998, 146–147) describes the elite debates in 1994 about forming a new Russian party to contest the next election. At the time, the calculation ultimately made was that even if this ethnic sectarian party did not succeed, it would enhance the chances of a Russian to enter the Knesset on a mainstream party's list. Here we see actors on the ground explicitly embracing the theoretical argument that even ultimately unsuccessful sectarian parties may influence the strategies of mainstream catch-all parties.

8. Conclusion: Party System Fragmentation and Beyond

1992 and 1996 Knessets, this is where their accommodation topped out—a strategy falling short of full accommodation. Perhaps not coincidentally, in 1981, Sephardi parties once again won seats in the Knesset. While their contribution to Sephardi representation has been limited by their size, and even today is dwarfed by that of the mainstream parties, it quickly became nontrivial: by 1999, one-third of the Sephardi legislators in the Knesset hailed from sectarian parties. Today, the Sephardi presence in the legislature approaches what is normatively desirable, as discussed earlier. However, this is only because of the Sephardim sent to the Knesset by Sephardi sectarian parties. Figure 8.2 shows a similar story with respect to the cabinet, except that by the late 1980s, mainstream parties were surprisingly playing a fully accommodative strategy towards the Sephardim. As a result, the inclusion of Sephardi sectarian parties in the government since then has led the Sephardim to be overrepresented at the executive level.

Accordingly, Sephardi sectarian parties have sometimes made important, if not critical, contributions to both a Sephardi legislative and executive descriptive presence. In light of the initial electoral success of Sephardi sectarian parties and the continual appearance of new, if unsuccessful, ones during Israel's first few decades, the gradually more accommodative strategy mainstream parties have played towards the group seems consistent with the optimists' argument that sectarian parties spur accommodation by mainstream parties, although the evidence is far from conclusive. And indeed, prominent commentators have attributed the increase in Sephardi ethnic representation in the mainstream parties to the variety of ethnically based organizations that existed in Israel's early years (e.g., Herzog 1986, 297). Yet in the 1980s, the leveling off at less than parity of Sephardi representation in the mainstream parties' legislative contingents shows the limits of this influence. In fact, if the Knesset elected in 1992 is viewed as a high-water mark instead of an aberration, the Sephardi presence in mainstream parties began a decline in 1996, precisely when the electoral success of Sephardi sectarian parties exploded. This suggests that, in keeping with the pessimists' argument, ultimately sectarian parties may lead mainstream catch-all parties to write off a new social group, at least to some extent. A better assessment of this argument will come only with the passage of time, however, given the recent occurrence and short duration of the downturn in Sephardi representation. From the perspective of the Sephardim in Israel, then, the at best moderately successful sectarian parties that have sought to provide them with democratic representation may be empirically viewed as both a limited blessing (à la the optimists) and a curse (à la the pessimists).

But what about the Russians? Here sectarian parties have played a much more important role in supplying descriptive representation. From 1996 onwards, with the exception of the 2003 Knesset, Russian sectarian parties have provided more representation to Russians than mainstream parties have—and even in 2003, they provided only slightly less than half of the total Russian legislators. In fact, prior to 1996, when Russian sectarian parties first obtained representation in the Knesset, only one Russian (from the earlier 1970s wave of immigration, not the 1990s wave) had received a Knesset seat on a mainstream party list. Mainstream parties began to provide more representation to Russians beginning in 1996. Perhaps not coincidentally, this followed the appearance of several Russian parties and the electoral success of one of them. As time passed, mainstream party strategy became even more accommodative: in 1992, less than one percent of their legislative contingent was Russian; by 2009, almost seven percent was. Nevertheless, at the legislative level, Russian parties initially supplied virtually all Russian representation and still supply a substantial amount today. At the executive level, the role of Russian parties has been even more important: with the exception of the thirtieth government, all Russian cabinet ministers have come from Russian sectarian parties. Hence, Russian sectarian parties have played a critical role in securing a Russian presence at both the legislative and executive levels in Israel. The evidence also suggestively supports the optimists' argument that sectarian parties have spurred mainstream catch-all parties to play a more accommodative strategy towards the Russians. To date, then, Russian sectarian parties seem to have borne out the predictions of the optimists.

United States

African American elites have also been well aware of the debate between the optimistic and pessimistic camps. However, because of the extremely adversarial strategies the major parties adopted towards African Americans during some periods, such as the mid-twentieth century, African Americans had little choice but to strike out on their own (Walton 1985). At the same time, in contrast to the Israeli case, an examination of Figures 8.3 and 8.4 reveals that African American sectarian parties have not played a significant role in providing descriptive representation to the group. This is a result of their never having managed to win legislative seats at the federal (national) level, and only rarely at the state level (e.g., one seat in both Mississippi from 1967 to 1975 and Alabama from 1970 to 1974). Instead, an African American presence in both the federal and state legislatures has been provided by mainstream catch-all parties. The same can obviously be said of the executive. As discussed earlier, while the African American share of the mainstream parties' legislative and executive contingents historically often fell below the normatively desirable level, near-parity with their share of the electorate has been achieved since the 1990s—the closest a new ethnic group has come to achieving parity.

But this is not to say that African American sectarian parties have had no impact from a representational perspective. Supporting the optimists' argument, it cannot be a coincidence that the appearance and electoral success of these parties during the Civil Rights era in the most segregationist states of the Old South, such as Mississippi, was almost immediately followed by the Democratic party branches of these states embracing more accommodative

8. Conclusion: Party System Fragmentation and Beyond

strategies. In fact, commentators have traced state party reforms in the late 1960s and early 1970s to a desire to head off further challenges by African American sectarian parties (e.g., Lawson 1985, 200-201). Whether African American parties were genuinely separate organizations or "satellites" of one of the major political parties, with the latter being the most common situation, all shared the goal of influencing the major parties; this influence has also been their ultimate legacy, like that of most third parties in the United States (Walton 1972). Accordingly, while African American sectarian parties have not directly provided African Americans with meaningful descriptive representation, they have nevertheless played an important role in that they have altered the strategies of mainstream parties, as predicted by the optimists.

8.5 QUO VADIS?

Fragmentation is not the only dimension of the party system worth studying. The political agenda, party positions, and descriptive representation are three other prominent, and normatively important, dimensions. Just as increasing a democracy's social heterogeneity by adding new groups to its citizenry sometimes shapes the number of political parties contesting its elections, so too will increasing its social heterogeneity sometimes shape these other dimensions of the party system.

Here the focus was upon descriptive representation. The empirical investigation was preliminary, but still allows for some tentative conclusions to be drawn. Some of the evidence presented was cross-national: changes in the gender, socioeconomic status, and ethnicity of legislators following extensions in the franchise. Other evidence drew upon the two case studies of Israel and the United States. Overall, all of these changes in social heterogeneity do appear to lead to changes in the heterogeneity of the policy-making class. Cross-nationally, as the franchise has expanded to include women, the lower socioeconomic classes, and once-excluded ethnic groups, the sociodemographic face of politics has been transformed. Similarly, as the franchise has expanded to include African Americans in the United States, and as Jews from different ethnic backgrounds have immigrated to Israel, the presence of these groups in the legislature and executive has increased. But all is not rosy. Nowhere has normative parity between a group's share of the electorate and its share of the political class been achieved. Moreover, the progress that has been made has been slow in coming. There is also great variance across countries. With respect to the ethnic groups studied here, it is ironically the United States with its restrictive electoral system, usually believed to discourage minority representation, that has come the closest to achieving parity.[23]

---

[23] Of course, the United States fares less well with respect to the descriptive representation of other groups, such as women. Nevertheless, its success in providing representation to African Americans in recent years is noteworthy. I will return to this point later.

Yet an obvious question was raised by this study of the relationship between social heterogeneity and descriptive representation, one that begged for a return to what had been my secondary research question throughout most of the book: sectarian political parties. Do sectarian parties help or hinder new social groups' efforts to secure a physical presence in the halls of political power? Bringing the discussion full circle, I finally explored this important issue. If the formation of sectarian parties is indeed an intervening factor shaping the other more normative dimensions of the party system, this has implications for constitutional engineers. Not surprisingly, optimists and pessimists have squared off over this issue, offering positive and negative assessments, respectively, of the role of sectarian parties. The position I took here was that this question was at heart an empirical one.

Primarily drawing upon my two case studies for evidence, I found more empirical support for the optimists' arguments. Sectarian ethnic parties in Israel have often directly provided significant amounts of descriptive representation to new social groups. Moreover, the successful appearance of sectarian parties—even if fleeting, as in the United States—seems to have spurred mainstream parties to adopt more accommodative strategies. Yet it is important to note that sectarian parties are certainly not necessary in order for a new social group to secure descriptive representation. To see this, one needs only to look at the case of African Americans in the United States. Further, in states where African American parties did not form, let alone achieve electoral success (e.g., Georgia), mainstream parties adopted accommodative strategies on their own, without a sectarian party "push." In other words, the pessimists' arguments are not completely without merit. Nevertheless, the sectarian party "push" in segregationist states like Mississippi probably significantly hastened the process as compared to what it otherwise would have been, which is to the good. Finally, while the case of the Sephardim in Israel suggests that sectarian party success may lead mainstream parties to play a somewhat less accommodative strategy towards a group, mainstream parties still provide extensive representation to the Sephardim. Ultimately, the passage of time will better reveal the extent to which this pessimistic prediction is realized.

Accordingly, the net preliminary evidence suggests that where conditions have been favorable for sectarian parties to emerge in equilibrium, they have both directly and indirectly, through their effect on mainstream parties, contributed to the representation of new latent social groups. Where conditions have not been favorable for sectarian parties to emerge in equilibrium, they have indirectly contributed. But even here, it is not the case that changes in society have had no impact upon the party system. It is true that the impact of increasing social heterogeneity has not taken the form of equilibrium party system fragmentation, that is, the successful and long-run emergence of sectarian parties. Rather, as hypothesized earlier à la Stoll (2011), social heterogeneity has instead affected the other, more normative dimensions of the party system, such as the characteristics of party personnel. In other words, as expected in a democracy, when society changes, the party system does too, with all that that implies for public policy and other outcomes of the political process.

8.5.1 IMPLICATIONS FOR FUTURE RESEARCH

To begin drawing the book to a close, I briefly explore the implications of my findings for future research. While this study is the most comprehensive look at the relationship between social heterogeneity and the party system to date, work remains to be done.

As mentioned earlier, one important way in which future researchers might build upon this study is to utilize multilevel models to explore the effect of social heterogeneity at two levels: the electoral district and the nation as a whole. Multilevel modeling should be the wave of the future because different political institutions act as constraints at these different levels and the size of new latent social groups usually varies from one district to another, as well as from the districts to the aggregate. However, the prerequisite for estimating such models is district-level data on social heterogeneity. Building upon the work of Moser and Scheiner (2012), who have gathered district-level data on ethnic heterogeneity for a small sample of countries at a single point in time, district-level data needs to be gathered for different types of heterogeneity, different countries, and different elections over a long period of time. While this will be a substantial undertaking, it is not an impossible one.

There are other areas in the realm of measurement where improvements can be made. First, while my measures of social heterogeneity improve upon existing measures, they still fall short of the ideal in several ways. For one, my index of social heterogeneity, which combined heterogeneity along the different historically important divisions, was time invariant. In the future, it may be possible to gather the necessary time series data to construct a longitudinal version of this index, which would be preferable. For another, my index did not take into account the cross-cuttingness of the different divisions. Building upon the work of Selway (2009), it may eventually be possible to do so. Second, it would be helpful to extend Hicken and Stoll's (2009) data on the horizontal centralization of policy-making authority in the national legislature, both internally and externally. Given the limited historical range of the data available for this variable, I was able to quantitatively test my hypothesis about the conditioning effect of the regime type only using presidential elections as the unit of analysis. With a longer historical time series, the hypotheses could also be quantitatively tested using legislative elections. Third, new measures of the electoral system currently in development, such as Kedar's (2011), which differentiate between the district and aggregate levels, will better enable us to test hypotheses about how this political institution does or does not condition the effect of social heterogeneity. Fourth, it may also be the case that in the future, better cross-national and time series measures of party system openness will be developed. This would allow scholars to revisit the issue of the empirical support for my hypothesis about this variable.

Outside of the realm of measurement, there is also much work needed regarding the relationship between social heterogeneity and the other, more normative dimensions of the party system, as I have argued in this final chapter. The bulk of this book has followed the existing literature in studying how social heterogeneity shapes the fragmentation of the party system. Yet there are very good normative, practical, and theoretical reasons for turning our collective lenses upon the other dimensions of the party system, from the political agenda to descriptive representation. This includes studying what, if any, role sectarian parties play in linking these dimensions to social heterogeneity. As discussed here at length, the preliminary evidence suggests that sectarian parties are more beneficial than not in facilitating the representation of new social groups, even though they are not necessary. But also as discussed here at length, this evidence is preliminary. Studying the role of sectarian parties in facilitating the representation of ethnic minorities in cross-national perspective is likely to be the most fruitful avenue for future exploration. This will involve substantial data-gathering efforts, but like the collection of district-level data on social heterogeneity, the prospective payoffs are large enough to justify the effort.

8.5.2 Implications for Constitutional Engineers

In earlier chapters, I argued that whether a new latent social group successfully manages to form a sectarian party ultimately depends upon a variety of factors outside of the control of policy-makers, from the group's size to the strategies existing parties choose to adopt. But I also argued that political institutions matter. And political institutions are under policy-makers' control. Given my finding that sectarian political parties appear to be beneficial from a normative democratic perspective, even though the evidence is admittedly preliminary, I close the book by discussing the implications for constitutional engineers.

One implication is that the regime type should not overly concentrate policy-making authority. The political institutional reforms in the constitutional engineer's tool kit for avoiding overconcentration are legion: for example, at least some decentralization to subnational levels of government or internally structuring the national legislature so that smaller political parties and the opposition still have some influence over policy. However, this does not mean that maximal decentralization and divided powers must be the name of the game. Sectarian political parties are not the panacea that the advocates of the consensus model of democracy often paint them to be (e.g., Lijphart 1999): as the discussion here has revealed, they are not *necessary* to secure the representation of new social groups. Moreover, as those who have followed the debate between the advocates of the consensus and majoritarian models are well aware, the desire for representation must be balanced with other concerns such as efficiency. Each polity must choose for itself which balance to strike. Nonetheless, within the range of the representation–efficiency trade-offs deemed acceptable, constitutional engineers can and should err on the side of dispersed authority. Of course, how dispersed policy-making authority is, and hence how small a new social group may be and still be able to credibly pursue sectarian representation, will vary from polity to polity with the polity's chosen ideal point on the representation–efficiency continuum. For socially heterogeneous polities, such as those that have experienced high levels of immigration in the past or that have engaged in ethnic discrimination in the franchise, erring on the side of dispersing policy-making authority seems particularly advisable.

The implications for the design of the electoral system are less straightforward. One might conclude, with the advocates of the consensus model of democracy, that permissive electoral systems should be employed. It is true that on average, permissive electoral systems pose a lower barrier to entry and hence facilitate the successful particization of smaller new groups. However, the case of African Americans in the United States demonstrates that restrictive electoral systems do not necessarily bar sectarian parties seeking to represent minorities from the electoral arena. Restrictive electoral systems can also deliver remarkably good representational results, as a comparison of the Israeli and United States cases reveals. For restrictive electoral systems to function in this manner, however, either new social groups must be geographically concentrated so that they are a majority in some electoral districts—the case for African Americans, although it will obviously not be the case for all new groups—or there need to be many very small electoral districts. Ironically, assembly size is a feature of the electoral system that used to attract more attention than it does today, with most scholars now viewing the district magnitude as the "decisive factor" (Taagepera and Shugart 1989, 112).

Accordingly, it may be time to turn back the clock: with larger assemblies increasing proportionality and hence facilitating sectarian representation, both political scientists and constitutional engineers should pay more attention to how many legislators there are, particularly if the electoral system is restrictive.[24] While efficiency concerns will obviously place limits on how large legislatures can become, there is probably room for many countries to bolster democratic representation by increasing the sizes of their legislatures.[25] This means that the devil is in the details of the electoral

---

[24] See, for example, the pride of place accorded to this variable in Lijphart's (1994) classic study. While the literature has mostly focused on how assembly size affects proportionality in permissive electoral systems, as he notes, see Taagepera and Shugart (1989) for some extensions to restrictive systems.

[25] An example is provided by Conley and Stevens's (2011) recent article in the *New York Times*, which argued that expanding the size of the United States' House of Representatives would increase democratic representation. Yet more than two decades ago, Taagepera and Shugart (1989) drew attention to how undersized the House was: that is, to how historically high the

system design. Of course, in choosing an electoral system, there are also trade-offs that must be made. The take-away message here is that majoritarian electoral systems, which deliver benefits such as constituency ties that proportional representation systems do not, need not be dismissed out of hand by those who value democratic representation.

Yet perhaps most importantly, the case of African Americans in the United States also demonstrates that the regime type is at least as important as the electoral system. In keeping with the overarching theme of this book, constitutional engineers should accordingly not focus all of their energies upon the electoral system. Rather, they should devote as much energy, if not more, to the regime type itself.

A final institutional mechanism that deserves mention in passing as an alternative to encouraging (or at least not discouraging) the formation of sectarian parties is the use of quotas for political parties' legislative slates. Quotas have been used with great success to increase women's representation in legislatures around the world (e.g., Jones 2009). In a slightly different format, quotas in the form of reserved seats have also ensured legislative representation of ethnic (e.g., the Maori in New Zealand) and socioeconomic (that is, Dalits in India) minorities. However, the disadvantage of quotas, as opposed to broader political institutional reforms of the sort described here, is that the underrepresented group must be known a priori. This makes quotas a reactive tool.

Reforms to the electoral system and political regime, by way of contrast, proactively open the door for *any* new latent social group to form and back a sectarian party. Given the preliminary evidence assembled here, this in turn is likely to help the group shape the more normative dimensions of the party system. Such an exercise of voice, when party systems change in response to changes in society, is what democracy is ultimately about.

---

current ratio of population to representatives is. While a few political scientists have continued to beat the drums (see, for example, Matthew Shugart's "Fruits & Votes" blog entries of August 29, 2005 and September 18, 2009 at www.fruitsandvotes.com), there has been surprisingly little academic, and certainly little popular, attention to this important issue. Matters are obviously even worse when it comes to the Senate.

A Additional Material for the Quantitative Analyses in Chapter 4

This appendix presents additional materials for the cross-national time series quantitative analyses in Chapter 4.

First, Table A.1 presents alternative versions of the two models from the legislative elections analysis, which are part of the sensitivity analysis reported in the main text. These models use a different measure of territorial gain.

Second, Table A.2 presents the cases for the presidential elections analysis. Tables A.3 and A.4 collectively present five additional models for the presidential elections analysis, which are part of the sensitivity analysis reported in the main text. Finally, Figures A.1–A.4 present quantities derived from the fourth and fifth of these models: the estimated marginal and conditional effects of ethnic heterogeneity.

A. Additional Material for the Quantitative Analyses in Chapter 4

	Model 1a	Model 2a
Intercept	1.7***	0.57
	(0.46)	(0.78)
Electorate (%)	0.015***	
	(0.0049)	
Majoritarian	−0.31	1.3*
	(0.43)	(0.72)
Territory	0.000013***	0.000012***
	(0.0000017)	(0.0000017)
Foreign (%)	0.044**	0.065***
	(0.017)	(0.018)
Electorate (%) × Majoritarian	0.0025	
	(0.0054)	
Territory × Majoritarian	0.0000069	0.0000014***
	(0.0000017)	(0.0000047)
Foreign (%) × Majoritarian	−0.051***	−0.047***
	(0.015)	(0.016)
Economic		0.59
		(0.54)
Gender		0.046
		(0.32)
Ethnic		1.7***
		(0.51)
Economic × Majoritarian		−0.14
		(0.55)
Gender × Majoritarian		0.29
		(0.34)
Ethnic × Majoritarian		−1.9***
		(0.53)
N	639	733
Root MSE	1.0	0.98
R^2	0.55	0.58

Table A.1: Coefficients and robust (Newey-West) standard errors for variants of Models 1 and 2 of the legislative elections analysis. Models 1a and 2a both use an alternate measure of territorial gain. The dependent variable is the effective number of electoral parties. Country fixed effects are not shown. Significance codes are for two-sided tests: 0.001, ***; 0.05, **; 0.10, *.

A. Additional Material for the Quantitative Analyses in Chapter 4

Country	Elections	Country	Elections
Argentina	10	Lithuania	2
Armenia	3	Macedonia	2
Austria	10	Madagascar	1
Benin	2	Malawi	2
Brazil	6	Mali	2
Bulgaria	2	Mexico	1
Cape Verde	2	Moldova	1
Central African Republic	2	Mongolia	2
Chile	7	Namibia	2
Colombia	12	Nicaragua	3
Republic of Congo	2	Niger	1
Costa Rica	13	Nigeria	3
Croatia	3	Panama	8
Dominican Republic	6	Peru	6
Ecuador	10	Philippines	9
El Salvador	4	Poland	3
Finland	9	Portugal	6
France	6	Romania	3
Ghana	1	Russia	3
Guatemala	3	Sierra Leone	1
Haiti	2	Slovakia	1
Honduras	1	Slovenia	2
Iceland	15	Sri Lanka	2
Ireland	9	Ukraine	3
Israel	2	United States	14
South Korea	3	Venezuela	10
Kyrgyzstan	2	Zambia	2

Table A.2: The number of elections per country used to estimate Model 3 of the presidential elections analysis. Model 4 adds two elections in Guyana and one election in Comoros.

265

A. Additional Material for the Quantitative Analyses in Chapter 4

	Model 3a	Model 3b	Model 4a
Intercept	36**	50***	53***
	(15)	(15)	(13)
Social Heterogeneity	−51**	−77***	−75***
	(24)	(23)	(19)
Social Heterogeneity^2	25**	38***	36***
	(12)	(11)	(9.1)
Social Heterogeneity^3	−3.8*	−6.1***	−5.3***
	(2.0)	(1.7)	(1.4)
Presidential Powers/Regime Type	−2.3*	−3.8***	−28***
	(1.4)	(1.3)	(7.7)
Presidential Powers^2	−0.040***	−0.039***	
	(0.013)	(0.013)	
Presidential Powers^3	0.0012***	0.0011***	
	(0.00036)	(0.00037)	
Social Heterogeneity ×	3.8*	6.3***	42***
Presidential Powers/Regime Type	(2.1)	(1.9)	(11)
Social Heterogeneity^2 ×	−1.7*	−3.0***	−19***
Presidential Powers/Regime Type	(1.0)	(0.89)	(5.2)
Social Heterogeneity^3 ×	0.26	0.47***	2.8***
Presidential Powers/Regime Type	(0.16)	(0.14)	(0.77)
Plurality	55	−0.47**	−0.51***
	(77)	(0.18)	(0.16)
Asia	−0.67	0.13	0.13
	(0.44)	(0.36)	(0.42)
Latin America	0.68**	0.98***	−0.081
	(0.31)	(0.26)	(0.39)
Eastern Europe	0.19	0.62**	0.066
	(0.35)	(0.28)	(0.34)
Africa	0.0037	0.36	0.23
	(0.40)	(0.40)	(0.43)
Other (Pacific/Caribbean Islands)	−1.0***	−0.80***	−1.0***
	(0.27)	(0.25)	(0.32)

Table A.3: Coefficients and robust (Newey-West) standard errors for variants of Models 3 and 4 of the presidential elections analysis. Model 3a adds interactions between social heterogeneity and a dummy variable for plurality electoral systems, while Models 3b and 4a substitute a dummy variable for transitional elections ("Transition") for the latter. A version of Table 4.3. Significance codes are for two-sided tests: 0.001, ***; 0.05, **; 0.10, *. Continued on next page.

	Model 3a	Model 3b	Model 4a
Social Heterogeneity × Plurality	−75		
	(110)		
Presidential Powers/Regime Type × Plurality	−4.8		
	(5.1)		
Social Heterogeneity^2 × Plurality	31		
	(49)		
Social Heterogeneity^3 × Plurality	−4.1		
	(7.2)		
Social Het. × Pres. Powers /Regime Type × Plurality	6.8		
	(7.2)		
Social Het.^{2} × Pres. Powers /Regime Type × Plurality	−3.1		
	(3.2)		
Social Het.^{3} × Pres. Powers /Regime Type × Plurality	0.44		
	(0.48)		
Transition		−27	−34*
		(24)	(19)
Social Heterogeneity × Transition		42	50*
		(38)	(30)
Presidential Powers/Regime Type × Transition		3.8	27*
		(2.4)	(14)
Social Heterogeneity^2 × Transition		−22	−24
		(18)	(15)
Social Heterogeneity^3 × Transition		3.5	3.5
		(2.9)	(2.3)
Social Het. × Pres. Powers /Regime Type × Transition		−5.7	−39*
		(3.7)	(21)
Social Het.^{2} × Pres. Powers /Regime Type × Transition		2.8	18*
		(1.8)	(9.7)
Social Het.^{3} × Pres. Powers /Regime Type × Transition		−0.43	−2.6*
		(0.27)	(1.5)
N	242	242	245
Root MSE	1.0	1.0	1.1
R^2	0.25	0.25	0.21

Table A.3: Continued from previous page.

A. Additional Material for the Quantitative Analyses in Chapter 4

	Model 3c	Model 4b
Intercept	0.82**	0.77**
	(0.41)	(0.37)
Ethnic Fractionalization	24***	24***
	(7.2)	(5.8)
Ethnic Fractionalization^2	−70***	−64***
	(20)	(19)
Ethnic Fractionalization^3	52***	48***
	(16)	(16)
Presidential Powers/Regime Type	0.34***	1.4***
	(0.12)	(0.33)
Presidential Powers^2	−0.025*	
	(0.013)	
Presidential Powers^3	0.00070*	
	(0.00037)	
Ethnic Fractionalization × Presidential Powers/Regime Type	−2.0***	−16***
	(0.60)	(3.5)
Ethnic Fractionalization^2 × Presidential Powers/Regime Type	5.5***	40***
	(1.6)	(10)
Ethnic Fractionalization^3 × Presidential Powers/Regime Type	−3.9***	−28***
	(1.2)	(8.6)
Plurality	−0.71***	−0.60***
	(0.17)	(0.15)
Asia	−0.13	−0.23
	(0.33)	(0.39)
Latin America	0.77***	0.40*
	(0.20)	(0.22)
Eastern Europe	0.15	0.095
	(0.27)	(0.29)
Africa	−0.25***	−0.12
	(0.36)	(0.53)
Other (Pacific/Caribbean Islands)	−0.45	−0.61**
	(0.31)	(0.28)
N	242	245
Root MSE	1.1	1.1
R^2	0.22	0.18

Table A.4: Coefficients and robust (Newey-West) standard errors for variants of Models 3 and 4 of the presidential elections analysis. Models 3c and 4b use ethnic fractionalization instead of the index of social heterogeneity. A version of Table 4.3. Significance codes are for two-sided tests: 0.001, ***; 0.05, **; 0.10, *.

A. Additional Material for the Quantitative Analyses in Chapter 4

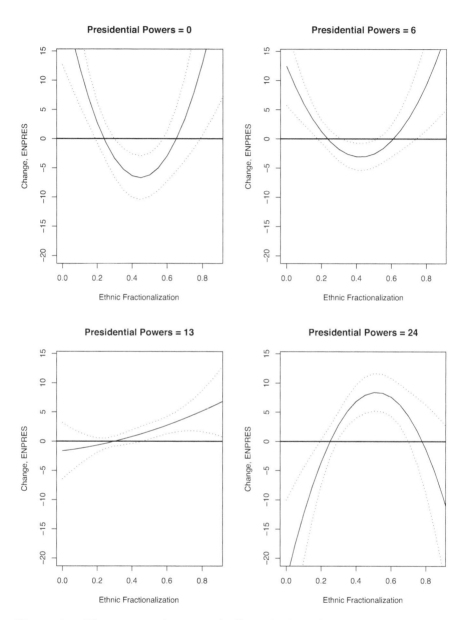

Figure A.1: The estimated marginal effect of ethnic fractionalization on the effective number of presidential candidates from Model 3c. A version of Figure 4.1. 95% two-sided confidence intervals are plotted around the conditional effects.

A. Additional Material for the Quantitative Analyses in Chapter 4

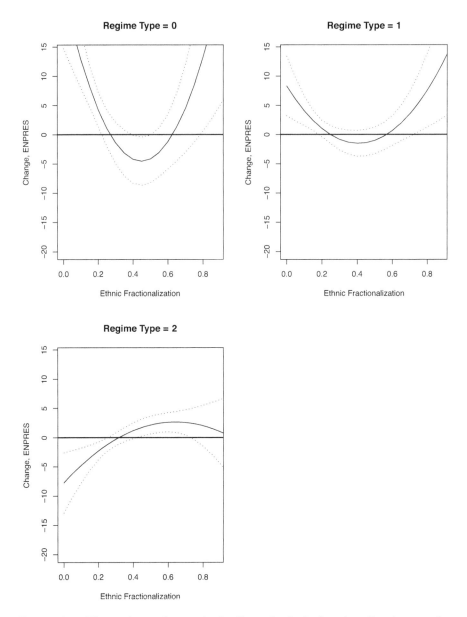

Figure A.2: The estimated marginal effect of ethnic fractionalization on the effective number of presidential candidates from Model 4b. A version of Figure 4.2. 95% two-sided confidence intervals are plotted around the conditional effects.

A. Additional Material for the Quantitative Analyses in Chapter 4

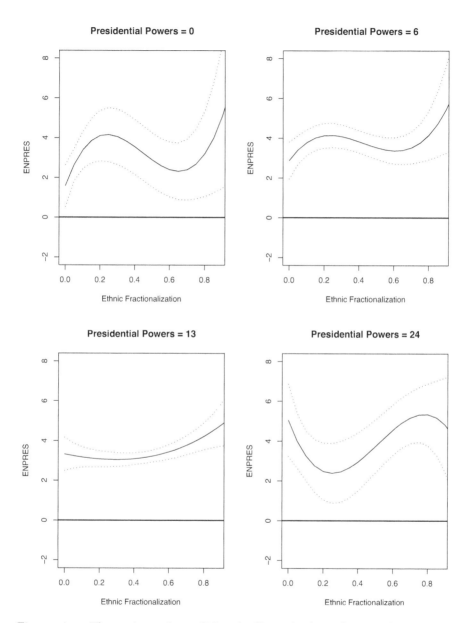

Figure A.3: The estimated conditional effect of ethnic fractionalization on the effective number of presidential candidates from Model 3c. A version of Figure 4.3. 95% two-sided confidence intervals are plotted around the conditional effects.

A. Additional Material for the Quantitative Analyses in Chapter 4

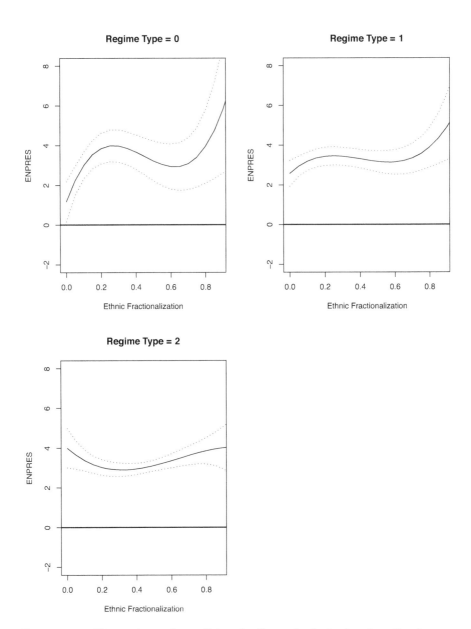

Figure A.4: The estimated conditional effect of ethnic fractionalization on the effective number of presidential candidates from Model 4b. A version of Figure 4.4. 95% two-sided confidence intervals are plotted around the conditional effects.

B Demography in Israel

This appendix presents estimates of a group's share of the *total* electorate of Israel. This is because non-Jews (such as Arab Israelis) became part of the electorate with Israel's statehood, which means that party vote shares include Arab votes. Consequently, in order to compare apples with apples when evaluating party success, a party's share of the vote must be compared to a group's share of the total (not just the Jewish) electorate. Nevertheless, I usually also provide estimates of a group's share of the *Jewish* electorate, as well as estimates of a group's share of the population (both total and Jewish). The data discussed in this appendix is used in Chapters 5, 6, and 8.

B.1 SEPHARDIM

B.1.1 The Sephardim as a Whole

Table B.1 presents three estimates of the Sephardi share of the *total* Israeli population and the *total* Israeli electorate for each election year: a conservative estimate, a generous estimate, and a middle-of-the-road estimate. In parentheses, it also presents equivalent estimates of the Sephardi share of the *Jewish* population and the *Jewish* electorate.

These estimates are all derived from Israeli Central Bureau of Statistics (CBS) publications, most notably from the yearly *Statistical Abstract of Israel*, which has been published since 1949. These publications in turn draw upon state record-keeping enterprises such as the Population Registration of November 8, 1948 and the May/June 1961 census. Sephardi is defined as those non-Arabs (usually Jews—see the following discussion) who have African or Asian origin, as discussed in the text.

There are four detailed issues concerning the construction of this data that are worth noting. First, because year-end data was more reliably available than average year data, year-end data was used where it was available, which was through 1992. Second, prior to the 1995 census, non-Arab Christians and those not classified by religion were lumped together with the Arab instead of with the Jewish population; the number of these "others" was small. However, with the 1990s wave of Russian immigration, the number of persons in the latter category—mostly non-Jewish family members of

	Conservative		Generous		Middle	
Election	Population, Percent Sephardi	Electorate, Percent Sephardi	Population, Percent Sephardi	Electorate, Percent Sephardi	Population, Percent Sephardi	Electorate, Percent Sephardi
1949	16 (18)	16 (18)	40 (46)	25 (28)	28 (32)	21 (23)
1951	25 (28)	24 (26)	47 (53)	32 (35)	36 (40)	28 (31)
1955	25 (28)	27 (30)	54 (60)	36 (40)	39 (44)	32 (35)
1959	25 (28)	30 (33)	57 (64)	41 (45)	41 (46)	36 (39)
1961	38 (43)	34 (37)	43 (48)	36 (40)	41 (46)	35 (38)
1965	41 (46)	36 (40)	46 (52)	39 (43)	44 (49)	38 (41)
1969	41 (48)	37 (41)	47 (55)	40 (44)	44 (52)	38 (43)
1973	40 (47)	37 (42)	48 (56)	41 (45)	44 (52)	39 (43)
1977	39 (46)	38 (43)	49 (58)	42 (47)	44 (52)	40 (45)
1981	37 (45)	39 (44)	50 (60)	43 (49)	44 (52)	41 (47)
1984	36 (44)	38 (45)	50 (61)	42 (51)	43 (52)	40 (48)
1988	35 (42)	40 (46)	52 (63)	46 (54)	43 (53)	43 (50)
1992	31 (37)	37 (43)	49 (60)	44 (51)	40 (49)	40 (47)
1996	28 (34)	35 (41)	48 (60)	43 (51)	38 (47)	39 (46)
1999	26 (32)	34 (39)	48 (59)	43 (50)	37 (45)	38 (45)
2003	23 (29)	31 (37)	48 (59)	43 (51)	36 (44)	37 (44)
2006	22 (29)	30 (38)	48 (64)	44 (56)	35 (46)	37 (47)
2009	21 (28)	30 (37)	50 (66)	46 (58)	36 (47)	38 (48)

Table B.1: Three sets of estimates of the Sephardi share of the total population and electorate. In parentheses are estimates of the Sephardi share of Israel's Jewish population and electorate. Source: based on CBS (1967); CBS (1969); and CBS SA, various.

B. Demography in Israel

Jewish immigrants—shot up. As a result, from 1995 onwards, this category of persons was broken out and sometimes included with the Jewish population ("Jews and others"). Because many persons in the "other" category are Russian immigrants, and seemingly closer to the Jewish than to the Arab community, I have counted them as Jews and as Sephardim (when called for) where possible, which was in 1999 and 2003. However, this was not possible for 1996, 2006, or 2009. Third, due to the way in which age groups are constructed by the Central Bureau of Statistics (e.g., one age group consists of fifteen- to nineteen-year-olds), the electorate is operationally defined as those with an age of at least twenty, even though the voting age is eighteen. I thus err on the conservative side when it comes to the electorate. Erring in the other direction, that is, operationally defining the electorate as those with an age of at least fifteen, increases the Sephardi share of the electorate in the early years (specifically, through 1984) and decreases it thereafter. Because a smaller Sephardi share of the electorate favors party success as I have defined it, I use the conservatively defined (twenty and up) electorate. However, the difference between the two operational definitions is small (specifically, at most two percentage points), which means that my conclusions are substantively unaffected by this operational decision. Fourth, data was not available for 1999, so I use 1998 data instead.

The three sets of estimates exist to deal with the unfortunate fact that the Israeli government tracks ethnicity only for two generations, as discussed in the text: third-generation Israelis, that is, the Israeli-born of Israeli-born fathers, are simply classified as belonging to the ethnic category "Israeli origin".[1] My simple tripartite solution takes three different approaches to dealing with third-generation Israelis, whose ethnicity is unknown. The first approach is conservative: not to classify any third-generation Israelis as Sephardi. Hence, my conservative estimates err on the side of caution and under-estimate the true numbers of Sephardim. The second approach, conversely, is generous: to classify all third-generation Israelis as Sephardi. My generous estimates consequently overestimate the true numbers of Sephardim. These two sets of estimates together provide both lower and upper bounds on the Sephardi shares of the electorate and population. Finally, the third approach is "middle-of-the-road": to divide third-generation Israelis equally between the Sephardi and Ashkenazi categories. Because some third-generation Israelis are Sephardi and some are Ashkenazi, this approach should best approximate reality. Not surprisingly, of the three sets of estimates, the middle-of-the-road ones seem the most empirically sound in that they are commensurate with other scholars' findings.[2]

---

[1] Friedlander et al. (2002) represent one recent heroic attempt to address this problem: they used a special data file linking a sample of individuals surveyed in the 1995 census to their parents' households in the 1983 census. Based on their data, about one-third of third-generation Israelis aged fifteen to forty-four were Sephardi in 1995. However, this approach cannot provide me with the time series data that I need.

[2] For example, Smooha (1978, 177) estimated that the Sephardim were 42 percent of the eligible Jewish electorate compared to a slim majority of the Jewish population in 1970. In both

B. *Demography in Israel*

Finally, there is an obvious discontinuity in most of the estimates, particularly the conservative and generous ones, from 1959 to 1961. This is because prior to the 1961 census, the Israeli government did not even track second-generation ethnicity, that is, the origin of an Israeli-born citizen's father. Instead, only first-generation ethnicity, that is, the origin of foreign-born Israelis, was recorded. This means that prior to 1961, only first-generation Sephardim are classified as Sephardim using the conservative approach; conversely, first-generation Sephardim *plus* all second- and third-generation Israelis (that is, all native-born Israelis, whose ethnicity is unknown) are classified as Sephardim using the generous approach.

B.1.2 Subgroups of the Sephardim

Because some parties targeted subgroups of the Sephardim such as the Yemeni community, estimates of these groups' shares of the electorate and population are also needed.

Using the same data sources described earlier, I arrive at the conservative estimates presented by Table B.2 for Yemenis and North Africans, the two subgroups that sectarian parties targeted in Israel's first few decades. These estimates are conservative, as just discussed, because ethnicity is known for the foreign-born (that is, first-generation Israelis) only through 1973[3] and for first- and second-generation Israelis only (that is, not for third-generation Israelis) from 1977 onwards. As a result, prior to 1977, only first-generation Yemenis (Africans) are classified as Yemenis (Africans), whereas from 1977 onwards, only first- and second-generation Yemenis (Africans) are classified as Yemenis (Africans). This change in how many generations back ethnicity is tracked accounts for the discontinuity in the estimates between 1973 and 1977. Note that for North Africa, data is available only for Africa as a whole, which includes Egypt. However, Egypt aside, North Africa and Africa are in fact reasonably equivalent because there were few sub-Saharan African immigrants to Israel, as discussed in the text.[4] Yemen includes Aden, North Yemen, and South Yemen.

Last but not least, an Ethiopian party ran in the 2006 election. Table B.2 accordingly also presents conservative estimates of Ethiopian population and electorate shares from 1992 onwards, when data on the number of first- and second-generation Israelis with Ethiopian origin becomes available.

1969 and 1973, the middle-of-the-road estimates put the Sephardi proportions of the Jewish electorate and population at 43 and 52 percent, respectively, almost spot on Smooha's estimates. The conservative and generous estimates are further off, with the former undershooting and the latter overshooting.

[3]While figures for the Sephardim as a whole begin to include second-generation Israelis in 1961, figures by specific country and continent of origin are either not available or include the foreign-born only through 1973.

[4]The exception is South Africa, but as a European settler state, it is included in the "continent" of Europe and the Americas, not Africa.

B. Demography in Israel

Election	Population, Percent Yemeni	Electorate, Percent Yemeni	Population, Percent African	Electorate, Percent African	Population, Percent Ethiopian	Electorate, Percent Ethiopian
1949	4.7 (5.4)	4.6 (5.0)	4.7 (5.4)	4.2 (4.7)	N/A	N/A
1951	4.1 (4.6)	4.2 (4.6)	6.3 (7.0)	5.8 (6.3)	N/A	N/A
1955	3.6 (4.0)	4.3 (4.7)	8.5 (9.6)	8.5 (9.3)	N/A	N/A
1959	3.0 (3.3)	4.1 (4.5)	11 (12)	12 (13)	N/A	N/A
1961	2.8 (3.1)	4.1 (4.5)	11 (12)	13 (14)	N/A	N/A
1965	N/A	N/A	N/A	N/A	N/A	N/A
1969	2.0 (2.3)	3.6 (4.0)	12 (14)	19 (21)	N/A	N/A
1973	1.7 (2.0)	3.0 (3.3)	11 (13)	17 (20)	N/A	N/A
1977	4.5 (5.3)	4.8 (5.4)	19 (23)	21 (24)	N/A	N/A
1981	4.1 (5.0)	4.8 (5.5)	19 (22)	18 (21)	N/A	N/A
1984	4.0 (4.8)	4.7 (5.6)	18 (22)	18 (21)	N/A	N/A
1988	3.6 (4.5)	4.9 (5.7)	18 (22)	19 (22)	N/A	N/A
1992	3.1 (3.7)	4.4 (5.1)	16 (20)	19 (22)	1.0 (1.2)	0.90 (1.1)
1996	2.7 (3.3)	4.0 (4.7)	15 (18)	18 (21)	1.1 (1.3)	1.1 (1.4)
1999	2.5 (3.1)	3.7 (4.4)	14 (17)	17 (20)	1.2 (1.4)	1.1 (1.2)
2003	2.2 (2.7)	3.3 (3.9)	13 (16)	16 (19)	1.2 (1.5)	1.2 (1.4)
2006	2.0 (2.7)	3.1 (3.9)	12 (16)	16 (20)	1.4 (1.8)	1.3 (1.6)
2009	1.9 (2.5)	2.9 (3.6)	12 (16)	16 (20)	1.4 (1.9)	1.4 (1.7)

Table B.2: The estimates of Sephardi subgroups' shares of the total population and electorate. In parentheses are estimates of their shares of Israel's Jewish population and electorate. Source: based on CBS (1967); CBS (1969); and CBS SA, various.

B. Demography in Israel

B.2 RUSSIANS

The Russian share of both the *total* electorate and population is calculated in a manner similar to that described above. These estimates are presented in Table B.3. Estimates of the Russian share of the *Jewish* electorate and population are shown in parentheses, as before. The earliest year for which I present data is 1973, given that Russians begin arriving in Israel in substantial numbers only in 1972.

Three notes regarding these estimates are in order. First, in the interest of providing the most conservative demographic estimates because doing so favors party success (see the earlier discussion), I operationally define the electorate to be those whose age is at least fifteen. This operational definition yields smaller estimates of the Russian share of the population and electorate than does defining the electorate to be those who are at least twenty. As with the Sephardim, however, the difference between the measures resulting from these two operational definitions is not substantively meaningful: for the Russians, the difference is always less than one percentage point.

Second, I provide two sets of estimates in Table B.3: one including only post-1989 Russian immigrants, and one additionally including Russians who immigrated between 1968 and 1980. As usual, I refer to the former group as the "1990s" Russians and the latter group as the "1970s" Russians. I calculate population and electorate shares both with and without the 1970s Russians for three reasons: because I have only rough estimates of how many of this group were of voting age (more on this momentarily); because I have data only on the first generation (that is, I lack estimates of the number of this group's children), which means that my estimates are conservative ones; and because most of the surveys that I use to estimate party success are of post-1989 Russian immigrants. As can be seen from the table, the differences in the two sets of estimates are quite small, which is not surprising given the relatively small number of Russians who immigrated in the 1970s.

Third, as already noted, I have unfortunately been unable to find a breakdown of the 1970s Russians by age group in the official government sources described earlier. However, Gitelman (1982, 77) supplies the proportion of Russians immigrating in the peak years of 1972–1975 who were under the age of fifteen: 18.5 percent. I simply deflate the number of Russian immigrants by this percentage to obtain an estimate of the Russian electorate for 1973, although this is obviously a far from perfect solution. Given that all Russians who were younger than fifteen when immigrating in the 1972–1975 period will have been fifteen or older by 1990 and hence part of the electorate, all 1970s Russians are included in the Russian electorate from 1992 onwards. For the elections between 1973 and 1992, I estimate the Russian electorate by deflating the number of Russians using the linearly interpolated percentage under fifteen (with the two end points of the line being 18.5 percent in 1975 and 0 percent in 1990).

The estimates in Table B.3 closely correspond to the estimates of various scholars. For example, in 1992, Gitelman and Goldstein (2002, 142) esti-

B. *Demography in Israel*

Election	Population, Percent Russian: 1970s and 1990s	Electorate, Percent Russian: 1970s and 1990s	Population, Percent Russian: 1990s Only	Electorate, Percent Russian: 1990s Only
1973	2.5 (2.9)	3.0 (3.4)	0.0	0.0
1977	3.4 (4.0)	4.2 (4.8)	0.0	0.0
1981	4.0 (4.8)	5.4 (6.2)	0.0	0.0
1984	3.9 (4.7)	5.1 (6.2)	0.0	0.0
1988	3.6 (4.4)	5.2 (6.1)	0.0	0.0
1992	10 (13)	13 (15)	7.3 (8.9)	8.4 (9.9)
1996	12 (15)	15 (18)	9.5 (12)	11 (13)
1999	15 (18)	18 (21)	12 (15)	14 (16)
2003	16 (20)	19 (22)	14 (17)	16 (18)
2006	15 (20)	18 (26)	13 (17)	15 (21)
2009	15 (20)	17 (22)	13 (17)	14 (18)

Table B.3: Estimates of the Russian share of the total population and electorate. In parentheses are estimates of the Russian share of the *Jewish* population and electorate. Source: based on CBS SA, various, and Gitelman (1982).

mated that 1990s Russians immigrants comprised 8 percent of the electorate, whereas I estimated them to comprise about 8.5 percent.

C Sephardi and Russian Sectarian Parties and Their Success in Israel

This appendix presents information about the Sephardi and Russian sectarian parties that have contested elections in Israel. It also provides further detail about the methodology used to measure the success of these parties. Chapters 5, 6, and 8 all make use of this data.

C.1 SEPHARDI PARTIES

Tables C.1, C.2, and C.3 list the Sephardi sectarian parties competing in Israeli elections from 1949 to 2009; their vote shares; and their Knesset seats obtained. New parties are shown in italics for each election. A new party is defined as one that does not show substantial continuity from the preceding election ($t - 1$) to the current one (t): it is either completely new at t; has split off from a previously existing ($t - 1$) party; or is a merger of previously existing parties ($t - 1$) that does not exactly recreate a party that existed at $t - 2$.

C.2 RUSSIAN PARTIES

Table C.4 lists the Russian sectarian parties competing in Israeli elections from 1981 to 2009; their vote shares; and their Knesset seats obtained. New parties are shown in italics for each election, where new parties are defined as before.

C.3 MEASURING PARTY SUCCESS I: ASSUMPTIONS FOR COMPARING ELECTORATE SHARES TO VOTE SHARES

Measuring party success by comparing a party's vote share to the targeted group's share of the electorate requires me to make a single assumption:

1949	% Votes	Seats	1951	% Votes	Seats
National Union of Sephardim	3.5	4	Sephardi and Oriental Communities	1.7	2
Yemenite Association	1.0	1	Yemenite Association	1.2	1
			Israeli Faithful	0.59	0
Total Sephardi	4.5	5	Total Sephardi	3.5	3
1955	% Votes	Seats	1959	% Votes	Seats
Sephardi and Oriental Communities	0.82	0	*Yemenite Faction*	0.18	0
Yemenite Association	0.29	0	*National Sephardi*	0.32	0
Sons of Yemen Movement	0.29	0	*National Union of Sephardim & Orientals*	0.25	0
			Union of Independent N. African Immigrants	0.85	0
Total Sephardi	1.4	0	Total Sephardi	1.6	0
1961	% Votes	Seats	1965	% Votes	Seats
Justice & Fraternity	0.32	0	*Young Israel*	0.16	0
Yemenite Immigrants	0.0	0	*Fraternity*	0.93	0
Total Sephardi	0.32	0	Total Sephardi	1.1	0

Table C.1: Knesset vote shares and seats (120 total) for Sephardi political parties, 1949–1965. New parties shown in italics. Source: classification of parties, various, including Herzog (1983, 1986); election results, CBS (1956), CBS (1964), and CBS (1967–1974).

1969	% Votes	Seats	1973	% Votes	Seats
Young Israel	0.15	0	Yemenis	0.20	0
			Black Panthers	0.85	0
			Blue & White Panthers	0.38	0
			Movement for Social Equality	0.65	0
			Popular Movement	0.070	0
Total Sephardi	0.15	0	Total Sephardi	2.2	0

1977	% Votes	Seats	1981	% Votes	Seats
House of Israel	0.54	0	Tami	2.3	3
Coalition of Workers & Neighborhoods	0.14	0	The Unity Party	0.067	0
Zionist Panthers	0.10	0	Your People	0.024	0
Social Zionist Renewal	0.83	0	One Israel	0.19	0
			Tent Movement	0.028	0
Total Sephardi	1.6	0	Total Sephardi	2.6	3

1984	% Votes	Seats	1988	% Votes	Seats
Shas	3.1	4	Shas	4.7	6
Tami	1.5	1			
New Indian Immigrants	0.27	0			
Your People	0.035	0			
Total Sephardi	4.9	5	Total Sephardi	4.7	6

Table C.2: Knesset vote shares and seats (120 total) for Sephardi political parties, 1969–1988. New parties shown in italics. Source: classification of parties, various, including Herzog (1983, 1986, 1995); election results, CBS (1967–1974), and CBS (1981–1997).

1992	% Votes	Seats	1996	% Votes	Seats
Shas	4.9	6	Shas	8.5	10
			Telem Emuna	0.42	0
Total Sephardi	4.9	6	Total Sephardi	8.9	10
1999	% Votes	Seats	2003	% Votes	Seats
Shas	13	17	Shas	8.2	11
			Love of Israel	0.17	0
Total Sephardi	13	17	Total Sephardi	8.4	11
2006	% Votes	Seats	2009	%Votes	Seats
Shas	9.5	12	Shas	8.5	11
One Future	0.45	0			
Total Sephardi	10	12	Total Sephardi	8.5	11

Table C.3: Knesset vote shares and seats (120 total) for Sephardi political parties, 1992–2006. New parties shown in italics. Source: classification of parties, various, including Herzog (1995); election results, CBS (1981–1997), Knesset (1999), Knesset (2003), Knesset (2006), and Knesset (2009).

1981	% Votes	Seats	1984	% Votes	Seats
List for Immigration	0.36	0	*Immigration & Young*	0.28	0
Total Russian	0.36	0	Total Russian	0.28	0

1992	% Votes	Seats	1996	% Votes	Seats
Democracy & Immigration (DA)	0.45	0	*Israel b'Aliya*	5.7	7
Pensioners & Immigrants (Yad b'Yad)	0.32	0	*Unity & Immigration*	0.75	0
Movement for Israel Renewal (Tali)	0.05	0			
Total Russian	0.75	0	Total Russian	6.5	7

1999	% Votes	Seats	2003	% Votes	Seats
Yisrael b'Aliya	5.2	6	Yisrael b'Aliya	2.2	2
Israel Beiteinu	2.6	4	Israel Beiteinu/National Union	5.5	7
Hope (Nadezhda)	0.22	0	*Citizen & State (Ezrach Umedina)*	0.050	0
Heart of Immigrants (Lev Olim)	0.19	0	*Progressive Liberal (Leeder)*	0.027	0
Total Russian	8.3	10	Total Russian	7.7	9

2006	% Votes	Seats	2009	Votes	Seats
Israel Beiteinu	9.0	11	Israel Beiteinu	12	15
Heart of Immigrants (Lev Olim)	0.056	0	*Heart of Immigrants (Lev Olim)*	0.019	0
Progressive Liberal (Leeder)	0.019	0	*Renewed Israel*	0.076	0
Total Russian	9.1	11	Total Russian	12	15

Table C.4: Knesset vote shares and seats (120 total) for Russian political parties, 1981–2009. New parties shown in italics. Source: classification of parties, various, including Herzog (1986) and Herzog (1995); election results, CBS (1981–1997), Knesset (1999), Knesset (2003), Knesset (2006), and Knesset (2009).

C. Sephardi and Russian Sectarian Parties and Their Success in Israel

that only members of the group that a sectarian party seeks to represent voted for that party. In other words, I assume that a sectarian party's votes do not come from members of other groups. This assumption seems prima facie reasonable: why would individuals who do not belong to the targeted group vote for the targeting party?

Chandra (2004) also made two other assumptions: first, that a group's share of the population is proportional to its share of the electorate; and second, that the various groups have similar turnout rates. The first of these assumptions is not necessary for my study because I was able to obtain estimates of groups' shares of the electorate. The second is a more complicated issue. Relatively greater numbers of a group's eligible voters not voting, that is, groups having unequal turnout, strikes me as reflecting a lack of support for the sectarian party that is competing. In other words, it is part of the story that I want to tell. Hence, I do not believe that equal turnout needs to be assumed, although I will present some evidence about turnout rates.

C.3.1 ONLY GROUP MEMBERS VOTE FOR GROUP PARTIES

Evidence exists that the vast majority of Shas's votes have come from the Sephardi community, although it has garnered some support from other groups (such as from Arab Israelis, as discussed in the text). For example, given the votes that Willis (1995, 131) reports Shas attracted from other social groups in the 1992 election, 81 percent of Shas's votes came from the Sephardi community—a substantial percentage.

Even more substantial evidence exists that the parties identified as Russian sectarian parties have almost exclusively drawn their votes from the Russian immigrant community. To offer just a few examples, in the 1999 election, Gitelman and Goldstein (2002, 158) estimate that only 3,705 of Israel b'Aliya's 171,705 votes (approximately two percent of its total votes) came from non-Russians, while Khanin (2004, 175) estimates this percentage to be four percent. Khanin also estimates that Russians supplied 95 percent of Israel Beiteinu's votes in this election, and 99 percent of the votes of the smaller Russian parties (Nadezhda and Lev). Similarly, in 2003, Goldstein and Gitelman (2005, 253) estimate that 100 percent of Israel b'Aliya's votes came from the Russian sector (Khanin's estimate is 89 percent), while 69 percent of Israel Beiteinu/National Union's did (Khanin's estimate is higher this time: 72 percent). Note that it is not surprising that approximately 30 percent of the latter's votes came from the non-Russian sector, given the coalition between the Russian Israel Beiteinu and the non-Russian National Union. Khanin again estimates that the small Russian parties in the 2003 election received effectively all of their votes from Russians.

C.3.2 EQUAL TURNOUT

Regarding the Sephardim, Lissak (1972, 277) found that turnout in the 1969 election was about ten percentage points higher in the subprecincts of Tel

Aviv, Jerusalem, and Haifa that were populated mostly by Ashkenazim relative to those populated mostly by Sephardim. Similarly, Avner (1975, 209) used a post-election survey to estimate that 42 percent of first-generation Sephardim did not vote in the 1973 election as compared to 37 percent of first-generation Ashkenazim; in the second generation, nonvoting rates were 10 percent and 8.5 percent, respectively. But these do not appear to be substantively meaningful differences, which supports Smooha's (1978, 106) argument that the Sephardi voting rate does not significantly differ from the national average.

Regarding the Russians, polls prior to the 1992 election found that 70 (Reich, Wurmser, and Dropkin 1994, 137) to 75 percent (Fein 1995, 163) planned to vote. This turnout rate is about ten percentage points lower than has been typical in Israeli elections; specifically, the overall Jewish turnout rate in 1992 was 77 percent (Gitelman 1995, 74). Hence, while it seems likely that fewer Russians voted in 1992 than did other Jewish Israelis, the differences in turnout between the two groups do not seem substantively significant. More recently, Gitelman and Goldstein (2002, 158) argued that Russians typically turn out to vote at high rates similar to those of the electorate at large. For example, in 1999, they estimate that approximately 480,000 Russians voted (ibid.), which yields a turnout rate of approximately 80 percent (given that I estimate the Russian electorate to have been approximately 600,000 in 1999). This is a comparable figure to that for the electorate as a whole: 79 percent (Arian and Shamir 2002, 4). Even in 2003, when Khanin (2004, 171) argues that Russian turnout fell relative to that of the overall electorate, the differences in turnout were not substantial (61 versus 69 percent, respectively).

C.4 MEASURING PARTY SUCCESS II: SURVEY DATA

Israeli National Elections Studies (INES) were usually conducted in several waves or phases. Where available, I utilize the post-election phase of the survey; when there is no post-election phase, I use the pre-election phase that is closest to the date of the election. For pre-election surveys, the question usually runs along the lines of, "If the election were held today, for which party would you vote?"; for post-election surveys, it usually asks, "For which party did you vote in the last election?" The 1996 survey was the first to include Arabs, although the Jewish and Arab subsamples are presented in separate data files; prior to 1996, only Jews were surveyed, and subsequent to 1996, both Jews and Arabs were surveyed and the responses are included in a single data file.

C.4.1 Sephardim

Table C.5 identifies the Israeli National Election Studies (INES) phase and questions used to generate the data on Sephardi party success appearing in Table 5.5.

As with the demographic data, I define Sephardi ethnicity conservatively

Election	Phase	Post-election?	Questions	Comments
1965	Phase 3 of 1969 INES (October-November)	Yes	Knesset party vote in 1965 (c7); Place of birth and father's place of birth (c45)	Ethnicity question includes option of "Irrelevant," which 0.7% chose; Jewish sample
1969	Phase 3 (October-November)	Mixed	Knesset party vote (b48); Place of birth and father's place of birth (c45)	Ethnicity question includes option of "Irrelevant," which 0.7% chose; Jewish sample
1973	Phase 5 (January 1974)	Yes	Party interviewee voted for in last elections (h54); Place of birth/father's place of birth (h64)	Jewish sample
1977	Phase 4 (June)	Yes	Party interviewee voted for in 1977 elections (c15); Place of birth of interviewee/father (c29)	Jewish sample
1981	Phase 3 (May-June)	No	Party interviewee would vote for if elections held today (b89); Place of birth/father's place of birth (b140)	Jewish sample
1984	N/A	No	Party interviewee would vote for it elections held today (a41); Place of birth/father's place of birth (a49)	Jewish sample

Table C.5: The phases of and questions from the Israeli National Election studies used to generate the Sephardi party success data of Table 5.5. Continued on next page.

Election	Phase	Post-election?	Questions	Comments
1988	N/A	No	Interviewee's vote if elections held now (g22); Place of birth (g68)	Full sample, not panel; Jewish sample
1992	N/A	No	Vote if elections were held today (i41); Place of birth (i52)	Jewish sample
1996	N/A	No	Vote for party if elections held today (ccc23); Continent of birth/of father (ccc59)	Jewish sample
1999	Phase 1 (April-May)	No	Party vote if elections held today (c12); Continent of birth/origin (c26)	Post-election phase 2 lacks place of birth question; complete sample
2003	N/A	No	Respondent party vote if elections held today (B63); Place of birth (B77)	Complete sample
2006	N/A	Yes	List voted for in last election (d6); Origin in categories (origin)	Complete sample
2009	N/A	Yes	List voted for in last elections (3); Ethnic origin of father coded into 11 categories (V179A)	Complete sample

Table C.5: Continued from previous page.

C. Sephardi and Russian Sectarian Parties and Their Success in Israel

through the second generation. All INES include a question that classifies individuals by both their and their father's place of birth, although the exact categories vary from year to year. For example, in 1969, respondents were divided into six categories of origin,[1] while in 2006, a more fine-grained twelve-category schema was employed.[2] I collapse these categories as necessary in order to divide respondents into the two ethnic categories of Sephardim and non-Sephardim. As before, Sephardim are those who were either (i) born in Asia or Africa or (ii) born in Israel, but whose father was born in Asia or Africa. All others are non-Sephardim, including all third-generation Israelis; respondents who declared their origin irrelevant in 1969; and respondents who placed themselves in what was effectively a residual "other" category in 1973 and 1977. I note that some INES (such as that of 1984) also include a question asking if the respondent self-identified with either the Ashkenazim or Sephardim; however, because Chapter 5 concerns itself only with latent group membership, I rely on the ascriptive trait of origin question instead.

But it is not clear that this conservative definition favors party success, as it does when comparing vote shares to electorate shares. Whether it does effectively hinges upon the extent to which the preferences of third-generation Sephardim differed from the preferences of first- and second-generation Sephardim, as well as the proportion of third-generation Israelis who are Sephardim. To address this issue, Table C.6 presents a revised version of the last two columns of Table 5.5 that instead adopts a generous definition. In this table, all those who are not first- or second-generation Ashkenazim are classified as Sephardim, which includes all third-generation Israelis and those placed in the miscellaneous categories. As a comparison of the original Table 5.5 and the new Table C.6 reveal, grouping these individuals with the known (up to the second generation) Sephardim usually depresses the reported vote for Sephardi parties instead of raising it.

C.4.2 RUSSIANS

Table C.7 summarizes the Israel National Election Studies (INES) phase and questions used to generate the data on Russian party success appearing in Table 5.7.

The problem with the INES is that it is only for the 2003, 2006, and 2009 elections that there are questions that explicitly identify respondents who were Russian immigrants in the 1990s (either post-1988 or post-1989). The fact that these questions do not identify the children of these immigrants is not a problem because their children are not yet of voting age. What is a

---

[1]These categories are: irrelevant; native of Asia or North Africa; native of Europe or Anglo-Saxon countries; native Israeli, father born in Asia or North Africa; native Israeli, father born in Europe or Anglo-Saxon countries; and native Israeli, father also native Israeli.

[2]These categories are: native of North Africa; native of Asia; native of Eastern Europe; native of West and Central Europe; native of America, Australia, or South Africa; native of Israel, father also born in Israel; and native of Israel, father born in North Africa, etc.

C. *Sephardi and Russian Sectarian Parties and Their Success in Israel*

Election	Percent Voting for Individual Sephardi Parties	Percent Collectively Voting for Sephardi Parties
1965	"An ethnic party": 0.50; "Another party": 3.2	3.7
1969	"An ethnic party": 2.5	2.5
1973	"Other": 0.50	0.50
1977	"Other": 0.50	0.50
1981	"Abu Hatzira's list" [Tami]: 1.2; "An ethnic party": 0.30; "Other party": 0.30	1.8
1984	Agudat Yisrael + Shas: 1.2; Tami: 0.30; "Ethnic party": 0.10; "Other party": 0.6	2.2
1988	Shas: 2.4; "Other": 0.0	2.4
1992	Shas: 2.6; "Other party": 1.0	3.6
1996	Shas: 1.9; "Another party": 0.2	2.1
1999	Shas: 3.6; "Another party": 0.0	3.6
2003	Shas: 6.1; Love of Israel: 0.0	6.1
2006	Shas: 10	10
2009	Shas: 7.7	7.7

Table C.6: A version of the last two columns of Table 5.5, which evaluates the success of Sephardi parties in Israel using survey data when membership in the Sephardi ethnic category is defined generously. For each election, the proportion of total Sephardim surveyed voting for individual Sephardi parties is shown, as well as the percentage collectively voting for Sephardi parties (the sum of the individual party vote shares). Source: Israeli National Election Studies, 1969–2009.

C. Sephardi and Russian Sectarian Parties and Their Success in Israel

Election	Phase	Post-election?	Questions	Comments
1999	2003 INES	Yes	Vote in 1999 Knesset elections (B70); Russian immigrant after 1988 (B81)	Complete sample
2003	N/A	No	Respondent party vote if elections held today (B63); Russian immigrant after 1988 (B81)	Complete sample
2006	N/A	Yes	List voted for in last election (d6); Russian immigrant after 1989 (c62)	Complete sample
2009	N/A	Yes	List voted for in last election (3); Immigrant from USSR from 1989 and on (V178)	Complete sample

Table C.7: The phases of and questions from the Israeli National Election studies used to generate the Russian party success data of Table 5.7 for 1999, 2003, 2006, and 2009.

problem is that these questions obviously do not allow for the identification of 1970s Russian immigrants and their children, the latter being of voting age by the 1990s. Note that there is a question in the 2003 INES that asks about the respondent's vote in the 1999 Knesset election, as shown in Table C.7. However, using this 2003 question as a source of data for 1999 raises obvious concerns.

Fortunately, data about the Russian sector's voting behavior is available from sources other than the INES. Numerous surveys of this community, particularly nationwide exit polls, have been conducted, although they have usually also focused upon the immigrants of the 1990s wave. The partial exception is 2009, when no nationwide exit poll was conducted and the only non-INES-based survey data of which I am aware is Khanin (2009). Unfortunately, there is often a large discrepancy between the INES results and the other surveys for the election years for which INES data is available (see Table 5.7). In light of the greater external validity that these other surveys, such as exit polls, have been shown to possess, that is, their close correspondence to actual election results (see, for example, Gitelman and Goldstein 2002), I place greater stock in them than in the INES, which is why they underlie my discussion in the main text.

D Demography and the Franchise in the United States

This appendix presents more information about the estimates of the African American share of the United States' population and theoretical electorate appearing in Chapters 7 and 8.

For both the national and state levels, where election year data had not been compiled by demographers from the decennial censuses, I linearly interpolated data for noncensus election years using the surrounding decennial censuses as the end points.

D.1 NATIONAL-LEVEL ESTIMATES

My estimates of the African American share of the national population and of the theoretical electorate appear in Table 7.1 and Figure 7.1.

To construct these estimates, I generally began with national totals and, if necessary, subtracted noncontributing states. For example, for 1862 and 1864, the populations, African American populations, and theoretical electorates of the eleven Confederate states were subtracted from the national totals; for 1866, the same was done with the exception of Tennessee, which had been readmitted to the Union; and for 1868, Mississippi, Georgia, Texas, and Virginia only were subtracted from the national totals because they had not yet been readmitted to the Union.

For 1860–1866, the African American theoretical electorate consisted solely of those African Americans of the enfranchised age and gender in Maine, Massachusetts, New Hampshire, Rhode Island, and Vermont. For subsequent election years, matters became more complicated and required several assumptions of varying validity. These assumptions were: (i) all African Americans in the former Confederate states were enfranchised from 1868 until 1908 (with the exception of Georgia, Mississippi, Texas, and Virginia in 1868), disenfranchised from 1910 until 1964, and again enfranchised from 1965 onwards; (ii) no non–African Americans were disenfranchised in the former Confederate states; and (iii) outside of the former Confederate states, all African Americans were enfranchised from 1870 onwards. For example, using these assumptions, the African American theoretical electorate from 1910 through 1964 consisted of African Americans of the enfranchised age and gender in the non–former Confederate states, so I subtracted the African American theoretical electorates of the former Confederate states from the national totals.

As discussed in the main text, however, in reality both African Americans and lower-class whites were gradually disenfranchised in the former Confederate states from 1877 until 1910; many African Americans were disenfranchised in southern border states not formally part of the Confederacy, such as Oklahoma; and not all African Americans in the South were disenfranchised, particularly after the 1940s. To elaborate regarding the latter, for example, Kousser (1984) notes that many middle- to upper-class, well-educated African Americans remained on southern electoral roles into the twentieth century, and according to Keyssar (2001, 202), 25 percent of African Americans in the South were registered to vote by 1956. In contrast to the approach taken to estimate the Sephardi share of the Israeli electorate, the net effect of these assumptions is at times to overestimate (as in the 1880s) and at times to underestimate (as in the 1950s) the African American share of the electorate. However, at this time, the data simply does not exist to proceed in any other way.

Other restrictions on the franchise, such as literacy requirements in some northern states, are ignored due to the difficulty of gathering this data at the state level, let alone the difficulty of aggregating all of these state-level restrictions up to the national level.

D.2 STATE-LEVEL ESTIMATES

Figure D.1 shows the African American proportion of the population and of the theoretical electorate for all states, not just for the selected states appearing in Figure 7.2.

There are two differences in the construction of these state-level estimates. First, for the quantitative analysis of Chapter 7, it is important to distinguish between the extensive but not complete African American disenfranchisement in the South from 1910 to 1964 and the early, pre-1868 situation of complete disenfranchisement. Accordingly, the African American share of the theoretical electorate in the former Confederate states is set at two percent from 1910 to 1964. I base this admittedly rough figure on Keyssar (2001, 199), which is almost certainly an underestimate for many Southern states in the 1950s and early 1960s.

Second, when reporting the voting-age and gendered population, the 1880 and 1890 censuses unfortunately did not break out African Americans from other "colored" racial groups (defined in these censuses to also include Chinese, Japanese, and "Indians"). At the national level, these other groups

D. Demography and the Franchise in the United States

are small enough that this does not have a noticeable effect on the estimates; however, at the state level, some states have large enough populations of these groups to substantially affect the estimates. For example, while the African American share of California's population in 1880 is 0.70 percent, the "colored" share of California's theoretical electorate in this same year is 20 percent. Accordingly, for western states with large Asian and Native American populations, where the African American share of the population and the "colored" share of the theoretical electorate diverge by more than one percentage point in 1880 and 1890, the African American share of the population is used instead. These states are California, Montana, Nevada, Oregon, Washington, and Wyoming.

D. Demography and the Franchise in the United States

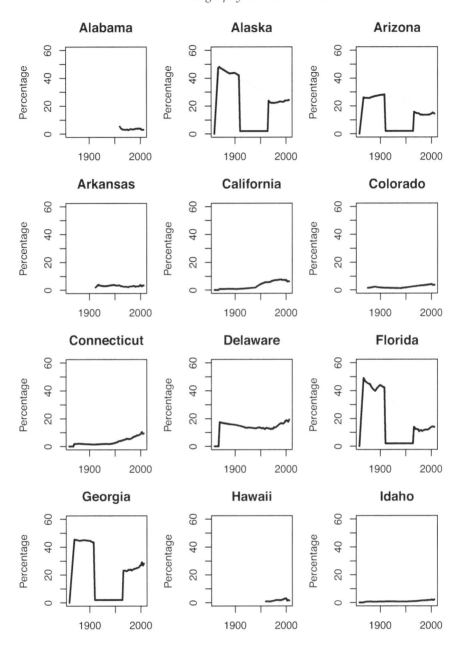

Figure D.1: The African American proportion of the population [gray line] and of the theoretical electorate (that is, the voting-age, race, and gendered population) [black line] for all states from 1860 through 2006. Continued on next page. Source: see Table 7.2.

D. Demography and the Franchise in the United States

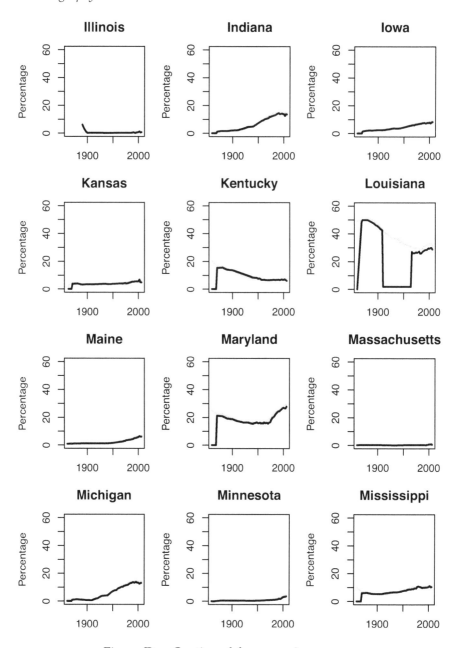

Figure D.1: Continued from previous page.

D. Demography and the Franchise in the United States

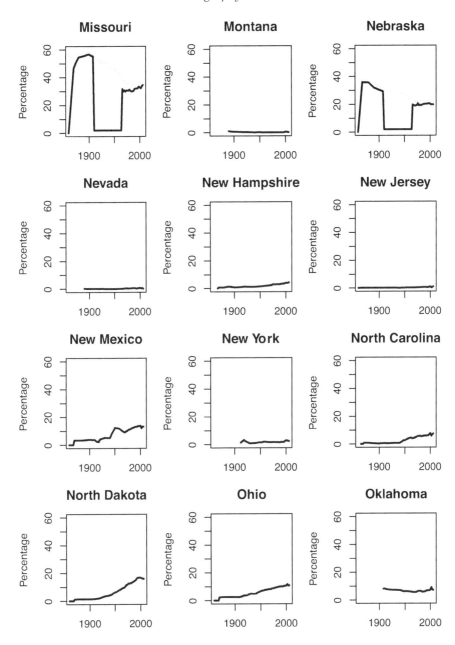

Figure D.1: Continued from previous page.

D. Demography and the Franchise in the United States

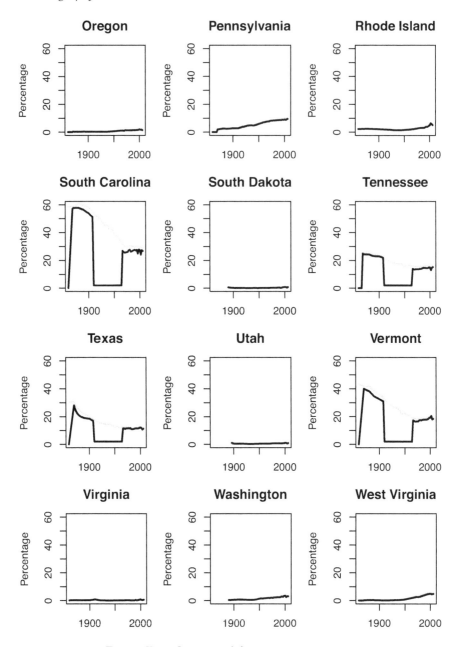

Figure D.1: Continued from previous page.

D. Demography and the Franchise in the United States

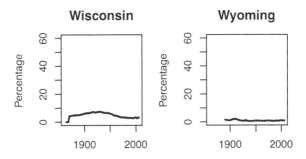

Figure D.1: Continued from previous page.

D.3 HOUSE DISTRICT ESTIMATES

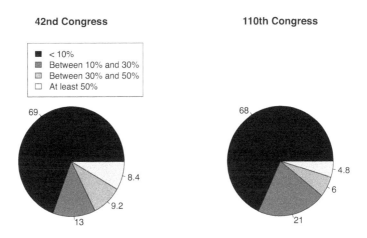

Figure D.2: Variation in the racial demography of congressional districts: the percentage of House districts for the 42nd (1870) and 110th (2006) Congress with theoretical electorates less than 10 percent African American; between 10 and 30 percent African American; between 30 and 50 percent African American; and at least 50 percent African American. Source: 1870, Parsons, Beach, and Dubin (1986); 2006, US Census Bureau (2000a).

E African American Descriptive Representation in the United States

This appendix presents data on the descriptive representation of African Americans in the United States. This data is used in the United States case study in Chapter 7, as well as in Chapter 8. Specifically, Figure E.1 displays the proportion of African American major party state and federal representatives for all states, not just the states selected for display in Figure 7.4.

As noted in the main text, this data was collected from a variety of primary and secondary sources. At the federal level, my starting point was the list of African American legislators in CQ (2010), which I cross-checked and supplemented for recent years with information from other sources such as the House's "Black Americans in Congress" website (www.baic.house.gov). The total number of House seats allocated to each state is from the *Official Congressional Directory* (U.S. Congress 1887–2008).

At the state level, primary sources include publications of the state legislatures themselves, such as class photos, membership rosters, and data compilations, such as North Carolina General Assembly (n.d.); publications of other state agencies, such as Texas State Library and Archives Commission (2002); and publications of state legislative black caucuses, such as Maryland Legislative Black Caucus and General Assembly (2010). Secondary sources include the various publications of the Joint Center for Political and Economic Studies, such as the *National Roster of Black Elected Officials* (Joint Center for Political Studies 1970–1982), supplemented for partisanship by the Council of State Government's *State Elective Officials and the Legislatures* (Council of State Governments 1969–1993); National Conference of State Legislatures (n.d.); scholarly studies, such as those of Brown (1998) and Menifield and Shaffer (2005); various newspapers; and more. State legislative seat totals are from Dubin (2007). Official state data was privileged over other sources. A complete list of sources for each state is available upon request.

E. *African American Descriptive Representation in the United States*

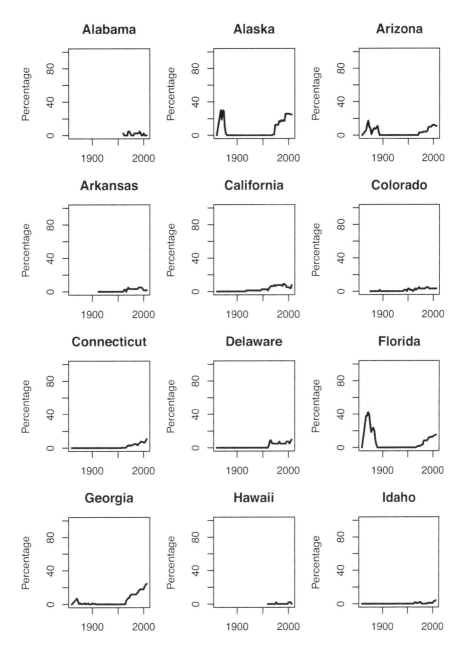

Figure E.1: The proportion of African American major party state [black line] and federal [grey line] representatives (that is, lower house legislators) for all states from 1860 through 2006. Continued on next page. Source: see Chapter 7 main text.

E. African American Descriptive Representation in the United States

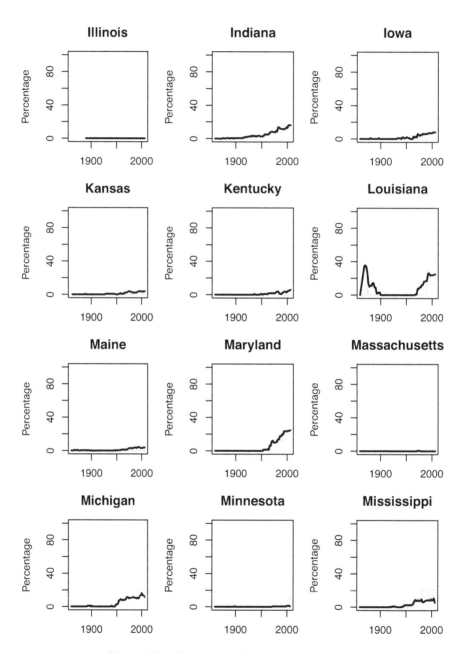

Figure E.1: Continued from previous page.

E. African American Descriptive Representation in the United States

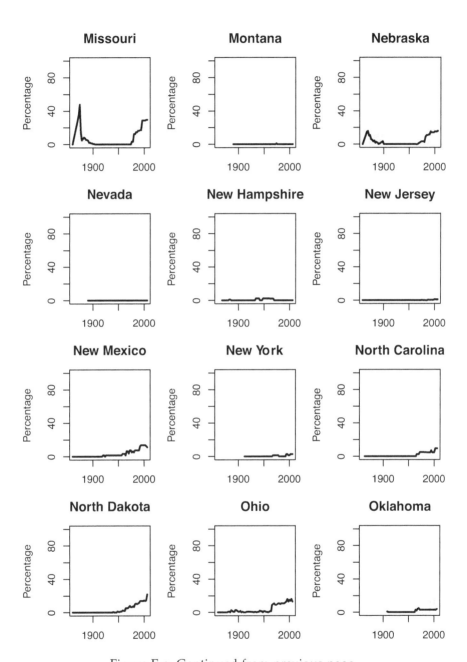

Figure E.1: Continued from previous page.

303

E. African American Descriptive Representation in the United States

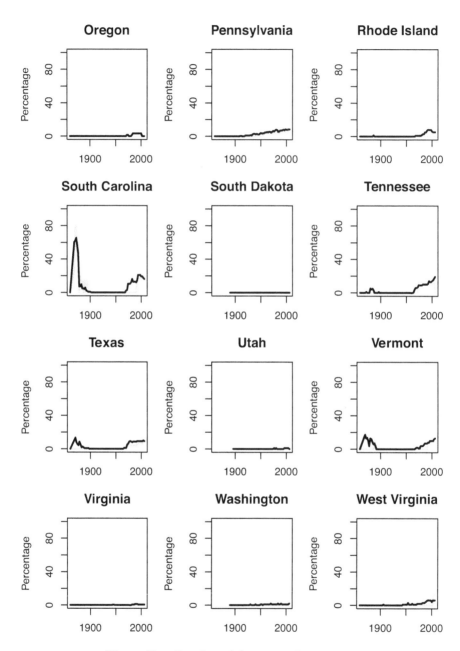

Figure E.1: Continued from previous page.

E. African American Descriptive Representation in the United States

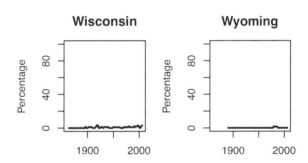

Figure E.1: Continued from previous page.

Bibliography

Aberbach, Joel D., Robert D. Putnam, and Bert A. Rockman. 1981. *Bureaucrats and Politicians in Western Democracies*. Cambridge, MA: Harvard University Press.

Acemoglu, Daron and James A. Robinson. 2000. "Why Did the West Extend the Franchise? Democracy, Inequality, and Growth in Historical Perspective." *The Quarterly Journal of Economics* 115: 1167–1199.

Adams, James, Michael Clark, Lawrence Ezrow, and Garrett Glasgow. 2004. "Understanding Change and Stability in Party Ideologies: Do Parties Respond to Public Opinion or to Past Election Results?" *British Journal of Political Science* 34: 589–610.

Adams, John. 1852–1865. Letter to John Penn. In *Works*, Vol. IV, 205. Boston: Little, Brown and Co. Quoted in Hana Pitkin, *The Concept of Representation* (Berkeley and Los Angeles: University of California Press, 1967), 60.

Ahuja, Amit. 2008. "Mobilizing Marginalized Citizens: Ethnic Parties without Ethnic Movements." Ph.D. diss., University of Michigan.

Aidt, T. S., Jayasri Dutta, and Elena Loukoianova. 2006. "Democracy Comes to Europe: Franchise Extension and Fiscal Outcomes 1830–1938." *European Economic Review* 50: 249–283.

Al-haj, Majid. 2002. "Identity Patterns among Immigrants from the Former Soviet Union in Israel: Assimilation vs. Ethnic Formation." *International Migration* 40 (2): 49–69.

———. 2004. "The Political Culture of the 1990s Immigrants from the Former Soviet Union in Israel and Their Views toward the Indigenous Arab Minority: A Case of Ethnocratic Multiculturalism." *Journal of Ethnic and Migration Studies* 30: 681–696.

Aldrich, John H. 1995. *Why Parties? The Origin and Transformation of Party Politics in America*. Chicago: University of Chicago Press.

Alesina, A., A. Devleeschauwer, W. Easterly, S. Kurlat, and R. Wacziarg. 2003. "Fractionalization." *Journal of Economic Growth* 8: 155–194.

Alesina, Alberto, Nouriel Roubini, and Gerald D. Cohen. 1997. *Political Cycles and the Macroeconomy*. Cambridge, MA: MIT Press.

Alt, James, and Robert Lowry. 1994. "Divided Government, Fiscal Institutions, and Budget Deficits: Evidence from the States." *American Political Science Review* 88: 811–828.

Bibliography

Alvarez, Mike, José Antonio Cheibub, Fernando Limongi, and Adam Przeworski. 1996. "Classifying Political Regimes." *Studies in Comparative International Development* 31 (2): 3–36.

———. 1999. "ACLP Political and Economic Database." Retrieved March 2005 from www.ssc.upenn.edu/%7Echeibub/data/Default.htm.

Amorim Neto, Octavio, and Gary Cox. 1997. "Electoral Institutions, Cleavage Structures, and the Number of Parties." *American Journal of Political Science* 41: 149–174.

Annett, A. 2001. "Social Fractionalization, Political Instability, and the Size of Government." *International Monetary Fund Staff Papers* 48: 561–592.

Arian, Asher. 2005. *Politics in Israel: The Second Republic*. 2nd ed. Washington, DC: CQ Press.

Arian, Asher, and Michal Shamir. 1999. "Introduction." In *The Elections in Israel: 1996*, ed. Asher Arian and Michal Shamir. Albany, NY: SUNY Press.

———. 2002. "Introduction." In *The Elections in Israel: 1999*, ed. Asher Arian and Michal Shamir. Albany, NY: SUNY Press.

Aronoff, Myron J. 1993. *Power and Ritual in the Israel Labor Party: A Study in Political Anthropology*. 2nd rev. ed. Armonk, NY: M. E. Sharpe.

———. 2000. "The 'Americanization' of Israeli Politics: Political and Cultural Change." *Israel Studies* 5 (1): 92–127.

Austen-Smith, David, and Jeffrey Banks. 1988. "Elections, Coalitions and Legislative Outcomes." *American Political Science Review* 82: 405–422.

Australia. Bureau of Statistics. 2008. *Australian Historical Population Statistics*. Catalog Number 3105.0.65.001. Canberra: Australian Bureau of Statistics. Retrieved July 2009 from http://www.abs.gov.au.

Australia. EC (Electoral Commission). 2006. *History of the Indigenous Vote*. Kingston: National Capital Printers. Retrieved July 2009 from http://www.ace.gov.au.

Avner, Uri. 1975. "Voter Participation in the 1973 Elections." In *The Elections in Israel - 1973*, ed. Asher Arian. Israel: Jerusalem Academic Press.

Bargsted, Matias A., and Orit Kedar. 2009. "Coalition-Targeted Duvergerian Voting: How Expectations Affect Voter Choice under Proportional Representation." *American Journal of Political Science* 53: 307–323.

Bartolini, Stefano. 2000. *The Political Mobilization of the European Left, 1860–1980*. New York: Cambridge University Press.

Bartolini, Stefano, and Peter Mair. 1990. *Identity, Competition, and Electoral Availability: The Stabilization of European Electorates, 1885–1985*. New York: Cambridge University Press.

Beck, Nathaniel, and Jonathan Katz. 1995. "What to Do (and Not to Do) with Time-Series Cross-Section Data." *American Political Science Review* 89: 634–647.

Behar, Moshe. 2009. "What's in a Name? Socio-terminological Formations and the Case for 'Arabized Jews.'" *Social Identities* 15: 747–771.

Bendor, Jonathan. 2001. "Bounded Rationality in Political Science." In *International Encyclopedia of Social and Behavioral Sciences*, ed. Neil J. Smelser and

Paul B. Baltes. New York: Elsevier.
Benoit, Kenneth. 2002. "The Endogeneity Problem in Electoral Studies: A Critical Re-Examinatioin of Duverger's Mechanical Effect." *Electoral Studies* 21 (34–35): 35–46.
Benoit, Kenneth, and Michael Laver. 2006. *Party Policy in Modern Democracies.* London: Routledge.
Berman, Sheri. 1998. *The Social Democratic Moment: Ideas and Politics in the Making of Interwar Europe.* Cambridge, MA: Harvard University Press.
Bick, Etta. 1997. "Sectarian Party Politics in Israel: The Case of Yisrael Ba'Aliya, the Russian Immigrant Party." *Israel Affairs* 4 (1): 121–145.
Birnir, Johanna Kristin. 2007. *Ethnicity and Electoral Politics.* New York: Cambridge University Press.
Blais, Andrew, and Marc Andrew Bodet. 2006. "Does Proportional Representation Foster Closer Congruence between Citizens and Policymakers?" *Comparative Political Studies* 39: 1243–1262.
Bloomfield, Gerald T. 1984. *New Zealand: A Handbook of Historical Statistics.* Boston: G. K. Hall & Co.
Bogdanor, Vernon. 1993. "The Electoral System, Government, and Democracy." In *Israeli Democracy under Stress,* ed. Ehud Sprinzak and Larry Diamond. Boulder, CO: Lynne Rienner Publishers.
Brady, Henry E., and Cynthia S. Kaplan. 2000. "Categorically Wrong? Nominal versus Graded Measures of Ethnic Identity." *Studies in Comparative International Development* 35 (3): 56–91.
———. 2009. "Conceptualizing and Measuring Ethnic Identity." In *Measuring Identity: A Guide for Social Scientists,* ed. Rawi Abdelal, Yoshiko Herrera, Alastair Iain Johnson and Rose McDermott. New York: Cambridge University Press.
Brambor, Thomas, William Roberts Clark, and Matt Golder. 2006. "Understanding Interaction Models: Improving Empirical Analyses." *Political Analysis* 14: 63–82.
Brancati, Dawn. 2008. "The Origins and Strengths of Regional Parties." *British Journal of Political Science* 38: 135–159.
Brichta, Avraham. 1998. "The New Premier-Parliamentary System in Israel." *Annals of the American Academy of Political and Social Science* 555: 180–192.
———. 2001. *Political Reform in Israel: The Quest for a Stable and Effective Government.* Brighton, UK: Sussex Academic Press.
Brown, Canter. 1998. *Florida's Black Public Officials, 1867–1924.* Tuscaloosa, AL: University of Alabama Press.
Brubaker, Rogers. 1992. *Citizenship and Nationhood in France and Germany.* Cambridge, MA: Harvard University Press.
Bruhn, Kathleen. 2009. "Electing Extremists? How the Selection Rules You Use Affect the Candidates You Get." Paper presented at the National Conference of the Midwest Political Science Association, Chicago, April 2–5.
Budge, Ian, Hans-Dieter Klingemann, Andrea Volkens, Judith Bara, and Eric Tanenbaum, eds. 2001. *Mapping Policy Preferences: Estimates for Parties, Elec-*

Bibliography

tors, and Governments 1945–1998. New York: Oxford University Press.
Burnham, Walter Dean. 1986. "Those High Nineteenth-Century American Voting Turnouts: Fact or Fiction?" *Journal of Interdisciplinary History* 16: 613–644.
———. 2007. "Triumphs and Travails in the Study of American Voting Participation Rates, 1788–2006." *The Journal of the Historical Society* 7: 505–519.
Butler, David, and Donald Stokes. 1969. *Political Change in Britain: Forces Shaping Electoral Choice.* New York: St. Martin's Press.
Campbell, Donald T., and H. Laurence Ross. 1968. "The Connecticut Crackdown on Speeding: Time-Series Data in Quasi-Experimental Analysis." *Law and Society Review* 3: 33–54.
Canada. EC (Elections Canada). Andrew Matheson. 2006. "Seeking Inclusion: South Asian Political Representation in Suburban Canada." *Electoral Insight* (December). Ottawa: Elections Canada. Retrieved July 2009 from http://www.elections.ca.
Canada. OCEO (Office of the Chief Electoral Officer of Canada). 2007. *A History of the Vote in Canada.* Ottawa: Elections Canada. Retrieved July 2009 from http://www.elections.ca.
Canada. SC (Statistics Canada). 1983. *Historical Statistics of Canada.* 2nd ed. Ottawa: Statistics Canada. Retrieved July 2009 from http://www.statcan.gc.ca.
Canon, David. 2002. "Electoral Systems and the Representation of Minority Interests in Legislatures." In *Legislatures: Comparative Perspectives on Representative Assemblies,* ed. Gerhard Loewenberg, Perverill Squire, and D. Roderick Kiewiet. Ann Arbor: The University of Michigan Press.
Caramani, Daniele. 2004. *The Nationalization of Politics: The Formation of National Electorates and Party Systems in Western Europe.* New York: Cambridge University Press.
Carroll, Susan J., ed. 2001. *The Impact of Women in Public Office.* Bloomington: Indiana University Press.
Carstairs, Andrew McLaren. 1980. *A Short History of Electoral Systems in Western Europe.* London: George Allen & Unwin.
Carter, Susan B., Scott Sigmund Gartner, Michael R. Haines, Alan L. Olmstead, Richard Sutch, and Gavin Wright. 2006. *Historical Statistics of the United States.* Millennial Edition Online. Cambridge University Press. Retrieved July 2009 from hsus.cambridge.org.
Caul, Miki. 1999. "Women's Representation in Parliament: The Role of Political Parties." *Party Politics* 5: 79–98.
Caul Kittilson, Miki. 2008. "Representing Women: The Adoption of Family Leave in Comparative Perspective." *Journal of Politics* 70: 323–334.
CBS (Central Bureau of Statistics). See Israel. CBS (Central Bureau of Statistics).
Chandra, Kanchan. 2004. *Why Ethnic Parties Succeed: Patronage and Ethnic Head Counts in India.* South Asian ed. New York: Cambridge University Press.

Chandra, Kanchan, and Cilanne Boulet. 2003. "A Model of Change in an Ethnic Demography." Unpublished manuscript.
Chesterton, G. K. 1936. *As I Was Saying*. New York: Dodd, Mead & Company.
Chhibber, Pradeep K., and Ken Kollman. 1998. "Party Aggregation and the Number of Parties in India and the United States." *The American Political Science Review* 92: 329–342.
———. 2004. *The Formation of National Party Systems: Federalism and Party Competition in Canada, Great Britain, India and the United States*. Princeton, NJ: Princeton University Press.
Ciment, James. 2000. "The Civil War and Reconstruction, 1854–1877." In *The Encyclopedia of Third Parties in America*, Vol. 1, ed. Immanuel Ness and James Ciment. Armonk, NY: Sharpe Reference.
Clark, William, and Matt Golder. 2006. "Rehabilitating Duverger's Theory: Testing the Mechanical and Strategic Modifying Effect of Electoral Laws." *Comparative Political Studies* 39: 679–708.
Cleveland, William. 2000. *A History of the Modern Middle East*. 2nd ed. Boulder, CO: Westview Press.
Cohen, Asher, and Bernard Susser. 2000. *Israel and the Politics of Jewish Identity: The Secular-Religious Impasse*. Baltimore, MD: Johns Hopkins University Press.
Cohen, Michael D., James G. March, and Johan P. Olsen. 1972. "A Garbage Can Model of Organizational Choice." *Administrative Science Quarterly* 17 (1): 1–25.
Cohen, Yinon. 2002. "From Haven to Heaven: Changing Patterns of Immigration to Israel." In *Challenging Ethnic Citizenship: German and Israeli Perspectives on Immigration*, ed. Daniel Levy and Yfaat Weiss. New York: Berghahn Books.
Conley, Dalton, and Jacqueline Stevens. 2011. "Build a Bigger House." Op-Ed. *New York Times*, January 23.
Council of State Governments. 1969–1993. *State Elective Officials and the Legislatures*. Supplement/Directory I. Lexington, KY: Council of State Governments.
Cox, Gary. 1997. *Making Votes Count: Strategic Coordination in the World's Electoral Systems*. New York: Cambridge University Press.
———. 1999. "Electoral Rules and Electoral Coordination." *Annual Review of Political Science* 2: 145–161.
Cox, Gary, and Jonathan S. Knoll. 2003. "Ethnes, Fiscs and Electoral Rules: The Determinants of Party System Inflation." Paper presented at the Annual Meeting of the American Political Science Association, August 28–31.
CQ (Congressional Quarterly). 1987. *Presidential Elections since 1789*. 4th ed. Washington, DC: Congressional Quarterly.
———. 2010. *American Political Leaders, 1789–2009*. Washington, DC: CQ Press.
Dahl, Robert A. 1966. *Political Oppositions in Western Democracies*. New Haven, CT: Yale University Press.

Bibliography

.5in 1971. *Polyarchy: Participation and Opposition*. New Haven, CT: Yale University Press.

Dalton, Russell J. 1996. *Citizen Politics: Public Opinion and Political Parties in Advanced Western Democracies*. 2nd ed. Chatham, NJ: Chatham House.

Dalton, Russell J., Scott C. Flanagan, and Paul Allen Beck, eds. 1984. *Electoral Change in Advanced Industrial Democracies: Realignment or Dealignment?* Princeton, NJ: Princeton University Press.

Dawson, Michael. 1994. *Behind the Mule: Race and Class in African-American Politics*. Princeton, NJ: Princeton University Press.

Deegan-Krause, Kevin. 2007. "New Dimensions of Political Cleavage." *Oxford Handbook of Political Science*. Oxford: Oxford University Press.

De Mesquita, Ethan Bueno. 2000. "Strategic and Nonpolicy Voting: A Coalitional Analysis of Israeli Electoral Reform." *Comparative Politics* 33: 63–80.

De Tocqueville, Alexis. 1969. *Democracy in America*. Translated by George Lawrence and edited by J. P. Mayer. New York: Perennial, Harper Collins.

Dickson, Eric S., and Kenneth Scheve. 2010. "Social Identity, Electoral Institutions, and the Number of Candidates." *British Journal of Political Science* 40: 349–375.

Diskin, Abraham. 1999. "The New Political System in Israel." *Government and Opposition* 34: 498–515.

Diskin, Hanna, and Abraham Diskin. 1995. "The Politics of Electoral Reform." *International Political Science Review* 16: 31–45.

Doorenspleet, Renske. 2000. "Reassessing the Three Waves of Democratization." *World Politics* 52: 384–406.

Doron, Gideon, and Barry Kay. 1995. "Reforming Israel's Voting Schemes." In *The Elections in Israel: 1992*, ed. Asher Arian and Michal Shamir. Albany, NY: SUNY Press.

Dowding, Keith, and Desmond King. 1995. "Introduction." In *Preferences, Institutions and Rational Choice*, ed. Keith Dowding and Desmond King. Oxford: Clarendon Press.

Downs, Anthony. 1957. *An Economic Theory of Democracy*. New York: Harper and Row.

Dubin, Michael J. 1998. *United States Congressional Elections, 1788–1997: The Official Results of the Elections of the 1st through 105th Congresses*. Jefferson, NC: McFarland & Company.

———. 2007. *Party Affiliations in the State Legislatures: A Year by Year Summary, 1796–2006*. Jefferson, NC: McFarland & Company, Inc.

Duverger, Maurice. 1963. *Political Parties: Their Organization and Activity in the Modern State*. New York: Wiley.

———. 1980. "A New Political System Model: Semi-Presidential Government." *European Journal of Political Research* 8: 165–187.

Eckstein, Harry. 1975. "Case Study and Theory in Political Science." In *Handbook of Political Science*, Vol. 1, *Political Science: Scope and Theory*, ed. Fred I. Greenstein and Nelson W. Polsby. Reading, MA: Addison-Wesley.

Edmonds, Helen G. 1973. *The Negro and Fusion Politics in North Carolina*.

Reissued ed. New York: Russell & Russell.

Eley, Geoff. 2002. *Forging Democracy: The History of the Left in Europe, 1850–2000*. New York: Oxford University Press.

Enyedi, Zsolt. 2008. "The Social and Attitudinal Basis of Political Parties: Cleavage Politics Revisited." *European Review* 16: 287–304.

Fearon, James. 1999. "Why Ethnic Politics and 'Pork' Tend to Go Together." Paper presented at the University of Chicago Conference on Ethnic Politics and Democratic Stability, Chicago, May 21–23.

———. 2003. "Ethnic Structure and Cultural Diversity by Country." *Journal of Economic Growth* 8: 195–222.

Fearon, James, and David Laitin. 2003. "Ethnicity, Insurgency, and Civil War." *American Political Science Review* 97: 75–90.

Fein, Aharon. 1995. "Voting Trends of Recent Immigrants from the Former Soviet Union." In *The Elections in Israel 1992*, ed. Asher Arian and Michael Shamir. Albany, NY: SUNY Press.

Feinstein, Brian D., and Eric Schickler. 2008. "Platforms and Partners: The Civil Rights Realignment Reconsidered." *Studies in American Political Development* 22: 1–31.

Filippov, Michel, Peter Ordeshook, and Olga Shvetsova. 1999. "Party Fragmentation and Presidential Elections in Post-communist Democracies." *Constitutional Political Economy* 10 (1): 3–26.

Fiorina, Mo. 1995. "Rational Choice, Empirical Contributions, and the Scientific Enterprise." *Critical Studies* 9 (1-2): 85–94.

Fish, M. Steven, and Matthew Kroenig. 2009. *The Handbook of National Legislatures: A Global Survey*. New York: Cambridge University Press.

Flora, Peter. 1983. *State, Economy, and Society in Western Europe 1815–1975: A Data Handbook*, Vol. 1, *The Growth of Mass Democracies and Welfare States*. Frankfurt: Campus Verlag.

Foner, Eric. 1993. *Freedom's Lawmakers: A Directory of Black Officeholders during Reconstruction*. New York: Oxford University Press.

———. 2002. *Reconstruction: America's Unfinished Revolution, 1863–1877*. First Perennial Classics ed. New York: Perennial Classics.

Foweraker, Joe. 1995. *Theorizing Social Movements*. London: Pluto Press.

Friedlander, Dov, and Calvin Goldscheider. 1979. *The Population of Israel*. New York: Columbia University Press.

Friedlander, Dov, Barbara S. Okun, Zvi Eisenbach, and Lilach Lion Elmakias. 2002. "Immigration, Social Change and Assimilation: Educational Attainment among Birth Cohorts of Jewish Ethnic Groups in Israel, 1925–29 to 1965–69." *Population Studies* 56: 135–150.

Frohlich, Norman, and Joe Oppenheimer. 1970. "I Get By with a Little Help from My Friends." *World Politics* 23: 104–120.

Frohlich, Norman, Joe Oppenheimer, and Oran Young. 1971. *Political Leadership and Collective Goods*. Princeton, NJ: Princeton University Press.

Frye, Hardy T. 1980. *Black Parties and Political Power: A Case Study*. Boston: G. K. Hall.

Bibliography

Frye, Tim, Joel Hellman, and Joshua Tucker. 2000. "Data Base on Political Institutions in the Post-Communist World." Ohio State University.

Geddes, Barbara. 2003. *Paradigms and Sand Castles: Theory Building and Research Design in Comparative Politics.* Ann Arbor: University of Michigan Press.

Gibson, Campbell, and Kay Jung. 2002. *Historical Census Statistics on Population Totals by Race, 1790 to 1990, and by Hispanic Origin, 1970 to 1990, for the United States, Regions, Divisions, and States.* Working Paper Series No. 56. Washington, DC: Population Division, U.S. Census Bureau.

Gitelman, Zvi. 1982. *Becoming Israelis: Political Resocialization of Soviet and American Immigrants.* New York: Praeger Publishers.

———. 1995. *Immigration and Identity: The Resettlement and Impact of Soviet Immigrants on Israeli Politics and Society.* Wilstein Institute Research Report. Los Angeles: Susan and David Wilstein Institute of Jewish Policy Studies.

———. 2004. "The 'Russian Revolution' in Israel." In *Critical Issues in Israeli Society,* ed. Alan Dowty. Westport, CT: Praeger Publishers.

Gitelman, Zvi, and Ken Goldstein. 2002. "The 'Russian' Revolution in Israeli Politics." In *The Elections in Israel 1999,* ed. Asher Arian and Michal Shamir. Albany, NY: SUNY Press.

Golder, Matt. 2005. "Democratic Electoral Systems around the World, 1946–2000." *Electoral Studies* 24: 103–121.

———. 2006. "Presidential Coattails and Legislative Fragmentation." *American Journal of Political Science* 50: 34–48.

Golder, Matt, and Jacek Stramski. 2010. "Ideological Congruence and Electoral Institutions." *American Journal of Political Science* 54: 90–106.

Goldscheider, Calvin. 2002a. "Ethnic Categorizations in Censuses: Comparative Observations from Israel, Canada, and the United States." In *Census and Identity: The Politics of Race, Ethnicity, and Language in National Censuses,* ed. David I. Kertzer and Dominique Arel. Cambridge: Cambridge University Press.

———. 2002b. *Israel's Changing Society: Population, Ethnicity, and Development.* 2nd ed. Boulder, CO: Westview Press.

Goldstein, Ken, and Zvi Gitelman. 2005. "From 'Russians' to Israelis?" In *The Elections in Israel 2003,* ed. Asher Arian and Michal Shamir. Albany, NY: SUNY Press.

Grofman, Bernard, ed. 1998. *Race and Redistricting in the 1990s.* New York: Agathon Press.

Grofman, Bernard, and Lisa Handley. 1989. "Minority Population and Black and Hispanic Congressional Success in the 1970s and 1980s." *American Politics Quarterly* 17: 436–445.

Grofman, Bernard, and Arend Lijphart, eds. 1986. *Electoral Laws and Their Political Consequences.* New York: Agathon Press.

Habyarimana, James, Macartan Humphreys, Daniel N. Posner, and Jeremy M. Weinstein. 2007. "Why Does Ethnic Diversity Undermine Public Goods Provision?" *American Political Science Review* 101: 709–725.

Hacohen, Dvora. 2003. *Immigrants in Turmoil: Mass Immigration to Israel and Its Repercussions in the 1950s and After.* Translated by Gila Brand. Syracuse, NY: Syracuse University Press.

Hall, Peter A. 1986. *Governing the Economy: The Politics of State Intervention in Britain and France.* New York: Oxford University Press.

Hall, Peter A., and Robert J. Franzese. 1998. "Mixed Signals: Central Bank Independence, Coordinated Wage Bargaining, and European Monetary Union." *International Organization* 52: 505–535.

Harmel, Robert, and John D. Robertson. 1985. "Formation and Success of New Parties: A Cross-National Analysis." *International Political Science Review* 6 (4): 501–523.

Harris, Michael, and Gideon Doron. 1999. "Assessing the Electoral Reform of 1992 and Its Impact on the Elections of 1996 and 1999." *Israel Studies* 4 (2): 16–39.

Hartlyn, Jonathan, Jennifer McCoy, and Thomas Mustillo. 2008. "Electoral Governance Matters: Explaining the Quality of Elections in Contemporary Latin America." *Comparative Political Studies* 41: 73–98.

Hazan, Reuven Y. 1996. "Presidential Parliamentarism: Direct Popular Election of the Prime Minister, Israel's New Electoral and Political System." *Electoral Studies* 15: 21–37.

———. 1997a. "Executive-Legislative Relations in an Era of Accelerated Reform: Reshaping Government in Israel." *Legislative Studies Quarterly* 22: 329–350.

———. 1997b. "Three Levels of Elections in Israel in 1996: Party, Parliamentary and Prime Ministerial." *Representation* 34: 240–249.

———. 1998. "Political Reform and the Committee System in Israel: Structural and Functional Adaptation." *The Journal of Legislative Studies* 4 (1): 163–187.

———. 1999a. "Religion and Politics in Israel: The Rise and Fall of the Consociational Model." *Israel Affairs* 6 (2): 109–137.

———. 1999b. "Yes, Institutions Matter: The Impact of Institutional Reform on Parliamentary Members and Leaders in Israel." *The Journal of Legislative Studies* 5 (3/4): 303–326.

———. 1999c. "The Electoral Consequences of Political Reform: In Search of the Center of the Israeli Party System." In *The Elections in Israel: 1996*, ed. Asher Arian and Michal Shamir. Albany, NY: SUNY Press.

———. 2000. "The Unintended Consequences of Extemporaneous Electoral Reform: The 1999 Elections in Israel." *Representation* 37: 39–47.

———. 2001. "The Israeli Mixed Electoral System: Unexpected Reciprocal and Cumulative Consequences." In *Mixed-Member Electoral Systems: The Best of Both Worlds?*, ed. Matthew Soberg Shugart and Martin Wattenberg. New York: Oxford University Press.

Hazan, Reuven Y., and Abraham Diskin. 2000. "The 1999 Knesset and Prime Ministerial Elections in Israel." *Electoral Studies* 19: 628–637.

Hazan, Reuven Y., and Gideon Rahat. 2000. "Representation, Electoral Reform, and Democracy: Theoretical and Empirical Lessons from the 1996 Elections in Israel." *Comparative Political Studies* 33: 1310–1336.

Herzog, Hanna. 1983. "The Ethnic Lists in Election 1981: An Ethnic Political Identity?" In *The Elections in Israel: 1981*, ed. Asher Arian. Israel: Ramot Publishing Co.

———. 1984. "Ethnicity as a Product of Political Negotiation: The Case of Israel." *Ethnic and Racial Studies* 7 (4): 517–533.

———. 1985a. "Social Construction of Reality in Ethnic Terms: The Case of Political Ethnicity in Israel." *International Review of Modern Sociology* 15 (1): 41–57.

———. 1985b. "Ethnicity as a Negotiated Issue in the Israeli Political Order: The "Ethnic Lists" to the Delegates' Assembly and the Knesset (1920–1977)." In *Studies in Israeli Ethnicity: After the Ingathering*, ed. Alex Winograd. New York: Gordon and Breach Science.

———. 1986. "Political Factionalism: The Case of Ethnic Lists in Israel." *Western Political Quarterly* 39: 285–303.

———. 1995. "Penetrating the System: The Politics of Collective Identities." In *The Elections in Israel: 1992*, ed. Asher Arian and Michal Shamir. Albany, NY: SUNY Press.

Hetherington, Marc J., and Bruce A. Larson. 2009. *Parties, Politics and Public Policy in America*. 11th ed. Washington, DC: CQ Press.

Hicken, Allen. 2009. *Building Party Systems in Developing Democracies*. New York: Cambridge University Press.

Hicken, Allen, and Heather Stoll. 2008. "Electoral Rules and the Size of the Prize: How Political Institutions Shape Presidential Party Systems." *Journal of Politics* 70: 1109–1127.

———. 2009. "Legislative Policy-making Authority, the Number of Parties and Party System Aggregation." Paper presented at the National Conference of the Midwest Political Science Association, Chicago, April 2–5.

———. 2011. "Presidents and Parties: How Presidential Elections Shape Coordination in Legislative Elections." *Comparative Political Studies* 44: 854–883.

———. 2013. "Are All Presidents Created Equal? Presidential Powers and the Shadow of Presidential Elections." *Comparative Political Studies* 46 (3). Forthcoming.

Hinich, Melvin J., and Michael C. Munger. 1997. *Analytical Politics*. New York: Cambridge University Press.

Hirschman, Albert O. 1970. *Exit, Voice, and Loyalty: Responses to Decline in Firms, Organizations, and States*. Cambridge, MA: Harvard University Press.

Hochschild, Jennifer L., and John H. Mollenkopf. 2009. *Bringing Outsiders In: Transatlantic Perspectives on Immigrant Political Incorporation*. Ithaca, NY: Cornell University Press.

Hooghe, Liesbet, Gary Marks, and Carole J. Wilson. 2004. "Does Left/Right Structure Party Positions on European Integration?" In *European Integra-*

tion and Political Conflict, ed. Gary Marks and Marco R. Steenbergen. Cambridge: Cambridge University Press.

Hoppen, K. Theodore. 1985. "The Franchise and Electoral Politics in England and Ireland 1832–1885." *History* 70: 202–217.

Horowitz, Dan, and Moshe Lissak. 1978. *Origins of the Israeli Polity.* Chicago: University of Chicago Press.

———. 1989. *Trouble in Utopia: The Overburdened Polity of Israel.* Albany, NY: SUNY Press.

Horowitz, Donald. 1985. *Ethnic Groups in Conflict.* Berkeley: University of California Press.

Horowitz, Tamir. 1999. "Determining Factors of the Vote among Immigrants from the Former Soviet Union." In *The Elections in Israel: 1996*, ed. Asher Arian and Michal Shamir. Albany, NY: SUNY Press.

Hug, Simon. 2001. *Altering Party Systems: Strategic Behavior and the Emergence of New Political Parties in Western Democracies.* Ann Arbor: University of Michigan Press.

IDEA (International Institute for Democracy and Electoral Assistance). 2009. "Voter Turnout Database." Revised May 2009. Retrieved July 2009 from `http:www.idea.int/vt/`.

Imai, Kosuke, Gary King, and Olivia Lau. 2007. "Relogit: Rare Events Logistic Regression for Dichotomous Dependent Variables." In *Zelig: Everyone's Statistical Software.* Retrieved April 2012 from `http://gking.harvard.edu/zelig`.

INES (Israeli National Election Studies). 1969–2009. Retrieved April 2008 and April 2012 from `http://www.ines.tau.il/elections.html`.

Inglehart, Ronald. 1984. "The Changing Structure of Political Cleavages in Western Society." In *Electoral Change in Advanced Industrial Democracies: Realignment or Dealignment?*, ed. Russell J. Dalton, Scott C. Flanagan, and Paul Allen Beck. Princeton, NJ: Princeton University Press.

Inglehart, Ronald, and Rudy B. Andeweg. 1993. "Change in Dutch Political Cultures: A Silent or a Silenced Revolution." *West European Politics* 16 (3): 345–361.

IPU (Inter-Parliamentary Union). 2009. *Women in National Parliaments, World Classification, Situation as of 31 October 2009.* Retrieved November 2009 from `http://www.ipu.org/wmn-3/arc/classif311009.htm`.

Israel. CBS (Central Bureau of Statistics). 1956. *Tots'ot ha-behirot la-Keneset ha-shelishit yela-rashuyot ha-mekomiyot* (in Hebrew). Special Series No. 51. Jerusalem.

———. 1961. *Tots'ot ha-behirot la-Keneset ha-revi'it yela-rashuyot ha-mekomiyot* (in Hebrew). Special Series No. 111. Jerusalem.

———. 1964. *Tots'ot ha-behirot la-Keneset ha-hamishit* (in Hebrew). Special Series No. 166. Jerusalem.

———. 1967. *Development of the Jewish Population in Israel 1948–1964, Part A.: Development by Sex, Age, Continent of Birth and Period of Immigration.* Special Series No. 215. Jerusalem.

———. 1967–1974. *Results of Elections to the [–]th Knesset and to Local Authorities* (in Hebrew). Special Series No. 216, 309, and 461. Jerusalem.

———. 1969. *Development of the Jewish Population in Israel 1948–1964, Part B.: Born Abroad by Sex, Age and Country of Birth.* Special Series No. 274. Jerusalem.

———. 1981–1997. *Results of Elections to the [–]th Knesset* (in Hebrew). Special Series No. 553, 680, 775, 855, 925, and 1054. Jerusalem.

Israel. CBS (Central Bureau of Statistics). SA. *Statistical Abstract of Israel.* 1949/50–2011. Jerusalem.

Israel. Knesset. 1999. "1999 Election Results (Final)." Retrieved June 2008 from http://www.knesset.gov.il/elections/eindex.html.

———. 2003. "Elections for the 16th Knesset (National Elections Results)." Retrieved June 2008 from http://www.knesset.gov.il/elections16/eng/results/regions.asp.

———. 2006. "Elections for the 17th Knesset (National Results)." Retrieved June 2008 from http://www.knesset.gov.il/elections17/eng/Results/main_results_eng.asp.

———. 2009. "Eighteenth Knesset." Retrieved September 2009 from http://www.knesset.gov.il.

Iversen, Torben. 1998. "Wage Bargaining, Central Bank Independence, and the Real Effects of Money." *International Organization* 52: 469–504.

Jenkins, J. Craig, Davidd Jacobs, and Jon Agnone. 2003. "Political Opportunities and African-American Protest, 1948–1997." *American Journal of Sociology* 109: 277–303.

Johnson, Kimberly. 2010. *Reforming Jim Crow: Southern Politics and State in the Age before* Brown. New York: Oxford University Press.

Joint Center for Political Studies. 1970–1982. *National Roster of Black Elected Officials.* Washington, DC: Joint Center for Political Studies.

Jones, Mark. 1994. "Presidential Election Laws and Multipartism in Latin America." *Political Research Quarterly* 47: 41–57.

———. 1997. "Racial Heterogeneity and the Effective Number of Candidates in Majority Runoff Elections: Evidence from Louisiana." *Electoral Studies* 16: 349–358.

———. 1999. "Electoral Laws and the Effective Number of Candidates in Presidential Elections." *Journal of Politics* 61: 171–184.

———. 2004. "Electoral Institutions, Social Cleavages, and Candidate Competition in Presidential Elections." *Electoral Studies* 23: 73–106.

———. 2009. "Gender Quotas, Electoral Laws, and the Election of Women: Evidence from the Latin American Vanguard." *Comparative Political Studies* 42: 56–81.

Kalyvas, Stathis N. 1996. *The Rise of Christian Democracy in Europe.* Ithaca, NY: Cornell University Press.

Kaplan, Gisela. 1992. *Contemporary Western European Feminism.* London: UCL Press, Allen and Unwin.

Kark, Ruth, and Joseph B. Glass. 2003. "Eretz Israel/Palestine, 1800–1948."

In *The Jews of the Middle East and North Africa in Modern Times,* ed. Reeva Spector Simon, Michael Menachem Laskier, and Sara Reguer. New York: Columbia University Press.

Kedar, Orit. 2005. "Why Moderate Voters Prefer Extreme Parties: Policy Balancing in Parliamentary Elections." *American Political Science Review* 99: 185–199.

———. 2006. "How Voters Work around Institutions: Policy Balancing in Staggered Elections." *Electoral Studies* 25: 509–527.

———. 2011. "Electoral Systems and District Magnitude: Beyond the Median." Paper presented at the National Conference of the Midwest Political Science Association, Chicago, March 31–April 3.

Kenig, Ofer. 2005. "The 2003 Elections in Israel: Has the Return to the 'Old' System Reduced Party System Fragmentation?" *Israel Affairs* 11: 552–566.

Kenig, Ofer, and Shlomit Barnea. 2009. "The Selection of Ministers in Israel: Is the Prime Minister 'A Master of His Domain'?" *Israel Afairs* 15: 261–278.

Kenig, Ofer, Reuven Hazan, and Gideon Rahat. 2005. "The Political Consequences of the Introduction and Repeal of the Direct Elections for the Prime Minister." In *The Elections in Israel: 2003,* ed. Asher Arian and Michael Shamir. New York: Transaction Books.

Key, V. O. 1964. *Politics, Parties and Pressure Groups.* 5th ed. New York: Thomas Y. Crowell.

Keyssar, Alexander. 2001. *The Right to Vote: The Contested History of Democracy in the United States.* New York: Basic Books.

Kezdi, Gabor. 2004. "Robust Standard Error Estimation in Fixed-Effects Panel Models." *Hungarian Statistical Review,* Special English Volume 9: 95–116.

Khanin, Vladimir. 2001. "Israeli 'Russian' Parties and the New Immigrant Vote." In *Israel at the Polls 1999,* ed. Daniel J. Elazar and M. Ben Mollov. Portland, OR: F. Cass.

———. 2004. "The Israeli 'Russian' Community and Immigrants Party Politics in the 2003 Elections." *Israel Affairs* 10 (4): 146–180.

———. 2009. "Israeli Russian Voting Trends in the 2009 Knesset Elections." Herzliya Pituach, Israel: Friedrich Ebert Stiftung. Retrieved April 2012 from http://www.fes.org.il/src/KhaninRussianVotingTrends.pdf.

Kinder, Donald R., and Thomas R. Palfrey, eds. 1993. *Experimental Foundations of Political Science.* Ann Arbor: University of Michigan Press.

King, Gary, James E. Alt, Nancy Burns, and Michael Laver. 1990. "A Unified Model of Cabinet Dissolution in Parliamentary Democracies." *American Journal of Political Science* 34: 846–871.

King, Gary, Robert O. Keohane, and Sidney Verba. 1994. *Designing Social Inquiry: Scientific Inference in Qualitative Research.* Princeton, NJ: Princeton University Press.

King, Gary, and Langche Zeng. 2001. "Explaining Rare Events in International Relations." *International Organization* 55: 693–715.

Kirchheimer, Otto. 1966. "The Transformation of the Western European

Bibliography

Party Systems." In *Political Parties and Political Development,* ed. Joseph LaPalombara and Myron Weiner. Princeton, NJ: Princeton University Press.

Kitschelt, Herbert. 1986. "Political Opportunity Structures and Political Protest: Anti-nuclear Movements in Four Democracies." *British Journal of Political Science* 16: 57–85.

———. 1989. *The Logics of Party Formation: Ecological Politics in Belgium and West Germany.* Ithaca, NY: Cornell University Press.

Kitschelt, Herbert, with Anthony J. McGann. 1997. *The Radical Right in Western Europe: A Comparative Analysis.* Ann Arbor: University of Michigan Press.

Kleppner, Paul. 1982. *Who Voted? The Dynamics of Electoral Turnout, 1870–1980.* New York: Praeger.

Knesset. See Israel. Knesset.

Knight, Jack. 1992. *Institutions and Social Conflict.* New York: Cambridge University Press.

Konstantinov, Vladimir. 2008. "The Immigration from the Former Soviet Union and the Elections in Israel, 1992–2006: Is a 'Third Israel' Being Created?" In *The Elections in Israel: 2006,* ed. Asher Arian and Michal Shamir. New Brunswick, NJ: Transaction Publishers.

Kop, Yaakov, and Robert E. Litan. 2002. *Sticking Together: The Israeli Experiment in Pluralism.* Washington, DC: Brookings Institution Press.

Kousser, J. Morgan. 1975. *The Shaping of Southern Politics: Suffrage Restriction and the Establishment of the One-Party South, 1880–1910.* Second printing. New Haven, CT: Yale University Press.

———. 1984. "The Undermining of the First Reconstruction: Lessons for the Second." In *Minority Vote Dilution,* ed. Chandler Davidson. Washington, DC: Howard University Press.

Krupavicius, Algis, and Irmina Matonyte. 2003. "Women in Lithuanian Politics: From Nomenklatura Selection to Representation." In *Women's Access to Political Power in Post-Communist Europe,* ed. Richard E. Matland and Kathleen A. Montgomery. Oxford: Oxford University Press.

Kruschke, Earl R. 1991. *Encyclopedia of 3rd Parties in the United States.* Santa Barbara, CA: ABC-CLIO.

Laakso, Markku, and Rein Taagepera. 1979. "Effective Number of Parties: A Measure with Application to Western Europe." *Comparative Political Studies* 12: 3–27.

Laitin, David. 1986. *Hegemony and Culture: Politics and Religious Change among the Yoruba.* Chicago: University of Chicago Press.

———. 2001. "The Political Science Discipline." Paper presented at the Annual Meeting of the American Political Science Association, San Francisco, August 29–September 2.

Laitin, David, and Daniel Posner. 2001. "The Implications of Constructivism for Constructing Ethnic Fractionalization Indices." *APSA-CP Newsletter* 12 (Winter): 13–17.

Lasswell, Harold D. 1936. *Politics: Who Gets What, When, How.* New York:

McGraw Hill.

Lawson, Steven F. 1985. *Southern Blacks and Electoral Politics, 1965–1982.* New York: Columbia University Press.

Laybourn, Keith. 1999. *Modern Britain since 1906: A Reader.* London: I. B. Tauris & Co.

Lijphart, Arend. 1971. "Comparative Politics and the Comparative Method." *American Political Science Review* 65: 682–693.

———. 1981. "Political Parties: Ideologies and Programs." In *Democracy at the Polls: A Comparative Study of Competitive National Elections,* ed. David Butler, Howard R. Penniman, and Austin Ranney. Washington, DC: American Enterprise Institute for Public Policy Research.

———. 1984. *Democracies: Patterns of Majoritarian and Consensus Government in Twenty-One Countries.* New Haven, CT: Yale University Press.

———. 1990. "The Political Consequences of Electoral Laws, 1945–85." *American Political Science Review* 84: 481–496.

———. 1993. "Israeli Democracy and Democratic Reform in Comparative Perspective." In *Israeli Democracy under Stress,* ed. Ehud Sprinzak and Larry Diamond. Boulder, CO: Lynne Rienner Publishers.

———. 1994. *Electoral Systems and Party Systems: A Study of Twenty-Seven Democracies, 1945–1990.* Oxford: Oxford University Press.

———. 1999. *Patterns of Democracy.* New Haven, CT: Yale University Press.

Lipset, Seymour Martin. 1960. *Political Man.* London: Heinemann.

Lipset, Seymour Martin, and Gary Marks. 2000. *It Didn't Happen Here: Why Socialism Failed in the United States.* New York: W. W. Norton.

Lipset, Seymour Martin, and Stein Rokkan. 1967. "Cleavage Structures, Party Systems, and Voter Alignments: An Introduction." In *Party Systems and Voter Alignments: Cross-National Perspectives,* ed. Seymour Martin Lipset and Stein Rokkan. New York: Free Press.

Lissak, Moshe. 1972. "Continuity and Change in the Voting Patterns of Oriental Jews." In *The Elections in Israel: 1969,* ed. Alan Arian. Israel: Jerusalem Academic Press.

Loewenberg, Gerhard, and Samuel C. Patterson. 1979. *Comparing Legislatures.* Boston: Little, Brown and Company.

Lovenduski, Joni. 1986. *Women and European Politics: Contemporary Feminism and Public Policy.* Brighton, UK: Wheatsheaf Books.

Lublin, David. 1997. *Congressional District Demographic and Political Data.* American University, Washington, DC. Accessed October 2010 at http://web.mit.edu/17.251/www/data_page.html.

Mackie, Thomas T., and Richard Rose. 1991. *The International Almanac of Electoral History.* 3rd ed. Washington, DC: Congressional Quarterly.

Madrid, Raul. 2005. "Indigenous Voters and Party System Fragmentation in Latin America." *Electoral Studies* 24: 689–707.

Mahler, Gregory S. 1997. "The Forming of the Netanyahu Government: Coalition Formation in a Quasi-Parliamentary Setting." *Israel Affairs* 3 (3): 3–27.

Bibliography

———. 2011. *Politics and Government in Israel: The Maturation of a Modern State*. 2nd ed. Lanham, MD: Rowman & Littlefield.

Mansbridge, Jane. 1999. "Should Blacks Represent Blacks and Women Represent Women? A Contingent 'Yes'." *Journal of Politics* 61: 628–657.

Manza, Jeff, and Clem Brooks. 1999. *Social Cleavages and Political Change*. New York: Oxford University Press.

March, James, and Johan Olsen. 1984. "The New Institutionalism: Organizational Factors in Political Life." *American Political Science Review* 78: 734–749.

Maryland Legislative Black Caucus and General Assembly, Department of Legislative Services. 2010. *Those on Whose Shoulders We Stand: A Historical Roster of the Legislative Black Caucus of Maryland, 1970–2010*. Retrieved November 2010 from http://dlslibrary.state.md.us/publications/Joint/Misc/HRLBCM_2010.pdf.

Matland, Richard E. 2003. "Women's Representation in Post-Communist Europe." In *Women's Access to Political Power in Post-Communist Europe*, ed. Richard E. Matland and Kathleen A. Montgomery. Oxford: Oxford University Press.

Matland, Richard E., and Kathleen A. Montgomery, eds. 2003. *Women's Access to Political Power in Post-Communist Europe*. Oxford: Oxford University Press.

Matthew, H. C. G., R. I. McKibbin, and J. A. Kay. 1976. "The Franchise Factor in the Rise of the Labour Party." *English Historical Review* 91: 723–752.

McAdam, Doug. 1982. *Political Process and the Development of Black Insurgency, 1930–1970*. Chicago: University of Chicago Press.

McDonald, Michael D., and Ian Budge. 2005. *Elections, Parties, Democracy: Conferring the Median Mandate*. New York: Oxford University Press.

McDonald, Michael P., and Samuel L. Popkin. 2001. "The Myth of the Vanishing Voter." *American Political Science Review* 95: 963–974.

Meguid, Bonnie. 2005. "Competition between Unequals: The Role of Mainstream Party Strategy in Niche Party Success." *American Political Science Review* 99: 347–359.

———. 2008. *Party Competition between Unequals: Strategies and Electoral Fortunes in Western Europe*. New York: Cambridge University Press.

Menifield, Charles E., and Stephen D. Shaffer, eds. 2005. *Politics in the New South: Representation of African Americans in Southern State Legislatures*. Albany, NY: SUNY Press.

Metcalf, Lee Kendall. 2000. "Measuring Presidential Power." *Comparative Political Studies* 33: 660–685.

Michels, Robert. [1911] 1962. *Political Parties: A Sociological Study of the Oligarchical Tendencies of Modern Democracy*. New York: Free Press.

Moe, Terry M. 1990. "Political Institutions: The Neglected Side of the Story." *Journal of Law, Economics & Organization* 6 (Special Issue): 213–253.

Moe, Terry M., Jonathan Bendor, and Kenneth Shotts. 2001. "Recycling the Garbage Can: An Assessment of the Research Program." *American Political*

Science Review 95: 169–191.
Monroe, Burt L., and Ko Maeda. 2004. "Rhetorical Idea Point Estimation: Mapping Legislative Speech." Paper presented at the Society for Political Methodology Summer Meeting, Stanford University, Palo Alto, CA, July 29–31.
Montalvo, Jose, and Marta Reynal-Querol. 2001. "The Effect of Ethnic and Religious Conflict on Growth." PRPES (Project on Religion, Political Economy, and Society) Working Paper No. 4, Weatherhead Center for International Affairs, Harvard University.
Moser, Robert G. 2003 "Electoral Systems and Women's Representation: The Strange Case of Russia." In *Women's Access to Political Power in Post-Communist Europe,* eds. Richard E. Matland and Kathleen A. Montgomery. Oxford: Oxford University Press.
Moser, Robert, and Ethan Scheiner. 2012. *Electoral Systems and Political Context: How Electoral System Effects Differ in New and Established Democracies.* New York: Cambridge University Press.
Mozaffar, Shaheen, James R. Scarritt, and Glen Galaich. 2003. "Electoral Institutions, Ethnopolitical Cleavages, and Party Systems in Africa." *American Political Science Review* 97: 379–390.
Munck, Geraldo. 2004. "Tools for Qualitative Research." In *Rethinking Social Inquiry: Diverse Tools, Shared Standards,* ed. Henry E. Brady and David Collier. Lanham, MD: Rowman & Littlefield.
Nachmias, David, and Itai Sened. 1999. "The Bias of Pluralism: The Redistributive Effects of the New Electoral Law." In *The Elections in Israel: 1996,* ed. Asher Arian and Michal Shamir. Albany, NY: SUNY Press.
National Conference of State Legislatures. n.d. "African-American Legislators, 1992–2009." Retrieved November 2010 from `http://www.ncsl.org`.
Ness, Immanuel, and James Ciment, eds. 2000. *The Encyclopedia of Third Parties in America.* Vols. 1–3. Armonk, NY: Sharpe Reference.
Newey, Whitney K., and Kenneth D. West. 1987. "A Simple, Positive-Definite, Heteroskedasticity and Autocorrelation Consistent Covariance Matrix." *Econometrica* 55: 703–708.
Norris, Pippa. 1993. "Conclusions: Comparing Legislative Recruitment." In *Gender and Party Politics,* ed. Joni Lovenduski and Pippa Norris. London: Sage.
Norris, Pippa, and Joni Lovenduski. 1995. *Political Recruitment: Gender, Race and Class in the British Parliament.* New York: Cambridge University Press.
North, Douglass. 1990. *Institutions, Institutional Change and Economic Performance.* Cambridge: Cambridge University Press.
North Carolina General Assembly. n.d. Legislative Library. *North Carolina African-American Legislators, 1969–2009.* Retrieved November 2010 from `http://www.ncga.state.nc.us/library/Documents/African-Americans.pdf`.
Olson, Mancur. 1965. *The Logic of Collective Action.* Cambridge, MA: Harvard University Press.

Bibliography

———. 1971. Foreword to *The Logic of Collective Action: Public Goods and the Theory of Groups.* Rev. ed. New York: Schocken Books.
Ordeshook, Peter, and Olva Shvetsova. 1994. "Ethnic Heterogeneity, District Magnitude, and the Number of Parties." *American Journal of Political Science* 38: 100–123.
Ortiz, Paul. 2005. *Emancipation Betrayed: The Hidden History of Black Organizing and White Violence in Florida from Reconstruction to the Bloody Election of 1920.* Berkeley: University of California Press.
Ottolenghi, Emanuele. 1999. "Immobility, Stability and Ineffectiveness: Assessing the Impact of Direct Election of the Israeli Prime Minister." *The Journal of Legislative Studies* 5 (1): 35–53.
———. 2001. "Why Direct Election Failed in Israel." *Journal of Democracy* 12 (4): 109–122.
———. 2002. "Explaining Systemic Failure: The Direct Elections System and Israel's Special Elections of February 2001." *Israel Affairs* 8 (3): 134–156.
———. 2004. "Choosing a Prime Minister: Executive-Legislative Relations in Israel in the 1990s." *Journal of Legislative Studies* 10: 263–277.
———. 2007. "The 2006 Election and the Legacy of the Direct Election System." *Israel Affairs* 13: 455–475.
Parsons, Stanley B., William W. Beach, and Michael J. Dubin. 1986. *United States Congressional Districts and Data, 1843–1883.* New York: Greenwood Press.
Parsons, Stanley B., Michael J. Dubin, and Karen Toombs Parsons. 1990. *United States Congressional Districts, 1883–1913.* New York: Greenwood Press.
Paxton, Pamela, Jennifer Green, and Melanie Hughes. 2008. "Women in Parliament, 1945–2003: Cross-National Dataset." Retrieved November 2009 from htt://www.icpsr.umich.edu.
Paxton, Pamela, and Melanie M. Hughes. 2007. *Women, Politics, and Power: A Global Perspective.* Thousand Oaks, CA: Pine Forge Press.
Peled, Yoav. 1992. "Ethnic Democracy and the Legal Construction of Citizenship: Arab Citizens of the Jewish State." *American Political Science Review* 86: 432–443.
Peres, Yochanan, and Sara Shemer. 1984. "The Ethnic Factor in Elections." In *The Roots of Begin's Success: The 1981 Israeli Elections*, ed. Dan Caspi, Abraham Diskin, and Emanuel Gutmann. London: Croom Helm.
Peres, Yochanan, Efraim Yuchtman (Yaar) and Rivka Shafat. 1975. "Predicting and Explaining Voters' Behavior in Israel." In *The Elections in Israel: 1973*, ed. Asher Arian. Israel: Jerusalem Academic Press.
Peretz, Don, and Sammy Smooha. 1981. "Israel's Tenth Knesset Elections: Ethnic Upsurgence and Decline of Ideology." *Middle East Journal* 35: 506–526.
Perman, Michael. 2001. *Struggle for Mastery: Disfranchisement in the South, 1888-1908.* Chapel Hill, NC: University of North Carolina Press.
Philippov, Michael. 2008. "1990s Immigrants from the FSU in Israeli Elec-

tions 2006: The Fulfillment of the Political Dreams of Post-Soviet Man?" In *The Elections in Israel: 2006,* ed. Asher Arian and Michal Shamir. New Brunswick, NJ: Transaction Publishers.

Phillips, Anne. 1995. *The Politics of Presence.* Oxford: Clarendon Press.

Phillips, John A., and Charles Wetherell. 1995. "The Great Reform Act of 1832 and the Political Modernization of England." *American Historical Reveiw* 100: 411–436.

Pitkin, Hanna. 1967. *The Concept of Representation.* Berkeley and Los Angeles: University of California Press.

Plott, Charles. 1991. "Will Economics Become an Experimental Science?" *Southern Economic Journal* 57: 901–920.

Portes, Alejandro, Christina Escobar, and Renelinda Arana. 2009. "Divided or Convergent Loyalties?: The Political Incorporation Process of Latin American Immigrants in the United States." *International Journal of Comparative Sociology* 50: 103–136.

Posner, Daniel. 2004a. "Measuring Ethnic Fractionalization in Africa." *American Journal of Political Science* 48: 849–863.

———. 2004b. "The Political Salience of Cultural Difference: Why Chewas and Tumbukas Are Allies in Zambia and Adversaries in Malawi." *American Political Science Review* 98: 529–545.

———. 2005. *Institutions and Ethnic Politics in Africa.* New York: Cambridge University Press.

Powell, G. Bingham. 1982. *Comparative Democracies: Participation, Stability and Violence.* Cambridge, MA: Harvard University Press.

———. 2000. *Elections as Instruments of Democracy: Majoritarian and Proportional Visions.* New Haven, CT: Yale University Press.

———. 2004. "Political Representation in Comparative Politics." *Annual Review of Political Science* 7: 273–296.

Przeworski, Adam, Michael E. Alvarez, Jose Anonio Cheibub, and Fernando Limongi. 2000. *Democracy and Development: Political Institutions and Material Well-Being in the World.* New York: Cambridge University Press.

Przeworski, Adam, and John Sprague. 1986. *Paper Stones: A History of Electoral Socialism.* Chicago: University of Chicago Press.

Pugh, Martin. 1982. *The Making of Modern British Politics, 1867–1939.* New York: St. Martin's Press.

Rae, Douglas. 1967. *The Political Consequences of Electoral Laws.* New Haven, CT: Yale University Press.

Rae, Douglas, and Michael Taylor. 1970. *The Analysis of Political Cleavages.* New Haven, CT: Yale University Press.

Rahat, Gideon. 2001. "The Politics of Reform in Israel: How the Israeli Mixed System Came to Be." In *Mixed-Member Electoral Systems: The Best of Both Worlds?,* ed. Matthew Soberg Shugart and Martin Wattenberg. New York: Oxford University Press.

———. 2004. "The Study of the Politics of Electoral Reform in the 1990s: Theoretical and Methodological Lessons." *Comparative Politics* 36 (4): 461–

Bibliography

479.

Rahat, Gideon, Reuven Y. Hazan, and Richard S. Katz. 2008. "Democracy and Political Parties: On the Uneasy Relationships between Participation, Competition and Representation." *Party Politics* 14: 663–683.

Rallings, Colin, and Michael Thrasher. 2007. *British Electoral Facts 1832–2006.* Aldershot, UK: Ashgate Publishing.

Reed, Steven R. 1990. "Structure and Behavior: Extending Duverger's Law to the Japanese Case." *British Journal of Political Science* 20: 335–356.

Reed, Steven R., and Michael Thies. 2001. "The Consequences of Political Reform in Japan." In *Mixed-Member Electoral Systems: The Best of Both Worlds?*, ed. Matthew Soberg Shugart and Martin P. Wattenburg. New York: Oxford University Press.

Reich, Bernard, Meyrav Wurmser, and Noah Dropkin. 1994. "Playing Politics in Moscow and Jerusalem: Soviet Jewish Immigrants and the 1992 Knesset Elections." In *Israel at the Polls, 1992,* ed. Daniel Elazar and Shmuel Sandler. Lanham, MD: Rowman & Littlefield.

Reingold, Beth. 2008. "Women as Officeholders: Linking Descriptive and Substantive Representation." In *Political Women and American Democracy,* ed. Christina Wolbrecht, Karen Beckwith, and Lisa Baldez. New York: Cambridge University Press.

Rice, Roberta, and Donna Lee Van Cott. 2006. "The Emergence and Performance of Indigenous Peoples' Parties in South America." *Comparative Political Studies* 39: 709–732.

Riker, William. 1986. *The Art of Political Manipulation.* New Haven, CT: Yale University Press.

Roeder, Philip. 2001. "Ethnolinguistic Fractionalization (ELF) Indices, 1961 and 1985." Retrieved July 2009 from http://weber.ucsd.edu/~proeder/elf.htm.

Rogowski, Ronald. 2004. "How Inference in the Social (but Not the Physical) Sciences Neglects Theoretical Anomaly." In *Rethinking Social Inquiry: Diverse Tools, Shared Standards,* ed. Henry E. Brady and David Collier. Lanham, MD: Rowman & Littlefield.

Rose, Richard. 1980. *Do Parties Make a Difference?* Berkeley: University of California Press.

Rouhana, Nadim N. 1997. *Palestinian Citizens in an Ethnic Jewish State: Identities in Conflict.* New Haven, CT: Yale University Press.

Rule, Wilma, and Joseph F. Zimmerman, eds. 1994. *Electoral Systems in Comparative Perspective: Their Impact on Women and Minorities.* Westport, CT: Greenwood Press.

Sacks, Harvey. 1992. *Lectures on Conversation.* Vols. I & II. Oxford: Basil Blackwell.

Said, Edward. 1978. *Orientalism.* New York: Vintage Books.

Salisbury, Robert. 1969. "An Exchange Theory of Interest Groups." *Midwest Journal of Political Science* 13: 1–32.

Samuels, David J., and Matthew S. Shugart. 2010. *Presidents, Parties, Prime*

Ministers. New York: Cambridge University Press.

Sartori, Giovanni. 1969. "From the Sociology of Politics to Political Sociology." In *Politics and the Social Sciences,* ed. Seymour Martin Lipset. New York: Oxford University Press.

———. 1976. *Parties and Party Systems: A Framework for Analysis.* Vol. 1. New York: Cambridge University Press.

———. 1997. *Comparative Constitutional Engineering: An Inquiry into Structures, Incentives and Outcomes.* 2nd ed. New York: New York University Press.

Saunders, Robert. 2007. "The Politics of Reform and the Making of the Second Reform Act, 1848–1867." *The Historical Journal* 50: 571–591.

Schattschneider, E. E. 1942. *Party Government.* New York: Holt, Rinehart and Winston.

———. 1960. *The Semi-Sovereign People: A Realist's View of Democracy in America.* New York: Holt, Rinehart and Winston.

Searle, G. R. 2004. *A New England? Peace and War, 1886–1918.* Oxford: Clarendon Press.

Segev, Tom. 1998. *1949: The First Israelis.* 1st Holt Paperbacks ed. New York: Henry Holt and Company.

Selway, Joel. 2009. "Constitutions, Cross-cutting Cleavages and Coordination: The Provision of Public Goods in Developing Countries." Ph.D. diss., University of Michigan.

Selznick, Philip. 1949. *TVA and the Grass Roots: A Study of Politics and Organization.* Berkeley: University of California Press.

Shafir, Gershon, and Yoav Peled. 2002. *Being Israeli: The Dynamics of Multiple Citizenship.* New York: Cambridge University Press.

Shama, Avraham, and Mark Iris. 1977. *Immigration without Integration: Third World Jews in Israel.* Cambridge, MA: Schenkman Publishing.

Shamir, Michal, and Asher Arian. 1983. "The Ethnic Vote in Israel's 1981 Elections." In *The Elections in Israel: 1981*, ed. Asher Arian. Israel: Ramot Publishing Co.

Shenhav, Yehouda. 2006. *The Arab Jews: A Postcolonial Reading of Nationalism, Religion, and Ethnicity.* Stanford, CA: Stanford University Press.

Shepsle, Kenneth, and Barry Weingast. 1987. "The Institutional Foundations of Committee Power." *American Political Science Review* 81: 85–104.

Shugart, Matthew. 1995. "The Electoral Cycle and Institutional Sources of Divided Presidential Government." *American Political Science Review* 89: 327–343.

———. 1999. "Presidentialism, Parliamentarism and the Provision of Collective Goods in Less-Developed Countries." *Constitutional Political Economy* 10: 53–88.

———. 2005. "Semi-Presidential Systems: Dual Executive and Mixed Authority Patterns." *French Politics* 3 (3): 323–351.

Shugart, Matthew, and John Carey. 1992. *Presidents and Assemblies: Constitutional Design and Electoral Dynamics.* New York: Cambridge University

Bibliography

Press.
Shugart, Matthew Soberg, and Martin P. Wattenberg, eds. 2001. *Mixed-Member Electoral Systems: The Best of Both Worlds?* New York: Oxford University Press.
Shuval, Judith. 1989. "The Structures and Dilemmas of Israeli Pluralism." In *The Israeli State and Society: Boundaries and Frontiers,* ed. Baruch Kimmerling. Albany, NY: SUNY Press.
Siaroff, Alan. 2003. "Varieties of Parliamentarianism in the Advanced Industrial Democracies." *International Political Science Review* 24: 445–464.
Siegel, Dina. 1998. *The Great Immigration: Russian Jews in Israel.* New York: Berghahn Books.
Simon, Reeva Spector. 2003. "Iraq." In *The Jews of the Middle East and North Africa in Modern Times,* ed. Reeva Spector Simon, Michael Menachem Laskier, and Sara Reguer. New York: Columbia University Press.
Singer, Matthew M., and Laura B. Stephenson. 2009. "The Political Context and Duverger's Theory: Evidence at the District Level." *Electoral Studies* 28: 480–491.
Smith, Stuart Tyson. 2008. "Ethnicity and Empire: The Political and Social Articulation of Identity in Ancient Egypt's Nubian Colony." Paper presented at the Annual Conference of the Theoretical Archaeology Group, Southampton, UK, December 15–17.
Smooha, Sammy. 1978. *Israel: Pluralism and Conflict.* Berkeley: University of California Press.
Stellman, Henri. 1996. "Electing a Prime Minister and a Parliament: The Israeli Election 1996." *Parliamentary Affairs* 49: 648–660.
Stimson, James, Michael MacKuen, and Robert Erikson. 1995. "Dynamic Representation." *American Political Science Review* 89: 543–565.
Stoll, Heather. 2004. "Social Cleavages, Political Institutions, and Party Systems: Putting Preferences Back into the Fundamental Equation of Politics." Ph.D. diss., Stanford University.
———. 2008. "Social Cleavages and the Number of Parties: How the Measures You Choose Affect the Answers You Get." *Comparative Political Studies* 41: 1439–1965.
———. 2010. "Elite Level Conflict Salience and Dimensionality in Western Europe: Concepts and Empirical Findings." *West European Politics* 33: 445–473.
———. 2011. "Dimensionality and the Number of Parties in Legislative Elections." *Party Politics* 17: 405–430.
Strom, Kaare. 1984. "Minority Governments in Parliamentary Democracies." *Comparative Political Studies* 17: 199–227.
———. 1990a. "A Behavioral Theory of Competitive Political Parties." *American Journal of Political Science* 34: 565–598.
———. 1990b. *Minority Government and Majority Rule.* New York: Cambridge University Press.
Susser, Bernard. 1997. "The Direct Election of the Prime Minister: A Balance

Sheet." *Israel Affairs* 4 (1): 237–257.
Svarlik, Bo. 2002. "Party and Electoral System in Sweden." In *The Evolution of Electoral and Party Systems in the Nordic Countries,* ed. Bernard Grofman and Arend Lijphart. New York: Agathon Press.
Swers, Michele L. 2002. *The Difference Women Make: The Policy Impact of Women in Congress.* Chicago: University of Chicago Press.
Swirski, Shlomo. 1989. *Israel: The Oriental Majority.* Translated by Barbara Swirski. Midsomer Norton, UK: Zed Books.
Taagepera, Rein. 1997. "Effective Number of Parties for Incomplete Data." *Electoral Studies* 16: 145–151.
———. 1999. "The Number of Parties as a Function of Heterogeneity and Electoral System." *Comparative Political Studies* 32: 531–548.
———. 2007. *Predicting Party Sizes: The Logic of Simple Electoral Systems.* Norfolk, UK: Oxford University Press.
Taagepera, Rein, and Matthew Shugart. 1989. *Seats and Votes: The Effects and Determinants of Electoral Systems.* New Haven, CT: Yale University Press.
Tanner, Duncan. 1983. "The Parliamentary Electoral System, the 'Fourth' Reform Act and the Rise of Labour in England and Wales." *Historical Research* 56: 205–219.
Tavits, Margit. 2006. "Party System Change: Testing a Model of New Party Entry." *Party Politics* 12: 99–119.
Tepe, Sultan, and Roni Baum. 2008. "Shas' Transformation to 'Likud with Kippa'? A Comparative Assessment of the Moderation of Religious Parties." In *The Elections in Israel: 2006,* ed. Asher Arian and Michal Shamir. New Brunswick, NJ: Transaction Books.
Texas State Library and Archives Commission and State Preservation Board. 2002. "Forever Free: Nineteenth Century African-American Legislators and Constitutional Convention Delegates of Texas." Retrieved November 2010 from http://www.tsl.state.tx.us/exhibits/forever/index.html.
Thomson, Robert. 1999. "The Party Mandate: Election Pledges and Government Actions in the Netherlands, 1986–1998." Ph.D. diss., University of Groningen.
Torgovnik, Efraim. 1986. "Ethnicity and Organizational Catchall Politics." In *The Elections in Israel: 1984,* ed. Asher Arian and Michal Shamir. New Brunswick, NJ: Transaction Books.
Treisman, Daniel. 2002. "Defining and Measuring Decentralization: A Global Perspective." Unpublished manuscript.
———. 2008. "Decentralization Dataset." Retrieved September 2009 from http://www.sscnet.ucla.edu/polisci/faculty/treisman.
Truman, David. 1958. *The Governmental Process.* New York: Alfred A. Knopf.
Tsebelis, George. 1995. "Decision Making in Political Systems: Veto Players in Presidentialism, Parliamentarism, Multicameralism and Multipartyism." *British Journal of Political Science* 25: 289–325.
Tsebelis, George, and Jeanette Money. 1997. *Bicameralism.* New York: Cam-

Bibliography

bridge University Press.

Tsur, Yaron. 2007. "The Brief Career of Prosper Cohen: A Sectorial Analysis of the North African Jewish Leadership in the Early Years of Israeli Statehood." In *Sephardic Jewry and Mizrahi Jews*, ed. Peter Y. Medding. New York: Oxford University Press.

UN (United Nations). PD (Department of Economic and Social Affairs, Population Division). 2009. "Trends in International Migrant Stock: The 2008 Revision." Retrieved July 2009 from http://esa.un.org/migration/.

UN (United Nations). SD (Department of Economic and Social Affairs, Statistics Division). 1997. *Demographic Yearbook, Historical Supplement*. Retrieved July 2009 from http://unstats.un.org/unsd/Demographic/Products/dyb/dybhist.htm.

U.S. (United States). Census Bureau. 1860–1960. *Census of Population and Housing*.

———. 1948. *Estimates of the Population of Voting Age, by States: 1948*. Report P25-15.

———. 1954–1962. *Estimates of the Civilian Population of Voting Age for States: November [–]*. Reports P25-100, P25-143, P25-185, P25-221, P25-255.

———. 1965. *Estimates of the Population of the Voting Age and of the Percent Voting in General Elections 1920–1960*. Report P25-315. Retrieved September 2010 from http://www.census.gov/population/socdemo/voting/p25-315.pdf.

———. 1966–2006. *Voting and Registration in the Election of November [–]*. Reports P20-174, P20-192, P20-228, P20-253, P20-293, P20-322, P20-344, P20-370, P20-383, P20-405, P20-414, P20-440, P20-453, P20-466, PPL-25RV, P20-504, P20-523RV, P20-542, P20-552, P20-556, and P20-557.

———. 1968–2000. *Projections of the Population of Voting Age, for States: November [–]*. Reports P25-342, P25-479, P25-526, P25-626, P25-732, P25-879, P25-916, P25-948, P25-1019, P25-1059, P25-1085, P25-1117, P25-1132, 1996 [no report number] and 2000 [no report number].

———. 1970. *1970 Population of Voting Age for States*. Report PC(S1)-3. Retrieved September 2010 from http://www.census.gov/population/www/socdemo/voting/pcs1-3.html.

———. 1975. *Historical Statistics of the United States: Colonial Times to 1970*. Washington, DC: Government Printing Office. Retrieved July 2009 from http://www.census.gov/prod/www/abs/statab.html.

———. 1990. *Historical Annual Time Series of State Population Estimates and Demographic Components of Change: 1900 to 1990 Total Population Estimates*. Retrieved September 2010 from http://www.census.gov/popest/archives/1980s/80s_st_totals.html.

———. 2000a. *2000 Census of Population and Housing, 110th Congressional District Summary File (100-Percent)*. Retrieved November 2010 from http://factfinder.census.gov/servlet/DatasetMainPageServlet?_lang=en. Washington, DC: U.S. Census Bureau.

———. 2000b. *Resident Population Estimates of the United States by Sex, Race and Hispanic Origin: April 1, 1990 to July 1, 1999, with Short-Term Projection to November 1, 2000.* Retrieved September 2010 from http://www.census.gov/popest/archives/1990s/nat-srh.txt.

———. 2000c. *1990 to 1999 Annual Time Series of State Population Estimates by Race and Hispanic Origin, July 1 [–].* Retrieved September 2010 from http://www.census.gov/popest/archives/1990s/St_race_hisp.html.

———. 2002. *Historical Census Statistics on Population Totals by Race, 1790 to 1990, and by Hispanic Origin, 1970 to 1990, for the United States, Regions, Divisions and States.* Working Paper Series No. 56. Washington, DC: U.S. Census Bureau, Population Division.

———. 2006. *Historical Census Statistics on the Foreign-born Population of the United States: 1850 to 2000.* Working Paper No. 81. Washington, DC: U.S. Census Bureau, Population Division.

———. 2008. *Current Population Survey, Voting and Registration, Historical Time Series Tables.* Retrieved September 2010 from http://www.census.gov/population/www/socdemo/voting.html.

———. 2009a. *Annual Estimates of the Resident Population for the United States, Regions, States, and Puerto Rico: April 1, 2000 to July 1, 2009.* Retrieved September 2010 from http://www.census.gov/popest/states/NST-ann-est.html.

———. 2009b. *International Data Base (IDB).* Retrieved July 2009 from http://www.census.gov.ipc/www/idb/index.php.

———. 2009c. *Annual Estimates of the Resident Population by Sex, Race and Hispanic Origin for [State]: April 1, 2000 to July 1, 2009.* Retrieved September 2010 from http://www.census.gov/popest/states/asrh/SC_EST2009-03.html.

U.S. (United States). Congress. 1887–2008. *Official Congressional Directory.* Washington, D.C.: U.S. Goverment Printing Office.

U.S. (United States). House of Representatives. 1920–2006. *Statistics of the Congressional [and Presidential] Election of [–].* Compiled from Official Sources by [–], Clerk of the House of Representatives. Washington, DC. Retrieved from http://clerk.house.gov/member_info/electionInfo/index.html.

Uzee, Philip. 1950. "Republican Politics in Louisiana, 1877–1900." Ph.D. diss., Lousiana State University.

Valelly, Richard M. 2004. *The Two Reconstructions: The Struggle for Black Enfranchisement.* Chicago: University of Chicago Press.

Van Cott, Donna Lee. 2000. "Party System Development and Indigenous Populations in Latin America: The Bolivian Case." *Party Politics* 6: 155–174.

———. 2005. *From Movements to Parties in Latin America: The Evolution of Ethnic Politics.* New York: Cambridge University Press.

van der Veen, Maurits, and David Laitin. 2004. "Modeling the Evolution of Ethnic Demography." Paper presented at the Ninth World Conference of the Association for the Study of Nationalities, Columbia University, New

Bibliography

York, April 15–17.

Varshney, Ashutosh. 1998. *Democracy, Development, and the Countryside: Urban–Rural Struggles in India.* New York: Cambridge University Press.

Wagner, Richard. 1966. "Pressure Groups and Political Entrepreneurs: A Review Article." *Papers on Non-Market Decision Making* 1: 161–170.

Walker, Jack. 1994. *Mobilizing Interest Groups in America.* Ann Arbor: University of Michigan Press.

Walton, Hanes, Jr. 1969. *The Negro in Third Party Politics.* Philadelphia: Dorrance & Company.

———. 1972. *Black Political Parties: An Historical and Political Analysis.* New York: The Free Press.

———. 1975. *Black Republicans: The Politics of the Black and Tans.* Metuchen, NJ: Scarecrow Press.

———. 1985. *Invisible Politics: Black Political Behavior.* Albany, NY: SUNY Press.

———. 2000a. "United Citizens Party, 1969-1970s." In *The Encyclopedia of Third Parties in America*, Vol. 3, ed. Immanuel Ness and James Ciment. Armonk, NY: Sharpe Reference.

———. 2000b. "Afro-American Party, 1960s." In *The Encyclopedia of Third Parties in America*, Vol. 1, ed. Immanuel Ness and James Ciment. Armonk, NY: Sharpe Reference.

———. 2000c. "Black and Tan Republican Parties, 1860–1960s." In *The Encyclopedia of Third Parties in America*, Vol. 1, ed. Immanuel Ness and James Ciment. Armonk, NY: Sharpe Reference.

Walton, John K. 1993. *The Second Reform Act.* Methuen & Co., 1983. Reprint, London: Routledge.

Ware, Alan. 1996. *Political Parties and Party Systems.* New York: Oxford University Press.

Wilkerson, Isabel. 2010. *The Warmth of Other Suns: The Epic Story of America's Great Migration.* New York: Random House.

Willis, Aaron P. 1995. "Shas—The Sephardic Torah Guardians: Religious 'Movement' and Political Power." In *The Elections in Israel: 1992,* ed. Asher Arian and Michal Shamir. Albany, NY: SUNY Press.

Wolendorp, Jaap, Hans Keman, and Ian Budge. 1993. "Party Government in 20 Democracies." *European Journal of Political Research* 24: 1–119.

Woodward, C. Vann. 1960. *The Burden of Southern History.* Baton Rouge, LA: Louisiana State University Press.

World Bank Group. DDG (Development Data Group). 2009. "World Development Indicators Online." Retrieved July 2009 from `http://go.worldbank.org/U0FSM7AQ40`.

World Bank Group. HSRP (Human Security Report Project). 2008. *miniAtlas of Human Security.* World Bank Publications. Retrieved July 2009 from `http://www.miniatlasofhumansecurity.info/en/access.html`.

World Bank Group. PSG (Public Sector Group). n.d. "Fiscal Decentralization Indicators." Retrieved February 2007 from `http://www1.wodlrbank.org/`

publicsector/decentralization/fiscalindicators.htm.

Yanow, Dvora. 1999. "From What Edah Are You? Israeli and American Meanings of 'Race-Ethnicity' in Social Policy Practices." *Israel Affairs* 5 (2): 183–199.

Yiftachel, Oren, and Erez Tzfadia. 2004. "Between Periphery and 'Third Space': Identity of Mizrahim in Israel's Development Towns." In *Israelis in Conflict: Hegemonies, Identities and Challenges,* ed. Adriana Kemp, David Newman, Uri Ram and Oren Yiftachel. Brighton, UK: Sussex Academic Press.

Zuckerman, Alan. 1975. "Political Cleavage: A Conceptual and Theoretical Analysis." *British Journal of Political Science* 5: 231–248.

Index

African American political parties
    Black and Tans, *see* Black and Tans
    Formation (entry) of, 198–200, 210–234
    Mississippi Freedom Democrats, *see* Mississippi Freedom Democrats
    National Democratic Party of Alabama, *see* National Democratic Party of Alabama
    Peace and Freedom party, *see* Peace and Freedom party
    Presidential elections, in, 211, 215–216, 218–219, 224, 228–230
    Quantitative models of entry and success of, 224–229
    Role in providing descriptive representation, 256–258
    Subnational elections, in, 211, 230–231, 249, 251, 256
    Success of, 10, 14, 18, 198–200, 212–224, 228–234, 239, 262
African Americans
    Descriptive representation of, 19, 222, 249–252
    Enfranchisement and disenfranchisement of (*see also* United States, franchise), 10, 18, 198–209, 237
    Identity and politicization of, 220–221, 226–228, 233
    Migration, Great of, 198, 202, 205, 207, 220, 221, 231, 233, 249
    Organization and leadership of, 221, 231
    Size (share of population and electorate) of, 15, 202–209, 219–220, 225–226, 228, 231–232, 238
Ashkenazim
    Definition of, 130–132, 136
    Immigration to Israel of, 130, 132
    Size (share of population and electorate) of, 134–135
Assembly size, 261–262

Black and Tans, 210–214, 216, 230, 233

Catch-all political parties, 14, 41, 144–145, 159, 252, 253

d'Hondt electoral formula, 4, 124, 163
Democratic party, 3, 201–202, 218–219, 221–225, 230, 233, 239, 256
Descriptive representation
    African Americans, of, *see* African Americans, descriptive representation
    Definition of, 16, 240–242
    Ethnic minorities, of, 240, 241, 244–245
    Relationship to social heterogeneity, 16, 235–236, 241–242, 257
    Russians, of, *see* Russians, descriptive representation
    Sectarian parties, role in providing, *see* Sectarian parties, role in providing descriptive representation
    Sephardim, of, *see* Sephardim, descriptive representation

Index

Socioeconomic class, of, 240, 241, 243–244, 253–254
Women, of, 240–244, 253

Effective number
   Electoral parties, of, 26, 33–34, 92–101, 103, 123, 126, 135, 139, 141, 209, 240
   Ethnic groups, of (*see also* Ethnic fractionalization; Fractionalization, index; Israel, effective number of ethnic groups; United States, effective number of ethnic groups), 60, 80
   Legislative parties, of, 26, 139
   Presidential candidates, of, 102–103, 107–120, 122–123
   Religious groups, of, 80
Electoral system (*see also* Israel, electoral system; United States, electoral system), 4–6, 8–9, 11–12, 14–16, 18, 19, 22–23, 26–27, 32–33, 35, 45–48, 56–58, 71–73, 91–103, 107–111, 122–123, 235–238, 259, 261–262
Ethnic division, 78–81, 86
Ethnic fractionalization (*see also* Effective number, ethnic groups), 60, 80, 85–87, 107, 117–120

Foreign policy division, 78–79, 83–84, 86
Fractionalization, index of (*see also* Effective number), 80
Franchise (*see also* United States, franchise), 23–26, 63–70, 87, 93–101, 121–123, 237
Fundamental equation of politics, 2, 13

Hare, LR electoral formula, 5, 163

Immigration (*see also* Israel, general immigration; Israel, Russian immigration; Israel, Sephardi immigration), 73–77, 87, 93–101, 121–122, 237
Index of social heterogeneity (*see also* Ethnic division; Foreign policy division; Post-materialist division; Religious division; Socioeconomic division; Urban–rural division), 17, 77–79, 84–89, 107–121
Israel
   Arab citizens of, 68, 127–128, 134–135, 137, 153, 244
   Descriptive representation in (*see also* Russians, descriptive representation; Sephardim, descriptive representation), 244–249
   Effective number of ethnic groups in, 134–135, 137–138
   Electoral system of, 4–5, 9–10, 22, 124–126, 159, 161–165, 195–196
   Existing party strategies in, 175–184, 195–196
   General immigration to, 9–10, 127–129, 132
   Law of Return, 127–128
   Party system fragmentation in, 3–5, 9–11, 126, 127, 138–141, 159–162, 194–195
   Party system openness of, 162, 184–185, 195–196
   President–parliamentary regime of, *see* Israel, regime type
   Presidential coattails in, 172–175
   Regime type of, 6, 19, 110, 124, 126, 162, 166–175, 195, 239
   Religious political parties in, 138, 152–153, 164, 176–179, 181–184
   Russian immigration to, 9, 18, 125, 127, 129, 135–138, 159, 161–162, 194
   Russian political parties in, *see* Russian political parties
   Sephardi immigration to, 9, 18, 125, 127, 129, 132–135, 159, 161–162, 194

Index

Sephardi political parties in, *see* Sephardi political parties
Social heterogeneity of, 9–11, 17–18, 125–138, 159–162, 194–195
Israel b'Aliya party, 155–158, 173, 183, 194
Israel Beiteinu party, 144, 155–158, 171, 173, 182, 183

Kadima party, 138, 165, 175–184, 194

Labor party, 138, 150–151, 155–158, 168–169, 172–173, 175–185, 189, 194
Latent social groups, *see* Social groups and their characteristics, politicization
Lieberman, Avigdor, 144, 155, 171, 173, 182, 248
Likud party, 138, 145, 150–152, 155–158, 168–169, 172–173, 175–185, 194

Mississippi Freedom Democrats, 213, 214, 216
Mizrachim, *see* Sephardim
Multilevel modeling, 259

National Association for the Advancement of Colored People (NAACP), 221, 224
National Democratic Party of Alabama, 211, 213, 214, 216
New institutionalism, 2–3, 6–8, 13, 236
Number of political parties, *see* Party system fragmentation

Particization, *see* Social groups and their characteristics, politicization
Party system
    Definition of, 3
    Descriptive representation of, *see* Descriptive representation
    Dimensions of, 3, 16, 22, 235–236, 239–240, 257, 260
    Fragmentation of, *see* Party system fragmentation
    Importance of, 3, 240
    Openness of, *see* Party system openness
Party system fragmentation
    Definition of, 3, 33
    Operational definition of (*see also* Effective number, electoral parties; Effective number, presidential candidates), 33, 92, 103, 123
    Quantitative models of, 90–91, 95–101, 108–121
    Relationship to social heterogeneity (*see also* Electoral system; Party system openness; Prior social heterogeneity; Regime type; Social groups and their characteristics; Strategies of existing parties), 8–16, 22–23, 26–27, 32–35, 56–58, 90–91, 120–123, 235–241, 260
    Theory (summary) of, 35, 57
Party system openness (*see also* Israel, party system openness; United States, party system openness), 15, 23, 35, 44–45, 56–57, 91, 96, 106–110, 122, 237–238, 259–260
Peace and Freedom party, 210–211, 213, 214, 216, 220, 228, 230
Political institutions, *see* Electoral system; New institutionalism; Regime type
Politicization, *see* Social groups and their characteristics, politicization
Post-materialist division, 78–79, 83, 86
Preferences, 1–2, 6–13, 38
Presidential coattails (*see also* Israel, presidential coattails; United States, presidential coattails), 5, 51
Presidential elections (*see also* African American political parties, presidential elections), 15, 17, 90–91, 101–123, 236
Presidential powers, 104–106, 108–120,

337

Index

122
Presidential prize, size of, *see* Regime type
Presidentialism, *see* Regime type
Prior social heterogeneity, 15, 23, 35, 52–57, 91, 107–120, 122, 237–238

Quasi-experiment, 18, 91, 125–126, 162, 168, 195, 199, 232
Quotas, 262

Regime type (*see also* Israel, regime type; United States, regime type), 5–6, 12, 15–16, 23, 35, 48–52, 56–58, 91, 103–106, 108–120, 122, 237–238, 259–261
Religious division, 78–81, 86
Republican party, 3, 200–201, 218–219, 221–225, 230, 233, 239
Russian political parties
    Formation (entry) of, 139, 153–156, 159–160, 163, 168–169
    Israel b'Aliya, *see* Israel b'Aliya party
    Israel Beiteinu, *see* Israel Beiteinu party
    Leadership of, 154–156, 181–182, 186–187
    Lieberman, Avigdor, *see* Lieberman, Avigdor
    Organizational resources of, 186–188
    Role in providing descriptive representation, 254–256, 258
    Sharansky, Natan, *see* Sharansky, Natan
    Success of, 10, 14, 18, 33, 127, 141, 153, 156–172, 175, 181–190, 193–197, 239
Russians
    Central Asia and Caucasus subgroup of, 136–137, 155–156, 158–159, 178, 182, 193
    Definition of, 135–136
    Descriptive representation of, 19, 182–183, 245–249
    Identity and politicization of, 162, 188–190, 193–196
    Immigration to Israel of, *see* Israel, Russian immigration
    Organization and leadership of, 186–188
    Political parties of, *see* Russian political parties
    Religiosity of, 135, 181–182, 193–194
    Size (share of population and electorate) of, 137–138, 164–165, 195
    Voting behavior of, 156–159

Sectarian political parties
    As mechanism relating social heterogeneity to party system fragmentation, 13–16, 22–23, 27, 33–35, 56–58, 103, 123, 126, 235–239
    Definition of, 14, 22, 141–142
    Definition of success of, 142–143, 210
    Operational definition of, 143–144, 209–210
    Operational definition of success of, 147–150, 215–216, 228
    Role in providing descriptive representation, 16, 236, 252–254, 257–260
Sephardi political parties
    Ethiopian political parties, 153, 165
    Formation (entry) of, 139, 145–147, 151–152, 163, 168–169
    Leadership of, 145–146, 176–177, 183, 186–187
    North African political parties, 151, 152, 165, 191
    Organizational resources of, 146, 176, 186, 188
    Role in providing descriptive representation, 254–255, 258
    Shas, *see* Shas party
    Success of, 10, 18, 127, 141, 146–153, 161–172, 175–181, 183–197, 239

338

Index

Tami, *see* Tami party
Yemeni political parties, 151, 165, 191
Sephardim
  Definition of, 130–132
  Descriptive representation of, 19, 177–181, 245–249
  Discrimination faced by, 132, 176, 180, 185, 187, 190–191
  Identity and politicization of, 162, 188–193, 195–196
  Immigration to Israel of, *see* Israel, Sephardi immigration
  Organization and leadership of, 186–188
  Political parties of, *see* Sephardi political parties
  Religiosity of, 130, 133, 152–153, 176–177, 180, 191
  Size (share of population and electorate) of, 134–135, 147–149, 164–165, 195
  Voting behavior of, 148–153, 159, 185
Sharansky, Natan, 154–155, 173, 183
Shas party, 148, 149, 151–153, 156, 160, 176–178, 182, 188–189, 192–193
Social cleavages, 8–9, 11, 28–29
Social divisions, *see* Ethnic division; Foreign policy division; Post-materialist division; Religious division; Social cleavages; Socioeconomic division; Urban–rural division
Social groups and their characteristics
  Politicization (*see also* African Americans, identity and politicization; Russians, identity and politicization; Sephardim, identity and politicization), 15, 23, 29–38, 56–57, 91, 236–238
  Size (*see also* African Americans, size; Russians, size; Sephardim, size), 15, 23, 35, 39–40, 56–58, 91, 162, 236–238
  Types of attributes, 15, 17–18, 23, 29–30, 35, 38–39, 56–57, 59, 91, 162–163, 219, 236–238
Social heterogeneity
  Cross-sectional index of, *see* Index of social heterogeneity
  Definition of, 11–14, 28–32
  External dimensions of change of, *see* Franchise; Immigration; Territory
  Historical dimensions of (*see also* Franchise; Immigration; Territory), 13–14, 17, 61–62, 87, 93–95, 121–122, 237
  Longitudinal measures of, *see* Social heterogeneity, historical dimensions
  Measurement of, general problems, 11–12, 59–61, 87–89, 101–102, 126, 259
  Nonlinearity of relationship with party system fragmentation, *see* Prior social heterogeneity
  Relationship to descriptive representation, *see* Descriptive representation, relationship to social heterogeneity
  Relationship to party system fragmentation, *see* Party system fragentation, relationship to social heterogeneity
Socioeconomic division, 78–79, 82–83, 86
Strategies of existing parties (*see also* Israel, existing party strategies; United States, existing party strategies), 12, 15, 23, 35, 41–44, 56–57, 103, 237–238

Tami party, 148, 149, 151–152, 176–178
Territory, 70–71, 87, 93–101, 121–122, 237

United States

339

Index

    Civil Rights movement, 10, 202–203, 209, 216, 221, 239, 256
    Civil War, 10, 198, 200, 203, 211, 217
    Democratic party, *see* Democratic party
    Descriptive representation in (*see also* African Americans, descriptive representation), 245, 249–252
    Effective number of ethnic groups in, 202–205
    Electoral system of, 4–5, 9–11, 198–200, 217, 229–234
    Existing party strategies in, 221–224, 227–228, 231, 233
    Franchise in (*see also* African Americans, enfranchisement and disenfranchisement), 24, 64–65, 68–70, 198–203
    Party system fragmentation in, 3–5, 9–11, 198–200, 209, 232–234
    Party system openness of, 218–219, 231
    Presidential coattails in, 51–52, 218, 228–229, 232–233
    Reconstruction, 10, 14, 200–202, 205, 207, 209–211, 217, 221–222, 224, 233, 239, 249
    Reconstruction, Second (*see also* Civil Rights movement), 202, 207, 211, 222
    Regime type of, 6, 198, 217–218, 230–231, 262
    Republican party, *see* Republican party
    Social heterogeneity of, 9–11, 17–18, 198–209, 232–234
    Voting Rights Act, 202, 205, 219, 249, 252
Urban–rural division, 78–79, 81–82, 86

Voice, 1, 3, 7, 9, 13, 62, 63, 262

For EU product safety concerns, contact us at Calle de José Abascal, 56–1°,
28003 Madrid, Spain or eugpsr@cambridge.org.

www.ingramcontent.com/pod-product-compliance
Ingram Content Group UK Ltd.
Pitfield, Milton Keynes, MK11 3LW, UK
UKHW040414060825
461487UK00006B/499